ASP.NET Web API 2 Recipes

A Problem-Solution Approach

Filip Wojcieszyn

Apress®

ASP.NET Web API 2 Recipes: A Problem Solution Approach

ISBN-13 (pbk): 978-1-4302-5980-0

ISBN-13 (electronic): 978-1-4302-5981-7

Publisher: Heinz Weinheimer
Lead Editor: Gwenan Spearing
Technical Reviewer: Fabio Claudio Ferracchiati
Editorial Board: Steve Anglin, Mark Beckner, Ewan Buckingham, Gary Cornell, Louise Corrigan, Jim DeWolf, Jonathan Gennick, Jonathan Hassell, Robert Hutchinson, Michelle Lowman, James Markham, Matthew Moodie, Jeff Olson, Jeffrey Pepper, Douglas Pundick, Ben Renow-Clarke, Dominic Shakeshaft, Gwenan Spearing, Matt Wade, Steve Weiss
Coordinating Editor: Christine Ricketts
Copy Editor: Mary Behr
Compositor: SPi Global
Indexer: SPi Global
Artist: SPi Global
Cover Designer: Anna Ishchenko

Distributed to the book trade worldwide by Springer Science+Business Media New York, 233 Spring Street, 6th Floor, New York, NY 10013. Phone 1-800-SPRINGER, fax (201) 348-4505, e-mail orders-ny@springer-sbm.com, or visit www.springeronline.com. Apress Media, LLC is a California LLC and the sole member (owner) is Springer Science + Business Media Finance Inc (SSBM Finance Inc). SSBM Finance Inc is a Delaware corporation.

For information on translations, please e-mail rights@apress.com, or visit www.apress.com.

Apress and friends of ED books may be purchased in bulk for academic, corporate, or promotional use. eBook versions and licenses are also available for most titles. For more information, reference our Special Bulk Sales–eBook Licensing web page at www.apress.com/bulk-sales.

Any source code or other supplementary material referenced by the author in this text is available to readers at www.apress.com. For detailed information about how to locate your book's source code, go to www.apress.com/source-code/.

This book is dedicated to the .NET open source community.

Contents at a Glance

Contents

About the Author

Filip Wojcieszyn is a popular ASP.NET blogger (`www.starthweb.com`), a Microsoft ASP.NET MVP, a prolific open source contributor, coordinator at the scriptcs project, and a member of the ASP.NET Web API advisory group. He specializes in the ASP.NET web stack and modern web technologies. He is experienced in delivering robust web solutions in a corporate context and has worked on projects in many corners of the world including Canada, Switzerland, Finland, Poland, and Scotland.

You can follow Filip on Twitter @filip_woj.

About the Technical Reviewer

Fabio Claudio Ferracchiati is a senior consultant and a senior analyst/developer using Microsoft technologies. He works for Blu Arancio (`www.bluarancio.com`). He is a Microsoft Certified Solution Developer for .NET, a Microsoft Certified Application Developer for .NET, a Microsoft Certified Professional, and a prolific author and technical reviewer. Over the past ten years, he's written articles for Italian and international magazines and coauthored more than ten books on a variety of computer topics.

Acknowledgments

This book would never have been possible without Maja, the love of my life. Without her wonderful heart, unbelievable support, and patience, I would never have managed to get anything done.

I would especially like to thank Jon Galloway, Henrik Frystyk Nielsen, and Dan Roth. Without Jon's support, and the nudge he gave me, I would not be where I am right now with my career, and for that I will always be grateful. Henrik, one of the fathers of HTTP and a true legend in the industry, has always supported my community activities and was always available and ready to share his tremendous knowledge. Dan has made sure that the Web API team is one of the most open and discussion-oriented teams in all of Microsoft. A number of current and past members of the ASP.NET team have also been very helpful to me, and I would like to thank them all: Yishai Galatzer, Kiran Challa, Brad Wilson, Youssef Moussaoui, and many others—even David Fowler with his crazy ideas!

A big thank you goes to my scriptcs friends, spearheaded by Glenn Block, who has been urging me to write this book since the early days and without whom the ASP.NET Web API framework would not exist in the first place, and Justin Rusbatch.

There are many amazing individuals in the ASP.NET Web API community who have been both inspirational and extremely supportive of me over the past couple of years: Pedro Felix, Ryan Riley, Brock Allen, Dominick Baier, Darrel Miller, Pablo Cibraro, Tugberk Ugurlu, and Ali Kheyrollahi, to name just a few. They are not only fantastic experts in the Web API area, but more importantly, they are terrific people who I am honored to be able to call friends.

I would also like to thank my friends at Climax Media, who gave me a chance and believed in me like no other company ever did. It's truly a great place to work.

Obviously this book would never have happened without the great support from Apress and my editors, Gwenan and Christine, who have been fantastic throughout the entire process.

Last but not least, a thank you to my family and to my best friend, Michał Mytnik, for putting up with me whining, complaining, and constantly moving from place to place for many years, which I can imagine has been a herculean task.

Introduction

Like all of us in this industry, I have been through a ton of programming or framework-centric books in my career as a developer. Without a doubt, my favorite type has always been a recipe-style book. It might be my low attention span or simply my urge to solve problems rather than read through abstract discussions, but I really enjoy the no-nonsense, straight-to-the-point format of such publications.

I started working with Web API back when it was still WCF Web API. I started blogging about it in the early beta days of the framework, at the beginning of 2012, at which time the name had already changed to ASP.NET Web API. Since then I have produced almost 100 blog posts on virtually all aspects of working with ASP.NET Web API, written a fair share of technical articles, been involved in a number of open-source initiatives focused around the framework, and been a speaker at plenty of events. But most importantly, I have grown to know Web API better than my own backyard.

I had some really wonderful feedback from readers and the amazing Web API community, so at some point I started thinking about producing a recipe-style book, as it would feel like a natural extension of the material from the blog. A number of plans and approaches were drafted and discussed, and things eventually came to fruition last winter, when this book was officially announced.

It has never been my intention to write an A-Z compendium or reference book about ASP.NET Web API. Instead, I reveled in the opportunity to use the problem-solution format of the recipe-style book. In my mind, it makes the book a much more enjoyable read, as you can cherry-pick the things you are interested in, rather than go through the entire book in a linear fashion.

You will not find theoretical divagations about architecture or abstract academic discussions about REST in this book. Instead, I focus on the problems stated in each recipe and how to solve them with ASP.NET Web API. The book dissects what is going on under the hood in the framework and shows you how to push ASP.NET Web API to its absolute limits. It is also a framework-centric book; it focuses on how to do things specifically with ASP.NET Web API 2.

Each of the 103 recipes in the book has dedicated source code illustrating the technique or problem discussed in the recipe. To make it easier to follow the book in a non-linear fashion, the solutions are not dependent on each other. Each example is simple, straight to the point, and entirely self-contained. This allows for the important bits to clearly stand out.

Due to the nature of the format of the book, the space available for each recipe is constrained, and as such, some of the topics cannot be covered in depth. In those cases, I lay out the basics to help you get started, and then point to extra resources and further reading.

There were many recipe-style books that helped me in my career, and I sincerely hope that this book will help you become a better ASP.NET Web API programmer, too. If at least a single recipe helps you avoid some headache that the framework might have given you before, I will be absolutely thrilled.

CHAPTER 1

■ ■ ■

Web API in ASP.NET

This chapter discusses using ASP.NET Web API on top of IIS, within the ASP.NET runtime. The recipes covered in this chapter deal with ASP.NET runtime specifics and, unless noted otherwise, the solutions presented here cannot be extended onto other Web API hosts.

You will learn how to do the following:

- Use ASP.NET Web API in the same process as ASP.NET MVC or ASP.NET Web Forms (Recipes 1-1 and 1-2)

- Deal with HTML forms and validation (Recipes 1-3 and 1-6)

- Link between MVC and Web API controllers (Recipe 1-4)

- Use scaffolding to rapidly bootstrap ASP.NET Web API projects (Recipe 1-5)

- Introduce ASP.NET-based CSRF (Cross-Site Request Forgery) protection to your Web API (Recipe 1-7)

- Work with traditional ASP.NET sessions in ASP.NET Web API (Recipe 1-8)

On the other hand, all of the host-agnostic features of Web API (routing, model binding, content negotiation, security, exception handling, and many others) are covered in detail in the upcoming chapters.

1-1. Add ASP.NET Web API to an MVC Application

Problem

You would like to integrate ASP.NET Web API into your ASP.NET MVC project.

Solution

ASP.NET Web API used to be automatically bundled in MVC project templates in Visual Studio 2012. Since Visual Studio 2013, you compose your ASP.NET web application using the new *One ASP.NET* project wizard, based on Microsoft's concept of a unified ASP.NET platform, where you can select the relevant components, such as MVC and Web API. This is shown in Figure 1-1.

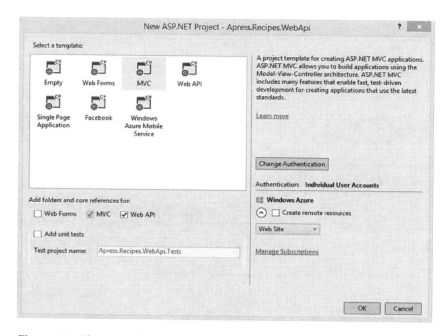

Figure 1-1. *The One ASP.NET project wizard, with MVC and Web API in a single project*

Interestingly, if you choose the Web API project template, MVC will be automatically bundled into it as well, as ASP.NET Web API Help Pages rely on MVC to serve content.

You can also add Web API to any existing MVC project by installing it from NuGet.

```
Install-Package Microsoft.AspNet.WebApi
```

Semantically, both approaches to including Web API in an ASP.NET web application project are equivalent because the project wizard simply installs ASP.NET Web API from NuGet too.

How It Works

Under the hood, ASP.NET Web API is built around an asynchronous HTTP handler called System.Web. IHttpAsyncHandler, which is shown in Listing 1-1. Handlers are the backbone of ASP.NET; they are classes that can intercept and handle HTTP requests made to the web server and respond to the client with the relevant response.

Listing 1-1. Definiton of IHttpAsyncHandler

```
public interface IHttpAsyncHandler : object, IHttpHandler
{
    System.IAsyncResult BeginProcessRequest(HttpContext context, System.AsyncCallback cb,
    object extraData);
    void EndProcessRequest(System.IAsyncResult result);
}
```

In fact, this is not much different from the architecture of the ASP.NET MVC framework, which also sits on top of an HTTP handler. As a result, while both frameworks are complex pieces of software engineering, they are not any more special than regular IHttpHandler or IHttpAsyncHandler implementations that you might have created in the past to handle your various custom HTTP-based tasks.

The outline of the Web API IHttpAsyncHandler HttpControllerHandler and its public members is shown in Listing 1-2.

Listing 1-2. Public Members of HttpControllerHandler

```
public class HttpControllerHandler : HttpTaskAsyncHandler
{
    public HttpControllerHandler(RouteData routeData);
    public HttpControllerHandler(RouteData routeData, HttpMessageHandler handler);

    public override Task ProcessRequestAsync(HttpContext context);
}
```

The main difference between MVC and Web API is that since version 2 of the framework, the Web API handler, HttpControllerHandler, is a subclass of HttpTaskAsyncHandler, while the MVC version, MvcHandler, implements IHttpAsyncHandler directly. HttpTaskAsyncHandler is .NET 4.5 only, which is the only .NET version supported by Web API 2.

When you run both MVC and Web API in the same ASP.NET process, ASP.NET will use the HttpApplication. MapRequestHandler event to determine which of the HTTP handlers will be selected to handle the incoming request. At this stage, route matching happens, and the request flows through the IRouteHandler relevant for the selected route. The sole purpose of IRouteHandler is to produce an IHttpHandler that can handle the request.

If the IRouteHandler is HttpControllerRouteHandler (Web API route), then the Web API path will be chosen and the request will end up in the HttpControllerHandler. Conversely, if the route handler is MvcRouteHandler, then the MVC path takes over via MvcHandler.

The Code

With the setup showed in this recipe, ASP.NET MVC and ASP.NET Web API will run in the same process so they can easily share state, such as static objects or Global.asax events. Additionally, the web.config is common for both frameworks.

Listing 1-3 shows two controllers, an MVC controller and a Web API controller, which can coexist side by side in a single ASP.NET web application. Notice that since they are located in different namespaces, they can even have the same name. Moreover, it's perfectly fine for them to share the same model (DTO) when necessary.

Listing 1-3. Sample MVC and Web API Controllers

```
public class Book
{
    public int Id { get; set; }
    public string Author { get; set; }
    public string Title { get; set; }
    public string Link { get; set; }
}
```

```
namespace Apress.Recipes.WebApi.Controllers.Mvc
{
    public class BooksController : Controller
    {
        public ActionResult Details(int id)
        {
            var book = Books.List.FirstOrDefault(x => x.Id == id);
            if(book == null) return new HttpNotFoundResult();

            return View(book);
        }
    }
}

namespace Apress.Recipes.WebApi.Controllers.WebApi
{
    public class BooksController : ApiController
    {
        public Book GetById(int id)
        {
            var book = Books.List.FirstOrDefault(x => x.Id == id);
            if (book == null) throw new HttpResponseException(HttpStatusCode.NotFound);

            return book;
        }
    }
}
```

The key to avoiding conflict between the frameworks is a careful route setup; to facilitate that, by default ASP.NET Web API will occupy URI space under /api, while all of the other root-level URLs will be handled by MVC. Typically Web API routes are defined in the WebApiConfig static class against the HttpConfiguration object and its Route property, while MVC routes are defined in the static RouteConfig class, directly against the System.Web.RouteCollection. The default route definitions for both frameworks are shown in Listing 1-4.

Listing 1-4. Default Routing for Web API and MVC

```
//Web API routing configuration
public static class WebApiConfig
{
    public static void Register(HttpConfiguration config)
    {
        // Web API configuration and services

        // Web API routes
        config.MapHttpAttributeRoutes();
```

```
        config.Routes.MapHttpRoute(
            name: "DefaultApi",
            routeTemplate: "api/{controller}/{id}",
            defaults: new { id = RouteParameter.Optional }
        );
    }
}

//MVC routing configuration
public class RouteConfig
{
    public static void RegisterRoutes(RouteCollection routes)
    {
        routes.IgnoreRoute("{resource}.axd/{*pathInfo}");

        routes.MapRoute(
            name: "Default",
            url: "{controller}/{action}/{id}",
            defaults: new { controller = "Home", action = "Index", id = UrlParameter.Optional }
        );
    }
}
```

Chapter 3 is dedicated to routing, but with the setup from Listing 1-4, the following endpoints are now exposed by your ASP.NET application:

- /api/books/{id} will route to ASP.NET Web API

- /books/details/{id} will route to ASP.NET MVC

1-2. Add ASP.NET Web API to a Web Forms Application

Problem

You would like to integrate ASP.NET Web API into your ASP.NET Web Forms application.

Solution

For new Web Forms projects, in Visual Studio 2013, you can simply choose to include ASP.NET Web API in the new One ASP.NET project wizard, as shown in Figure 1-2.

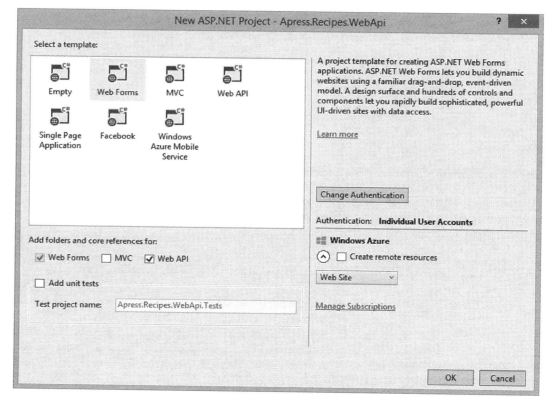

Figure 1-2. *ASP.NET project wizard, with Web Forms and Web API hosted side by side*

Since ASP.NET Web API is available on NuGet, it can also easily be added to an existing Web Forms solution:

```
Install-Package Microsoft.AspNet.WebApi
```

The same applies to using Visual Studio 2012; you can just create a new Web Forms project, and throw in Web API through NuGet.

How It Works

Similarly to using ASP.NET Web API alongside MVC, adding it to a Web Forms project results in Web API running in the same ASP.NET process as the Web Forms application.

Installing the `Microsoft.AspNet.WebApi` NuGet package into your ASP.NET project will add a `WebApiConfig` static class to the `App_Start` folder. It is used for configuring ASP.NET Web API and declaring ASP.NET Web API routes.

Additionally, the following line, invoking the Web API configuration, gets added to the `Application_Start` block of the `Global.asax`:

```
GlobalConfiguration.Configure(WebApiConfig.Register);
```

Running Web API inside a Web Forms application is no different than running it inside an MVC application; each request will still be handled by a relevant `IHttpHandler`. This could either be the Web API-specific `HttpControllerHandler`, or a Web Forms-supplied handler. Web Forms map the ASPX extension to

PageHandlerFactory, which in turn produces the relevant IHttpHandler to handle the HTTP request. The default building block of a Web Forms application, a System.Web.UI.Page class, is indeed an IHttpHandler too, and that's how it's capable of acting as request processor.

The engine and architecture behind ASP.NET Web API is discussed in detail in Recipe 1-1.

The Code

Listing 1-5 shows a sample model class plus an ApiController and a Web Forms Page class sharing it to present the data.

Listing 1-5. Sample Model, Web Forms Page, and a Web API Controller

```
public class Book
{
    public int Id { get; set; }
    public string Author { get; set; }
    public string Title { get; set; }
}

public partial class _Default : Page
{
    protected void Page_Load(object sender, EventArgs e)
    {
        int id;
        if (Int32.TryParse((string)Page.RouteData.Values["id"], out id))
        {
            var book = Books.List.FirstOrDefault(x => x.Id == id);
            if (book == null)
            {
                Response.StatusCode = 404;
                return;
            }

            ltlAuthor.Text = book.Author;
            ltlTitle.Text = book.Title;
            hplLink.NavigateUrl = "/api/books/" + book.Id;
        }

        Response.StatusCode = 404;
    }
}

public class BooksController : ApiController
{
    public Book GetById(int id)
    {
        var book = Books.List.FirstOrDefault(x => x.Id == id);
        if (book == null) throw new HttpResponseException(HttpStatusCode.NotFound);

        return book;
    }
}
```

It is a convention to place ApiControllers inside a Controller folder in your solution, but it is by no means a requirement; any public implementation of IHttpController available in the current AppDomain, as long as it uses a Controller suffix in the name, is going to be discovered at runtime and deemed suitable to handle HTTP requests.

As is the case with running Web API and MVC side by side, when using Web Forms routing, you have to be careful not to cause conflicts between routes intended to be handled by Web API and those intended to be leading to ASPX pages. Listing 1-6 shows a sample routing setup for both Web Forms and Web API. ASP.NET Web API routing is done in this case in the static WebApiConfig class, while Web Forms routing is configured in the static RouteConfig.

Listing 1-6. Web API Routing and Web Forms Routing, Side by Side

```
public static class RouteConfig
{
    public static void RegisterRoutes(RouteCollection routes)
    {
        var settings = new FriendlyUrlSettings();
        settings.AutoRedirectMode = RedirectMode.Permanent;
        routes.EnableFriendlyUrls(settings);

        routes.MapPageRoute(
        "book-route",
        "book/{id}",
        "~/default.aspx");
    }
}

public static class WebApiConfig
{
    public static void Register(HttpConfiguration config)
    {
        // Web API configuration and services

        // Web API routes
        config.MapHttpAttributeRoutes();

        config.Routes.MapHttpRoute(
            name: "DefaultApi",
            routeTemplate: "api/{controller}/{id}",
            defaults: new { id = RouteParameter.Optional }
        );
    }
}
```

1-3. Accept an HTML Form

Problem

You would like to create an ASP.NET Web API endpoint that's capable of handling HTML forms (data posted as application/x-www-form-urlencoded).

Solution

You can create a controller action that accepts a model that's structured like the HTML form you are going to handle, and rely on ASP.NET Web API to perform the model binding for you. The properties on the model must match the names of the keys used in the HTTP request.

```
public HttpResponseMessage Post(RegistrationModel model)
{
    //omitted for brevity
}
```

Alternatively, you can use System.Net.Http.Formatting.FormDataCollection as the only parameter on the action; the framework will then pass the form data as a key-value collection, allowing you to manually handle the form exactly how you'd want to.

```
public HttpResponseMessage Post(FormDataCollection form)
{
    //omitted for brevity
}
```

How It Works

Submitting form-URL-encoded data is a common requirement when building web applications with ASP.NET Web API, or, even more so, when you are using Web API to facilitate your existing web application (MVC, Web Forms, or any other technology).

ASP.NET Web API uses MediaTypeFormatters to extract data from the body of HttpRequestMessage and pass it to the relevant action selected to handle the request. Chapter 4 is dedicated to model binding and working with formatters, so here I will only touch on the concepts directly related to handling HTML forms.

Two of the out-of-the-box formatters are capable of handling forms: FormUrlEncodedMediaTypeFormatter, used for binding FormDataCollection on requests with application/x-www-form-urlencoded content type, and JQueryMvcFormUrlEncodedFormatter, also used for the same content type, but also capable of binding to models (DTOs). From a design perspective, the latter subclasses the former.

Using FormDataCollection, instead of a model, as your action parameter will not only give you access to the raw form, but also instruct ASP.NET Web API to not perform any validation. Other special Types excluded from input validation are System.Xml.XmlNode, Newtonsoft.Json.Linq.JToken, System.Xml.Linq.XObject, System.Type, and byte[].

By default, Web API reads the body of the request only once, so when using a model to bind to form data, that model should encapsulate all of the form fields. In other words, out of the box, it is not possible to pass some of the fields as part of the request body and some in the URL, and expect the framework to try to automatically reconcile them into a single model. This is a dangerous spot for MVC developers because that's exactly the behavior they are used to. It is, however, possible to force Web API into such MVC-style parameter binding; this is discussed in Recipe 4-4.

If your form handles binary data, such as uploading files, then the form will be submitted as multipart/form-data instead. ASP.NET Web API does not provide any built-in MediaTypeFormatter to handle that; however, it is still relatively easy to work with forms submitted that way. This is done by using the `MultipartFormDataStreamProvider` directly against the contents of the `HttpRequestMessage`. The technique is shown in Listing 1-7. Dealing with file uploads is beyond the scope of this recipe, though; it is separately discussed in Recipe 4-11.

Listing 1-7. Accessing Form Data of a Multipart Request

```
public async Task Post()
{
    if (!Request.Content.IsMimeMultipartContent())
    {
        throw new HttpResponseException(Request.CreateResponse(HttpStatusCode.NotAcceptable,
            "This request is not properly formatted"));
    }

    var streamProvider = new MultipartFormDataStreamProvider("d:/uploads/");
    await Request.Content.ReadAsMultipartAsync(streamProvider);

    //here you can access streamProvider.FormData which
    //is an instance of FormDataCollection
}
```

■ **Note** The functionality discussed in this recipe is not ASP.NET-specific and can be used beyond web-hosted Web APIs. However, you usually have to deal with traditional HTML forms when running Web API as part of an ASP.NET web application.

The Code

Listing 1-8 shows a simple HTML form that can be submitted to an ASP.NET Web API endpoint, both as a regular form and from JavaScript.

Listing 1-8. A Sample HTML Form

```
<form role="form" method="post" action="/api/form" enctype="application/x-www-form-urlencoded">
    <div class="form-group">
        <label for="name">Name</label>
        <input type="text" class="form-control" name="name" placeholder="Enter name">
    </div>
    <div class="form-group">
        <label for="email">Email</label>
        <input type="email" class="form-control" name="email" placeholder="Enter email">
    </div>
    <div class="radio">
        <label>
            <input type="radio" name="gender" value="female" checked>
            Female
        </label>
    </div>
```

```
    <div class="radio">
        <label>
            <input type="radio" name="gender" value="male">
            Male
        </label>
    </div>
    <button type="submit" class="btn btn-default">Submit</button>
    <button id="postJS" class="btn btn-default">Send with JS</button>
</form>

<script type="text/javascript">
    $(function () {
        $("#postJS").on("click", function () {
            var data = {
                    name: $("input[name='name']").val(),
                    email: $("input[name='email']").val(),
                    gender: $("input[name='gender']:checked").val(),
            };

            $.ajax({
                data: data,
                datatype: "html",
                type: "POST",
                url: "/api/user"
            }).done(function (res) {
                //success handler
            });
        });
    });
</script>
```

Listing 1-9 shows two ASP.NET Web API actions that are capable of handling the form from Listing 1-8. The first one does it in a more traditional way, using FormDataCollection and manual data extraction, which is then used to populate a server side model. The second one relies on the framework to hydrate the model automatically.

Listing 1-9. Web API Controllers Handling the Form Data

```
public class UserModel
{
    public string Name { get; set; }
    public string Email { get; set; }
    public string Gender { get; set; }
}

public class FormController : ApiController
{
    public HttpResponseMessage Post(FormDataCollection form)
    {
        var user = new UserModel
        {
            Email = form["Email"],
```

```
            Name = form["Name"],
            Gender = form["Gender"]
        };

        //process user...
        //rest omitted for brevity
    }
}

public class UserController : ApiController
{
    public HttpResponseMessage Post(UserModel user)
    {
        //process user...
        //rest omitted for brevity
    }
}
```

1-4. Link from MVC Controller to API Controller and Vice Versa
Problem

You would like to create direct links from ASP.NET MVC controllers to ASP.NET Web API controllers and the other way round.

Solution

You can create links to controllers using an instance of System.Web.Http.Routing.UrlHelper, exposed on the base ApiController (as the Url property), as well as on the RequestContext, which is attached to an instance of HttpRequestMessage. To achieve this, you need to call the Link or Route method and pass in the name of the MVC route and the route defaults (controller name, action name, and relevant action parameters).

On the MVC controller side, System.Web.Mvc.UrlHelper, hanging off the base MVC base Controller class, is able to generate Web API links via the HttpRouteUrl method.

How It Works

It is a common requirement, when using ASP.NET Web API as part of an existing MVC application, to be able to cross link between the two types of controllers. When creating links to MVC controllers from Web API, you actually use the exact same methods as when creating links between Web API controllers: Link or Route on the UrlHelper. The reason why this is possible is that ASP.NET Web API will find the route by name, and then call the GetVirtualPath on that route to resolve a link to it. If the route happens to be registered as an MVC route, it will be of type System.Web.Route and its particular implementation of GetVirtualPath will be used. It's important to remember that the Link method will generate an absolute link, while the Route method will generate a relative one.

In the opposite direction, when linking from MVC to Web API, the HttpRouteUrl method is not an extension method introduced by the ASP.NET Web API assemblies, but rather a class member of UrlHelper, inside the System.Web.Mvc DLL. This helper uses a private constant called httproute, which is added to the RouteValueDictionary every time you use HttpRouteUrl. This way, a route can be identified as pointing to ASP.NET Web API.

■ **Note**　Recipe 3-12 is dedicated to further exploring and understanding the engine behind generating links to routes.

The Code

Imagine a sample web application dealing with books. Listing 1-10 shows a sample Book model, an in-memory representation of a repository of books and the API/MVC routing configuration. For demo purposes, it is fine to use the same model for both MVC and Web API endpoints. You'll use the artefacts declared in this listing to illustrate the cross-linking between Web API and MVC controllers.

Listing 1-10. An Example Model, Routing and In-Memory Repository

```
public class Book
{
    public int Id { get; set; }
    public string Author { get; set; }
    public string Title { get; set; }
    public string Link { get; set; }
}

public static class Books
{
    public static List<Book> List = new List<Book>
    {
        new Book {Id = 1, Author = "John Robb", Title = "Punk Rock: An Oral History"},
        new Book {Id = 2, Author = "Daniel Mohl", Title = "Building Web, Cloud, and Mobile Solutions
        with F#"},
        new Book {Id = 3, Author = "Steve Clarke", Title = "100 Things Blue Jays Fans Should Know
        & Do Before They Die"},
        new Book {Id = 4, Author = "Mark Frank", Title = "Cuban Revelations: Behind the Scenes in
        Havana "}
    };
}

public class RouteConfig
{
    public static void RegisterRoutes(RouteCollection routes)
    {
        routes.IgnoreRoute("{resource}.axd/{*pathInfo}");

        routes.MapRoute(
            name: "BookPage",
            url: "books/details/{id}",
            defaults: new { controller = "BooksPage", action = "Details" }
        );
    }
}
```

```
public static class WebApiConfig
{
    public static void Register(HttpConfiguration config)
    {
        config.Routes.MapHttpRoute(
            name: "DefaultApi",
            routeTemplate: "api/{controller}/{id}",
            defaults: new {id = RouteParameter.Optional}
            );
    }
}
```

The code responsible for creating the link to ApiController from MVC controller is shown in Listing 1-11. BooksPageController is the MVC controller responsible for dealing with books. To generate the link, you call a Link method on the UrlHelper, and pass in the relevant route defaults.

Listing 1-11. ASP.NET Web API ApiController Linking to MVC Controller

```
public class BooksController : ApiController
{
    public Book GetById(int id)
    {
        var book = Books.List.FirstOrDefault(x => x.Id == id);
        if (book == null) throw new HttpResponseException(HttpStatusCode.NotFound);

        book.Link = Url.Link("BookPage", new {controller = "BooksPage", action = "Details", id = id });
        return book;
    }
}
```

A link in the opposite direction, from ApiController to MVC controller, can be seen in Listing 1-12. In this case, an MVC-specific UrlHelper is used with the HttpRouteUrl extension method.

Listing 1-12. Linking to ASP.NET Web API from an MVC Controller

```
public class BooksPageController : Controller
{
    public ActionResult Details(int id)
    {
        var book = Books.List.FirstOrDefault(x => x.Id == id);
        if(book == null) return new HttpNotFoundResult();

        book.Link = Url.HttpRouteUrl("DefaultApi", new { controller = "Books", id = id });
        return View(book);
    }
}
```

1-5. Use Scaffolding with ASP.NET Web API

Problem

You'd like to rapidly bootstrap an ASP.NET Web API solution.

Solution

ASP.NET Scaffolding has supported ASP.NET Web API from the very beginning. To use scaffolding to add Web API controllers to your project, right-click the `Controllers` folder in your solution, and choose Add ➤ New Scaffold Item. From there, out of the box, you can select one of the following:

- Web API 2 Controller
- Web API 2 Controller with actions, using Entity Framework
- Web API 2 Controller with read/write actions
- Web API 2 OData Controller with actions, using Entity Framework

Additionally, scaffolding templates with attribute routing can be downloaded from NuGet:

```
Install-Package Microsoft.AspNet.WebApi.ScaffolderTemplates.AttributeRouting.CSharp
```

How It Works

The proper, full name for the scaffolding functionality is ASP.NET Scaffolding, and it is a T4-based code generation framework for ASP.NET. T4, a Text Template Transformation Toolkit, is a template-based code generator that has been part of Visual Studio since version 2005.

Visual Studio 2013 introduced support for the excellent Scaffolded Items feature, allowing you to quickly generate bootstrapping code for your ASP.NET applications. With Visual Studio 2013 Update 2, some terrific extensibility points have been added, introducing the possibility for template customizations, giving you the ultimate flexibility when it comes to code generation.

The built-in scaffolding templates are installed in your Visual Studio installation folder, and can be customized from there. For example, if you use the standard Program Files folder, that would be `C:\Program Files (x86)\ Microsoft Visual Studio 12.0\Common7\IDE\Extensions\Microsoft\Web\Mvc\Scaffolding\Templates`. If you modified any of the templates there, the changes will obviously have a global effect. If you would like to customize the templates on a per project basis, there are two ways to do so:

- Install SideWaffle (`sidewaffle.com`), a Visual Studio extension dedicated to template management. Then use the regular "add" dialog, and choose Web ➤ SideWaffle ➤ ASP.NET Scaffolding T4. This will create a new `CodeTemplates` folder in your solution, containing the copies of all of the global scaffolding templates, which you can edit there to suit your solution's needs.

- Copy all of the files from the global scaffolding templates folder to your ASP.NET project manually, into a top-level folder named `CodeTemplates` (name is important). This copies both C# and VB.NET templates, but you can get rid of the ones you don't need by hand. Make sure to include the files into your project.

The Code

Let's walk through a basic scaffolding process for a Web API controller with Entity Framework Code First model. The model is shown in Listing 1-13.

Listing 1-13. A Sample EF Code First Model

```
public class Team
{
    public int Id { get; set; }
    public string Name { get; set; }
    public DateTime FoundingDate { get; set; }
    public string LeagueName { get; set; }
}
```

After adding the model, you need to rebuild your project before you can proceed to the scaffolding dialog; EF would rely on reflection on your web application DLL. Afterwards, you can proceed to the Add ➤ Scaffolded Item ➤ Web API ➤ Web API 2 Controller with actions, using Entity Framework. The dialog is shown in Figure 1-3.

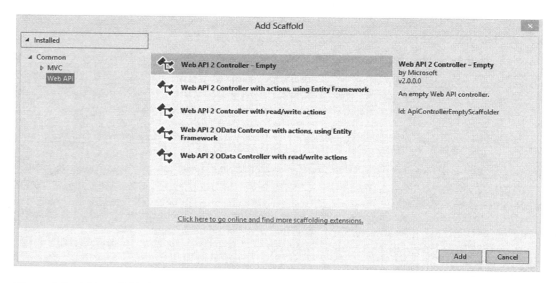

Figure 1-3. *Add scaffolded item dialog*

You then proceed to the dialog shown in Figure 1-4, where you must choose your model, through its fully qualified name (there is a dropdown available, listing all the classes in your solution), an Entity Framework DataContext (a dropdown will list available contexts, if any exist, or you can create one directly from there), also with a fully qualified name, and the desired name of your controller. You can check the *Use async controller actions* checkbox to force the scaffolding engine into generating asynchronous actions and using asynchronous methods against the EF DataContext.

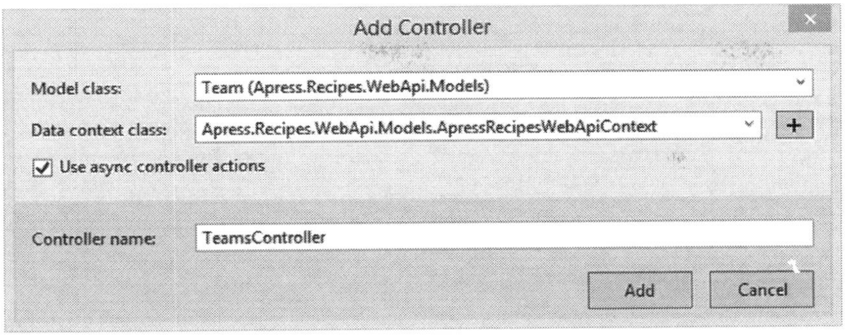

Figure 1-4. *Second step of creating a controller through scaffolding*

The generated controller (stripped of namespaces to save on space) is shown in Listing 1-14. It is a perfectly usable HTTP endpoint, which will be picked up by the default centralized routing. The create action (POST) will respond to the client with the 201 status code, and include a link to the newly created resource in the Location header (thanks to using the CreatedAtRoute method). The update action (PUT) even handles a potential DbUpdateConcurrencyException.

Listing 1-14. A Web API Controller with EF Actions, Generated Through Scaffolding

```
public class TeamsController : ApiController
{
    private ApressRecipesWebApiContext db = new ApressRecipesWebApiContext();

    // GET: api/Teams
    public IQueryable<Team> GetTeams()
    {
        return db.Teams;
    }

    // GET: api/Teams/5
    [ResponseType(typeof(Team))]
    public async Task<IHttpActionResult> GetTeam(int id)
    {
        Team team = await db.Teams.FindAsync(id);
        if (team == null)
        {
            return NotFound();
        }

        return Ok(team);
    }
```

```csharp
// PUT: api/Teams/5
[ResponseType(typeof(void))]
public async Task<IHttpActionResult> PutTeam(int id, Team team)
{
    if (!ModelState.IsValid)
    {
        return BadRequest(ModelState);
    }

    if (id != team.Id)
    {
        return BadRequest();
    }

    db.Entry(team).State = EntityState.Modified;

    try
    {
        await db.SaveChangesAsync();
    }
    catch (DbUpdateConcurrencyException)
    {
        if (!TeamExists(id))
        {
            return NotFound();
        }
        else
        {
            throw;
        }
    }

    return StatusCode(HttpStatusCode.NoContent);
}

// POST: api/Teams
[ResponseType(typeof(Team))]
public async Task<IHttpActionResult> PostTeam(Team team)
{
    if (!ModelState.IsValid)
    {
        return BadRequest(ModelState);
    }

    db.Teams.Add(team);
    await db.SaveChangesAsync();

    return CreatedAtRoute("DefaultApi", new { id = team.Id }, team);
}
```

```
// DELETE: api/Teams/5
[ResponseType(typeof(Team))]
public async Task<IHttpActionResult> DeleteTeam(int id)
{
    Team team = await db.Teams.FindAsync(id);
    if (team == null)
    {
        return NotFound();
    }

    db.Teams.Remove(team);
    await db.SaveChangesAsync();

    return Ok(team);
}

protected override void Dispose(bool disposing)
{
    if (disposing)
    {
        db.Dispose();
    }
    base.Dispose(disposing);
}

private bool TeamExists(int id)
{
    return db.Teams.Count(e => e.Id == id) > 0;
}
}
```

Now, suppose that you have added scaffolding templates to your solution in one of the ways described in the "How It Works" section. You may now proceed to customizing them however you wish. An example of forcing all new ASP.NET Web API controller classes to inherit from a specific base class is shown in Listing 1-15. You'll modify the Controller.cs.t4 from the CodeTemplates/ApiControllerEmpty folder to ensure that each new controller does not inherit from ApiController, but instead subclass ApiBaseController, which is a fairly typical requirement in larger projects, as lots of Web API developers like to introduce their own base class for controllers.

Listing 1-15. Forcing a Web API Controller Created Through Scaffolding Templates to Always Inherit from ApiBaseController

```
<#@ template language="C#" HostSpecific="True" #>
<#@ output extension="cs" #>
<#@ parameter type="System.String" name="ControllerName" #>
<#@ parameter type="System.String" name="Namespace" #>
using System;
using System.Collections.Generic;
using System.Linq;
using System.Net;
using System.Net.Http;
using System.Web.Http;
```

```
namespace <#= Namespace #>
{
    public class <#= ControllerName #> : ApiBaseController
    {
    }
}
```

If you now go to Add ➤ Scaffolded Item ➤ Web API ➤ Web API 2 Controller Empty, the generated code will look as shown in Listing 1-16, inheriting from ApiBaseController instead of ApiController.

Listing 1-16. A Controller Generated from the Customized Scaffolding Template

```
using System;
using System.Collections.Generic;
using System.Linq;
using System.Net;
using System.Net.Http;
using System.Web.Http;

namespace Apress.Recipes.WebApi.Controllers
{
    public class SampleController : ApiBaseController
    {
    }
}
```

You could use this technique to introduce a wide array of customizations, including custom namespaces, injecting your own services, or forcing the actions to be asynchronous.

■ **Tip**   Instead of merely modifying the existing ones, you can also create new, completely independent scaffolding templates. You can learn more at the official .NET Web Development and Tools group blog at

http://blogs.msdn.com/b/webdev/archive/2014/04/03/creating-a-custom-scaffolder-for-visual-studio.aspx.

1-6. Add Model Validation
Problem

You would like ASP.NET Web API to perform validation against your models, and share some validation logic with ASP.NET MVC.

Solution

ASP.NET Web API supports the same validation mechanism as ASP.NET MVC: validation through attributes from System.ComponentModel.DataAnnotations. It's enough to just decorate your models with relevant validation attributes, and the framework will respect them.

For fine grained validation, you may choose to implement IValidatableObject (from System.ComponentModel.DataAnnotations) on your model. If all validation attributes successfully pass, ASP.NET Web API will then invoke the Validate method of that interface, allowing you to further inspect the entity. This is the same behavior as in MVC, and you can even use the same DTOs for both Web API and MVC.

A variation of this approach is to use a third-party library called FluentValidation (FluentValidation on NuGet) for building powerful validation scenarios. In this case, you would still implement IValidatableObject on your models, except it would need to rely on FluentValidation validators, rather than having the validation logic embedded. Those validators can also be shared between Web API and MVC.

■ **Tip** The validation behavior of ASP.NET Web API is the same across different hosts.

How It Works

In order to perform validation of models that are read from the body of HTTP requests, ASP.NET Web API relies on an IBodyModelValidator service. The outline of that interface is shown in Listing 1-17, and while it's a replaceable service, normally it's enough for you to use the default implementation, DefaultBodyModelValidator, which is enabled in HttpConfiguration automatically.

Listing 1-17. Definition of IBodyModelValidator

```
public interface IBodyModelValidator
{
    bool Validate(object model, Type type, ModelMetadataProvider metadataProvider,
    HttpActionContext actionContext, string keyPrefix);
}
```

The Validate method on the DefaultBodyModelValidator is invoked when a service called FormatterParameterBinding performs the binding of the body of the HTTP request to the parameter on the action that's handling the request. It recursively validates the entire object graph, validating each property and nested property against a relevant validation provider. For data annotation support, Web API uses DataAnnotationsModelValidatorProvider. If your model is annotated with WCF-style DataMemberAttributes, then the framework uses DataMemberModelValidatorProvider instead.

Finally, your model may implement IValidatableObject, a validation interface that exposes a single method, as shown in Listing 1-18. In this case, the model itself is providing additional validation logic. ASP.NET Web API will invoke that Validate method on an IValidatableObject, as long as all other validations (attribute based) pass.

Listing 1-18. Definition of the IValidatableObject

```
public interface IValidatableObject
{
    IEnumerable<ValidationResult> Validate(ValidationContext validationContext);
}
```

The validation result is represented in ASP.NET Web API by ModelStateDictionary, which is available as the ModelState property on the base ApiController. This is the exact same concept as in ASP.NET MVC, but the object is different because Web API uses its own version from the System.Web.Http.ModelBinding namespace. ModelStateDictionary exposes the IsValid property, which can be checked to determine the status of the model from inside of an action.

Data annotations as a validation mechanism are also integrated really well into the ASP.NET Web API Help Page, where they provide a semantic description of your API endpoint. That will be discussed in detail in Recipe 7-11.

■ **Tip**   It is a good practice to use a different model for requests to your API to that which you use for the responses. For example, an entity ID is typically needed only on the response model, as in the request can be read from the URI if needed.

The Code

Listing 1-19 shows a model with several annotations: RequiredAttribute, MaxLengthAttribute, and RangeAttribute. You are then able to use ModelState to check the state of the validation inside of the controller, and issue the appropriate response to the client.

Listing 1-19. A Sample Web API Model

```
public class Album
{
    public int Id { get; set; }

    [Required(ErrorMessage = "Artist is required")]
    [MaxLength(30)]
    public string Artist { get; set; }

    [Required(ErrorMessage = "Title is required")]
    [MaxLength(40)]
    public string Title { get; set; }

    [Range(0, 10, ErrorMessage = "Rating in the range of 0-10 is required.")]
    public int Rating { get; set; }
}

public class AlbumController : ApiController
{
    public HttpResponseMessage Post(Album album)
    {
        if (!ModelState.IsValid)
        {
            throw new HttpResponseException(Request.CreateErrorResponse(HttpStatusCode.BadRequest,
            ModelState));
        }

        //omitted for brevity
    }
}
```

The code responsible for dealing with ModelState, and in general with validation verification, can easily be extracted from the controller into a common, reusable filter; this will be discussed further in Recipe 5-4.

Now, consider the following scenario. What if you'd like to introduce an extra property on the model, called Starred, and extend the validation of the model so that at least one of the two (Rating or Starred) is required? While this type of entanglement between two properties is difficult to express with data annotations, it is where IValidateableObject can help. You can use the Validate method of the interface to inspect the state of the entire model and return the relevant ValidationResult based on that. The modified example is shown in Listing 1-20.

Listing 1-20. A Modified ASP.NET Web API Validation, Relying on IValidateableObject

```
public class Album : IValidatableObject
{
    public int Id { get; set; }

    [Required(ErrorMessage = "Artist is required")]
    [MaxLength(30)]
    public string Artist { get; set; }

    [Required(ErrorMessage = "Title is required")]
    [MaxLength(40)]
    public string Title { get; set; }

    public int? Rating { get; set; }

    public bool? Starred { get; set; }

    public IEnumerable<ValidationResult> Validate(ValidationContext validationContext)
    {
        if (!(Rating.HasValue && Rating > 0 && Rating < 10) || (Starred.HasValue && Starred.Value))
        {
            yield return new ValidationResult("You must set either the Rating in the 0-9 range or
            Starred flag.");
        }
    }
}
```

As you can see, you are free to combine the data annotations with custom logic from within the Validate method. In this particular example, if your request does not contain either of the two properties that are tied together (Rating or Starred), you can expect the validation to fail and the result to be as shown in Listing 1-21.

Listing 1-21. A Sample Invalid Request and a Response from Validation Performed via IValidateableObject

```
POST /api/album HTTP 1.1
Content-Type: application/json
{"artist":"Rancid", "title":"And Out Come The Wolves"}

Status Code: 400 Bad Request
Content-Length: 130
Content-Type: application/json; charset=utf-8
Date: Tue, 13 May 2014 19:06:31 GMT
{
    "Message": "The request is invalid.",
    "ModelState": {
        "album": [
            "You must set either the Rating in the 0-9 range or Starred flag."
        ]
    }
}
```

You can take validation a step further and introduce FluentValidation support to your Web API service. To get started, install FluentValidation from NuGet.

```
Install-package FluentValidation
```

Instead of embedding the validation logic into the entity itself, like you initially did, you'll just make it reference a FluentValidation validator, and invoke it within the Validate method. This way, all the validation logic can be externalized; as a result, you can not only move out the former logic contained in the Validate method, but also get rid of the DataAnnotations attributes. The previous example modified to work with FluentValidation is shown in Listing 1-22.

Listing 1-22. FluentValidation Validator Incorporated into IValidateableObject

```
public class TrackValidator : AbstractValidator<Track>
{
    public TrackValidator()
    {
        RuleFor(track => track.Artist).Length(0, 30).WithMessage("Artist is required");
        RuleFor(track => track.Artist).Length(0, 40).WithMessage("Title is required");
        RuleFor(track => track.Starred).NotNull().Equal(x => true).Unless(track => track.Rating.
        HasValue && track.Rating > 0 && track.Rating < 10);
        RuleFor(track => track.Rating).NotNull().GreaterThan(0).LessThan(10).Unless(track => track.
        Starred.HasValue && track.Starred.Value);
    }
}


public class Track : IValidatableObject
{
    public int Id { get; set; }

    public string Artist { get; set; }

    public string Title { get; set; }

    public int? Rating { get; set; }

    public bool? Starred { get; set; }

    public IEnumerable<ValidationResult> Validate(ValidationContext validationContext)
    {
        var validator = new TrackValidator();
        var result = validator.Validate(this);
        return result.Errors.Select(item => new ValidationResult(item.ErrorMessage, new[]
        { item.PropertyName }));
    }
}
```

In terms of functionality, the above example is equivalent to that from Listing 1-20; FluentValidation rules have been configured on a relevant validator to correspond to the behavior provided earlier by data annotations, while the presence of the IValidateableObject interface ensures that this particular validator is getting invoked.

1-7. Use CSRF Protection

Problem

You'd like to include CSRF (Cross-Site Request Forgery) protection against the data submitted from your MVC pages to the ASP.NET Web API endpoints.

Solution

ASP.NET already includes CSRF protection functionality, through the use of `System.Web.Helpers.AntiForgery` class (part of `System.Web.WebPages`).

It will generate two tokens: a cookie token and a string-based one that can be embedded into a form or a request header (in case of AJAX). To prevent CSRF attacks, form submissions and AJAX requests sent to the API must include both of the tokens that will get validated on the server side.

In ASP.NET Web API, it's typical to implement a cross cutting concern like anti-CSRF token validation as a `MessageHandler`.

How It Works

To generate a token within the context of MVC application, you call the `AntiForgeryToken HtmlHelper` extension method from inside a form.

```
<form id="myForm">
@Html.AntiForgeryToken()
//other fields
</form>
```

This helper uses the `AntiForgery` class under the hood. It writes a cookie token to the response, and generates a field named __RequestVerificationToken, which will be sent alongside your form data.

To validate the token on the server side, you call the static `Validate` method on the `AntiForgery` class. If it's called without parameters, it will use `HttpContext.Current` and try to extract the tokens from the relevant cookie and from the request body, assuming that the body is indeed a form and that a __RequestVerificationToken is present there.

The method is `void` so if the request validates successfully, nothing happens; otherwise, an `HttpAntiForgeryException` is thrown. You can catch that and return a relevant response to the client (for example an HTTP 403 Forbidden status code).

An alternative approach is to call `Validate` method and manually pass in both tokens. It is then up to you to retrieve them from the request; for example, it could be from the headers. This approach is also free of the dependency on the `HttpContext`.

For Web API, a custom message handler responsible for CSRF token validation can intercept every request as soon as it enters the Web API, perform the necessary checks, and continue with the pipeline execution, or, in case the request is invalid, short-circuit an error response (immediately return an error status code).

The Code

An example of a `MessageHandler` that performs the CSRF validation is shown in Listing 1-23. The code has two paths: one for AJAX requests and one for all other requests, which are simply assumed to be form submissions. If it's an AJAX request, you attempt to retrieve the token from the request header and the cookie token from the cookies collection sent alongside the request. In all other cases, the parameterless `Validate` method is used, so you rely on the framework to extract the tokens on its own.

If the validation fails, the client gets an immediate 403 Forbidden response.

Listing 1-23. Anti-CSRF Message Handler

```
public class AntiForgeryHandler : DelegatingHandler
{
    protected override async Task<HttpResponseMessage> SendAsync(
        HttpRequestMessage request,
        CancellationToken cancellationToken)
    {
        string cookieToken = null;
        string formToken = null;

        if (request.IsAjaxRequest())
        {
            IEnumerable<string> tokenHeaders;
            if (request.Headers.TryGetValues("__RequestVerificationToken", out tokenHeaders))
            {
                var cookie = request.Headers.GetCookies(AntiForgeryConfig.CookieName).
                FirstOrDefault();

                if (cookie != null)
                {
                    cookieToken = cookie[AntiForgeryConfig.CookieName].Value;
                }

                formToken = tokenHeaders.FirstOrDefault();
            }
        }

        try
        {
            if (cookieToken != null && formToken != null)
            {
                AntiForgery.Validate(cookieToken, formToken);
            }
            else
            {
                AntiForgery.Validate();
            }

        }
        catch (HttpAntiForgeryException)
        {
            return request.CreateResponse(HttpStatusCode.Forbidden);
        }

        return await base.SendAsync(request, cancellationToken);
    }
}
```

The handler is then registered against the `HttpConfiguration` to globally protect your API.

```
config.MessageHandlers.Add(new AntiForgeryHandler());
```

Building an anti-CSRF shield as a message handler is not the only way. You could just as well take the same code and place it inside a filter which you can then selectively apply to the relevant actions (similarly to how validation is done with filters, which is discussed in Recipe 5-4). A message handler, instead of being globally used, can also be attached to specific routes only. This is discussed in Recipe 3-9.

HttpRequestMessage does have a built-in way for checking if the request is an AJAX request, so the code uses a simple extension method to facilitate that, relying on the X-Requested-With header, which most of the JavaScript frameworks automatically send. That method is shown in Listing 1-24.

Listing 1-24. An Extension Method Checking if the HttpRequestMessage is an AJAX One

```
public static class HttpRequestMessageExtensions
{
    public static bool IsAjaxRequest(this HttpRequestMessage request)
    {
        IEnumerable<string> headers;
        if (request.Headers.TryGetValues("X-Requested-With", out headers))
        {
            var header = headers.FirstOrDefault();
            if (!string.IsNullOrEmpty(header))
            {
                return header.ToLowerInvariant() == "xmlhttprequest";
            }
        }

        return false;
    }
}
```

A simple form and an AJAX request, both utilizing the anti-CSRF tokens, are shown in Listing 1-25. In the case of a traditional form, the HTML helper renders a hidden input field and anti-forgery token is submitted alongside the form data automatically. In the case of an AJAX request, you explicitly read the token value from the rendered hidden input field, and attach it to the request in a custom header field.

Listing 1-25. Using the Anti-CSRF Protection in a Form and AJAX Request That Is Submitted to ASP.NET Web API

```
//HTML form
    <form id="form1" method="post" action="/api/form" enctype="application/x-www-form-urlencoded">
        @Html.AntiForgeryToken()
        <div>
            <label for="name">Name</label>
        </div>
        <div>
            <input type="text" name="name" value="Some Name" />
        </div>
        <div>
            <button id="postData" name="postData">Post form</button>
        </div>
    </form>
```

27

```
//AJAX form
    @Html.AntiForgeryToken()
    <input id="itemJS" type="text" disabled="disabled" name="text" value="some text" />
    <div>
        <button id="postJS" name="postJS">Post JS</button>
    </div>
    <script type="text/javascript">
            $(function () {
                $("#postJS").on("click", function () {
                    $.ajax({
                        dataType: "json",
                        data: JSON.stringify({ name: $("#itemJS").val() }),
                        type: "POST",
                        headers: {
                            "__RequestVerificationToken": $("#jsData input[name='__
                            RequestVerificationToken']").val()
                        },
                        contentType: "application/json; charset=utf-8",
                        url: "/api/items"
                    }).done(function (res) {
                        alert(res.Name);
                    });
                });
            });
    </script>
```

1-8. Add Support for Session State

Problem

Your web application, built around ASP.NET Web API, requires you to use the session to store some user-specific context on the server side.

Solution

ASP.NET Web API does not support sessions out of the box, as it does not rely at all on System.Web. It also tries to break away from artificial, non-HTTP like concepts, and session is one of them (HTTP is stateless, after all).

However, if you are running your ASP.NET Web API within the ASP.NET runtime, you can still enable session support. There are two ways to do it: globally, for the entire API, or locally, for specific routes only.

To enable session globally, you need to explicitly set the session behavior as SessionStateBehavior.Required in the Global.asax.

```
protected void Application_PostAuthorizeRequest()
{
    HttpContext.Current.SetSessionStateBehavior(SessionStateBehavior.Required);
}
```

To do it per route, you can introduce a route handler that implements IRequiresSessionState. Then, such a handler can be attached to specific Web API routes, enabling session state on requests to those routes.

How It Works

In the default ASP.NET Web API templates, you are guided to declare your routes in a static WebApiConfig class, against an instance of HttpConfiguration. However, it is possible to define Web API routes against the System.Web.RouteCollection too, in the same place where you define MVC routes, as the framework ships with an extension method allowing you to do just that.

While MapHttpRoute overloads are typically used as if they are void, in fact the method does return an instance of a newly declared route; it's just that the result of the invocation of the method is typically thrown away. In the case of the route declared directly against System.Web.RouteCollection, the return would be a System.Web.Route object, to which you are able to assign an IRouteHandler.

When running on top of ASP.NET, the ASP.NET Web API framework uses the same mechanism to ensure API-bound requests will reach it; it assigns HttpControllerRouteHandler to each Web API route. HttpControllerRouteHandler, in the GetHttpHandler method, returns an instance of HttpControllerHandler, which is the entry point to the ASP.NET Web API pipeline. HttpControllerHandler, albeit very complex (it's the heart of Web API), is simply a traditional IHttpAsyncHandler (an async version of the old school IHttpHandler) under the hood.

You can enforce session presence on an IHttpHandler by making it implement an IRequiresSessionState marker interface. ASP.NET will explicitly enable session state for each route handler implementing that interface.

Alternatively, on the global scale, calling the HttpContext.Current.SetSessionStateBehavior method and passing in SessionStateBehavior.Required explicitly enables a session for the current HttpContext. The SetSessionStateBehavior method must be called before the AcquireRequestState event.

The Code

As you have probably concluded already, you'll need to customize two classes: HttpControllerHandler and HttpControllerRouteHandler. You'll create a custom SessionHttpControllerHandler that implements IRequiresSessionState and a custom SessionHttpControllerRouteHandler that simply acts as a factory that returns SessionHttpControllerHandler, instead of the default type. These are shown in Listing 1-26.

Listing 1-26. Customized HttpControllerHandler and HttpControllerRouteHandler

```
public class SessionControllerHandler : HttpControllerHandler, IRequiresSessionState
{
    public SessionControllerHandler(RouteData routeData)
        : base(routeData)
    { }
}

public class SessionHttpControllerRouteHandler : HttpControllerRouteHandler
{
    protected override IHttpHandler GetHttpHandler(RequestContext requestContext)
    {
        return new SessionControllerHandler(requestContext.RouteData);
    }
}
```

You should now move your route definition from WebApiConfig to the RouteConfig class, as you need to perform it against RouteCollection. Then, SessionHttpControllerRouteHandler should be set as the RouteHandler on the created route. This is shown in Listing 1-27.

Listing 1-27. Registering Web API Routes Against System.Web.RouteCollection

```
public static void RegisterRoutes(RouteCollection routes)
{
    routes.IgnoreRoute("{resource}.axd/{*pathInfo}");

    //Web API with session
    routes.MapHttpRoute(
        name: "DefaultApi",
        routeTemplate: "api/{controller}/{id}",
        defaults: new { id = RouteParameter.Optional }
        ).RouteHandler = new SessionHttpControllerRouteHandler();

    //MVC
    routes.MapRoute(
        name: "Default",
        url: "{controller}/{action}/{id}",
        defaults: new { controller = "Home", action = "Index", id = UrlParameter.Optional }
    );
}
```

If you are feeling really adventurous, there is one more trick you may want to perform, which will allow you to not have to move your route registration into RouteConfig, and still perform it against HttpConfiguration, from WebApiConfig. Moreover, it will also automagically enable session for all of your Web API routes.

When you register the routes through Web API configuration, they will all be registered against the underlying RouteTable as routes with the singleton HttpControllerRouteHandler.Instance as the route handler. This allows ASP.NET to forward all of the calls to Web API routes, to the Web API pipeline. That singleton is actually a Lazy<HttpCo ntrollerRouteHandler>. You could, at your application startup, swap that singleton instance with a different subclass (in your case SessionHttpControllerRouteHandler), which will allow you to continue registering your routes against HttpConfiguration, and will ensure every single Web API route uses SessionHttpControllerRouteHandler, which in turn means that they all have access to session state. This simple reflection-based trick is shown in Listing 1-28.

Listing 1-28. Arbitrarily Enabling Session on All ASP.NET Web API Routes Through a Reflection Trick

```
public static class WebApiConfig
{
    public static void Register(HttpConfiguration config)
    {
        var httpControllerRouteHandler = typeof(HttpControllerRouteHandler).GetField("_instance",
                    BindingFlags.Static | BindingFlags.NonPublic);

        if (httpControllerRouteHandler != null)
        {
            httpControllerRouteHandler.SetValue(null,
                new Lazy<HttpControllerRouteHandler>(() => new SessionHttpControllerRouteHandler(),
                true));
        }

        config.Routes.MapHttpRoute(
            name: "DefaultApi",
            routeTemplate: "api/{controller}/{id}",
```

```
            defaults: new {id = RouteParameter.Optional}
            );
        config.MapHttpAttributeRoutes();
    }
}
```

Now, just as proof that this is indeed working, let's put together a simple ApiController that will simulate dice throwing. It will give you a random 1-6 value, as well as the result of the previous throw, coming from the session. This is shown in Listing 1-29.

Listing 1-29. A Sample ApiController Relying on Session State

```
public class DiceResult
{
    public int NewValue { get; set; }
    public int LastValue { get; set; }
}

public class DiceController : ApiController
{
    public DiceResult Get()
    {
        var newValue = new Random().Next(1, 7);

        object context;
        if (Request.Properties.TryGetValue("MS_HttpContext", out context))
        {
            var httpContext = context as HttpContextBase;
            if (httpContext != null && httpContext.Session != null)
            {
                var lastValue = httpContext.Session["LastValue"] as int?;
                httpContext.Session["LastValue"] = newValue;

                return new DiceResult
                {
                    NewValue = newValue,
                    LastValue = lastValue ?? 0
                };
            }
        }

        return new DiceResult { NewValue = newValue};
    }
}
```

Notice that you retrieve HttpContext from the HttpRequestMessage Properties dictionary, from the MS_HttpContext key. This is a more testable way than directly accessing System.Web.HttpContext.Current.

CHAPTER 2

■ ■ ■

ASP.NET Web API Outside of IIS

In this chapter, I'll go beyond the classic scenario of hosting ASP.NET Web API on IIS. ASP.NET Web API, despite its name, is entirely independent from the ASP.NET runtime. You can embed Web API into almost any .NET process, namely console applications or Windows services, as well as class libraries that can be plugged into an existing pre-defined architecture in Microsoft Azure.

The goal of this chapter is to provide a compact, yet comprehensive overview of the various options that are available to you. You will learn how to do the following:

- Self-host ASP.NET Web API using the WCF hosting adapter (Recipe 2-1)

- Host ASP.NET Web API on top of OWIN (Open Web Interface for .NET) (Recipe 2-2)

- Host within a console application and Windows Services (Recipes 2-1 and 2-2)

- Host ASP.NET Web API in Microsoft Azure, as part of Azure Mobiles Services or in an Azure Worker Role (Recipes 2-3 and 2-5)

- Rapidly wireframe ASP.NET Web API projects with scriptcs (Recipe 2-4)

- Build Web APIs with F# (Recipe 2-6)

ASP.NET Web API can also be hosted entirely in memory, without even touching the networking stack; however, this will be discussed in detail in Recipe 11-7, as its primary use case is for testing.

2-1. Self-Host ASP.NET Web API

Problem

You would like to run your Web API without IIS and the ASP.NET runtime, using Web API's self-hosting capabilities.

Solution

The package enabling Web API self-hosting, using a Windows Communication Foundation hardened core, is available on NuGet:

```
Install-Package Microsoft.AspNet.WebApi.SelfHost
```

To run a self-hosted ASP.NET Web API (Listing 2-1), you need to create an instance of an HttpSelfHostConfiguration and pass it into an instance of HttpSelfHostServer, which will create the WCF channel stack responsible for the HTTP interaction of your Web API service.

Listing 2-1. Self-Hosting a Web API

```
var address = "http://localhost:900";
var config = new HttpSelfHostConfiguration(address);
//configure the HttpConfiguration as you wish

var server = new HttpSelfHostServer(config)
server.OpenAsync().Wait();
Console.WriteLine("Server running at {0}. Press any key to exit", address);
Console.ReadLine();
```

How It Works

Since its first version, Web API has shipped with a self-hosted mode, which is based on HttpListener and allows you to run Web API services outside of ASP.NET. You can turn any .NET application into a Web API server, as long as it meets the following prerequisites:

- It can listen on a specific port, meaning that the URL and port had been reserved for the application with the relevant netsh command, or the application is running with elevated (admin) privileges.

- It is able to reference and utilize the WCF components that Web API self-host is built on, such as System.ServiceModel (for example, Windows Store applications cannot).

ASP.NET Web API self-host uses the WCF channel stack layer to obtain request messages from the underlying HTTP infrastructure. Internally, HttpSelfHostServer sets up an HttpBinding which is configured using the data provided through HttpSelfHostConfiguration. Then the HttpBinding is used to configure a WCF message channel stack, which is responsible for the communication with the operating system's networking stack; on Windows, that's HTTP.SYS (which would also be responsible for HTTP requests for IIS).

ASP.NET Web API self-host internally relies on an HttpListener class, which requires that any application that uses it to listen on a specific port fulfills one of two requirements:

- It runs with elevated privileges (it can then listen on any port).

- The account used to run the application has previously been granted explicit permission to listen on the port being used. This is the so called reservation.

Running the application using the administrator's identity is often not the best idea, so it's more common to go with the second option. You can use the netsh tool to reserve a URL for a specific user account, like so:

```
//add a URL reservation
netsh http add urlacl url=http://+:900/ user=filip-pc\filip

//remove a URL reservation
netsh http delete urlacl url=http://+:8080/
```

At application startup, HttpListener tries to register a URL to be able to receive HTTP requests, and if neither of the two preconditions is met (application is not running with elevated privileges or URL has not been reserved), you will encounter the following error at Web API startup:

System.ServiceModel.AddressAccessDeniedException: HTTP could not register URL http://+:900/...
Your process does not have access rights to this namespace

■ **Note** You can read more about HTTP Server API, Reservations, Registrations, and Routing at MSDN
http://msdn.microsoft.com/en-us/library/Aa364673.

Having to explicitly start the server by hand (as was shown in Listing 2-1) and being able to shut it down
at any time without exiting the host application are the key differences from using Web API in the ASP.NET
runtime. Under ASP.NET, the HttpServer instance handling your Web API HTTP interaction is statically
created by the GlobalConfiguration object the first time HttpControllerRouteHandler (a Web API-specific
HttpTaskAsyncHandler) is used.

HttpSelfHostConfiguration, shown in Listing 2-2, extends the default HttpConfiguration and introduces a few
of the WCF-specific properties along the way. As a consequence, a Web API host created using self-host is not always
100% portable to ASP.NET, and vice versa.

Listing 2-2. Definition of HttpSelfHostConfiguration

```
public class HttpSelfHostConfiguration : HttpConfiguration
{
    public HttpSelfHostConfiguration(string baseAddress);
    public HttpSelfHostConfiguration(Uri baseAddress);

    public Uri BaseAddress { get; }
    public System.ServiceModel.HttpClientCredentialType ClientCredentialType { get; set; }
    public System.ServiceModel.HostNameComparisonMode HostNameComparisonMode { get; set; }
    public int MaxBufferSize { get; set; }
    public int MaxConcurrentRequests { get; set; }
    public long MaxReceivedMessageSize { get; set; }
    public TimeSpan ReceiveTimeout { get; set; }
    public TimeSpan SendTimeout { get; set; }
    public System.ServiceModel.TransferMode TransferMode { get; set; }
    public System.IdentityModel.Selectors.UserNamePasswordValidator UserNamePasswordValidator
    { get; set; }
    public System.IdentityModel.Selectors.X509CertificateValidator X509CertificateValidator
    { get; set; }

    protected virtual System.ServiceModel.Channels.BindingParameterCollection
    OnConfigureBinding(HttpBinding httpBinding);
}
```

Additionally, HttpSelfHostConfiguration exposes a virtual OnConfigureBinding method which allows you to
tap into the mechanism of configuring the HttpBinding created by HttpSelfHostServer just before it gets used to set
up the WCF channel stack.

The ASP.NET Web API self-host defaults to 100 maximum concurrent requests per processor of your server;
you can adjust this by modifying the MaxConcurrentRequests property. Unless modified, the SendTimeout and
ReceiveTimeout settings default to 60 and 600 seconds, respectively.

HttpSelfHostConfiguration also exposes—contrary to the regular HttpConfiguration—a TransferMode setting, allowing you to *globally* define whether all communication with your Web API should be done in streamed or buffered mode. By default, TransferMode.Buffered is used; switching to Streamed mode also changes the native channel shape from IDuplexSessionChannel (used in buffered mode) to IRequestChannel and IReplyChannel. This is a considerable difference from the web host, as there you are able to influence the streaming/buffering setting on a per-request basis.

Finally, a critical difference between ASP.NET Web API web host and self-host is the fact that since self-host operates outside of the ASP.NET runtime, there is no global System.Web.HttpContext available. As a result, you have to be extremely careful when crafting your code and eliminate any references to HttpContext.Current.

The Code

Using ASP.NET Web API self-host is a great alternative to hosting on ASP.NET/IIS as it gives you the ability to create small, lightweight, focused services which are extremely easy to deploy and manage—either as console applications or Windows services.

As long as you are aware of some of the small differences mentioned earlier in this chapter, working with Web API in self-hosted mode is almost identical to working within the ASP.NET context. You still define the controllers, filters, message handlers, routes, and any other components of the Web API pipeline like you do on other hosts. The example, using self-host from a console application, is shown in Listing 2-3.

Listing 2-3. A Sample Console Application Using ASP.NET Web API Self-Host

```
class Program
{
    static void Main(string[] args)
    {
        var address = "http://localhost:900";
        var config = new HttpSelfHostConfiguration(address);
        config.MapHttpAttributeRoutes();

        using (var server = new HttpSelfHostServer(config))
        {
            server.OpenAsync().Wait();
            Console.WriteLine("Server running at {0}. Press any key to exit", address);
            Console.ReadLine();
        }

    }
}
```

■ **Tip** While Web API self-host is still being maintained and updated by Microsoft, it is generally recommended to use the Web API OWIN Self Host (Recipe 2-2) host instead, as it provides similar functionality with less restrictions and more flexibility.

2-2. Host ASP.NET Web API with OWIN

Problem

You'd like to use ASP.NET Web API on top of OWIN, the Open Web Interface for .NET.

Solution

To run a self-hosted (HttpListener-based) ASP.NET Web API using Project Katana, Microsoft's implementation of OWIN, use the Microsoft.AspNet.WebApi.OwinSelfHost NuGet package. To run ASP.NET Web API against other types of Katana-compatible servers, install the Microsoft.AspNet.WebApi.Owin NuGet package.

In either case, once installed, in order to inject the ASP.NET Web API middleware adapter, you need to create a Startup class with a single Configuration method, which takes in an IAppBuilder. You should then call the UseWebApi extension method and pass in the correctly configured Web API HttpConfiguration object, which is shown in Listing 2-4.

Listing 2-4. Sample Startup Class for Web API Katana Hosting

```
public class Startup
{
    public void Configuration(IAppBuilder appBuilder)
    {
        var config = new HttpConfiguration();

        //add routes, configure Web API
        config.MapHttpAttributeRoutes();

        appBuilder.UseWebApi(config);
    }
}
```

How It Works

OWIN, the Open Web Interface for .NET, is a community-driven specification defining a standard interaction between .NET web servers and .NET web applications.

As a consequence, OWIN helps to decouple the host (i.e. console application), the server (i.e. HttpListener) and the application framework from each other, effectively eliminating environmental dependencies from the applications, which in turn results in a much more portable and robust web application landscape and ecosystem in .NET. OWIN was originally inspired by the Rack interface used in Ruby as minimal contract between the server and a Ruby on Rails application.

The interface describing the application-server communication is reduced to one trivial delegate.

```
using AppFunc = Func<
        IDictionary<string, object>, // Environment
        Task>; // Done
```

The environment dictionary acts as a store for all requests (summarized in Table 2-1), response (summarized in Table 2-2) and all state data, and it's the responsibility of an OWIN-compatible server to populate it with relevant data which can then be consumed by the applications.

Table 2-1. *OWIN Request Environment Dictionary Keys. Source: Open Web Server Interface for .NET, v1.0.0,* `http://owin.org/spec/owin-1.0.0.html`*, Copyright: OWIN contributors, License: Creative Commons Attribution 3.0 Unported License*

Required	Key Name	Value Description
Yes	"owin.RequestBody"	A `Stream` with the request body, if any. `Stream.Null` MAY be used as a placeholder if there is no request body.
Yes	"owin.RequestHeaders"	An `IDictionary<string, string[]>` of request headers.
Yes	"owin.RequestMethod"	A string containing the HTTP request method of the request (e.g., "GET", "POST").
Yes	"owin.RequestPath"	A string containing the request path. The path MUST be relative to the root of the application delegate
Yes	"owin.RequestPathBase"	A string containing the portion of the request path corresponding to the root of the application delegate
Yes	"owin.RequestProtocol"	A string containing the protocol name and version (e.g. "HTTP/1.0" or "HTTP/1.1").
Yes	"owin.RequestQueryString"	A string containing the query string component of the HTTP request URI, without the leading "?" (e.g., "`foo=bar&baz=quux`"). The value may be an empty string.
Yes	"owin.RequestScheme"	A string containing the URI scheme used for the request (e.g., "http", "https")

Table 2-2. *Owin Response Environment Dictionary Keys. Source: Open Web Server Interface for .NET, v1.0.0,* `http://owin.org/spec/owin-1.0.0.html`*, Copyright: OWIN contributors, License: Creative Commons Attribution 3.0 Unported License*

Required	Key Name	Value Description
Yes	"owin.ResponseBody"	A Stream used to write out the response body, if any.
Yes	"owin.ResponseHeaders"	An `IDictionary<string, string[]>` of response headers.
No	"owin.ResponseStatusCode"	An optional int containing the HTTP response status code as defined in RFC 2616 section 6.1.1. The default is 200.
No	"owin.ResponseReasonPhrase"	An optional string containing the reason phrase associated the given status code. If none is provided, then the server SHOULD provide a default as described in RFC 2616 section 6.1.1
No	"owin.ResponseProtocol"	An optional string containing the protocol name and version (e.g. "HTTP/1.0" or "HTTP/1.1"). If none is provided, then the "owin.RequestProtocol" key's value is the default.

Due to this simplicity, lack of heavy external dependencies, asynchronous design, and a general no-frills approach, OWIN encourages and facilitates development of small, focused components (middleware) which can then be used across different frameworks. Moreover, OWIN-compatible applications are generally easily portable to different platforms.

While the OWIN specification does not define a specific way of declaring an OWIN entry point in an assembly or how to define a startup sequence, a de facto standard has emerged from Project Katana, in the form of a `Startup` class and an `IAppBuilder`.

Project Katana is a Microsoft's OWIN implementation and contains the following:

- a host (`OwinHost.exe`)

- a set of servers (`HttpListener`, `SystemWeb`)

- a number of middleware components (i.e. Authentication components)

Katana will try to find the developer's code by looking for a `Startup` class, based on the following order of precedence:

- Look at the `appSettings owin:AppStartup` as a type hint.

- Look at assembly-level attribute `OwinStartupAttribute`.

- Scan all `AppDomain` assemblies looking for a class named `Startup`.

Once the `Startup` type is found, it will try to call a configuration method matching the following signature:

```
void Configuration(IAppBuilder app)
```

And this is exactly the place where a developer can plug into the OWIN pipeline, and register his middleware or adapters for his web framework(s) of choice, as shown in Listing 2-5.

Listing 2-5. A Sample Startup Class and a Definition of IAppBuilder

```
public class Startup
{
    public void Configuration(IAppBuilder app)
    {
        app.Use(typeof(SomeMiddleware)); //register SomeMiddleware
        app.UseNancy(); //register NancyFx framework
    }
}

    public interface IAppBuilder
    {
        IDictionary<string, object> Properties { get; }
        IAppBuilder Use(object middleware, params object[] args);
        object Build(Type returnType);
        IAppBuilder New();
    }
```

ASP.NET Web API supports OWIN by providing an adapter class called `HttpMessageHandlerAdapter` between the OWIN Dictionary and its request/response-specific entries and the native Web API `HttpRequestMessage` and `HttpResponseMessage` types.

The UseWebApi extension method from Microsoft.AspNet.WebApi.Owin will internally set the default IHostBufferPolicySelector to OwinBufferPolicySelector, register HttpMessageHandlerAdapter as OWIN middleware, and plug in the default HttpServer. In case you want to customize the entry point to your Web API, you can plug in an alternative HttpServer too, using a different extension method:

```
public static IAppBuilder UseWebApi(this IAppBuilder builder, HttpConfiguration configuration)
public static IAppBuilder UseWebApi(this IAppBuilder builder, HttpServer httpServer)
```

■ **Tip** OwinBufferPolicySelector is discussed in more detail in Recipe 4-12.

The Code

The example in Listing 2-6 shows a Web API hosted using OWIN self-host within a Windows Service. This is a particularly useful solution due to the ease with which you can now manage such a Web API from different Windows tools and scripts.

Listing 2-6. Windows Service Utilizing Web API OWIN Self-Host

```
public class Startup
{
    public void Configuration(IAppBuilder appBuilder)
    {
        var config = new HttpConfiguration();
        config.MapHttpAttributeRoutes();

        appBuilder.UseWebApi(config);
    }
}

public partial class WebApiService : ServiceBase
{
    private IDisposable _owinHost;
    const string Address = "http://localhost:999/";

    public WebApiService()
    {
        InitializeComponent();

    }

    protected override void OnStart(string[] args)
    {
        _owinHost = WebApp.Start<Startup>(Address);
    }

    protected override void OnStop()
    {
        _owinHost.Dispose();
    }
}
```

The `WebApp` static class (Listing 2-7) is part of `Microsoft.Owin.Hosting` and is used to load and start a web application using the Katana self-host. You can either provide a `Startup` class that you have already created or define the behavior inline using `Action<IAppBuilder>`. As far as the host URL goes, you may provide a raw string representing the address or use a more elaborate `StartupOptions` to configure any extra settings.

Listing 2-7. Definition of the WebApp Class from Katana

```
public static class WebApp
{
    public static IDisposable Start<TStartup>(StartOptions options);
    public static IDisposable Start(StartOptions options);
    public static IDisposable Start<TStartup>(string url);
    public static IDisposable Start(string url);
    public static IDisposable Start(StartOptions options, Action<Owin.IAppBuilder> startup);
    public static IDisposable Start(string url, Action<Owin.IAppBuilder> startup);
}
```

The server started by the `WebApp.Start` returns an `IDisposable` which can be used to shut it down whenever necessary. To deploy such a Windows service, you need to add an `Installer`, which you can do by right-clicking on the Windows Service designer surface and choose the Add Installer option. The bare minimum that should be set are the name of the service as it will appear in the list of installed services, which is set through the Properties pane of the auto-generated `serviceInstaller1`, and the account used to run the service, set through the Properties of the auto-generated `serviceProcessInstaller1`.

The service can installed using `installutil` (the Visual Studio developer command prompt has it in the PATH variable already). Given that your Windows service project is called Apress.Recipes.WebApi, you'd call:

```
installutil Apress.Recipes.WebApi.exe
```

2-3. Host ASP.NET Web API in Azure Mobile Services
Problem

You want to host an HTTP API in Azure so that your service is monitored, scaled, and managed for you. Additionally, you would like to have built-in support for authentication and push notifications as you'd like your API to be used by a wide range of clients and devices.

Solution

You can take advantage of the excellent Azure Mobile Services (also known as ZUMO) offered by Microsoft Azure, allowing you to build rich application backends for all kinds of devices and platforms that have HTTP connectivity. Originally a Node.js-exclusive platform, since early 2014 Azure Mobile Services has been supporting .NET by providing an option to host ASP.NET Web API.

To create a new Azure Mobile Services, head off to the Microsoft Azure management portal and choose New ➤ Compute ➤ Mobile Service ➤ Create and then complete a short 2-step wizard like the one shown in Figure 2-1.

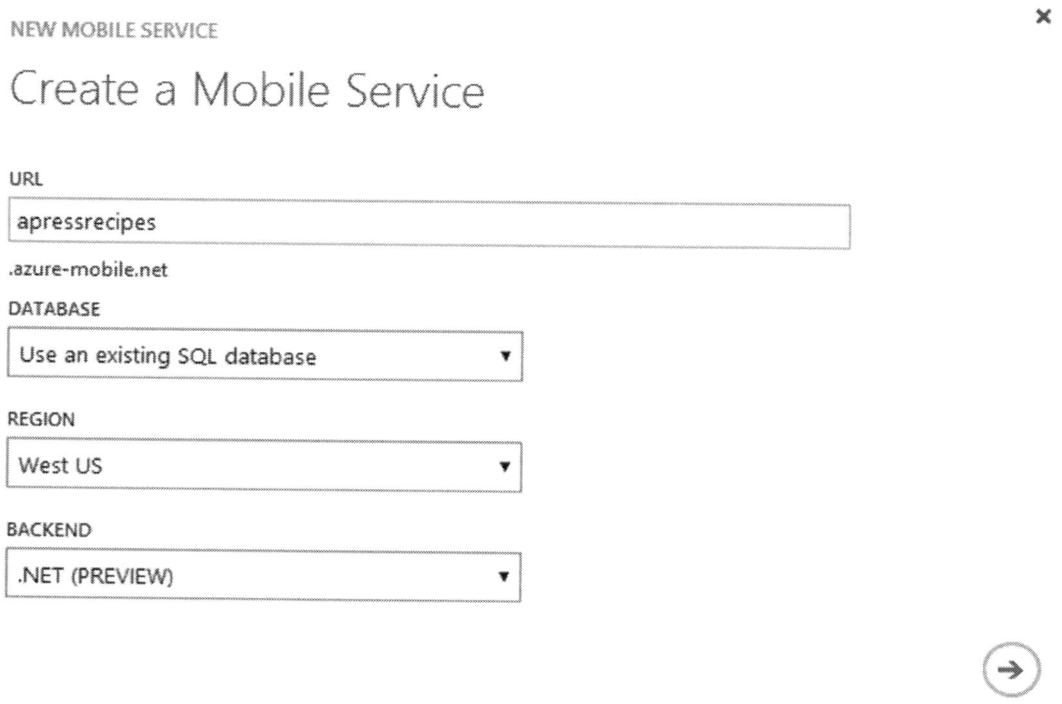

NEW MOBILE SERVICE   ✕

Create a Mobile Service

URL

    apressrecipes

.azure-mobile.net

DATABASE

    Use an existing SQL database   ▼

REGION

    West US   ▼

BACKEND

    .NET (PREVIEW)   ▼

                                                        (→)

Figure 2-1. *Creating a new .NET-based Azure Mobile Service*

You can then open up your new Mobile Service from the left-hand menu, and, after clicking "Connect an Existing App", download the snapshot of the service as a Visual Studio solution. This view is shown in Figure 2-2.

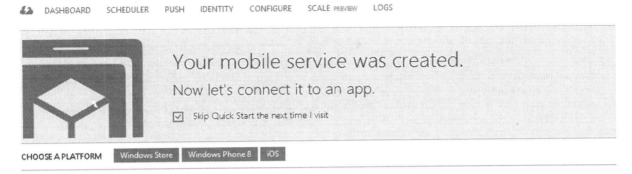

GET STARTED

▷ CREATE A NEW WINDOWS STORE APP

◢ CONNECT AN EXISTING WINDOWS STORE APP

Follow these steps to connect an existing application to your mobile service.

1 ### Download your service locally

Download and extract your personalized starter project.

Download

Add the mobile service project to your solution and build it.

Figure 2-2. *Downloading the sample .NET-based Azure Mobile Service*

The downloaded project can be used to develop your API locally; once you are happy with the end result, you can publish it back to Azure, using `MsDeploy` (your Mobile Service has an associated Publishing Profile which you can download from the Azure Management Portal) or through `git` deployment (also configurable in the portal).

■ **Note** Technically speaking, contrary to the chapter title, Azure Mobile Services actually use IIS under the hood. However, the extra features included in ZUMO are beyond the typical ASP.NET Web API that you might host on IIS yourself.

How It Works

In addition to being based on the familiar ASP.NET Web API, the .NET version of Azure Mobile Services adds most of the great features of the ZUMO platform, such as support for cross-device push notifications, support for scheduled jobs, and integration with the most popular authentication providers.

The out-of-the-box Azure Mobile Services Web API setup is built and configured around the following:

- OWIN pipeline
- Entity Framework and integration with SQL Azure
- Autofac for dependency injection

- Web API tracing to SystemDiagnostics.Trace

- OData support

- Integration with popular authentication providers (Google, Twitter, Microsoft, Facebook)

- Integration with push services for the major devices and with Azure Notification Hubs

Most of the extra features of Azure Mobile Services are baked into the Microsoft.WindowsAzure.Mobile. Service package.

To get the most out of Web API hosted in Azure Mobile Services, you should inherit your controllers from TableController or TableController<TData>. This base class exposes the ApiServices property, which you can use to access all of the terrific features of ZUMO. The definition of that type is shown in Listing 2-8.

Listing 2-8. Definition of ApiServices

```
public class ApiServices : IDisposable
{
    public ApiServices(HttpConfiguration config);

    public virtual HttpConfiguration Config { get; set; }
    public virtual ITraceWriter Log { get; set; }
    public virtual IDictionary<object, object> Properties { get; }
    public virtual PushClient Push { get; set; }
    public virtual ServiceSettingsDictionary Settings { get; set; }

    public void Dispose();
    protected virtual void Dispose(bool disposing);
}
```

ServiceSettingsDictionary is shown in Listing 2-9 and represents a de facto configuration of your Azure Mobile Services instance, including things like authentication providers keys/secrets, notification hubs setup, and connection string settings. Any values changed in the ServiceSettingsDictionary object at runtime will only stay in effect for the duration of the lifetime of the current System.AppDomain; if you wish to do it in a persistent manner, you should update them in the Azure Management Portal.

Listing 2-9. Definition of ServiceSettingsDictionary

```
public class ServiceSettingsDictionary : Dictionary<string, string>
{
    public ServiceSettingsDictionary();
    protected ServiceSettingsDictionary(SerializationInfo info, StreamingContext context);

    public virtual string AzureActiveDirectoryAudience { get; set; }
    public IDictionary<string, ConnectionSettings> Connections { get; }
    public virtual string FacebookAppId { get; set; }
    public virtual string FacebookSecret { get; set; }
    public virtual string GoogleAppId { get; set; }
    public virtual string GoogleSecret { get; set; }
    public virtual bool IsFacebookAuthenticationEnabled { get; }
    public virtual bool IsGoogleAuthenticationEnabled { get; }
    public virtual bool IsMicrosoftAccountAuthenticationEnabled { get; }
    public virtual bool IsTwitterAuthenticationEnabled { get; }
    public virtual string Key { get; set; }
```

```
    public virtual string MasterKey { get; set; }
    public virtual string MicrosoftAccountClientId { get; set; }
    public virtual string MicrosoftAccountClientSecret { get; set; }
    public virtual string Name { get; set; }
    public virtual string NotificationHubName { get; set; }
    public virtual string Schema { get; set; }
    public virtual string SubscriptionId { get; set; }
    public virtual string TwitterConsumerKey { get; set; }
    public virtual string TwitterConsumerSecret { get; set; }
    public static string GetSchemaName();
}
```

The PushClient exposed by the ApiServices allows you to send a notification payload to connected devices directly from the controller; note that they have to be implementing the marker IPushMessage interface. Each of the popular devices uses different technology for push notifications, but Mobile Services-hosted Web API makes it really to use all of them, providing a relevant implementation of IPushMessage for each of the platforms.

- iOS: Apple Push Notification Service (APNS) through ApplePushMessage type

- Android: Google Cloud Messaging for Chrome (GCM) through GooglePushMessage type

- Windows Phone: Microsoft Push Notifications Service (MPNS) through MpnsPushMessage type

- Windows 8: WPNS through WindowsPushMessage type

Authentication is supported via a number of external packages from the Microsoft.Owin.Security.* family. To enable authentication in your controller, simply add the [AuthorizeLevel(AuthorizationLevel.User)] (or any other appropriate level) attribute to your controller/action, which will enforce the access control restrictions on the connecting client. When running locally, ZUMO Web API will pick up the keys and secrets from web.config settings (see Listing 2-10), but once you deploy to Azure those will be overridden by the settings present in your Azure Management Portal.

Listing 2-10. Appropriate Key Names to Enable Authentication Support with Different Providers

```
<add key="MS_MicrosoftClientID" value="Overridden by portal settings" />
<add key="MS_MicrosoftClientSecret" value="Overridden by portal settings" />
<add key="MS_FacebookAppID" value="Overridden by portal settings" />
<add key="MS_FacebookAppSecret" value="Overridden by portal settings" />
<add key="MS_GoogleClientID" value="Overridden by portal settings" />
<add key="MS_GoogleClientSecret" value="Overridden by portal settings" />
<add key="MS_TwitterConsumerKey" value=" Overridden by portal settings " />
<add key="MS_TwitterConsumerSecret" value=" Overridden by portal settings " />
```

Interestingly, Azure Mobile Services Web API ships with Autofac baked in, so you get free dependency injection out of the box. You can register your own dependencies by passing a relevant Action<HttpConfiguration, ContainerBuilder> to the ServiceConfig.Initialize as shown in Listing 2-11.

Listing 2-11. Registering Custom Services Against Autofac in ZUMO

```
public static void Register()
{
    var options = new ConfigOptions();
    var config = ServiceConfig.Initialize(new ConfigBuilder(options, (httpConfig, autofac) =>
autofac.RegisterInstance(new MyService()).As<IService>()));
}
```

Finally, one of the great features of Azure Mobile Services is that it can be remotely debugged, meaning you can attach from a local Visual Studio to a live instance of your Web API in Azure and step through the code. This feature has to be enabled in your Azure Management Portal first, and you can then use the "Attach to Process" dialog and point it to the DNS name of your mobile service to allow you breakpoints to hit. Henrik Frystyk Nielsen, the architect of ASP.NET Web API and now the .NET backend for Azure Mobile Services, has a detailed blog post about this at `http://blogs.msdn.com/b/azuremobile/archive/2014/03/14/debugging-net-backend-in-visual-studio.aspx`.

■ **Tip** To learn more about the Azure Mobile Services platform head over to `www.windowsazure.com/en-us/develop/mobile/resources/` for excellent tutorials and references.

The Code

Aside from some of the differences and extra features just mentioned, Web API running in Azure Mobile is very much a typical Web API (at the time of writing at version 2.1) like you are accustomed to using. Almost all of the recipes used in this book are applicable and usable in Azure Mobile Services.

A sample controller from a default project that gets generated for each new ZUMO account is shown in Listing 2-12. You can immediately see that it's a typical Web API controller, with all familiar HTTP methods and Web API constructs such as `IHttpActionResult`. Interestingly, it even supports PATCH for partial updates of your entities.

Listing 2-12. Sample Controller from the Default ZUMO Project

```
public class TodoItemController : TableController<TodoItem>
{
    protected override void Initialize(HttpControllerContext controllerContext)
    {
        base.Initialize(controllerContext);
        apressrecipesContext context = new apressrecipesContext();
        DomainManager = new EntityDomainManager<TodoItem>(context, Request, Services);
    }

    // GET tables/TodoItem
    public IQueryable<TodoItem> GetAllTodoItems()
    {
        return Query();
    }

    // GET tables/TodoItem/48D68C86-6EA6-4C25-AA33-223FC9A27959
    public SingleResult<TodoItem> GetTodoItem(string id)
    {
        return Lookup(id);
    }

    // PATCH tables/TodoItem/48D68C86-6EA6-4C25-AA33-223FC9A27959
    public Task<TodoItem> PatchTodoItem(string id, Delta<TodoItem> patch)
    {
        return UpdateAsync(id, patch);
    }
```

```
// POST tables/TodoItem/48D68C86-6EA6-4C25-AA33-223FC9A27959
public async Task<IHttpActionResult> PostTodoItem(TodoItem item)
{
    TodoItem current = await InsertAsync(item);
    return CreatedAtRoute("Tables", new { id = current.Id }, current);
}

// DELETE tables/TodoItem/48D68C86-6EA6-4C25-AA33-223FC9A27959
public Task DeleteTodoItem(string id)
{
    return DeleteAsync(id);
}
}
```

The controller inherits from TableController<TData>, which was mentioned before. This class is actually constraining TData to ITableData, so if you want to use SQL Azure and the built-in Entity Framework Code First support, you need to make sure to implement that (see Listing 2-13). The extra attributes on that interface have been used to ensure uniform serialization across different platforms.

Listing 2-13. Definition of ITableData Interface

```
public interface ITableData
{
    [JsonProperty(PropertyName = "__createdAt")]
    DateTimeOffset? CreatedAt { get; set; }

    [JsonProperty(PropertyName = "__deleted")]
    bool Deleted { get; set; }

    string Id { get; set; }

    [JsonProperty(PropertyName = "__updatedAt")]
    DateTimeOffset? UpdatedAt { get; set; }

    [JsonProperty(PropertyName = "__version")]
    byte[] Version { get; set; }
}
```

While the default template is creating a database from scratch, it's worth noting that ITableData is using a regular version of Entity Framework (nothing Azure Mobile Services-specific there). As a result, you can quite easily connect to an existing DB instance too.

■ **Tip** You can also use Azure Mobile Services Web API with Azure Table Storage (WindowsAzure.MobileServices. Backend.Storage NuGet package) and MongoDB (WindowsAzure.MobileServices.Backend.Mongo package).

If you want to push some notifications to the client, you have to use the relevant IPushMessage type (mentioned before). Listing 2-14 shows an example of a push to an Android device.

Listing 2-14. Sample Push to Google Cloud Messaging

```
var message = new GooglePushMessage(new Dictionary<string, string> {{"message",
"Hello from Web API!"}}, TimeSpan.FromDays(1));

var result = await Services.Push.SendAsync(message);
Services.Log.Info(result.State.ToString());
```

2-4. Quick Prototypes with scriptcs
Problem

You'd like to quickly prototype or test out some of the ASP.NET Web API features, ideally without the hassle and overhead of having to go through the solution/project creation in Visual Studio.

Solution

The open source scriptcs project provides an excellent platform for rapidly prototyping and wireframing ASP.NET Web API projects from the convenience your favorite text editor.

■ **Caution**   This recipe assumes scriptcs is installed on your machine. You can find the installation instructions at the official scriptcs GitHub page at https://github.com/scriptcs/scriptcs#getting-scriptcs.

---

scriptcs supports self-hosting ASP.NET Web API through a Scriptcs.WebApi script pack (scriptcs extension). To get started, you first need to install the script pack from NuGet. The usual tool, NuGet.exe, is not even required, as scriptcs has a built in support for NuGet.

```
scriptcs -install Scriptcs.WebApi
```

Next, you need to create a *.csx script that will be your application file and pull the newly installed script pack into the context of your script using an ambient (global) Require<TScriptPack> method. Getting up and running with a Web API is as simple as shown in Listing 2-15.

Listing 2-15. Up and Running with ASP.NET Web API in scriptcs in Just Eight Lines of Code

```
//start.csx file
public class TestController : ApiController {
        public string Get() { return "Hello scriptcs!";}
}

var webApi = Require<WebApi>();
var server = webApi.CreateServer("http://localhost:900");
server.OpenAsync().Wait();
Console.ReadKey(); //prevent the application from exiting
```

This script will start a Web API server with a default route of {controller}/{id}. In order to execute the script, you simply pass it as an argument to the scriptcs CLI (command-line interface):

```
scriptcs script.csx
```

How It Works

scriptcs is a command-line-based tool that provides an execution engine wrapper and a rich pluggable pipeline for scripted C# code. By default, it uses Microsoft Roslyn (for Windows) and Mono.Csharp (for Mono) and their compiler-as-a-service capabilities to run your C# code; however, it can easily be replaced with compilers for alternative languages, such as F#, as long as they are CLR compatible.

scriptcs also gives you access to a rich ecosystem of community contributed script packs, such as the Web API script pack, which make lots of development tasks simpler. This mimics the Node.js world, where you compose an application from small, individual modules. scriptcs takes your scripted code and compiles it into an in-memory assembly, which is then invoked as if it was a regular DLL, albeit one that resides entirely in memory.

In addition to the execution of scripts, scriptcs also does a bunch of pre-processing work against your CSX file, allowing you do things like explicitly reference external assemblies or reference scripts from other scripts (just like you'd do in JavaScript).

■ **Tip** You can learn more about the specifics of writing scriptcs scripts at the project wiki at https://github.com/scriptcs/scriptcs/wiki.

CSX scripts are entirely project-less and can be written from any text editor in an extremely lightweight fashion. scriptcs ships with a plug-in for Sublime Text to provide basic syntax highlighting. In addition, scriptcs has a REPL mode (Read-Evaluate-Print-Loop), which is an interactive console for C# that can also be used for writing applications. This gives you a terrific chance to explore and play around with different APIs in an interactive fashion.

The concept of script packs, available via Require<TScriptPack>, is similar to Node.js and its require functionality, so if you are familiar with that, you should immediately feel comfortable in the scriptcs world. Since the C# semantics in scriptcs are a bit looser than in traditional C#, you don't need to define an entry point, such as a static void Main, as the entry point to your script is simply the first line of your script. The script pack will also take care of loading all of the relevant assemblies and importing the needed namespaces into the context of your script and expose some helper APIs for quickly creating a Web API server.

I've often found scriptcs indispensable for quick prototyping of ASP.NET Web API solutions, as well as for all kinds of demos. With its relaxed, scripted C# syntax and a large number of community extensions and script packs, you are able to get an ASP.NET Web API project up and running as quickly and smoothly as you'd have a Node.js solution.

The Code

You have already seen one simple example of running a Web API self-hosted server with scriptcs. In it, you relied on the default setup; however, the CreateServer method of the Web API script pack also has an overload that takes an HttpConfiguration for a more fine-tuned setup.

Listing 2-16 shows using an instance of HttpConfiguration to plug in a customized route and remove the XML formatter from the Web API that is being hosted from within a CSX script.

Listing 2-16. Sample CSX Script Creating a Self-Hosted ASP.NET Web API

```
public class TestController : ApiController {
        public string Get() { return "Hello scriptcs!";}
}

var webApi = Require<WebApi>();
var config = new HttpSelfHostConfiguration("http://localhost:900");
config.Routes.MapHttpRoute("MyRoute", "awesomeRoute", new {controller = "Test"});
config.Formatters.Remove(config.Formatters.XmlFormatter);
```

```
var server = webApi.CreateServer(config);
server.OpenAsync().Wait();

Console.ReadKey();
```

2-5. Host ASP.NET Web API in Azure Worker Role
Problem
You want to cloud-host a scalable ASP.NET Web API using a Microsoft Azure Worker Role.

Solution

Using the techniques presented earlier in this chapter, such as WCF self-hosting (Recipe 2-1) or Katana self-hosting (Recipe 2-2), it's possible to host and deploy an ASP.NET Web API solution to the cloud, to an Azure Worker Role. You simply need to follow the instructions from the relevant previous recipe, depending on the type of host you have chosen, except this time the host application will be an Azure Worker Role type of Visual Studio project.

To create such a project, you need to install Azure SDK first, which is available from `www.windowsazure.com/en-us/downloads/`, under .NET SDKs. This will result in a new project group called Cloud being added to your Visual Studio New Project dialog under the Visual C# section, as shown in Figure 2-3.

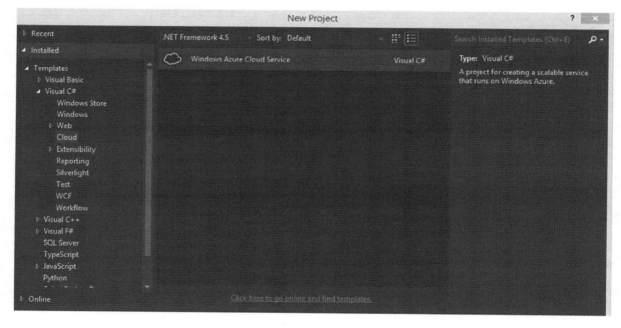

Figure 2-3. *Project Dialog for Windows Azure Cloud Service*

There is only a single choice, Windows Azure Cloud Service, available in this step, as you will choose the relevant project type in the next step (Figure 2-4); in your case, that's a Worker Role.

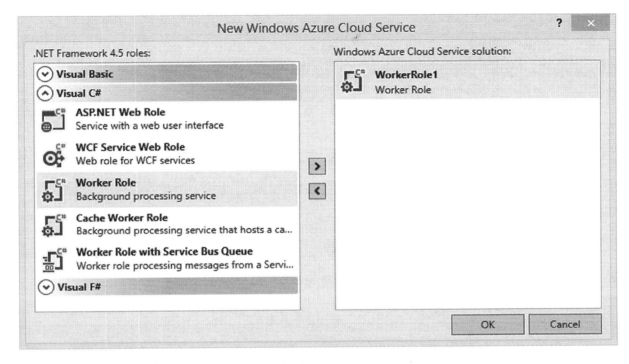

Figure 2-4. *Second step, choosing the type of Azure Service*

How It Works

Azure Workers are essentially virtual machines running Windows Server 2012 with IIS disabled. You can use them as part of any distributed architecture to run any code that exposes TCP/HTTP/HTTPS/UDP endpoints.

When you are developing a worker solution, Azure SDK allows you to run them locally using the service emulator, which is started automatically as soon as you start the program (F5) from Visual Studio. The emulator requires elevated privileges, so make sure to open Visual Studio as an administrator.

To create an Azure Worker, you need to inherit from an abstract class called RoleEntryPoint, which defines the start, stop, and run hooks, as shown in Listing 2-17.

Listing 2-17. Definition of RoleEntryPoint

```
public abstract class RoleEntryPoint
    {
        protected RoleEntryPoint();

        public virtual bool OnStart();
        public virtual void OnStop();
        public virtual void Run();
    }
}
```

In the case of a self-hosted Web API, you have to start the ASP.NET Web API server in the overridden OnStart method and shut down the overridden OnStop.

The Code

An example of OWIN self-hosting ASP.NET Web API within Azure Worker is shown in Listing 2-18. As you may have noticed, the code is very similar to hosting within a Windows Service (Recipe 2-2), as you also have to start and stop the Web API service in two separate methods and store the IDisposable reference in a private field.

Listing 2-18. Azure Worker Role, Running an OWIN Self-Hosted ASP.NET Web API

```
public class WorkerRole : RoleEntryPoint
{
    private IDisposable _app;

    public override void Run()
    {
        while (true)
        {
            Thread.Sleep(10000);
            Trace.TraceInformation("Working", "Information");
        }
    }

    public override bool OnStart()
    {
        ServicePointManager.DefaultConnectionLimit = 12;

        var endpoint = RoleEnvironment.CurrentRoleInstance.InstanceEndpoints["Default"];
        var url = string.Format("{0}://{1}", endpoint.Protocol, endpoint.IPEndpoint);

        _app = WebApp.Start(url, app =>
        {
            var config = new HttpConfiguration();
            config.MapHttpAttributeRoutes();

            app.UseWebApi(config);
        });

        return base.OnStart();
    }

    public override void OnStop()
    {
        if (_app != null)
        {
            _app.Dispose();
        }
        base.OnStop();
    }
}
```

In this example, you used the `Action<IAppBuilder>` instead of a `Startup` class to configure your OWIN pipeline, but obviously both approaches are applicable. Notice the specific way of referencing a port on which the API will run. Instead of hardcoding it in the code, you need to enable it as a public endpoint on the worker. This is done by going to the Worker Project properties and adding a new entry in the Endpoints tab (see Figure 2-5).

Figure 2-5. *Configuring endpoints in Azure Worker project*

You can then reference the endpoint through the static `InstanceEndpoints` dictionary, which returns an instance of a `RoleInstanceEndpoint`, a strongly typed wrapper around the settings you previously defined.

```
RoleEnvironment.CurrentRoleInstance.InstanceEndpoints["<ENDPOINT NAME>"];
```

2-6. Use ASP.NET Web API with F#

Problem

You are looking to go beyond C# and would like to build your ASP.NET Web API with F#.

Solution

F# is a first-class citizen in .NET and Visual Studio, and as a result, ASP.NET Web API can easily be created and maintained in F#. All of the examples in this entire book are completely compatible with F#, as long as you get used to the syntax and, more importantly, the mindset change that comes with moving to a functional programming language.

To convert the Azure Worker Web API example from Recipe 2-5 to F#, you first need to create an F# Azure Worker project. In the past, you used to have to create a C# worker project and an F# class library separately, and then swap the project IDs, since Azure SDK did not ship with native F# project templates. This has since changed, and in the second step of the Clouds Service project setup, you can now choose the F# template, as shown in Figure 2-6.

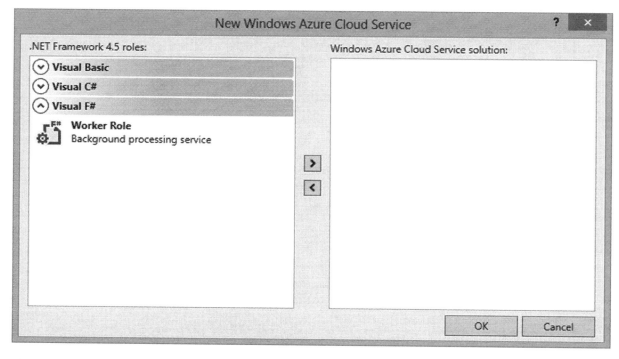

Figure 2-6. *Second step of creating an Azure Cloud Project, choosing the type of Azure Service using F#*

Given the nature of programming in F#, there is actually less code required even to run a basic ASP.NET Web API under F# than there is with C#, and the difference only gets bigger as you add more functionality to your API.

How It Works

There are a number of good reasons to switch from C# to F#:

- Code reduction: F# is much more concise and comes with much less syntactic noise (brackets, white space, punctuation, etc.). Moreover, the very nature of functional programming, such as the support for higher order functions or default immutability, can significantly reduce the amount of code.

- Fewer bugs: Smaller code base automatically translates into lower potential for errors; moreover, the inherent lack of nulls (native F# has no notion of null) can eliminate some of the more dreadful bugs you would normally encounter in C# programming.

- Immutability by default: As opposed to C#, where mutable state is the default, immutability is a great way to improve the correctness and coherence of your applications.

- Great, intuitive support for asynchronous and parallel programming.

- F# is an entirely open source language, with cross platform support.

- You can still interoperate with C# in a very rich way.

F# solves and improves some very annoying language deficiencies of C#, but going into details about F# is far beyond the scope of this book. You can always learn more about F# at the official site of the language, tryfsharp.org.

From the Web API perspective, aside from self-hosting with OWIN like you are doing in this recipe, you can also very easily use F# to build ASP.NET Web API on top of ASP.NET. F# community contributors have created F# Web Application templates for both MVC and Web API, which you can add to your Visual Studio by installing the F# MVC 5 extension from http://visualstudiogallery.msdn.microsoft.com/39ae8dec-d11a-4ac9-974e-be0fdadec71b.

The Code

Recipe 2-5 ported to F# is shown in Listing 2-19. You still need to install the same Microsoft.AspNet.WebApi.OwinSelfhost NuGet package, inherit from RoleEntryPoint, and override the three relevant methods (Run, OnStart, OnStop).

Since values in F# are immutable by default, you declare the webApp field as mutable, as you'll modify it from two different methods (start, stop).

Listing 2-19. ASP.NET Web API Azure Worker Written in F#

```
type WorkerRole() =
    inherit RoleEntryPoint()
    let mutable webApp = None

    override w.Run() =
        while(true) do
            Thread.Sleep(10000)
            Trace.TraceInformation("Working", "Information")

    override w.OnStart() =
        ServicePointManager.DefaultConnectionLimit <- 12

        let endpoint = RoleEnvironment.CurrentRoleInstance.InstanceEndpoints.["Default"]
        let uri = sprintf "%s://%O" endpoint.Protocol endpoint.IPEndpoint
        webApp <- Some(WebApp.Start(uri, fun app ->
            let config = new HttpConfiguration()
            config.MapHttpAttributeRoutes()
            app.UseWebApi(config) |> ignore
        ))

        base.OnStart()

    override w.OnStop() =
        match webApp with
        | Some x -> x.Dispose() |> ignore
        | None -> ()
        base.OnStop()
```

What's interesting if you compare the F# sample with the C# one is that you got rid of a null check in the OnStop methods and instead rely on an F# Option, which forces you to explicitly handle Some and None cases, as it wouldn't compile otherwise. This particular feature of F# can help you avoid almost all potential NullReferenceExceptions, and in itself is one of the great benefits of switching to F#.

In a couple of places you throw away the result of a given computation using |> ignore. That is because in F# everything is an expression, whereas in those particular cases you are interested in using those as statements only.

CHAPTER 3

■ ■ ■

Routing

This chapter introduces the concepts behind ASP.NET Web API routing mechanisms. It deals with centralized routing and direct (attribute) routing, which was introduced in version 2 of the framework.

You will learn how to do the following:

- Define routes using both routing engines (Recipes 3-1 and 3-2)
- Use default and optional route values, and apply routing constraints (Recipes 3-3, 3-4, and 3-5)
- Support remote procedure call (Recipe 3-6)
- Define greedy "catch-all" routes and prevent controller methods from becoming routes (Recipes 3-7 and 3-8)
- Apply a message handler to a specific route and use that technique to ignore certain routes (Recipes 3-9 and 3-10)
- Approach the problem of route localization using direct routing (Recipe 3-11)
- Generate links to your routes (Recipe 3-12)

There is an ongoing debate between ASP.NET Web API developers about whether routing setup should be a central concern (using centralized routing) or whether it should be closely tied to the resources (using attribute routing). Recipes in this chapter will cover both scenarios, letting you decide which routing mechanism you feel more comfortable with.

3-1. Define Centralized Routes
Problem

You would like to declare all of your routes in a single place.

Solution

Define a route by calling the MapHttpRoute extension method from the HttpRouteCollectionExtensions class, on the HttpRouteCollection, which is available off the HttpConfiguration object.

The most basic usage is to define a very generic route template, which will match all of the controllers through a {controller} placeholder. This is shown in Listing 3-1.

Listing 3-1. The Default ASP.NET Web API Route and a Basic Controller

```
config.Routes.MapHttpRoute(
    name: "DefaultApi",
    routeTemplate: "api/{controller}/{id}",
    defaults: new { id = RouteParameter.Optional }
);

public class OrdersController : ApiController
{
    public Order Get(int id)
    {
        //omitted for brevity
    }
}
```

In the routeTemplate, you can define your own placeholders such as {id} in Listing 3-1. It then has to match the name of a parameter in your action method, allowing ASP.NET Web API to extract a correct value from the URI of the HTTP request and pass into the method. And indeed, that is the case in the Get method on the OrdersController in Listing 3-1.

How It Works

Since its very first version, ASP.NET Web API has been using a centralized routing mechanism that's almost identical as that used by ASP.NET MVC.

ASP.NET Web API defines a number of variations of the MapHttpRoute method. The bare minimum required is a route template and a route name.

```
public static IHttpRoute MapHttpRoute(this HttpRouteCollection routes, string name,
string routeTemplate)
```

In addition to declaring simple basic routes, it is also possible to pass in defaults or constraints, or set a per-route message handler, all of which will be discussed later in this chapter. All those operations are done through the relevant MapHttpRoute overload.

```
public static IHttpRoute MapHttpRoute(this HttpRouteCollection routes, string name,
string routeTemplate, object defaults)
public static IHttpRoute MapHttpRoute(this HttpRouteCollection routes, string name,
string routeTemplate, object defaults, object constraints)
public static IHttpRoute MapHttpRoute(this HttpRouteCollection routes, string name,
string routeTemplate, object defaults, object constraints, HttpMessageHandler handler)
```

With route defaults you are able to point specific routes to relevant controllers directly; however, such routes need to be defined before generic routes such as the route from Listing 3-1. The reason for that is that route order matters because a route that will handle an incoming HTTP request is selected by scanning the route collection on every request. As soon as a first matching route template is found, the route is going to be used. Therefore, you will always need to declare the more specific routes before the generic ones.

In self-hosting scenarios, ASP.NET Web API maintains the route collection in the form of an IDictionary<string, IHttpRoute> inside an HttpRouteCollection class. In web hosting, ASP.NET Web API also provides extension methods for System.Web.Routing.RouteCollection so you can also define ASP.NET Web API routes directly on that. For example,

```
RouteTable.Routes.MapHttpRoute("DefaultApi", "api/{controller}")
```

This is possible because if you are hosting your Web API in the ASP.NET runtime, regardless of which extension method you use to declare your route, it would always end up getting added to the same underlying `RouteTable`. This is internally represented by a specialized subclass of `HttpRouteCollection` called `HostedHttpRouteCollection`, which, instead of maintaining routes in a dictionary (like in self-host), forwards all route look-ups to `System.Web.Routing.RouteCollection`.

ASP.NET Web API, contrary to ASP.NET MVC, uses HTTP verb-based dispatching to handle a request with a controller. In other words, the framework will select an action to handle your request based on the HTTP verb. The logic of the selection is as follows:

- The HTTP verb will be inferred from the method name if possible (i.e. `PostOrder`, `GetById`).

- The HTTP verb will be inferred from an attribute on an action (i.e. `HttpPutAttribute`, `HttpGetAttribute`).

- Action parameters have to match those defined on the route template.

As a result, the typical ASP.NET Web API route setup boils down to pointing to a resource, which can be called with various HTTP verbs, rather than a specific action only. Therefore, the single initial route defined in Listing 3-1 could potentially handle all of the following requests:

- GET `myapi.com/api/orders`

- POST `myapi.com/api/invoice`

- PUT `myapi.com/api/invoice/2`

▓ **Note**   It is still possible to use RPC in ASP.NET Web API. See Recipe 3-6 for more details.

The Code

Because of the HTTP verb-based dispatching logic used by ASP.NET Web API, unlike in ASP.NET MVC, it is very easy to trap yourself with an `AmbiguousMatchException`. For example, consider a Web API service using a generic route from Listing 3-1.

Even though the controller code shown in Listing 3-2 compiles (method signatures are unique), all three of them could potentially handle the same GET request, such as `/api/orders/1`.

Listing 3-2. Bad ASP.NET Web API controller

```
public class BadOrdersController : ApiController
{
    [HttpGet]
    public Order FindById(int id)
    {
        //omitted for brevity
    }

    public Order GetById(int id)
    {
        //omitted for brevity
    }
```

```
    public Order Get(int id)
    {
        //omitted for brevity
    }
}
```

On the same note, centralized routing makes it very tedious and unnatural when it comes to defining complex, hierarchical, or nested routes. Consider the following routing requirement:

- GET myapi.com/api/teams
- GET myapi.com/api/teams/1
- GET myapi.com/api/teams/1/players

With centralized routing it's possible to contain all three methods in the same controller; however, you have to be careful not to have routes 2 and 3 conflict with each other since both are a GET with a single ID parameter. The correct setup is shown in Listing 3-3. A specific route pointing to the /players/ segment of the URL is defined before the generic route.

Listing 3-3. Configuring Nested Routes with Centralized Routing

```
public class TeamsController : ApiController
{
    public Team GetTeam(int id)
    {
        //omitted for brevity
    }

    public IEnumerable<Team> GetTeams()
    {
        //omitted for brevity
    }

    public IEnumerable<Player> GetPlayers(int teamId)
    {
        //omitted for brevity
    }
}

config.Routes.MapHttpRoute(
    name: "players",
    routeTemplate: "api/teams/{teamid}/players",
    defaults: new { controller = "teams" }
);

config.Routes.MapHttpRoute(
    name: "DefaultApi",
    routeTemplate: "api/{controller}/{id}",
    defaults: new { id = RouteParameter.Optional }
);
```

The prevailing problem with this particular setup is that specialized routes, which handle only specific actions in a specific controller, become artificially disconnected from the controller and get mixed up with generic route definitions instead.

This is hardly ideal, and the bigger your application becomes, and the more complex your routing hierarchy is, the more likely you are to struggle with the maintenance and debugging of centralized routing. Therefore, it's often a better option to move to direct routing instead, which is discussed in Recipe 3-2 and in general in the rest of this chapter.

3-2. Define Direct Routes
Problem

You would like to declare your routes as close to the resources (controllers, actions) as possible.

Solution

Declare your routes directly at the resource level using attribute routing. You simply annotate your actions with a RouteAttribute, and pass it a relevant route template. The route template for attribute routing has similar semantics to that used with centralized routing: all route parameters should be in curly braces and match those available on the action. Route defaults, optional parameters, and constrains are all supported by direct routing, and will be discussed later in this chapter.

```
[Route("api/teams/{id}")]
public Team GetTeam(int id)
{
    //omitted for brevity
}
```

To enable attribute routing, you need to call the MapHttpAttributeRoutes extension method (HttpConfigurationExtensions) on your HttpConfiguration at the application startup.

```
config.MapHttpAttributeRoutes();
```

How It Works

A once popular open source library called Attribute Routing became part of core ASP.NET Web API in version 2 of the framework. It was brought in to solve a number of woes of the centralized routing mechanism as it allows you to declare the routes as attributes directly on the action or controller.

For many developers, attribute routing (also known as *direct routing*) is a more natural approach than centralized route setup, as it emphasizes a direct relationship between a Web API resource and a URI at which this resource should be reachable over HTTP. In fact, part of the appeal of other popular .NET web frameworks, such as ServiceStack or NancyFx, has been their ability to define routes as close to the actual resource as possible (inline with the resource).

When you call MapHttpAttributeRoutes at your application startup, you instruct ASP.NET Web API to scan all of your controllers for any route declarations.

Ultimately, routes declared with attribute routing are not much different from centralized routing; once found, they are added to the same route collection that centralized routing uses (see Recipe 3-1). The only difference is that direct routes (attribute-based routes) are added to the route collection as a single composite route (an internal SubRouteCollection type) under a common MS_attributerouteWebApi route key.

When processing each attribute route, the controller (HttpControllerDescriptor) or action (HttpActionDescriptor) that the direct route is specifically pointing to will be marked as only reachable via attribute routing. This is achieved by adding an MS_IsAttributeRouted to the Properties dictionary on either of those descriptor types.

Attribute routing exposes a number of hooks for customization of the routing process, which will be explored later in this chapter. In fact, you are not forced to use just RouteAttribute to annotate your controllers and actions with route definitions. By implementing IDirectRouteFactory, you are able to provide route definitions through custom attributes, or even non-attribute, centralized logic. The usage of IDirectRouteFactory and IDirectRouteProvider is discussed in Recipe 3-11 and later again in Recipe 6-8.

The Code

Contrary to centralized routing, the very nature of attribute routing, and its direct relationship with a controller and action, make it very simple to declare sophisticated, nested routes. An example is shown in Listing 3-4.

Listing 3-4. A Sample Controller with Attribute Routing Defined on It

```
public class TeamsController : ApiController
{
    [Route("api/teams/{id}")]
    public Team GetTeam(int id)
    {
        //omitted for brevity
    }

    [Route("api/teams")]
    public IEnumerable<Team> GetTeams()
    {
        //omitted for brevity
    }

    [Route("api/teams/{teamId}/players")]
    public IEnumerable<Player> GetPlayers(int teamId)
    {
        //omitted for brevity
    }
}
```

Attribute routing also allows you to declare a route prefix through RoutePrefixAttribute. It can only be declared on a controller level, and gives you a possibility to define a common prefix for all of the routes within this controller. Code from Listing 3-4, rewritten to use RoutePrefixAttribute, is shown in Listing 3-5. Notice that when a route prefix is present, all of the RouteAttributes specified on the action should now use route templates with the path relative to the prefix.

Listing 3-5. A Sample Controller with Attribute Routing and Route Prefix

```
[RoutePrefix("api/teams")]
public class TeamsController : ApiController
{
    [Route("{id}")]
    public Team GetTeam(int id)
    {
        //omitted for brevity
    }
```

```
[Route]
public IEnumerable<Team> GetTeams()
{
    //omitted for brevity
}

[Route("{teamId}/players")]
public IEnumerable<Player> GetPlayers(int teamId)
{
    //omitted for brevity
}
}
```

Similarly to centralized routing, attribute routing also relies on verb-based dispatching. Therefore, due to the naming convention (see Recipe 3-1 for more details on verb-based dispatching) all of the routes defined in Listings 3-4 and 3-5 will only work with the HTTP GET method.

To enable support for other types of HTTP verbs, you have to add additional actions to the controller, either with a name prefixed with that verb or annotated with a relevant HTTP verb attribute. Two types of POST actions and a PUT action are shown in Listing 3-6. They extend your TeamsController with the ability to create a Team resource, to create a Player resource within the context of a team (both POST), and to update a Team (PUT).

Listing 3-6. Defining Additional Actions, Supporting Other HTTP Verbs

```
[Route]
public HttpResponseMessage PostTeam(Team team)
{
    //omitted for brevity
}

[HttpPost]
[Route("{teamId}/players")]
public HttpResponseMessage AddPlayer(int teamId, Player player)
{
    //omitted for brevity
}

[Route("{id}")]
public HttpResponseMessage PutTeam(int id, Team team)
{
    //omitted for brevity
}
```

3-3. Set Default Route Values

Problem

You want to provide default values for the parameters used in your routes.

Solution

Regardless whether you are using attribute routing or centralized routing, ASP.NET Web API makes it very easy to define default values for a route. These are the values that will be automatically populated by the framework on every request in case the client making the request omits them.

For centralized routing, the `MapHttpRoute` extension method accepts default values as a third parameter in the form of an `IDictionary<string, object>` (also as anonymous object). The key (or property on the anonymous object) must match the parameter name as specified in the routing template.

```
config.Routes.MapHttpRoute(
    name: "DefaultApi",
    routeTemplate: "api/{controller}/{id}",
    defaults: new { id = VALUE }
);
```

In attribute routing, you define the default value directly inline in the route declaration.

```
[Route("items/{id:int=VALUE}")]
public HttpResponseMessage Get(int id) {}
```

Finally, for both types of routing, you can also supply the default value in the action signature itself.

```
public HttpResponseMessage Get(int id = VALUE) {}
```

How It Works

When using centralized routing, the default values declared on your route are used to hydrate the `IHttpRoute` object whenever the `Request.GetRouteData` method is called (by your code or by the framework code) to fill in the gaps, in case some of the parameters were omitted by the calling client.

For attribute routing, the process is the same, except there are some extra registration steps. At the start of your application, all routing attributes are used by the framework to produce concrete `RouteEntry` instances; this is done by calling the `CreateRoute` method on every `RouteAttribute` (or, more generally, `IDirectRouteFactory`) found on your controllers and actions. `CreateRoute` will internally invoke the `CreateBuilder` method of the `DirectRouteFactoryContext`. That operation uses an internal class called `InlineRouteTemplateParser` to parse the template defined in your route attribute and produce the relevant constraints and default values out of it. After that, the route is registered as if it was a centralized route with defaults and constraints specified.

The Code

Consider the three examples in Listing 3-7.

Listing 3-7. Sample Usage of Default Values in Routing

```
//centralized
    config.Routes.MapHttpRoute(
        name: "DefaultApi",
        routeTemplate: "{controller}/{id}",
        defaults: new { id = 100 }
    );

//attribute routing
[Route("items/{id:int=100}")]
public HttpResponseMessage Get(int id) {}

//inline
public HttpResponseMessage Get(int id = 100) {}
```

In each of the cases, the following two requests will be identical, and return the resource with the ID of 100:

- `myapi.com/items/`

- `myapi.com/items/100`

▓ **Caution**   Using default values can often result in very "greedy" routes. In the example above, there is no longer the possibility to retrieve all items using a parameterless `Get` method.

3-4. Set Optional Route Values

Problem

You want to create routes that have optional parameters that are matched regardless of whether the client supplies them or not.

Solution

ASP.NET Web API supports declaring optional route parameters for both centralized and attribute routing.

With centralized routing you can specify an optional parameter by giving it a default value of `RouteParameter.Optional` (which is semantically equivalent to the `UrlParameter.Optional` from ASP.NET MVC).

```
config.Routes.MapHttpRoute(
    name: "DefaultApi",
    routeTemplate: "api/{controller}/{param}",
    defaults: new { param = RouteParameter.Optional }
);
```

In attribute routing, you support optional parameters by suffixing them with a question mark. You then have to specify the default value.

```
[Route("items/{param?}")]
public HttpResponseMessage Get(int? param = null)
```

How It Works

Under the hood, support for optional parameters in ASP.NET Web API is a de facto variation of default route values support. RouteParameter, which can be seen in Listing 3-8, is actually an immutable type, implementing a null-pattern. It is only used by the framework for comparison purposes, to determine that this particular default value is actually representing an optional parameter.

Listing 3-8. Definition of RouteParameter

```
public sealed class RouteParameter
{
    public static readonly RouteParameter Optional = new RouteParameter();

    private RouteParameter()
    {
    }

    public override string ToString()
    {
        return String.Empty;
    }
}
```

On the attribute routing side of things, the parameter followed by a question mark will also be converted into a RouteEntry having the default value of RouteParameter.Optional.

At runtime, when an incoming HTTP request is handled by the framework, HttpRoutingDispatcher will remove all optional parameters that do not have a value from the route data. This is necessary to support both /resource and /resource/{optionalParameter}.

The Code

Listing 3-9 shows the usage of optional route values with attribute routing on an HTTP resource allowing the client to apply basic pagination.

Listing 3-9. Usage of Optional Parameters with Attribute Routing

```
[Route("orders/{skip?},{take?}")]
public HttpResponseMessage GetFiltered(int? skip = null, int? take = null)
{
    var query = orders.AsQueryable();
    if (skip.HasValue)
    {
        query = query.Skip(skip.Value);
    }

    if (take.HasValue)
    {
        query = query.Take(take.Value);
    }

    return Request.CreateResponse(HttpStatusCode.OK, query);
}
```

The same route, also with default parameters, using centralized routing is defined as shown in Listing 3-10.

Listing 3-10. Usage of Optional Parameters with Centralized Routing

```
config.Routes.MapHttpRoute(
    name: "OrdersFilter",
    routeTemplate: "orders/{skip},{take}}",
    defaults: new {skip = RouteParameter.Optional, take = RouteParameter.Optional}
);
```

3-5. Set Route Constraints
Problem

You need to restrict the values of some of the route parameters.

Solution

ASP.NET Web API allows you to work with route constraints through the IHttpRouteConstraint interface. IHttpRouteConstraint is applicable to both centralized and direct routing.

The framework ships with 18 implementations of this interface, allowing you to provide most common constraint types, such as restricting a route parameter to a relevant length, ensuring its value falls into a predefined range, or restricting it to being a specific data type. You can also introduce custom logic into route constraints by implementing the IHttpRouteConstraint interface yourself.

How It Works

IHttpRouteConstraint, an HTTP route constraint interface (definition shown in Listing 3-11), exposes a single Match method, which takes an HttpRequestMessage, IHttpRoute instance, parameter name, dictionary of route values, and the HttpRouteDirection (resolution or generation), and also ensures that this route should be matched based on the logic required by your application.

Listing 3-11. Definition of IHttpConstraint

```
public interface IHttpRouteConstraint
{
    bool Match(HttpRequestMessage request, IHttpRoute route, string parameterName,
               IDictionary<string, object> values, HttpRouteDirection routeDirection);
}
```

Constraints can also be compounded together using CompoundRouteConstraint, which takes a collection of IHttpRouteConstraint through its constructor. Table 3-1 provides an overview of all of the built-in constraints and shows their basic usage example.

Table 3-1. *All of the IHttpRouteConstraints Available Out of the Box in ASP.NET Web API*

Class	Direct Routing	Centralized Routing Example	Direct Routing Example
AlphaRouteConstraint	Alpha	new AlphaRouteConstraint()	{param:alpha}
BoolRouteConstraint	Bool	new BoolRouteConstraint()	{param:bool}
CompoundRouteConstraint	-	new CompoundRouteConstraint (new List<IHttpRouteConstraint> { new AlphaRouteConstraint(), new MaxLengthRouteConstraint(5) })	{text:alpha: maxlength(5)}
DateTimeRouteConstraint	datetime	new DateTimeRouteConstraint()	{param:datetime}
DecimalRouteConstraint	decimal	new DecimalRouteConstraint()	{param:decimal}
DoubleRouteConstraint	double	new DoubleRouteConstraint()	{param:double}
FloatRouteConstraint	float	new FloatRouteConstraint()	{param:float}
GuidRouteConstraint	guid	new GuidRouteConstraint()	{param:guid}
IntRouteConstraint	int	new IntRouteConstraint()	{param:int}
LengthRouteConstraint	length	new LengthRouteConstraint(10) new LengthRouteConstraint(10,20)	{param:length(10)} {param:length(10,20)}
LongRouteConstraint	long	new LongRouteConstraint()	{param:long}
MaxLengthRouteConstraint	maxlength	new MaxLengthRouteConstraint(10)	{param:maxlength(10)}
MaxRouteConstraint	max	new MaxRouteConstraint(1000)	{param:max(1000)}
MinLengthRouteConstraint	minlength	new MinLengthRouteConstraint(3)	{param:minLength(3)}
MinRouteConstraint	min	new MinRouteConstraint(1000)	{param:min(1000)}
OptionalRouteConstraint	-	RouteParameter.Optional	{param?}
RangeRouteConstraint	range	new RangeRouteConstraint(100,200)	{param: range(100,200)}
RegexRouteConstraint	regex	new RegexRouteConstraint("^\w+ ([-+.']\w+)*@\w+([-.]\w+)*\.\w+ ([-.]\w+)*)")	{param:regex(^\w+ ([-+.']\w+)*@\w+ ([-.]\w+)* \.\w+([-.]\w+)*)}
HttpMethodConstraint	-	new HttpMethodConstraint (HttpMethod.Get)	N/A

For attribute routing, the mapping between the inline version of the constraint and the actual Type is provided by DefaultInlineConstraintResolver. When you call MapHttpAttributeRoutes, ASP.NET Web API will actually use that resolver to convert the inline constraints to relevant IHttpRouteConstraint instances. To introduce certain constraint processing customizations, you can either modify the DefaultInlineConstraintResolver or implement the entire IInlineConstraintResolver yourself. In either case, you will have to pass the instance to the MapHttpAttributeRoutes method (there is an overload that allows this).

OptionalRouteConstraint is used to provide the optional parameter functionality, as discussed in Recipe 3-4, in conjunction with any other regular constraint. OptionalRouteConstraint will only evaluate the constraint if the value of the parameter is not RouteParameter.Optional.

The Code

For centralized routes, constraints are passed as a third parameter of the MapHttpRoute method. Similarly to defaults, discussed in Recipe 3-3, they are expected to be IDictionary<string, object>, but since the intention of the framework authors was to allow you to pass an anonymous object too, the actual type in the signature is simply an object. The name of the constrained parameter (dictionary key or property of the anonymous object) must be the same as in the route template and in the action signature.

```
config.Routes.MapHttpRoute(
    name: "DefaultApi",
    routeTemplate: "orders/{text}",
    constraints: new { text = new AlphaRouteConstraint() },
    defaults: null
);
```

With centralized routing, you can also define regular expression constraints inline as string, without having to use any IHttpRouteConstraint implementation. In the following example, the id is constrained to be a digit by an inline regular expression:

```
config.Routes.MapHttpRoute(
    name: "DefaultApi",
    routeTemplate: "size/{id}",
    constraints: new { id = "\d+" },
    defaults: null
);
```

Centralized routing can also accept routing constraints that constraint HTTP methods. This is done through a predefined httpMethod key and through the use of HttpMethodConstraint.

```
config.Routes.MapHttpRoute(
    name: "DefaultApi",
    routeTemplate: "size/{id}",
    constraints: new { httpMethod = new HttpMethodConstraint(HttpMethod.Get) },
    defaults: null
);
```

For direct routes, constraints are specified using the colon after the parameter name.

```
[Route("orders/{text:alpha}")]
public HttpResponseMessage Get(string text)
```

In order to combine constraints together, for centralized routing you need to wrap them in the CompoundRouteConstraint.

```
config.Routes.MapHttpRoute(
    name: "DefaultApi",
    routeTemplate: "orders/{text}",
    constraints: new { text = new CompoundRouteConstraint (new List<IHttpRouteConstraint>
                    {new AlphaRouteConstraint(), new MaxLengthRouteConstraint(5) } },
    defaults: null
);
```

For attribute routing, you can simply chain different constraints types with the colon; the framework will internally build up a CompoundRouteConstraint out of that.

```
[Route("orders/{text:alpha:maxlength(5)}")]
public HttpResponseMessage Get(string text)
```

A sample custom constraint, ensuring that the parameter is a valid email format, is shown in Listing 3-12. Since the route values are IDictionary<string, object>, there is a need to cast to the expected Type (in this case a string) before validating the constraint.

Listing 3-12. A Custom IHttpRouteConstraint, Validating if the Paramater Is a Valid Email Format

```
public class EmailRouteConstraint : IHttpRouteConstraint
{
    public bool Match(HttpRequestMessage request, IHttpRoute route, string parameterName,
                    IDictionary<string, object> values, HttpRouteDirection routeDirection)
    {
        object value;
        if (values.TryGetValue(parameterName, out value) && value != null)
        {
            var stringValue = value as string;
            if (stringValue == null) return false;

            try
            {
                var email = new MailAddress(stringValue);
                return true;
            }
            catch (FormatException)
            {
                return false;
            }
        }

        return false;
    }
}
```

You can use this constraint with centralized routing straight away like all of the built-in route constraints.

```
config.Routes.MapHttpRoute(
    name: "Email",
    routeTemplate: "{controller}/email/{text}",
    constraints: new { text = new EmailRouteConstraint() },
    defaults: null
);
```

However, with attribute routing, you use a short alias instead, and you probably noticed that it was not defined anywhere in the EmailRouteConstraint class. That's because this mapping between the shorthand name and a constraint Type is done against the DefaultInlineConstraintResolver that ASP.NET Web API uses to resolve the constraints, so you'll need to perform this additional step:

```
var constraintResolver = new DefaultInlineConstraintResolver();
constraintResolver.ConstraintMap.Add("email", typeof(EmailRouteConstraint));
config.MapHttpAttributeRoutes(constraintResolver);
```

With this in place, you can now use the email constraint just like all the default framework constraints.

```
[Route("orders/client/{text:email}")]
public HttpResponseMessage GetByClient(string text)
```

▓ **Caution**   Without that extra mapping step, the constraint would not only not have any effect, but the entire attribute routing would break for your ASP.NET Web API.

3-6. Define Remote Procedure Call Style Routes

Problem

You want to have RPC (Remote Procedure Call) routes in your ASP.NET Web API, instead of the default convention of verb-based dispatching.

Solution

When using centralized routing you can extend your route template to include the {action} token, which will require the client to specifically call a server-side method.

```
config.Routes.MapHttpRoute(
    name: "DefaultApi",
    routeTemplate: "api/{controller}/{action}/{id}",
    defaults: new { id = RouteParameter.Optional }
);
```

In this case, the client now has to call your HTTP endpoints in the following matter:

- myapi.com/api/orders/getall
- myapi.com/api/orders/getbyid/1

With attribute routing, since you are in direct control over the route appearance, you can just define such inline routes to match the name of the action method.

```
//the controller is OrdersController
[Route("orders/getbyid/{id}")]
public HttpResponseMessage Get(int id)
{
    //omitted for brevity
}
```

```
[Route("orders/getall")]
public HttpResponsesMessage GetAll()
{
    //omitted for brevity
}
```

Attribute routing also supports the {action} placeholder.

```
[RoutePrefix("direct")]
[Route("items/{action}")]
public class ItemsController : ApiController
    {
        //omitted for brevity
    }
```

Alternatively, it is possible to define a custom IDirectRouteFactory that will infer the controller and action name automatically for you, and only require you to pass the parameter part of the route template.

```
[RpcRoute("{id}")]
public HttpResponseMessage Get(int id)
{
    //omitted for brevity
}
```

How It Works

ApiControllerActionSelector is a Web API service that's responsible for selecting an action on the controller that will process the current HTTP request. Typically, an action is selected according to RESTful routing principles based on the HTTP verb (discussed already in Recipe 3-1). However, the selection process is relying on the RouteData too, and if RouteData contains an entry for the {action} placeholder, it is given precedence over the verb-based action selection.

Remember that introducing RPC routing will not prevent ASP.NET Web API from respecting HTTP verbs. Therefore, your remotely callable actions will still only be accessible through the HTTP verb they are prefixed with or annotated with via an attribute. If neither of those two conditions are met, then Web API will automatically assume that such an action is only a POST action.

When using the default ApiControllerActionSelector, you are not able to combine RPC and RESTful routing in the same controller; trying to do that will result in an ambiguous match exception. The reason is quite simple: imagine having two actions in the same controller, both responding to a GET request, except one is intended for RPC invocation and one is intended for RESTful invocation. ApiControllerActionSelector has no way of identifying which one is supposed to be RPC and treats both of them as equally good matches for a RESTful route, resulting in an ambiguous result.

For such advanced usage scenarios, the whole action selection process is customizable as it is interface based. You may implement your own IHttpActionSelector (Listing 3-13) and register it against HttpConfiguration.

Listing 3-13. Definition of IHttpActionSelector

```
public interface IHttpActionSelector
{
    HttpActionDescriptor SelectAction(HttpControllerContext controllerContext);
    ILookup<string, HttpActionDescriptor> GetActionMapping(HttpControllerDescriptor
    controllerDescriptor);
}
```

An extensive example of building a custom IHttpActionSelector and combining RESTful and RPC dispatching in a single controller for centralized routing is available in a blog post at www.strathweb.com/2013/01/magical-web-api-action-selector-http-verb-and-action-name-dispatching-in-a-single-controller/.

The Code

In centralized routing, the mere introduction of the {action} route segment will force ASP.NET Web API to treat those routes as RPC. You can even use {action} in route templates without the {controller} segment, as long as the controller will get provided by default. Similarly, {action} can be supplied its own default value too. An example setup of RPC is shown in Listing 3-14.

Listing 3-14. Example Setup of Centralized RPC Routing

```
config.Routes.MapHttpRoute(
    name: "LatestOrder",
    routeTemplate: "api/orders/getlatestorder"}",
    defaults: new { controller = "Orders", action = "GetLatestOrder" }
);
config.Routes.MapHttpRoute(
    name: "Orders",
    routeTemplate: "api/orders/{action}/{id}",
    defaults: new { controller = "Orders", id = RouteParameter.Optional }
);
config.Routes.MapHttpRoute(
    name: "DefaultApi",
    routeTemplate: "api/{controller}/{action}/{id}",
    defaults: new { id = RouteParameter.Optional }
);
```

The definition of a custom RpcRouteAttribute, an implementation of IDirectRouteFactory, which can be used for RPC-enabling attribute routing, is shown in Listing 3-15. In the CreateRoute method, you can use DirectRouteFactoryContext to access the relevant HttpActionDescriptor and HttpControllerDescriptor, from which you can pull out action name and controller name information. Those can then be arbitrarily used as part of the route creation, effectively forcing RPC-style routing through attribute routing.

Listing 3-15. Definition of RpcRouteAttribute

```
public class RpcRouteAttribute : Attribute, IDirectRouteFactory
{
    public RpcRouteAttribute() : this(string.Empty) {}

    public RpcRouteAttribute(string template)
    {
        Template = template;
    }

    public string Name { get; set; }

    public int Order { get; set; }

    public string Template { get; private set; }
```

```
RouteEntry IDirectRouteFactory.CreateRoute(DirectRouteFactoryContext context)
{
    var action = context.Actions.FirstOrDefault();
    var template = string.Format("{0}/{1}", action.ControllerDescriptor.ControllerName,
    action.ActionName);
    if (!string.IsNullOrWhiteSpace(Template))
    {
        template += "/" + Template;
    }
    var builder = context.CreateBuilder(template);

    builder.Name = Name;
    builder.Order = Order;
    return builder.Build();
    }
}
```

If you compare this RpcRouteAttribute to the built-in RouteAttribute, you'll immediately notice that the semantics of the Template property are now slightly different. In normal RouteAttribute, Template represents the entire route (or a route template, minus the route prefix segment), while in your RpcRouteAttribute, Template represents only the URL part after the controller and action names. Therefore, the usage is as shown in Listing 3-16.

Listing 3-16. Example Usage of RpcRouteAttribute

```
[RoutePrefix("direct")]
public class ItemsController : ApiController
{
    private static List<Item> items = new List<Item>
        {
            new Item {Id = 1, Name = "Filip"},
            new Item {Id = 2, Name = "Not Filip"}
        };

    [RpcRoute("{id:int}")]
    public Item Get(int id)
    {
        var item = items.FirstOrDefault(x => x.Id == id);
        if (item == null) throw new HttpResponseException(HttpStatusCode.NotFound);

        return item;
    }

    [RpcRoute]
    public IEnumerable<Item> GetAll()
    {
        return items;
    }
}
```

3-7. Create Catch-all Routes

Problem

You want to define a single route that will catch all of the requests regardless of the type and number of route parameters passed.

Solution

By preceding a parameter in the route template with an asterisk, for example {*params}, you are able to catch all of the requests, as long as the request URL matches the rest of the route template too. This technique is applicable to both centralized and attribute routing.

How It Works

If the entire route template is just {*params}, then the whole relative part of the request URL is passed to the action as a single string parameter. It can then be parsed or processed inside the action by hand.

In case there are some other route template segments preceding the catch-all parameter, then those are matched first, and afterwards the remaining portion of the URL is passed to the action as a string parameter.

▧ **Caution**　Since a parameter with an asterisk represents a catch-all segment, it must also be the last segment in your route template. For example {*params}/{id} does not make sense, as the value of id will never be read correctly because {*params} will greedily absorb all of the parameters.

These types of catch-all routes are typically needed when using ASP.NET Web API as a proxy that simply forwards the calls to some other system, or when trying to punch holes in the routing setup (this will be discussed in Recipe 3-10). It is also useful when you are allowing a client to compose URLs containing rich queries on the client side.

The Code

Listing 3-17 shows examples of catch-all routes for both centralized routing and attribute routing.

Listing 3-17. Catch-all ASP.NET Web API Routes

```
config.Routes.MapHttpRoute(
    name: "DefaultApi",
    routeTemplate: "{*params}"
);

public class ProxyController : ApiController
{
    [Route("{*params}")]
    public HttpResponseMessage Get(string params)
    {
        //omitted for brevity
    }
}
```

In both cases, the routes are infinitely greedy because they will handle all possible requests to your Web API services. For example,

- GET myapi.com/1

- GET myapi.com/hello

- GET myapi.com/www.google.com

- GET myapi.com/monday/filip/192.5

To allow coexistence of catch-all routes and regular routes, a common approach is to hide them behind a specific prefix. Consider the example from Listing 3-17 in a slightly modified version shown in Listing 3-18.

Listing 3-18. Catch-all ASP.NET Web API Routes—But Only for Requests for proxy/*

```
config.Routes.MapHttpRoute(
    name: "DefaultApi",
    routeTemplate: "proxy/{*params}"
);

public class ProxyController : ApiController
{
    [Route("proxy/{*params}")]
    public HttpResponseMessage Get(string params)
    {
        //omitted for brevity
    }
}
```

With this change, both of the route definitions can still catch all kinds of requests, but only as long as the relative part of the request URL starts with proxy, for example, myapi.com/proxy/www.google.com. All other types of requests can still be correctly handled by other controllers in your Web API.

3-8. Prevent Controller Methods from Inadvertently Becoming Web API Endpoints

Problem

You have a public method on a controller that should not be considered an action by ASP.NET Web API.

Solution

ASP.NET Web API, when operating both in regular HTTP-verb based dispatching mode and in RPC mode will rely on a convention for finding actions on a controller. By default, every public method on a controller will be considered an action. To prevent a public method from becoming an action, you have to decorate it with a NonActionAttribute.

How It Works

NonActionAttribute (see Listing 3-19) is a no-op class which itself doesn't do anything and is used merely as a marker.

Listing 3-19. Definition of NonActionAttribute

```
[AttributeUsage(AttributeTargets.Method, AllowMultiple = false, Inherited = true)]
public sealed class NonActionAttribute : Attribute
{
}
```

ApiControllerActionSelector, when finding valid candidates for actions on a controller internally performs the checks shown in Listing 3-20: it treats all public methods on the controller as potential actions, except for those that are special ones (i.e. constructors), that are declared on ApiController, IHttpController or that are decorated with NonActionAttribute.

Listing 3-20. ApiControllerActionSelector Filtering Rules for Action Selection

```
private static bool IsValidActionMethod(MethodInfo methodInfo)
{
    if (methodInfo.IsSpecialName)
    {
        return false;
    }

    if (methodInfo.GetBaseDefinition().DeclaringType.IsAssignableFrom(TypeHelper.ApiControllerType))
    {
        return false;
    }

    if (methodInfo.GetCustomAttribute<NonActionAttribute>() != null)
    {
        return false;
    }

    return true;
}
```

▩ **Caution** Since this logic exists internally in ApiControllerActionSelector, if you ever go ahead and implement your own IHttpActionSelector, you will have to ensure that similar logic exists there too.

ASP.NET Web API wraps every action candidate in a ReflectedHttpActionDescriptor class, which, among other things, is responsible for finding out which HTTP verb the action should handle. This is inferred from the method name or from a relevant attribute (HttpGetAttribute, HttpPostAttribute, etc.) that the method might be decorated with. If an action's name starts with a name of one of the major HTTP verbs (GET, POST, PUT, DELETE), ASP.NET Web API will consider this action suitable to handle those relevant types of HTTP requests.

Otherwise, such a method will be automatically given a capability of handling POST requests only. This is very important, and often overlooked by developers, who think that if they don't prefix their method name with a "Post", it will not be callable from the client side!

Solution

Listing 3-21 shows three action methods. The first one will be used by ASP.NET Web API to handle GET requests, and the second one will be used to handle POST requests (due to the lack of hint about any HTTP verb, POST is used by default). Finally, the third method is explicitly excluded from being treated as an action with the use of NonActionAttribute.

Listing 3-21. Example Usage of NonActionAttribute

```
//action considered relevant for GET
public string GetCustomer()
{
  //omitted for brevity
}

//action considered relevant for POST
public string ProcessCustomer()
{
  //omitted for brevity
}

//not an action
[NonAction]
public string GetCustomer()
{
  //omitted for brevity
}
```

3-9. Configure Route-Specific Message Handlers
Problem

You would like to restrict a message handler to only run against a specific route, rather than for every request.

Solution

A lot of ASP.NET Web API functionalities are built around message handlers. The real power of them is that they run globally and provide an easy mechanism for globally addressing some of the application concerns (such as security). However, there are situations where you'd like to use a handler to apply specific behavior to only a selected portion of an application.

It is possible to configure a message handler (DelegatingHandler) on a per-route basis, rather than registering globally in an HttpConfiguration object. There is an overload of the MapHttpRoute method in HttpRouteCollectionExtensions that allows you to do that.

```
public static IHttpRoute MapHttpRoute(this HttpRouteCollection routes, string name, string
routeTemplate, object defaults, object constraints, HttpMessageHandler handler);
```

▓ **Note**   You can only do this for centralized routes (not when using attribute routing).

How It Works

In the Web API pipeline, the additional per-route handler kicks in **after** all global message handlers run and just prior to HttpControllerDispatcher. A service called HttpRoutingDispatcher is responsible solely for recognizing whether a given route has a specific handler attached to it. If that's the case, the request will be handed off to that handler; otherwise, the processing continues normally towards the dispatching of controllers.

Route-specific handlers need to specify an InnerHandler that will take over afterwards. You have to either plug in another route-specific handler there, or hand back the request to the HttpControllerDispatcher, as shown in Listing 3-22. Using this technique, you could chain as many handlers on this route as you want, as long as you plug the HttpControllerDispatcher at the end; otherwise the request will never be able to reach any controller.

Listing 3-22. Applying a Per-Route Message Handler

```
config.Routes.MapHttpRoute(
    name: "DefaultApi",
    routeTemplate: "api/{controller}/{id}",
    defaults: new { id = RouteParameter.Optional },
    constraints: null,
    handler: new MyHandler() { InnerHandler = new HttpControllerDispatcher(config) }
);
```

You can only imagine the amount of flexibility this gives developers, especially in authentication-related situations where only specific routes have to be secured with some sort of an authentication mechanism (which would often be handled in Web API by message handlers).

The Code

Suppose you need to log all traffic against the routes /api/[something] but not /api/public/[something]. As a result, you need to have a message handler to apply only to a specific route, rather than globally to every request.

To begin with, let's take a simple API request logging handler, such as the one in Listing 3-23.

Listing 3-23. A Logging Message Handler That Will Be Applied to a Specific Route Only

```
public class Repository
{
    public static readonly List<string> Log = new List<string>();
}

public class WebApiUsageHandler : DelegatingHandler
{
    protected override async Task<HttpResponseMessage> SendAsync(HttpRequestMessage request,
        CancellationToken cancellationToken)
    {
        var apikey = request.GetQueryString("apikey");

        if (!string.IsNullOrWhiteSpace(apikey))
        {
            Repository.Log.Add(string.Format("{0} {1} {2}", apikey, request.Method, request.RequestUri));
            var result = await base.SendAsync(request, cancellationToken);
            Repository.Log.Add(string.Format("{0} {1}", apikey, result.StatusCode));
```

```
            return result;
        }

        return await base.SendAsync(request, cancellationToken);
    }
}
```

The actual implementation of the request/response logging is not important here; in this case an in-memory repository is just fine. You are really interested only in the mechanism that will allow you to apply this handler to specific routes. As mentioned, you do that against the ASP.NET Web API HttpConfiguration object, as shown in Listing 3-24.

Listing 3-24. Registering a Regular Default Route and a Route with a Handler Attached to It

```
config.Routes.MapHttpRoute(
    name: "PublicDefaultApi",
    routeTemplate: "api/public/{controller}/{id}",
    defaults: new { id = RouteParameter.Optional }
);

config.Routes.MapHttpRoute(
    name: "PrivateDefaultApi",
    routeTemplate: "api/{controller}/{id}",
    defaults: new { id = RouteParameter.Optional },
    constraints: null,
    handler: new WebApiUsageHandler() {
        InnerHandler = new HttpControllerDispatcher(config)
    }
);
```

If you run your application now,

- All /api/public/[something] routes do not log their requests/responses.

- All /api/[something] routes log their requests/responses because the handler executes only for these routes.

3-10. Ignore Routes
Problem

You have defined centralized routes that are very greedy, but you need to allow specific requests to pass through. Therefore, you'd like to ignore certain routes.

Solution

ASP.NET Web API provides a StopRoutingHandler, which is a message handler that you can attach to a specific route to force Web API to ignore it. The handler is part of System.Web.Http and was introduced into Web API with the 2.1 release. The presence of the StopRoutingHandler handler on a specific route forces HttpRoutingDispatcher to treat that route as non-existing.

▓ **Note**   ASP.NET MVC has its own version of a `StopRoutingHandler` (located in `System.Web`). If you are running ASP.NET Web API on top of a full ASP.NET runtime and have access to `System.Web` assembly, the MVC handler works for Web API too.

How It Works

It is common to look at ignoring routes if ASP.NET Web API is greedily catching the types of requests it should not process. These could be requests to static files that must be handled by the underlying web server, or, in case you are running an OWIN pipeline, calls designated to be handled by other OWIN middleware.

▓ **Note**   OWIN middleware processing is sequential, so if your ASP.NET Web API is registered first in the OWIN pipeline, you may often find a need to "punch holes" in the ASP.NET Web API routing by applying route ignoring.

`HttpRoutingDispatcher`, mentioned already in Recipe 3-9, is a specialized message handler that is responsible for inspecting the `IHttpRoute` of the route that was matched for the current request, and then delegating the processing to `HttpControllerDispatcher`. `HttpRoutingDispatcher` is being called by the `HttpServer`.

`HttpRoutingDispatcher` will check if the route has a per-route handler attached to it, and if it does and if it is of `StopRoutingHandler` type, it will treat the request as if there was no route matched for the request. This logic, from the ASP.NET We API source code, is highlighted in Listing 3-25.

Listing 3-25. Excerpt from Web API Source Code, Showing How StopRoutingHandler Is Used to Treat Matched Routes as If They Were Not Found

```
protected override Task<HttpResponseMessage> SendAsync(HttpRequestMessage request, CancellationToken
cancellationToken)
{
    IHttpRouteData routeData = request.GetRouteData();
    if (routeData == null)
    {
        routeData = _configuration.Routes.GetRouteData(request);
        if (routeData != null)
        {
            request.SetRouteData(routeData);
        }
    }

    if (routeData == null || (routeData.Route != null && routeData.Route.Handler is
        StopRoutingHandler))
    {
        request.Properties.Add(HttpPropertyKeys.NoRouteMatched, true);
        return Task.FromResult(request.CreateErrorResponse(
            HttpStatusCode.NotFound,
            Error.Format(SRResources.ResourceNotFound, request.RequestUri),
            SRResources.NoRouteData));
    }
```

```
        routeData.RemoveOptionalRoutingParameters();

        var invoker = (routeData.Route == null || routeData.Route.Handler == null) ?
            _defaultInvoker : new HttpMessageInvoker(routeData.Route.Handler, disposeHandler: false);
        return invoker.SendAsync(request, cancellationToken);
}
```

The Code

In order to configure route ignoring in your ASP.NET Web API, you can use one of the two syntax constructs.

The first one is similar to the example from Recipe 3-9, as it encompasses registering StopRoutingHandler as a per-route message handler for the route you wish to ignore. An example of that is shown in Listing 3-26. In that case, all requests matching the /content/* pattern will pass through Web API, while the rest will be caught by the greedy /{controller}/{id} generic route definition.

Listing 3-26. Ignoring Routes by Manually Attaching a StopRoutingHandler

```
config.Routes.MapHttpRoute("Content", "content/{*params}", null, null, new StopRoutingHandler());
config.Routes.MapHttpRoute("DefaultApi", "{controller}/{id}", new { id = RouteParameter.Optional });
```

A slightly simplified option is to use the IgnoreRoute extension method from the HttpRouteCollectionExtensions class. Under the hood, it does exactly the same thing: registers the specified route with the StopRoutingHandler attached to it. The example from Listing 3-26, converted to using the IgnoreRoute extension method, is shown in Listing 3-27.

Listing 3-27. Ignoring Routes by Using the IgnoreRoute Extension Method

```
config.Routes.IgnoreRoute("Content", "content/{*params}");
config.Routes.MapHttpRoute("DefaultApi", "{controller}/{id}", new { id = RouteParameter.Optional });
```

3-11. Localize Routes
Problem

You would like to be able to easily localize your routes to the different language versions that your application supports.

Solution

There are a number of ways one could go about implementing localized routing in ASP.NET Web API. Probably the most convenient approach is to utilize direct routing, as it provides two very useful hooks for plugging in custom logic that can extend the default route declaration and their runtime registration: IDirectRouteFactory and IDirectRouteProvider.

You can use IDirectRouteFactory to create a custom attribute that you'll use to annotate your actions with routes. In there, you can provide localization-aware logic that should be used when building a RouteEntry. You can even use that to inject culture-specific DataTokens into the route.

How It Works

IDirectRouteProvider gives you a possibility to customize the logic that's responsible for harvesting route attributes from the actions and controllers at the start of your ASP.NET Web API solution (when you call MapHttpAttributeRoutes). For example, you can trick ASP.NET Web API into thinking that the action is annotated with more route attributes than it actually is, which is perfect for localization, as you end up only needing a single route attribute on an action at compile time, but at runtime a number of routes, one for each language, can get registered.

As is often the case for ASP.NET Web API development, while IDirectRouteProvider is a simple interface, it is complex in terms of functionality, so it's typically more convenient to extend its default implementation, DefaultDirectRouteProvider, which contains a number of convenient virtual methods that can be overridden, than to implement it from scratch.

IDirectRouteFactory allows you to create custom attributes that can be consumed by ASP.NET Web API attribute routing engine as route declarations in place of the default RouteAttribute (that one is sealed so it cannot be extended).

In fact, a class implementing IDirectRouteFactory doesn't even have to be an Attribute, so theoretically you could build an "attribute routing" solution without using attributes at all (!), and rely, for example, on a centralized mechanism of IDirectRouteFactory assignment, and thus, route declaration.

Recipe 6-8, where you'll implement ASP.NET Web API versioning, will go into further details regarding working with IDirectRouteFactory.

IDirectRouteProvider is an important extensibility point, where custom logic responsible for converting HttpControllerDescriptor and its list of HttpActionDescriptor, into a collection of RouteEntry, can be provided. The default implementation, DefaultDirectRouteProvider, splits up the process into three steps:

- Retrieving IReadOnlyCollection<IDirectRouteFactory> from a controller

- Retrieving IReadOnlyCollection<IDirectRouteFactory> from an action

- Converting them into IReadOnlyCollection<RouteEntry> that originated from a controller and IReadOnlyCollection<RouteEntry> that originated from an action.

This is very convenient because you can override each and every step (each has a corresponding virtual method). All of the RouteEntries gathered in that process are later reconciled together and registered against your Web API.

Definitions (outlines) of both IDirectRouteFactory and IDirectRouteProvider interfaces, as well as the DefaultDirectRouteProvider, are shown in Listing 3-28.

Listing 3-28. Definitions of IDirectRouteFactory, IDirectRouteProvider, and DefaultDirectRouteProvider

```
public interface IDirectRouteFactory
{
    RouteEntry CreateRoute(DirectRouteFactoryContext context);
}

public interface IDirectRouteProvider
{
    IReadOnlyCollection<RouteEntry> GetDirectRoutes(HttpControllerDescriptor controllerDescriptor,
IReadOnlyCollection<HttpActionDescriptor> actionDescriptors, IInlineConstraintResolver
constraintResolver);
}

public class DefaultDirectRouteProvider : IDirectRouteProvider
{
    public DefaultDirectRouteProvider();
```

```
    public IReadOnlyCollection<RouteEntry> GetActionDirectRoutes(HttpActionDescriptor
actionDescriptor, IReadOnlyCollection<IDirectRouteFactory> factories, IInlineConstraintResolver
constraintResolver);

    public virtual IReadOnlyCollection<RouteEntry> GetDirectRoutes(HttpControllerDescri
ptor controllerDescriptor, IReadOnlyCollection<HttpActionDescriptor> actionDescriptors,
IInlineConstraintResolver constraintResolver);

    protected virtual IReadOnlyCollection<IDirectRouteFactory>
GetActionRouteFactories(HttpActionDescriptor actionDescriptor);

    protected virtual IReadOnlyCollection<RouteEntry>
GetControllerDirectRoutes(HttpControllerDescriptor controllerDescriptor,
IReadOnlyCollection<HttpActionDescriptor> actionDescriptors, IReadOnlyCollection<IDirectRouteFactor
y> factories, IInlineConstraintResolver constraintResolver);

    protected virtual IReadOnlyCollection<IDirectRouteFactory>
GetControllerRouteFactories(HttpControllerDescriptor controllerDescriptor);

    protected virtual string GetRoutePrefix(HttpControllerDescriptor controllerDescriptor);
}
```

The Code

Supporting localization can take many shapes or forms and it can also become a very complex solution, depending on your requirements. The approach used in this recipe is adequate to the nature of the recipe format; it is simplified, but it's a good foundation for being further extended and adapted to your needs.

Let's start by assuming that your route translation repository will take a format of a Dictionary<string, Dictionary<string, string>>, where the key is the route name, and the value is a dictionary composed of a key representing the language and a value representing the translated route. For convenience, you'll store all of the translations in a static property inside your custom IDirectRouteFactory.

The implementation of the IDirectRouteFactory, LocalizedRouteAttribute, is shown in Listing 3-29. It mirrors the look and structure of RouteAttribute, with three notable additions: the Culture property is present, the DataTokens entry "culture" is being added to every instance of a RouteEntry produced from this attribute, and finally there is a specialized GetLocalizedVersions method. It is responsible for creating instances of the LocalizedRouteAttribute for the current route that are relevant for all of the languages found in the localization dictionary. This way you only need to annotate your actions with LocalizedRouteAttribute once, and a route for each language is automatically registered.

Listing 3-29. LocalizedRouteAttribute, as a First Step to Supporting Localized Routes

```
public class LocalizedRouteAttribute : Attribute, IDirectRouteFactory
{
    public static Dictionary<string, Dictionary<string, string>>Routes = new Dictionary<string,
Dictionary<string, string>>();

    public IEnumerable<LocalizedRouteAttribute> GetLocalizedVersions()
    {
        if (string.IsNullOrWhiteSpace(Name)) yield break;
```

```csharp
        Dictionary<string, string> languageMap;
        if (Routes.TryGetValue(Name, out languageMap))
        {
        foreach (var entry in languageMap)
            {
            yield return new LocalizedRouteAttribute(entry.Value) { Culture = entry.Key};
            }
        }
    }

    public LocalizedRouteAttribute(string template)
    {
        Template = template;
    }

    public string Culture { get; set; }

    public string Name { get; set; }

    public int Order { get; set; }

    public string Template { get; private set; }

    RouteEntry IDirectRouteFactory.CreateRoute(DirectRouteFactoryContext context)
    {
        var builder = context.CreateBuilder(Template);

        builder.Name = Name;
        builder.Order = Order;
        builder.DataTokens = new Dictionary<string, object>();
        builder.DataTokens["culture"] = Culture ?? "en-US";
        return builder.Build();
    }
}
```

Note that LocalizedRouteAttribute and its static Routes dictionary containing translations rely on a route Name as a key, which means you'll need to define a name for every route you have. Alternatively, you could just use the route template as a key as well.

Another thing worth emphasizing is that in this solution, the assumption is that the default route language/culture is en-US. That is represented automatically by the route template defined directly on an action, so the dictionary of translations doesn't need to contain that version. Again, it's totally up to you how you choose to handle this.

By populating the DataTokens dictionary with the correct culture entry, you now have a very convenient hint that can facilitate the process of setting the relevant locale (Thread.Current.CurrentCulture) for your Web API requests. This can be done in any Web API component, such as a message handler, as long as the route has already been matched. There, you could retrieve the locale information from the RouteData DataTokens using the Request.GetRouteData method.

The next step is to introduce a custom IDirectRouteProvider, which will correctly harvest IDirectRouteFactory from actions (for simplicity, I am skipping controller-level declared routes in this example, but, through analogy, you can easily introduce that yourself). This is shown in Listing 3-30.

Listing 3-30. LocalizedDirectRouteProvider, Enabling Translated Routes

```
public class LocalizedDirectRouteProvider : DefaultDirectRouteProvider
{
    protected override IReadOnlyCollection<IDirectRouteFactory>
GetActionRouteFactories(HttpActionDescriptor actionDescriptor)
    {
        var routeAttributes = base.GetActionRouteFactories(actionDescriptor).ToList();
        foreach (var directRouteFactory in routeAttributes.Where(x => x is
        LocalizedRouteAttribute).ToList())
        {
            var localizedRoute = directRouteFactory as LocalizedRouteAttribute;
            if (localizedRoute != null)
            {
                routeAttributes.AddRange(localizedRoute.GetLocalizedVersions());
            }
        }

        return routeAttributes;
    }
}
```

The key aspect of this LocalizedDirectRouteProvider is that in the GetActionRouteFactories, instead of just returning the IDirectRouteFactories it can pick up statically from the HttpActionDescriptor as attributes, you also call your own method, GetLocalizedVersions, which will allow you to add a number of language-specific LocalizedRouteAttributes as if they were statically declared too.

The only thing left to do is to modify your call to MapHttpAttributeRoutes to take the LocalizedDirectRouteProvider into account when processing the routing attributes. Of course, you will also need to add some translations. An example of a controller with a couple of routes, as well as the setup of their translations into Polish and German, is shown in Listing 3-31.

Listing 3-31. A Sample Translation Infrastructure Setup in a Katana-Hosted Web API

```
public class Startup
{
    public void Configuration(IAppBuilder appBuilder)
    {
        var config = new HttpConfiguration();
        config.MapHttpAttributeRoutes(new LocalizedDirectRouteProvider());
        LocalizedRouteAttribute.Routes.Add("order", new Dictionary<string, string>
        {
            { "de-CH", "auftrag" },
            { "pl-PL", "zamowienie" }
        });

        LocalizedRouteAttribute.Routes.Add("orderById", new Dictionary<string, string>
        {
            { "de-CH", "auftrag/{id:int}" },
            { "pl-PL", "zamowienie/{id:int}" }
        });

        appBuilder.UseWebApi(config);
    }
}
```

```
public class OrdersController : ApiController
{
    [LocalizedRoute("order", Name = "order")]
    public HttpResponseMessage Get()
    {
        //omitted for brevity
    }

    [LocalizedRoute("order/{id:int}", Name = "orderById")]
    public HttpResponseMessage GetById(int id)
    {
        //omitted for brevity
    }
}
```

With this in place, all of the following routes are now operational and registered against your ASP.NET Web API service:

- myapi.com/order (English route)

- myapi.com/auftrag (German route)

- myapi.com/zamowienie (Polish route)

- myapi.com/order/{id} (English route)

- myapi.com/auftrag/{id} (German route)

- myapi.com/zamowienie/{id} (Polish route)

3-12. Generate a Link to the Route
Problem

You want to be able to generate links that point to specific routes, instead of hardcoding raw strings.

Solution

ASP.NET Web API supports route-bound link generation through the UrlHelper class. An instance of UrlHelper is available as a public Url property on the ApiController and on the RequestContext object on HttpRequestMessage.

To generate a link, you have to pass a route name and the relevant route values to one of the methods (Route or Link) exposed by UrlHelper.

```
var routeLink = Url.Link("GetTeamById", new {id = team.Id});
```

■ **Caution**　Do not confuse System.Web.Http.UrlHelper, used in ASP.NET Web API with System.Web.Mvc.UrlHelper, which is ASP.NET MVC-specific.

How It Works

Route values can be passed either as an anonymous object or as IDictionary<string, object>. If you declared your routes using centralized routing, each route already has a name; it's a prerequisite. If you used attribute routing, route name is not mandatory, so you will have to ensure that the route declaration, in addition to the route template, also provides a name through which it could be addressed. For example,

```
[Route("api/teams/{id}", Name = "GetTeamById")]
public Team GetTeam(int id)
```

The outline of UrlHelper is shown in Listing 3-32.

Listing 3-32. Definition of UrlHelper

```
public class UrlHelper
{
    public UrlHelper()
    public UrlHelper(HttpRequestMessage request)

    public HttpRequestMessage Request

    public virtual string Content(string path)
    public virtual string Route(string routeName, object routeValues)
    public virtual string Route(string routeName, IDictionary<string, object> routeValues)
    public virtual string Link(string routeName, object routeValues)
    public virtual string Link(string routeName, IDictionary<string, object> routeValues)
}
```

The difference between Route and Link methods is that Route generates a relative URL, while Link produces an absolute URL. Link will actually use Route internally and concatenate it with the RequestUri of the current HttpRequestMessage.

Content is an extra helper method that allows you to create an absolute URL off a string, which could either be a relative URL or a virtual path.

▨ **Tip** Since ASP.Net Web API 2, all methods on UrlHelper are virtual, therefore using it will not cripple the testability of your solution, as the return can always be mocked.

The Code

An example of using UrlHelper with attribute routing to generate a route-specific link is shown in Listing 3-33. In this particular case, a link to a newly created resource is created and returned to the user in the Location header.

Listing 3-33. Sample Use of UrlHelper

```
public class Team
{
    public int Id { get; set; }
    public string Name { get; set; }
}
```

```
public class TeamsController : ApiController
{
    //repository implementation is irrelevant
    private readonly field ITeamsRepository _teams;

    public TeamsController(ITeamsRepository teams)
    {
        _teams = teams;
    }

    [Route("api/teams/{id}", Name = "GetTeamById")]
    public Team GetTeam(int id)
    {
        var team = Teams.FirstOrDefault(x => x.Id == id);
        if (team == null) throw new HttpResponseException(HttpStatusCode.NotFound);

        return team;
    }

    [Route("api/teams")]
    public HttpResponseMessage PostTeam(Team team)
    {
        _teams.Add(team);

        var routeLink = Url.Link("GetTeamById", new {id = team.Id});
        var response = new HttpResponseMessage(HttpStatusCode.Created);
        response.Headers.Location = new Uri(routeLink);
        return response;
    }
}
```

The same code could be used with centralized routing, as long as the route name used to generate the link is changed to a name of a centrally defined route.

CHAPTER 4

■ ■ ■

Content Negotiation and Media Types

This chapter covers the concept of content negotiation, handling media types, and working with model binding. It also covers handling binary data and file uploads in ASP.NET Web API applications.

You will learn how to do the following:

- Request and respond with various media types (Recipes 4-1 and 4-2)

- Control model binding (Recipes 4-3 and 4-4)

- Customize content negotiation (Recipes 4-5, 4-6, and 4-9)

- Perform content negotiation by hand or bypass it (Recipes 4-7 and 4-8)

- Work with binary data (Recipe 4-10)

- Accept file uploads in your Web API application (Recipes 4-11, 4-12 and 4-13)

4-1. Request a Specific Media Type from ASP.NET Web API

Problem

You would like to know how to request a resource representation in a JSON or XML format from an ASP.NET Web API endpoint.

Solution

Out of the box, ASP.NET Web API supports the notion of content negotiation, which is the process of selecting the best representation (XML, JSON, etc.) for a given resource, provided there are multiple representations available.

The primary mechanism driving content negotiation is the **request header**; however, there are a few other criteria that the Web API team has decided to implement to make the whole process as intuitive as possible.

How It Works

Content negotiation is one of the key concepts at the heart of any modern web/HTTP framework, and not just ASP.NET Web API; many other .NET-based web frameworks such as NancyFx and ServiceStack support it.

This might be new to developers coming from an ASP.NET MVC background (which has no built-in content negotiation support), and those developers might wonder why they would ever need it. However, the notion of content negotiation is an intrinsic server-driven aspect of HTTP, and plays a vital role when using HTTP as an application protocol.

Content negotiation (**conneg**) was born when W3C released its RFC 2616 (Request For Comments), where conneg was defined for the first time. In short, it is the process of selecting the best representation (XML, JSON, etc.) for a given resource (as long as the resource has multiple representations to choose from). Moreover, any request may be subject to content negotiation, regardless of whether the request has been successfully fulfilled by the server or not—the only requirement being that the entity processed should have a body, as content negotiation applies to the format of the body.

In the same RFC 2616, W3C also provides a definition for **media type**, as being used "in the Content-Type (section 14.17) and Accept (section 14.1) header fields in order to provide open and extensible data typing and type negotiation." There are countless examples of media types; two of the most common ones in the ASP.NET Web API world are application/xml and application/json.

■ **Note** You can find the full text of RFC2616 at http://www.ietf.org/rfc/rfc2616.txt.

As a result, content negotiation determines, based on the client's request, which media type is going to be used to return an API response. In ASP.NET Web API, that boils down to the HTTP client engaging in content negotiation with the server, and based on the information available, selecting a relevant MediaTypeFormatter to process the body of the HTTP request message, extracting the underlying .NET object (data transfer object), and providing a meaningful response in the format the client can understand.

ASP.NET Web API will go through a series of steps when trying to match a relevant formatter. As soon as a match is found, the result is returned immediately and no further processing is done. This gives the developers a chance to declare their rules at different precedence levels. Let's walk through the conneg process.

The nature and specifics of MediaTypeFormatters are discussed in detail in Recipe 4-6. Out of the box, ASP.NET Web API ships with five formatters (System.Net.Http.Formatting namespace):

- JsonMediaTypeFormatter: For handling JSON. Uses JSON.NET but can be switched to DataContractJsonSerializer.

- BsonMediaTypeFormatter: For handling BSON (binary JSON). Uses JSON.NET.

- XmlMediaTypeFormatter: For handling XML. Uses DataContractSerializer (can be switched to XmlSerializer).

- FormUrlEncodedMediaTypeFormatter: For handling HTML form URL-encoded data.

- JQueryMvcFormUrlEncodedFormatter: For handling model-bound HTML form URL-encoded data.

The Code

The most straight forward way to take advantage of the automatic content negotiation process provided by ASP.NET Web API is to expose an action returning a concrete type rather than HttpResponseMessage or IHttpActionResult; see Listing 4-1.

Listing 4-1. A Sample ASP.NET Web API Controller

```
public class ItemsController : ApiController
{
    public IEnumerable<Item> Get()
    {
        return new List<Item>
```

```
    {
        new Item {Id = 1, Name = "Filip"},
        new Item {Id = 2, Name = "Not Filip"}
    };
  }
}
```

CONTENT NEGOTIATION WITH HTTPRESPONSEMESSAGE

If you use one of the `HttpResponseMessage` extension methods that `System.Web.Http` introduces, you can still work with `HttpResponseMessage` in your action methods and avoid having to bypass content negotiation, hard-code a formatter, or perform manual content negotiation (see Recipe 4-7).

```
public static HttpResponseMessage CreateResponse<T>(this HttpRequestMessage request, T
value);
public static HttpResponseMessage CreateResponse<T>(this HttpRequestMessage request,
HttpStatusCode statusCode, T value);
```

In this case, all you need to do is pass in your object instance; under the hood, the framework will perform content negotiation for you and create an HTTP response with a proper media type, which is exactly the process discussed in Recipe 4-7.

```
public HttpResponseMessage Get()
{
    //get myObjInstance from somehwere
    var response = Request.CreateResponse<ResponseDto>(HttpStatusCode.OK, myObjInstance);
    return response;
}
```

Such an approach lets you work closer to the metal than returning a concrete .NET object (a DTO) - as you do not relinquish your chance to interact with the fundamental HTTP concepts embodied by the `HttpResponseMessage` instance.

When a request flows into the ASP.NET Web API pipeline, the first things the framework will look at (and this is not something defined in any RFC, it's just a Web API convention) are the `MediaTypeMappings` (discussed in Recipe 4-9). However, they are disabled by default.

Since content negotiation is typically driven by the headers, your HTTP request should carry an `Accept` header to specify which media type you are expecting to receive in response.

```
GET /api/items/ HTTP/1.1
Accept: application/xml

GET /api/items/ HTTP/1.1
Accept: text/csv
```

If your HTTP request has a body—perhaps you want to create a new resource or update an existing one—and you skip the Accept header, ASP.NET Web API will look for the Content-Type header of your request's body to determine the response media type. This is very logical, as it creates symmetry between client and server behavior.

```
PUT /api/items/1 HTTP/1.1
Content-Type: application/json
Body: {"Id":"1", "Name":"MyItem"}
```

The final criterion is whether the selected MediaTypeFormatter can even serialize a specific type at all; if so, the first match is selected and used. Out of the box, it means that, at worst, the client will always get a JSON response.

However, such behavior is sometimes undesirable. Imagine a client requesting a text/pdf; if your Web API doesn't have a relevant formatter available, it will always respond with JSON, which might break the client. This behavior can be disabled (see Recipe 6-6).

4-2. Support Additional Media Types
Problem

You would like to support additional request and response formats in your ASP.NET Web API, not just the default ones of XML and JSON/BSON.

Solution

If you would like to allow the existing XML and JSON/BSON MediaTypeFormatters to work with different media types than the ones used by them by default (application/json, text/xml, application/xml), you can extend the SupportedMediaTypes property that each of the formatters exposes.

On the other hand, if you would like to introduce a completely new serialization format, like the ultra-fast Protocol Buffers (application/x-protobuf), you can extend the Formatters collection exposed by the HttpConfiguration with a new MediaTypeFormatter, in this case, a Protocol Buffers one.

A WebApiContrib project contains a lot of community-contributed formatters which can be installed from NuGet and are ready to be used in your project; ProtoBufFormatter is one of them.

How It Works

Formatters act as a bridge between HTTP and the CLR, serializing and deserializing output of and input into an ASP.NET Web API HTTP endpoint. As a result, the global Formatters collection on the HttpConfiguration is one of the finest Web API extensibility points, allowing developers to easily add more media types to the default XML/JSON support that Web API provides.

The formatter in ASP.NET Web API consists of three primary elements:

- A rule defining whether the HTTP input can be read (deserialized) into a .NET type.

- A rule defining whether a .NET type (output) can be written (serialized) into an HttpContent object (body of the HTTP message).

- Definitions of the methods that would do writing/reading to and from the HTTP content streams.

In other words, each formatter can specify whether it should participate in either reading requests, returning responses, or both. Additionally, it can be configured to work only with specific Types; after all, not every DTO can be represented in every media type. I cover the internals of a MediaTypeFormatter in Recipe 4-6.

The order of formatters in the global `Formatters` collection is important. If two or more formatters are suitable for handling the request/response, the content negotiation engine will pick the one registered first. As a consequence of this, the `JsonMediaTypeFormatter` is the default fallback mechanism because it is marked as supporting every single Type and is registered before the XML formatter.

The Code

Suppose you would like the XML formatter to also handle the `text/html` media type. In that case, you add an instance of a relevant `MediaTypeHeaderValue` to the `SupportedMediaTypes` collection of the `XmlMediaTypeFormatter`.

```
httpConfiguration.Formatters.XmlFormatter.SupportedMediaTypes.Add(new MediaTypeHeaderValue("text/html"));
```

To add support for the aforementioned Protocol Buffers formatter, you need to first install it from NuGet (`WebApiContrib.Formatting.ProtoBuf`), and then add to the `Formatters` collection on your `HttpConfiguration`.

```
httpConfiguration.Formatters.Insert(0, new ProtoBufFormatter());
```

In this case, since you added it at the beginning of the collection, and because it's internally configured to support all Types, it also becomes the default formatter if content negotiation cannot determine which formatter to use for a given HTTP request or response.

Other formatters available from WebApiContrib are listed in Table 4-1.

Table 4-1. *List of MediaTypeFormatters from the WebApiContrib Project*

Formatter	Adds support for	Media types
WebApiContrib.Formatting.Bson	BSON (binary JSON) – Web API prior to version 2.5 didn't have it	application/bson
WebApiContrib.Formatting.Html	Raw HTML	text/html application/xhtml application/xhtml+xml
WebApiContrib.Formatting.JavaScriptSerializer	JSON – replacement for JsonMediaTypeFormatter	application/json
WebApiContrib.Formatting.Jsonp	JSONP	text/javascript
WebApiContrib.Formatting.MsgPack	MessagePack	application/x-msgpack
WebApiContrib.Formatting.ProtoBuf	Protocol Buffers	application/x-protobuf
WebApiContrib.Formatting.Razor	HTML with Razor	text/html application/xhtml application/xhtml+xml
WebApiContrib.Formatting.ServiceStack	JSON – replacement for JsonMediaTypeFormatter, uses ServiceStack.Text serializer	application/json
WebApiContrib.Formatting.CollectionJson	Collection+JSON	application/vnd.collection+json
WebApiContrib.Formatting.Xlsx	Generates formatted Excel documents	application/vnd.ms-excel

In order to replace an existing formatter with a different one (i.e. `JsonMediaTypeFormatter` with `ServiceStackMediaTypeFormatter`) you simply need to remove the unnecessary one from the `Formatters` collection and add the new one.

```
config.Formatters.Remove(config.Formatters.JsonFormatter);
config.Formatters.Add(new ServiceStackTextFormatter());
```

4-3. Control Model Binding From URI and Body

Problem

You would like to change the default behavior of ASP.NET Web API, which reads basic parameters from the URI and complex ones from the body of the HTTP request.

Solution

ASP.NET Web API provides a number of places in which the model binding process can be customized:

- Through the use of [`FromBody`] and [`FromUri`] attributes, a given parameter can be forced to load from the body of the request or from the URI, respectively.

- A custom `TypeConverter` can provide instructions on converting a string to a custom Type.

- A custom [`ModelBinder`] attribute can define custom logic on determining how a set of data fed from `ValueProviders` should be converted into an action parameter.

- `ValueProviders` are more low-level than `ModelBinders` and can provide generic instructions on getting a specific value from an `HttpRequestMessage`.

- `ModelBinders` are specialized examples of a general mechanism called `HttpParameterBinding`, which can execute both as a model binder and as a `MediaTypeFormatter`.

■ **Note**   `ValueProviders` and custom `HttpParameterBinding`, due to their low-level nature, are typically more relevant when you are building framework plug-ins or extensions, and are rarely used in typical, everyday API development.

How It Works

The basic rules of parameter binding in ASP.NET Web API are as follows:

- Primitive and basic types are read from the URI using model binders: `int`, `string`, `boolean`, `Guid`, `DateTime`, `decimal`, and so on.

- Collections and complex types are read from the body of the HTTP request using a `MediaTypeFormatter` selected by performing content negotiation.

Additionally, as discussed in the next recipe, only a single thing can be read from a body.

The Code

Let's walk through the process of customizing Web API's default behavior through the use of [FromUri] and [FromBody], as well as writing custom TypeConverters and ModelBinders.

FromUri and FromBody

In order to force simple types to be bound from the body, you need to decorate them with a [FromBody] attribute. Bear in mind that the constraint of only a single thing being allowed to be read from the body of the HTTP request still applies. See Listing 4-2.

Listing 4-2. Correct and Incorrect Usage of [FromBody] Attribute

```
//correct
public void Post([FromBody]int id)
{
//omitted for brevity
}

//incorrect
public void Post([FromBody]int id, [FromBody]string name)
{
//omitted for brevity
}
```

One other thing to be aware of here is that ASP.NET Web API will bind over the entire body; therefore the whole content of the body has to be the required value (int in this case). This is shown in Listing 4-3.

Listing 4-3. Correct and Incorrect Request to and Endpoint Using [FromBody] on a Primitive Type

```
//correct
POST /api/my HTTP/1.1
Content-Type: application/json
Body: 7

//incorrect
POST /api/my HTTP/1.1
Content-Type: application/json
Body: {id: 7}
```

Similarly, with the [FromUri] attribute, you can force model binding of complex types from the URI, instead of a MediaTypeFormatter. This is very useful for GET requests, which by design cannot have a request body, as they allow you to pass in complex types from the URI directly. Consider a simple example using a wrapper for a simple search query (Listing 4-4).

Listing 4-4. Complex Object Which Will Be Read from URI and a Sample Action Binding It

```
public class SearchQuery
{
    public SearchQuery()
    {
        PageSize = 10;
    }
```

```
        public int PageIndex { get; set; }
        public int PageSize { get; set; }
        public string StartsWith { get; set; }
}

public HttpResponseMessage Get([FromUri]SearchQuery query)
{
    //omitted for brevity
    }
```

You can now very easily pass it from the client in the URI.

```
GET /api/search?PageIndex=1&PageSize=5&StartsWith=asp HTTP/1.1
Accept: application/json
```

 It's worth noting that in this case you can still have additional action parameters bound from the URI (the single parameter restriction applies to body only), so for example the following signature is still valid:

```
public HttpResponseMessage Get(int id, [FromUri]SearchQuery query)
```

TypeConverters

TypeConverters assume the responsibility of converting a string (raw value from an HTTP request) into a concrete Type. With that, a complex type can be treated as a simple type, since ASP.NET Web API passes a string to the converter, which outputs a complex type. You could alter your SearchQuery object to work with a TypeConverter by writing a SearchQuery-specific converter as shown in Listing 4-5.

Listing 4-5. A Sample TypeConverter

```
public class SearchQueryConverter : TypeConverter
{
    public override bool CanConvertFrom(ITypeDescriptorContext context, Type sourceType)
    {
        if (sourceType == typeof(string))
        {
            return true;
        }
        return base.CanConvertFrom(context, sourceType);
    }

    public override object ConvertFrom(ITypeDescriptorContext context,
        CultureInfo culture, object value)
    {
        if (value is string)
        {
            var parts = ((string)value).Split(',');
            if (parts.Length == 3)
```

```
        {
            int firstParsed;
            int secondParsed;
            if (Int32.TryParse(parts[0], out firstParsed) && Int32.TryParse(parts[1], out
            secondParsed))
            {
                return new SearchQuery
                {
                    PageIndex = firstParsed,
                    PageSize = secondParsed,
                    StartsWith = parts[2]
                };
            }
        }
    }
    return base.ConvertFrom(context, culture, value);
    }
}
```

In this example, it is assumed that the client will pass a comma-delimited structure of a SearchQuery object in the query string. The converter then tries to split it, and if all conditions are matched, a new instance of SearchQuery is passed into the action.

In addition to that, it's necessary to decorate the SearchQuery DTO with a TypeConverter attribute.

```
[TypeConverter(typeof(SearchQueryConverter))]
public class SearchQuery
```

As a result, you can now write actions taking in this DTO and have it populated automatically from the URI. You make requests to the API as follows:

```
GET /api/search?query=1,10,asp HTTP/1.1
Accept: application/json
```

ModelBinders

The final example in this recipe will show a ModelBinder, which is a slightly more flexible option than a TypeConverter, since, contrary to the latter one, it can be selectively applied. Moreover, a ModelBinder can be generic, rather than Type-specific. See Listing 4-6.

Listing 4-6. A Sample ModelBinder

```
public class CollectionModelBinder<T> : IModelBinder
{
    public bool BindModel(HttpActionContext actionContext, ModelBindingContext bindingContext)
    {
        var key = bindingContext.ModelName;
        var val = bindingContext.ValueProvider.GetValue(key);
        if (val != null)
        {
            var s = val.AttemptedValue;
            try
```

```
        {
            T[] result;
            if (s != null && s.IndexOf(",", StringComparison.Ordinal) > 0)
            {
                result = s.Split(new[] {","}, StringSplitOptions.None)
                        .Select(x => (T) Convert.ChangeType(x, typeof (T)))
                        .ToArray();
            }
            else
            {
            result = new[] {(T) Convert.ChangeType(s, typeof (T))};
            }

            bindingContext.Model = result;
            return true;
        }
        catch (InvalidCastException)
        {
            return false;
        }
        }
    return false;
    }
}
```

In this example, the binder will try to bind a collection of simple parameters (int, double, string, etc.) from a comma-delimited request. In case of a casting failure, the BindModel method will return false.

ModelBinder can be applied directly to the parameter of an action, which means only this specific occurrence of the action parameter will be bound using the binder.

```
public HttpResponseMessage Get([ModelBinder(typeof(CollectionModelBinder<int>))] IEnumerable<int>
numbers)
public HttpResponseMessage Get([ModelBinder(typeof(CollectionModelBinder<string>))]
IEnumerable<string> words)
```

The HTTP requests can now look like this:

```
GET /api/my?numbers=1,2,3,4 HTTP/1.1
Accept: application/json

GET /api/my?words=asp,net,web,api HTTP/1.1  Accept: application/json
```

It can also, similarly to TypeConverter, be applied on the DTO (however, in this example you are dealing with collection ModelBinder so there is no DTO to apply it to, unless you have a DTO extending one of the default .NET collections). Finally, it can also be registered globally against HttpConfiguration and its Services property.

4-4. ASP.NET MVC-style Parameter Bindingin ASP.NET Web API
Problem

You would like ASP.NET Web API to behave in the same way as ASP.NET MVC when performing parameter binding.

Solution

The entire process of parameter binding in ASP.NET Web API is controlled by a replaceable IActionValueBinder service. The WebApiContrib project provides an MvcActionValueBinder written by Microsoft's Mike Stall, which extends the DefaultActionValueBinder and introduces the MVC parameter binding semantics into ASP.NET Web API. You can download it and replace the default IActionValueBinder in your HttpConfiguration.

```
Install-package WebApiContrib
httpConfiguration.Services.Replace(typeof(IActionValueBinder), new MvcActionValueBinder());
```

How It Works

DefaultActionValueBinder introduces two major differences (or restrictions, if you will) when compared to the MVC parameter binding mechanism:

- A single model cannot be composed of values (fields) coming from both body and URI.

- Only a single thing can be read from a body, which means that if you want to accept two complex DTOs as an input to your action, you need to wrap them together in another type.

MvcActionValueBinder changes this behavior by reading the entire body of the request and treating it as a set of key-value pairs (assuming that the body is a FormDataCollection). All of the data gets saved in the request's Properties dictionary and is shared between the parameters; as a consequence, a number of parameters can be bound from the body.

The Code

Globally enabling MVC style binding is very easy, as it comes down to swapping the default implementation of IActionValueBinder with MvcActionValueBinder:

```
httpConfiguration.Services.Replace(typeof(IActionValueBinder), new MvcActionValueBinder());
```

However, this is hardly advisable, and ideally you'd like to have more granular control over this. Thankfully, you can also easily apply MvcActionValueBinder at the controller level through the use of a controller-scoped configuration (see Recipe 5-3) which is shown in Listing 4-7.

Listing 4-7. A Controller with MvcActionValueBinder Applied to It

```
public class MyComplexDto
{
    public string Message { get; set; }
    public int Id { get; set; }
}

[MvcBindingConfiguration(ActionValueBinder=typeof(MvcActionValueBinder))]
public class MyController : ApiController
{
    public void Post(MyComplexDto dto)
    {
    }
}
```

Listing 4-8 shows three different POST requests. The MVC-style model binding will work correctly in all of these cases, regardless of whether a given field is provided via the URI or the body.

Listing 4-8. Various Requests to an MVC-Style Binding Endpoint, All Resulting in the Same Model Being Passed into the Action

```
POST /api/my?Id=1&Message=hello HTTP/1.1

POST /api/my?Id=1 HTTP/1.1
Content-Type: application/x-www-form-url
Body: Message=hello

POST /api/my HTTP/1.1
Content-Type: application/x-www-form-url
Body: Message=hello&Id=1
```

4-5. Customize XML and JSON Responses
Problem

You would like to change some of the serialization settings on the default formatters, such as camel-casing JSON, enumeration handling, max depth, XML structure, etc.

Solution

In order to customize the output of both of the default formatters, you have to configure the underlying serializer in each of them. JsonMediaTypeFormatter uses JSON.NET under the hood, while XmlMediaTypeFormatter uses DataContractSerializer. Out of the box, Web API allows you to easily switch, through a boolean setting, to DataContractJsonSerializer and XmlSerializer, respectively.

Both formatters expose hooks for tapping into the process of serializer initialization, which can be overridden. What's more, the serialization settings are exposed too, which means some settings can be tweaked without having to re-instantiate the given formatter. This option is usually the fastest and simplest. On the other, removing a formatter, and adding back a new one, preconfigured with relevant settings, is also a viable option.

How It Works

To switch from JSON.NET to DataContractJsonSerializer, you need to set the UseDataContractJsonSerializer flag, while to switch from DataContractSerializer to XmlSerializer, you need to set the UseXmlSerializer flag.

```
httpConfiguration.Formatters.JsonFormatter.UseDataContractJsonSerializer = true;
httpConfiguration.Formatters.XmlFormatte.UseXmlSerializer = true;
```

ASP.NET Web API will look at these flags to determine what kind of formatter you wish to use. DataContractSerializer-based serializers for both JSON and XML operate on their default settings. For JSON handling with JSON.NET, Web API uses mostly JSON.NET defaults, except for two custom settings:

- MissingMemberHandling is set Ignore.
- TypeNameHandling is set to None.

XML handling with `XmlSerializer` is done through slightly customized `XmlWriterSettings`:

- `OmitXmlDeclaration` is set `true`.
- `CloseOutput` is set to `false`.
- `CheckCharacters` is set to `false`.

The Code

The following section will discuss the specifics of customizing JSON and XML formatters, respectively.

JSON

JSON.NET's `SerializerSettings` are exposed through the `JsonMediaTypeFormatter`'s `SerializerSettings` property. To globally tweak those, you can simply walk up to the registered JSON formatter and apply the necessary changes, as shown in Listing 4-9.

Listing 4-9. Customizing the Default JsonFormatter

```
config.Formatters.JsonFormatter.SerializerSettings.DateFormatHandling = DateFormatHandling.
IsoDateFormat;

config.Formatters.JsonFormatter.SerializerSettings.ReferenceLoopHandling = ReferenceLoopHandling.
Ignore;

config.Formatters.JsonFormatter.SerializerSettings.Formatting = Formatting.Indented;

config.Formatters.JsonFormatter.SerializerSettings.ContractResolver = new
CamelCasePropertyNamesContractResolver();
```

In this particular example, a number of JSON.NET-specific settings are set: treating all dates as ISO dates, indenting the JSON output, ignoring reference loops (helps with lazy loaded self-referencing entities), and applying camel casing. For all available settings, please refer to JSON.NET documentation at `http://james.newtonking.com/json`.

You could also set the entire `SerializerSettings` property in a single go, instead of dealing with individual properties, or even recreate the entire `JsonMediaTypeFormatter` with the relevant `SerializerSettings` object.

`JsonMediaTypeFormatter` also exposes a virtual `CreateJsonSerializer` method which can be overridden to provide the formatter with the properly configured JSON.NET serializer.

XML

Both XML serializers, `DataContractSerializer` and `XmlSerializer`, are created per `Type`. `XmlMediaTypeFormatter` exposes virtual methods responsible for creating instances of those which may be used to customize certain behaviors. These methods are also called only once per `Type`, since the formatter caches the resolved serializers.

```
public virtual XmlSerializer CreateXmlSerializer(Type type)
public virtual DataContractSerializer CreateDataContractSerializer(Type type)
```

While discussing the differences between `DataContractSerializer` and `XmlSerializer` is beyond the scope of this book (this is nothing ASP.NET Web API specific, as both belong to the core .NET framework), the rule of thumb is that `DataContractSerializer` is faster but `XmlSerializer` gives you more granular control over the output XML.

Listing 4-10 shows a simple example of a customized DataContractSerializer, which then has to be used to replace the default one.

Listing 4-10. Customizing the XML Formatter

```
public class MyXmlMediaTypeFormatter : XmlMediaTypeFormatter
{
    public virtual DataContractSerializer CreateDataContractSerializer(Type type)
    {
        var settings = new DataContractSerializerSettings
        {
            MaxItemsInObjectGraph = 20,
            PreserveObjectReferences = true
        };
        var mySerializer = new DataContractSerializer(type, settings);
        return mySerializer;
    }
}
```

```
httpConfiguration.Formatters.Remove(config.Formatters.XmlFormatter);
httpConfiguration.Formatters.Add(new MyXmlMediaTypeFormatter());
```

Customization of the XmlSerializer can be done in the same way, through overriding the CreateXmlSerializer method, but it can also be done by tweaking the XmlWriterSettings directly. For example:

```
httpConfiguration.Formatters.XmlFormatter.UseXmlSerializer = true;
httpConfiguration.Formatters.XmlFormatter.WriterSettings.OmitXmlDeclaration = false;
```

4-6. Write Your Own MediaTypeFormatter
Problem

You would like to create a custom formatter to handle an RSS media type (application/rss+xml), as it is not supported by ASP.NET Web API out of the box.

Solution

In order to facilitate handling of an RSS media type, you can build a custom MediaTypeFormatter and extend the default formatters collection. Subclassing a MediaTypeFormatter is an extremely powerful technique for extending ASP.NET Web API.

How It Works

The MediaTypeFormatter abstract class provides you four methods to override, as well as a couple of collections for fine-grained control over the behavior of your formatter. An overview of the members of this class is shown in Listing 4-11.

Listing 4-11. Overview of the Abstract MediaTypeFormatter Class

```
public abstract class MediaTypeFormatter
{
        public Collection<MediaTypeHeaderValue> SupportedMediaTypes { get; private set; }

        public Collection<Encoding> SupportedEncodings { get; private set; }

        public Collection<MediaTypeMapping> MediaTypeMappings { get; private set; }

        public virtual Task<object> ReadFromStreamAsync(Type type, Stream stream, HttpContentHeaders
        contentHeaders, IFormatterLogger formatterLogger)
           {
            // to be overriden
           }

        public virtual Task WriteToStreamAsync(Type type, object value, Stream stream,
        HttpContentHeaders contentHeaders, TransportContext transportContext)
           {
            // to be overriden
           }

        public abstract bool CanReadType(Type type);

        public abstract bool CanWriteType(Type type);
}
```

SupportedMediaTypes and SupportedEncodings collections allow you to further restrict the formatter to specific media types and encodings. These rules will be taken into account when Web API runs its content negotiation process to determine which formatter should be selected for a given request. Note that the read/write API is entirely asynchronous.

MediaTypeMappings are discussed in detail in Recipe 4-9.

The Code

In this example, the custom RSS MediaTypeFormatter will do all the heavy lifting for Web API, as it will convert the model returned by your controller's action into an RSS output type (application/rss+xml).

You will also utilize the CanReadType and CanWriteType methods. Since not every single possible .NET type can be converted into a meaningful RSS representation, you will introduce a constraint interface, IRss. The formatter will then check whether the model passed by the action implements the IRss interface as a prerequisite to perform the output conversion.

What's more, since you will only deliver content with RSS (never read from an RSS with this formatter), you will skip the deserialization process altogether, and make the formatter one-way only.

First, let's introduce an IRss contract and a sample model, as shown in Listing 4-12.

Listing 4-12. An IRss Constraint Interface and a Sample Model Implementing It

```
public interface IRss
{
    string Title { get; set; }
    string Description { get; set; }
    DateTime CreatedAt { get; set; }
```

```
    Uri Link { get; set; }
    string Author { get; set; }
}

public class Article : IRss
{
    public int ArticleId { get; set; }
    public Uri Link { get; set; }
    public string Title { get; set; }
    public string Description { get; set; }
    public string Content { get; set; }
    public DateTime CreatedAt { get; set; }
    public string Author { get; set; }
}
```

The formatter inherits from MediaTypeFormatter and can be found in Listing 4-13.

Listing 4-13. An Implementation of RssMediaTypeFormatter

```
public class RssMediaTypeFormatter : MediaTypeFormatter
{
        private readonly string rss = "application/rss+xml";

    public RssMediaTypeFormatter()
    {
    SupportedMediaTypes.Add(new MediaTypeHeaderValue(rss));
    }

    Func<Type, bool> typeisIRss = (type) => typeof(IRss).IsAssignableFrom(type);
    Func<Type, bool> typeisIRssCollection = (type) => typeof(IEnumerable<IRss>).
    IsAssignableFrom(type);

    public override bool CanReadType(Type type)
    {
        return false;
    }

    public override bool CanWriteType(Type type)
    {
        return typeisIRss(type) || typeisIRssCollection(type);
    }

    public override Task WriteToStreamAsync(Type type, object value, Stream writeStream,
    HttpContent content, TransportContext transportContext)
    {
        RssFeedBuilder builder;
        if (typeisIRss(type))
            builder = new RssFeedBuilder((IRss)value);
        else
         builder = new RssFeedBuilder((IEnumerable<IRss>)value);
```

```
        builder.BuildSyndicationFeed(writeStream, content.Headers.ContentType.MediaType);
        return Task.FromResult(0);
    }
}
```

In the constructor, you declare support for the application/rss+xml Accept header. Notice that the formatter is very specific: it will **only** work with application/rss+xml.

You have two simple predicates, which will check whether the DTO type returned from your actions is either IRss or IEnumerable<IRss>, and you use them in the CanReadType and CanWriteType methods of the formatter. These three conditions are used by ASP.NET Web API to determine whether a given formatter should take part in the HTTP response process.

The process of writing the actual HTTP response happens in the formatter's WriteToStreamAsync method, which uses a helper class called RssFeedBuilder (Listing 4-14) to convert the IRss into a RSS syndication feed (using .NETs Rss20FeedFormatter class from the System.ServiceModel.Syndication namespace).

Listing 4-14. Helper Class Performing the Actual Build-up of the RSS Feed

```
public class RssFeedBuilder
{
    private readonly IEnumerable<IRss> _items;
    private readonly string _feedTitle;

    public RssFeedBuilder(IRss item) : this(new List<IRss> { item })
    {}

    public RssFeedBuilder(IEnumerable<IRss> items, string feedTitle = "My feed")
    {
        _items = items;
        _feedTitle = feedTitle;
    }

    public void BuildSyndicationFeed(Stream stream, string contenttype)
    {
    List<SyndicationItem> items = new List<SyndicationItem>();
        var feed = new SyndicationFeed()
        {
            Title = new TextSyndicationContent(_feedTitle)
        };

        var enumerator = _items.GetEnumerator();
        while (enumerator.MoveNext())
        {
            items.Add(BuildSyndicationItem(enumerator.Current));
        }

        feed.Items = items;

        using (XmlWriter writer = XmlWriter.Create(stream))
        {
            Rss20FeedFormatter rssformatter = new Rss20FeedFormatter(feed);
            rssformatter.WriteTo(writer);
        }
    }
}
```

```
    private SyndicationItem BuildSyndicationItem(IRss singleItem)
    {
        var feedItem = new SyndicationItem()
        {
            Title = new TextSyndicationContent(singleItem.Title),
            BaseUri = singleItem.Link,
            LastUpdatedTime = singleItem.CreatedAt,
            Content = new TextSyndicationContent(singleItem.Description)
        };
        feedItem.Authors.Add(new SyndicationPerson() { Name = singleItem.Author });
        return feedItem;
    }
}
```

The final piece of the puzzle is to plug in the formatter into the Web API's HttpConfiguration.

```
httpConfiguration.Formatters.Insert(0, new RssMediaTypeFormatter());
```

You can now declare some controller actions that return an object or a collection of objects that implement IRss. A sample is shown in Listing 4-15. Such ASP.NET Web API endpoints can be requested by the client by passing in the Accept header application/rss+xml. This will match your formatter's SupportedMediaTypeMappings and therefore the ASP.NET Web API pipeline will select it to issue the response in RSS format.

Listing 4-15. Sample Controller Exposing Objects That Can Be Transformed by Web API into an RSS Feed

```
public class ValuesController : ApiController
{
    private readonly List<Article> _articles;

    public ValuesController()
    {
        _articles = new List<Article> {
            new Article {
                ArticleId = 1,
                Author = "Filip",
                CreatedAt = new DateTime(2012,10,25),
                Description = "Some text",
                Link = new Uri("http://www.strathweb.com/1"),
                Title = "Article One"
            },
            new Article {
                ArticleId = 2,
                Author = "Filip",
                CreatedAt = new DateTime(2012,10,26),
                Description = "Different text",
                Link = new Uri("http://www.strathweb.com/2"),
                Title = "Article Two"
            }
        };
    }
}
```

```
public IEnumerable<Article> Get()
{
    return _articles;
}

public Article Get(int id)
{
    return _articles.FirstOrDefault(i => i.ArticleId == id);
}
}
```

This controller still produces a typical XML/JSON output such as you might have come to expect from ASP.NET Web API, and it is RSS friendly.

4-7. Run Content Negotiation Manually

Problem

You would like to perform the content negotiation process by hand, rather than have ASP.NET Web API do it automatically for you.

Solution

In order to be able to run content negotiation .manually, you should use the current HttpConfiguration object and get an instance of the registered IContentNegotiator.

It exposes a Negotiate method that is used to determine which formatter and media type are supposed to be used to respond to the client's HTTP request. The Negotiate method returns information in the form of a ContentNegotiationResult class. See Listing 4-16.

Listing 4-16. Definition of ContentNegotiationResult

```
public class ContentNegotiationResult
{
    public MediaTypeFormatter Formatter { get; set; }
    public MediaTypeHeaderValue MediaType { get; set; }
}
```

How It Works

While it is not required too often, you may encounter scenarios where you'd benefit from being able to run content negotiation manually.

If your action doesn't return a POCO object but rather an HttpResponseMessage with some content, you will be required to specify a formatter. To avoid making this decision for the client in an arbitrary way, or simply guessing which one should be used, you can get a helping hand from IContentNegotiator.

Another common use case for manual content negotiation is situations when you want to respond to the client directly from an action filter/message handler, without allowing the request to get into any controller action itself. This mechanism, known as "short-circuiting" of responses, is common when implementing caching or API throttling solutions.

CACHING AND MANUAL CONTENT NEGOTIATION

When you build a caching solution based on action filters or message handlers, you want to cache each representation (version) of processed output (after content negotiation; so JSON, XML and so on) separately rather the just the raw DTO itself, as in that case you'd have to rerun serialization over and over.

Through the manual use of content negotiation you can determine on every request which version of the response the client should receive.

Whenever you return `HttpResponseMessage` or `IHttpActionResult` directly, Web API will not run content negotiation on its own anymore.

The Code

A simple example of manual content negotiation is shown in Listing 4-17. The best-match formatter and relevant media type are determined using the current instance of IContentNegotiator.

Listing 4-17. A Sample Action Performing Content Negotiation Manually

```
public HttpResponseMessage Get()
{
    var item = new MyType(); //whatever you want to return
    var negotiator = Configuration.Services.GetContentNegotiator();
    var result = negotiator.Negotiate(typeof(MyType), Request, Configuration.Formatters);

    var bestMatchFormatter = result.Formatter;
    var mediaType = result.MediaType.MediaType;

    return new HttpResponseMessage()
    {
    Content = new ObjectContent<MyType>(items, bestMatchFormatter, mediaType)
    };
}
```

This way, the relevant formatter will be used to serialize the response for the client. It is worth noting that this is semantically equivalent to the setup shown in Listing 4-18.

Listing 4-18. Sample Actions Relying on Automatic Content Negotiation

```
public MyType Get()
{
        var item = new MyType();
        return item;
    }

    public HttpResponseMessage Get()
    {
        //CreateResponse will run conneg internally
var result = Request.CreateResponse(HttpStatusCode.OK, new MyType());
        return item;
}
```

The major difference in this case is that working with the raw HttpResponseMessage allows you to work directly with HTTP concepts, instead of relying on the framework to do the translation to HTTP for you.

4-8. Bypass Content Negotiation

Problem

You would like to respond with a specific media type directly, rather than relying on ASP.NET Web API to produce the relevant response format for you.

Solution

There are a two ways to bypass the content negotiation engine in ASP.NET Web API. Instead of returning a type, you should use one of the following as a return type for your action:

- HttpResponseMessage
- IActionHttpResult (which is used to produce an HttpResponseMessage)

The outcome is that you are then free to work with HTTP concepts directly, and shape the outgoing HTTP response in any way you want.

How It Works

ASP.NET Web API will run content negotiation for all custom types returned for your actions. However, if you return an HttpResponseMessage, the pipeline allows it to pass through, simply returning it to the client.

The story is similar with IActionHttpResult, which was introduced in ASP.NET Web API 2. It's effectively an interface that acts as a generic factory for HttpResponseMessage. The interface declares only a single method, which produces a Task<HttpResponseMessage>. See Listing 4-19.

Listing 4-19. Definition of IHttpActionResult

```
public interface IHttpActionResult
{
    Task<HttpResponseMessage> ExecuteAsync(CancellationToken cancellationToken);
}
```

When Web API encounters a type implementing this interface as result of an executed action, instead of running content negotiation, it will call its only method (Execute) to produce the HttpResponseMessage, and then use that to respond to the client.

The Code

Let's have a look at some of the techniques mentioned above. The simplest possible example involves manually creating an HttpResponseMessage and choosing the formatter you'd like to use in place of the regular content negotiation process. This is shown in Listing 4-20.

Listing 4-20. A Sample HttpResponseMessage with an Arbitrary JSON Response

```
public class ResponseDto
{
    public string Message { get; set; }
}

    public HttpResponseMessage Get()
    {
        var message = new ResponseDto
        {
            Message = "hello world"
        };

        var result = new HttpResponseMessage(HttpStatusCode.OK)
        {
            Content = new ObjectContent<ResponseDto>(message, Configuration.Formatters.
            JsonFormatter)
        };

        return result;
    }
```

In this example, you explicitly say that the ResponseDto should be transferred to the client as a JSON, since you used the out-of-the-box JsonMediaTypeFormatter.

In most cases, bypassing content negotiation like this is not advisable, but in some situations you may be dealing with specific resources that only have a single, known-in-advance representation, such as HTML or PDF; then you can easily save your service a trip through the negotiation process.

Of course, if you do things like this often, it may become tedious to repeat the same code that sets up a specific HttpResponseMessage over and over again. Moreover, this approach might be difficult to unit test (more on that in Recipe 11-5). This is where IHttpActionResult comes into the picture, as it allows you to package the "recipes" for an HttpResponseMessage into reusable classes. In fact, the framework itself ships with plenty of IHttpActionResult implementations already; those are exposed as methods on the base ApiController.

The equivalent to the last piece of code, but with IHttpActionResult, is shown in Listing 4-21.

Listing 4-21. A Sample IHttpActionResult Response in JSON Format

```
public IHttpActionResult Get()
{
    var message = new ResponseDto
    {
        Message = "hello world"
    };

    return Json(message);
}
```

You use a helper method that hangs off the base ApiController, Json<T>(T content), which returns a JsonResult. As you can see, it is much simpler because you don't have to create the HttpResponseMessage by hand; it's done inside the JsonResult implementation.

Finally, let's look at creating a custom IHttpActionResult, which you can use as a way to bypass content negotiation for your specific media type.

Suppose you are interested in having a shortcut for returning text/plain responses (useful for demos and testing). Your IHttpActionResult would look like the code in Listing 4-22.

Listing 4-22. An IHttpActionResult Returning text/plain Response

```
public class PlainTextResult : IHttpActionResult
{
    private readonly string _text;
    private readonly Encoding _encoding;

    public PlainTextResult(string text, Encoding encoding)
    {
        _text = text;
        _encoding = encoding;
    }

    public Task<HttpResponseMessage> ExecuteAsync(CancellationToken cancellationToken)
    {
        var response = new HttpResponseMessage(HttpStatusCode.OK)
        {
            Content = new StringContent(_text, _encoding)
        };

        return Task.FromResult(response);
    }
}
```

In this example, you pass in some text and the relevant encoding directly from the action, which are later transformed into an HttpResponseMessage when the framework invokes the Execute method.

■ **Note**   StringContent defaults to content type header "text/plain" so there is no need to set it manually.

To use this custom IHttpActionResult in an action, you simply need to return a new instance of PlainTextResult.

```
public IHttpActionResult Get()
{
    return new PlainTextResult("hello world", Encoding.UTF8);
}
```

4-9. Control Media Types with MediaTypeMappings

Problem

You would like to be able to serve specific media types based on an extension in the URL, a query string, or a predefined request header.

Solution

ASP.NET Web API provides a feature called MediaTypeMappings, which allows you to fine-tune the regular content negotiation process (which out of the box, relies on Accept and Content-Type headers).

MediaTypeMappings have the highest precedence in content negotiation and let you quickly respond with a specific media type, as long as the condition defined in the mapping is met by the incoming request.

How It Works

ASP.NET Web API ships with three MediaTypeMappings which can be applied to any formatter. Each of the mappings lets you provide a different type of a condition.

- QueryStringMapping
- UriPathExtensionMapping
- RequestHeaderMapping

UriPathExtensionMapping tries to find an extension parameter in the route (representing an extension). This allows your resources to be targeted as if they physically existed; for example, the following will always respond with JSON/XML, respectively:

```
GET /api/items.json
GET /api/items.rss
```

This is especially useful if you want specific resources to look as if they were physical files on the server (consider actions that generate PDFs or images).

QueryStringMapping looks for a specific query parameter (which can be anything the developer defines):

```
GET /api/items?format=json
GET /api/items?format=rss
```

RequestHeaderMapping allows the calling client to specify the required media type through a predefined header field:

```
GET /api/items
ReturnType: json
```

■ **Tip**   The custom header used here, ReturnType, has no X- prefix on purpose. IETF (Internet Engineering Task Force) has deprecated it in 2012 (http://tools.ietf.org/search/rfc6648).

The Code

In order to register MediaTypeMapping against a formatter, ASP.NET Web API provides a few helper extension methods. Additionally, MediaTypeFormatter exposes a MediaTypeMappings collection as a property.

MediaTypeMappings can be applied to both the default Web API formatters and to the custom ones. The two default formatters, XML and JSON, hang off the HttpConfiguration so it can be done directly there, as shown in Listing 4-23.

Listing 4-23. Examples of Registering the MediaTypeMappings Against Existing Formatters

```
httpConfiguration.Formatters.JsonFormatter.AddUriPathExtensionMapping("json", "application/json");
    xmlConfiguration.Formatters.XmlFormatter.AddUriPathExtensionMapping("xml", "application/xml");

httpConfiguration.Formatters.JsonFormatter. AddQueryStringMapping("format", "json", "application/
json");
    xmlConfiguration.Formatters.XmlFormatter. AddQueryStringMapping("format", "xml", "application/
xml");

httpConfiguration.Formatters.JsonFormatter. AddRequestHeaderMapping("ReturnType", "json",
StringComparison. InvariantCultureIgnoreCase, false, "application/json");
    xmlConfiguration.Formatters.XmlFormatter. AddRequestHeaderMapping ("ReturnType", "xml",
StringComparison. InvariantCultureIgnoreCase, false, "application/xml");
```

While the same extension methods can be used to register relevant mapping against your own custom (non-default) formatters, ideally you would perform such setup from inside the formatter instead (see Listing 4-24).

Listing 4-24. Registering a Mapping from Within the Formatter

```
public class MyFormatter : MediaTypeFormatter
{
    public MyFormatter(string format)
    {
        AddUriPathExtensionMapping("myExtension", new MediaTypeHeaderValue(format));
    }
}
```

If you are working with UriPathExtensionMapping, you will additionally need to configure proper routes, as the default routes do not take the extension into account. To register extension-aware routes, you need to use the {ext} placeholder shown in Listing 4-25.

Listing 4-25. Registering Routes with an {extension} Placeholder for UriPathExtensionMapping

```
routes.MapHttpRoute(
  name: "Api UriPathExtension",
  routeTemplate: "api/{controller}.{ext}/{id}",
  defaults: new { id = RouteParameter.Optional, ext = RouteParameter.Optional }
);

routes.MapHttpRoute(
  name: "Api UriPathExtension ID",
  routeTemplate: "api/{controller}/{id}.{ext}",
  defaults: new { id = RouteParameter.Optional, ext = RouteParameter.Optional }
);
```

Finally, you can also implement your own custom mapping by inheriting from the `MediaTypeMapping` base class, which you can see in Listing 4-26.

Listing 4-26. A Sample Custom MediaTypeMapping

```
public class MyMediaTypeMapping : MediaTypeMapping
{
    protected override double OnTryMatchMediaType(HttpResponseMessage response)
    {
        HttpRequestMessage request = response.RequestMessage;
        //check whatever you want in the request to determine the response type
    }
}
```

In this case, you have to define the match accuracy by a `double` value, where 1.0 is the 100% accurate match.

4-10. Serve Binary Data from ASP.NET Web API

Problem

You would like to serve binary content directly from the API, rather than have it delivered by your underlying web server. It might be dynamically generated images, text files, or any other form of processed data, which is quite common in web frameworks.

Solution

There are four principle ways of returning binary data from Web API, and they are represented by four types derived from the base `HttpContent` class, which can be used to send a response to the client:

- `StreamContent`
- `ByteArrayContent`
- `MultipartContent`
- `PushStreamContent`

To set these types of content on the body, you have to move away from the usual mode of returning a DTO from controller actions (and letting the framework serialize it for you), and take full control over the pipeline by producing an `HttpResponseMessage` directly or leveraging `IHttpActionResult`. It is important to emphasize that once you do that, the response message will bypass all the `MediaTypeFormatters` you might have registered in your application.

This is done on purpose, as you certainly wouldn't want a formatter trying to serialize your binary data to JSON, for example.

How It Works

ASP.NET Web API, contrary to what the name may suggest, is not an API engine only, but rather a fully-fledged web framework (or rather, an HTTP framework) capable of doing much more than just exposing an entry point to your system in the form of API endpoints.

This approach to dealing with static files is also necessary when you are self-hosting ASP.NET Web API, as it will not have any other way of serving files because no underlying web server is involved (TCP/HTTP capabilities are provided using WCF core or `HttpListener`).

The Code

The following sections will discuss the usage of StreamContent, ByteArrayContent, and MultipartContent, and will briefly touch on PushStreamContent.

StreamContent

A simple example of using StreamContent to fetch a file from the local drive is shown in Listing 4-27. All you need to do is read the file stream from somewhere, create a new HttpResponseMessage, and set the stream to be the content of the response. Additionally, though not mandatory, you should provide Content-Type header with the media type relevant for a given file type.

Listing 4-27. A Sample Controller Serving Binary Data as StreamContent

```
public HttpResponseMessage Get(string filename)
{
    var path = Path.Combine(ROOT, filename);
    if (!File.Exists(path))
    throw new HttpResponseException(Request.CreateErrorResponse(HttpStatusCode.NotFound));

    var result = new HttpResponseMessage(HttpStatusCode.OK);
    var stream = new FileStream(path, FileMode.Open);
    result.Content = new StreamContent(stream);
    result.Content.Headers.ContentType = new MediaTypeHeaderValue("application/octet-stream");
    return result;
}
```

■ **Tip**   You do not have to explicitly close the FileStream as the framework will dispose of it for you.

With StreamContent you are able to facilitate most of the scenarios requiring binary data over HTTP. You could use those types of actions to replace traditional HTTP Handler-based solutions. This also mirrors the FileResult functionality that many developers are familiar with from ASP.NET Web MVC.

As mentioned before, if you are using a self-hosted version of Web API, you will not have the luxury of a web server that you can rely on for serving static files, so all files you'd like to use would have go through this type of endpoint.

■ **Note**   When using StreamContent, ASP.NET Web API will not buffer the response.

ByteArrayContent

Another way of serving binary data is through the use of ByteArrayContent. Because the concepts of Stream and byte[] are closely related, this is pretty much identical to the previous example. The main difference is that ASP.NET Web API will not buffer the response, which is a Stream, whereas the byte array is already buffered anyway.

You can easily imagine situations when the data you may want to return is already available as an array of bytes (rather than some sort of a MemoryStream which would need to be read). In such situations, the byte[] can be directly set as the content of the HttpResponseMessage, without the need of conversion to a Stream. See Listing 4-28.

Listing 4-28. A Sample Controller Serving Binary Data as ByteArrayContent

```
public HttpResponseMessage Get(string filename)
{
    byte[] data = GetFromSomewhere(filename);
    if (data = null)
    throw new HttpResponseException(Request.CreateErrorResponse(HttpStatusCode.NotFound));

    var result = new HttpResponseMessage(HttpStatusCode.OK);
    result.Content = new ByteArrayContent(data);
    result.Content.Headers.ContentType = new MediaTypeHeaderValue("application/octet-stream");
    return result;
}
```

MultipartContent

Multipart content allows you to package together a number of files and send them together with clear boundaries between the chunks of binary data representing each file. This in turn allows the consumer of the message to easily extract the relevant files. See Listing 4-29 for an example.

Listing 4-29. A Sample Controller Serving Binary Data as MultipartContent

```
public HttpResponseMessage Get(string file1, string file2)
{
        var fileA = new StreamContent(new FileStream(Path.Combine(ROOT,file1), FileMode.Open));
        fileA.Headers.ContentType = new MediaTypeHeaderValue("image/jpeg");

        var fileB = new StreamContent(new FileStream(Path.Combine(ROOT,file2), FileMode.Open));
        fileA.Headers.ContentType = new MediaTypeHeaderValue("image/jpeg");

        var result = new HttpResponseMessage(HttpStatusCode.OK);
        result.Content = new MultipartContent();
        result.Content.Add(fileA);
        result.Content.Add(fileB);

        return result;
}
```

While the example is very trivial, it illustrates the technique well. Inside MultipartContent you can also mix traditional ObjectContent with binary data, which is often used to transfer files along with some metadata.

PushStreamContent

Finally, you can also push down chunks of unbuffered data to the client asynchronously in the form of PushStreamContent. This used to be a distinct feature of Web API, as it requires IAsyncHttpHandler, and many other popular frameworks (ServiceStack, NancyFX) weren't originally built on one (this has since changed). Due to its unique nature, PushStreamContent is discussed in detail separately in Recipe 8-4.

4-11. Accept File Uploads

Problem

You would like to accept file uploads through your ASP.NET Web API service.

Solution

ASP.NET Web API exposes several implementations of the `MultipartStreamProvider` class to facilitate file uploads. In order to write directly to a path on the server, you can use

- `MultipartFileStreamProvider`, if you are creating an upload only endpoint.
- `MultipartFormDataStreamProvider`, if you are going to be dealing with HTML form and you expect the client to send a content-disposition header.

In order to write directly to the `MemoryStream` (no I/O), you can use

- `MultipartMemoryStreamProvider`.
- `MultipartFormDataStreamProvider`, if you know your client will not send a content-disposition header.

`MultipartFileStreamProvider` and `MultipartMemoryStreamProvider` are direct subclasses of an abstract `MultipartStreamProvider`, while `MultipartFormDataStreamProvider` further extends `MultipartFileStreamProvider`.

How It Works

The core responsibility of any implementation of `MultipartStreamProvider` is to convert the contents of incoming HTTP request into a `Stream`.

`MultipartFileStreamProvider` and `MultipartFormDataStreamProvider`, since their intent is file I/O, will try to write the content of the request into a `FileStream`. In other words, they will physically create a file on the server, and then expose the stream representing this file for the developer to process further. Additionally, `MultipartFormDataStreamProvider` will look for the filename in a `Content-Disposition` header. If this header is not present, it will not write to the disk directly (will not use `FileStream`), but will instead expose the uploaded file as a `MemoryStream` only.

`MultipartMemoryStreamProvider` will always load the contents of the uploaded file into a `MemoryStream`.

The Code

Let's explore the code that will allow you to accept file uploads on the disk and into memory in ASP.NET Web API.

Upload To Disk

The code to perform a simple disk-targeted upload is rather straightforward.

```
var streamProvider = new MultipartFileStreamProvider("d:/uploads/");
await Request.Content.ReadAsMultipartAsync(streamProvider);
//the file has been saved to disk now
```

MultipartFileStreamProvider doesn't have a parameterless constructor, as it expects you to pass in a path to which the uploaded file should be saved. The name of the file is automatically generated for security reasons, using the following snippet from the Web API source code:

```
String.Format(CultureInfo.InvariantCulture, "BodyPart_{0}", Guid.NewGuid());
```

You can customize this behavior by subclassing the provider and overriding the GetLocalFileName method (more about this in Recipe 4-13).

To make this example more suitable for real life usage, you can wrap the code in a controller (see Listing 4-30) and perform some basic integrity validation by checking if the incoming request is MimeMultipartContent. Notice that you completely skip any Web API model binding and formatters, as you deal with the raw HttpRequestMessage directly.

Listing 4-30. A Basic Controller Accepting Uploads to the Server's Disk Directly

```
public class MyController : ApiController
{
    public async Task Post()
    {
        if (!Request.Content.IsMimeMultipartContent())
                throw new HttpResponseException(Request.CreateResponse(HttpStatusCode.NotAcceptable,
"This request is not properly formatted"));

            var streamProvider = new MultipartFormDataStreamProvider("d:/uploads/");
            return await Request.Content.ReadAsMultipartAsync(streamProvider);
    }
}
```

The final step is to replace the hard-coded absolute upload path with a dynamic relative one. If you are using web hosting, you could do that by looking at System.Web.HttpContext.Current:

```
var path = HttpContext.Current.Server.MapPath("~/uploads/");
```

In self-hosted scenarios, the easiest way to determine current location is to grab it off the current Assembly:

```
var path = Assembly.GetExecutingAssembly().Location;
```

Upload To Memory

The code to accept a file upload directly into memory (Listing 4-31) is very similar, except the fact that once the file is loaded into a MemoryStream, it's up to you as the developer to handle it further. For example, you may wish to save the Stream to a database or upload it to cloud storage.

Listing 4-31. A Basic Controller Accepting Uploads to MemoryStream

```
public class MyController : ApiController
{
    public async Task Post()
    {
        if (!Request.Content.IsMimeMultipartContent())
                throw new HttpResponseException(Request.CreateResponse(HttpStatusCode.NotAcceptable,
"This request is not properly formatted"));

        var provider = new MultipartMemoryStreamProvider();
        await Request.Content.ReadAsMultipartAsync(provider);

        foreach (HttpContent ctnt in provider.Contents)
        {
            //now read individual part into STREAM
            var stream = await ctnt.ReadAsStreamAsync();

            if (stream.Length != 0)
            {
                //handle the stream here
            }
        }
    }
}
```

Once the provider loads the uploaded files into memory, you can access them by looping through the Contents property; it will be as big as the number of uploaded files by the client.

Interestingly, since ASP.NET Web API relies on the underlying host to deal with requests and their input streams, if you are web hosting and are comfortable with traditional ASP.NET request handling, you can rely on that too in your Web API uploads. This is shown in Listing 4-32.

Listing 4-32. Grabbing the Uploaded Stream Directly from the ASP.NET Request

```
Stream stream = HttpContext.Current.Request.GetBufferlessInputStream();
    byte[] bytes = new byte[32*1024];
    while ((n = stream.Read(bytes, 0, bytes.Length)) > 0)
    {
        //process stream
}
```

However, this is highly discouraged, and should only be used as a last resort.

IIS AND ASP.NET UPLOAD LIMITS

The default maximum IIS7 and IIS Express upload file size is 30 000 000 bytes (28.6MB). If you try to upload a larger file, the server response will be a 404.13 error. You can modify it with the maxAllowedContentLength web.config setting.

```
<system.webServer>
  <security>
    <requestFiltering>
```

```
      <requestLimits maxAllowedContentLength="2147483648" />
    </requestFiltering>
  </security>
</system.webServer>
```

Moreover, ASP.NET has its own upload file size limit of 4MB. It can be increased by tweaking the maxRequestLength setting in web.config.

```
<system.web>
  <httpRuntime maxRequestLength="2097152" />
</system.web>
```

4-12 Enable Bufferless Uploads

Problem

You are uploading large files to your Web API, and would like to allow uploads to be performed in a streamed mode, rather than being buffered.

Solution

You can provide a customized implementation of the IHostBufferPolicySelector (see Listing 4-33) to explicitly state whether ASP.NET Web API should use buffering for input and output streams. You are also able to provide a specific condition that has to be matched for a given behavior to kick in, meaning that parts of your API could be bufferless, while others not.

Listing 4-33. Definition of IHostBufferPolicySelector

```
public interface IHostBufferPolicySelector
{
    bool UseBufferedInputStream(object hostContext);
    bool UseBufferedOutputStream(HttpResponseMessage response);
}
```

How It Works

ASP.NET Web API in buffered mode holds the entire message in memory, until the transfer between the client and the server has completed. Streamed (bufferless) mode, on the other hand, only buffers the request/response headers, while the body is exposed as a stream which can be read in small chunks.

While ASP.NET Web API does a great job of providing a consistent experience between different types of its hosts (web host, self-host, OWIN host), the buffering story differs a lot between them.

The web host, and its WebHostBufferPolicySelector (web host-specific IHostBufferPolicySelector), relies on the underlying ASP.NET mechanisms. As a consequence, it can obtain the input stream in a bufferless manner any time you want, and you can decide on that on a per-request basis. However, out of the box, it's always buffering requests.

The self-host, which uses WCF under the hood, while it can also support streaming of the requests, can only have this set globally, for all requests. This particular type of host does not use any IHostBufferPolicySelector at all, and the customizations have to happen against the HttpSelfHostConfiguration itself.

The OWIN host utilizes `OwinBufferPolicySelector`, which by default does not buffer requests. However, since this behavior essentially relies on the underlying OWIN-compatible server and its capabilities, you may have to tweak it based on the type of environment you are using.

The Code

The code required to enable bufferless input from the client is specific to the type of host you are using: web host, self-host, or OWIN host.

Web Host

You can override `WebHostBufferPolicySelector`, since both of its methods are `virtual`. The exposed `hostContext` is nothing more than `HttpContextBase` which should be familiar from traditional ASP.NET projects. An example of it is shown in Listing 4-34.

Listing 4-34. A Sample WebHostBufferPolicySelector That Does Not Buffer Input for Specific Controllers

```
public class FileUploadBufferPolicySelector : WebHostBufferPolicySelector
{
    private static string[] _unbufferedControllers = new[2] { "image", "video" };

    public override bool UseBufferedInputStream(object hostContext)
    {
        var context = hostContext as HttpContextBase;

        if (context != null)
        {
            var controller = context.Request.RequestContext.RouteData.Values["controller"].ToString().
            ToLower();
            if (_unbufferedControllers.Contains(controller))
                return false;
        }

        return true;
    }

    public override bool UseBufferedOutputStream(HttpResponseMessage response)
    {
        return base.UseBufferedOutputStream(response);
    }
}
```

In this particular example, you designate two controller names, `ImageController` and `VideoController`, to have requests to them handled in a bufferless way. You can use the `HttpContextBase`, to which you have access, to pick up the controller name from the `RouteData`, and match it against your settings. By returning false from the `UseBufferedInputStream` method, you are able to tell Web API to stream the request rather than buffer it. Obviously you are free to choose the rules deciding on buffering as you wish, for example using headers instead.

```
┌─────────────────────────────────────────────────────────────────────────┐
│                       RESPONSE STREAMING                                  │
└─────────────────────────────────────────────────────────────────────────┘
```

In order to facilitate response (output) streaming (rather than buffering) you can simply override the UseBufferedOutputStream of the IHostBufferPolicySelector.

ASP.NET Web API will not buffer the output for StreamContent (see Recipe 4-10) and PushStreamContent (see Recipe 8-4) unless its Content-Length is already known. Additionally, when hosting using OWIN, setting the header Transfer-Encoding to chunked will also disable output buffering.

Registration of the IHostBufferPolicySelector happens against the HttpConfiguration object.

```
httpConfiguration.Services.Replace(typeof(IHostBufferPolicySelector), new
FileUploadBufferPolicySelector());
```

Self Host

Since WCF-based self-host does not use IHostBufferPolicySelector at all, the only way to control streaming/buffering of requests and responses is to use the global TransferMode setting exposed by HttpSelfHostConfiguration. It can be assigned any of the values of the System.ServiceModel.TransferMode enumeration; see Table 4-2.

Table 4-2. Available TransferModes and Their Behavior

Mode	Behavior
Streamed	Both request and response are streamed.
Buffered	Both request and response are buffered.
StreamedRequest	Only requests are streamed.
StreamedResponse	Only responses are streamed.

Unfortunately, this setting is global and there is no way to reliably modify it on a per-request basis, such as to provide different behavior for different endpoints or client scenarios.

```
selfHostConfiguration.TransferMode = TransferMode.Streamed;
```

OWIN Host

Enabling bufferless input is not required with OWIN host, since OwinBufferPolicySelector is streaming requests by default. However, you can still override its methods to control buffering, but bear in mind this might affect the behavior of your OWIN pipeline.

The usage with Microsoft's Project Katana, shown in Listing 4-35, is similar to WebHostBufferPolicySelector, except the hostContext object, instead of being HttpContextBase, is an IOwinContext (Project Katana specific context). It's relatively easy to adapt the previous example to OWIN; however, since the RouteData is not available through IOwinContext or its Request property (IOwinRequest), you have to resort to different mechanisms when determining if the request should be buffered. The following example is simply checking for /image/ and /video/ in the path, which is sufficient for illustration purposes, but in real life scenarios you will probably want to introduce a more elaborate condition check.

Listing 4-35. A Sample WebHostBufferPolicySelector That Does Not Buffer Input if a Specific URL Part Is Found

```
public class FileUploadBufferPolicySelector : OwinBufferPolicySelector
{
    private static string[] _unbufferedControllers = new[2] { "image", "video" };

    public override bool UseBufferedInputStream(object hostContext)
    {
        var context = hostContext as IOwinContext;

        if (context != null)
        {
            if (_unbufferedControllers.Any(x => context.Request.Uri.AbsolutePath.Contains("/" + x +
"/"));
                return false;
        }

        return true;
    }

    public override bool UseBufferedOutputStream(HttpResponseMessage response)
    {
        return base.UseBufferedOutputStream(response);
    }
}
```

When the ASP.NET Web API OWIN adapter encounters a policy selector that tells it to not buffer the request, under the hood it tries to pick up the key `server.DisableRequestBuffering` from the OWIN environment dictionary. Unless something modified it explicitly, it should contain an `Action` object representing a continuation to the next middleware.

4-13 Validate File Uploads
Problem

You are accepting file uploads to your ASP.NET Web API and would like to validate file extensions before proceeding with processing the uploaded files.

Solution

As you can learn in Recipe 4-11, you may use `MultipartMemoryStreamProvider` (in memory) or `MultipartFormDataStreamProvider` (directly to disk) to facilitate file uploads in Web API.

In order to provide some basic validation to the client's input, you can subclass these providers and override some of the base methods which allow you to inspect the headers of the incoming HTTP request.

If you inherit from `MultipartFormDataStreamProvider`, you should override the base `GetLocalFileName` or `GetStream`; if you inherit `MultipartMemoryStreamProvider`, you have to override the base `GetStream` method.

How It Works

When the client uploads a file to the web server, the file name is present in the HTTP request headers, under Content-Disposition.

```
Content-Disposition: attachment; filename="someFile.txt"
```

MultipartFormDataStreamProvider uses GetLocalFileName to provide the uploaded file with some file name. By default, the name will be random (not whatever the client provides) for security reasons. This is a method specific for this provider only.

```
public virtual string GetLocalFileName(System.Net.Http.Headers.HttpContentHeaders headers)
```

Both MultipartMemoryStreamProvider and MultipartFormDataStreamProvider also give you access to the headers in the GetStream method, which you could also use for inspecting the headers for ContentDisposition.

```
public virtual Stream GetStream(HttpContent parent, HttpContentHeaders headers)
```

All in all, by tapping into this process and overriding the relevant method, you are able to deny the upload if the extension doesn't match the requirements of your application.

The Code

The preferred way of doing the validation is to use the GetStream method, since, as it is run prior to reading the uploaded files from the HTTP request, it is more efficient in terms of memory footprint. This is shown in Listing 4-36.

Listing 4-36. An Example of a ValidatedMemoryStreamProvider. If the Extension of the Uploaded File Doesn't Match Your Requirement, You Simply Nullify the Stream.

```
public class ValidatedMemoryStreamProvider : MultipartMemoryStreamProvider
{
    private static string[] extensions = new[] { "jpg", "gif", "png"};

    public override Stream GetStream(HttpContent parent, HttpContentHeaders headers)
    {

            var filename = headers.ContentDisposition.FileName.Replace("\"", string.Empty);
            if (filename.IndexOf('.') < 0)
                    return Stream.Null;

            var extension = filename.Split('.').Last();

            return extensions.Any(i => i.Equals(extension, StringComparison.
            InvariantCultureIgnoreCase)) ? base.GetStream(parent, headers) : Stream.Null;
    }
}
```

The other option, available only for MultipartFormDataStreamProvider is, as shown in Listing 4-37. That is, to use GetLocalFileName and, in case the validation fails, throw an exception which needs to be appropriately handled outside of the provider.

Listing 4-37. An Example of a CustomMultipartFormDataStreamProvider

```
public class CustomMultipartFormDataStreamProvider : MultipartFormDataStreamProvider
{
        private static string[] extensions = new[] { "jpg", "gif", "png"};

        public CustomMultipartFormDataStreamProvider(string path) : base(path)
            {}

        public override string GetLocalFileName(HttpContentHeaders headers)
        {
                var filename = headers.ContentDisposition.FileName.Replace("\"", string.Empty);
                if (filename.IndexOf('.') < 0)
                        throw new Exception("No extension");

                var extension = filename.Split('.').Last();
                if (!extensions.Any(i => i.Equals(extension, StringComparison.
                InvariantCultureIgnoreCase))
                        throw new Exception("Extension not allowed!");

                return base.GetLocalFileName(headers);
        }
}
```

In either case, you have to remember that you are simply validating the filenames and extensions here, and in general the validity of the HTTP request—not the integrity of the data, as this is beyond scope here.

CHAPTER 5

■ ■ ■

Configuration and Customization

This chapter deals with configuring some of the features of ASP.NET Web API, as well as improving its processing pipeline with a number of convenient customizations. In the recipes that you will find in this chapter, I will address and deal with several common roadblocks that you might encounter when building a custom Web API solution.

In this chapter you will learn how to do the following:

- Apply rate limiting in ASP.NET Web API (Recipe 5-1)

- Configure support for controllers from external assemblies (Recipe 5-2)

- Apply controller-specific `HttpConfiguration` (Recipe 5-3)

- Validate requests with action filters, override filters, and control the filter execution order (Recipes 5-4, 5-5, 5-8, and 5-9)

- Add caching to your ASP.NET Web API services (Recipes 5-6 and 5-7)

- Customize the level of error details that Web API exposes (Recipe 5-10)

- Return HTML from ASP.NET Web API (Recipe 5-11)

- Deal with per-request storage requirements (Recipe 5-12)

5-1. Throttle ASP.NET Web API Calls

Problem

You are building a public API and need to introduce rate limiting.

Solution

WebApiContrib, which can be installed from NuGet, provides excellent support for request throttling.

```
install-package WebApiContrib
```

To enable throttling for your ASP.NET Web API, you need to provide the following:

- A timespan which should be used to count calls to the API

- A hit quota per client

- Optionally, an error message

The idea behind the WebApiContrib throttling implementation is to intercept every request as early as possible and then check how many times a client has accessed the API in a given timespan. If the predefined rate is exceeded, the client is issued a failed response immediately. Due to such design requirements, WebApiContrib throttling support is implemented as a message handler, which you add to your ASP.NET Web API processing pipeline.

This design also allows you to control at which place the throttling actually happens; for example, you may want to insert a caching handler or an authentication handler in front of it, so that cached responses will not count against client's quota.

How It Works

The throttling handler requires you to pass in a Timespan that will be used to count the API hits, and a Func<string, long> that should take a user identifier string and return a quota for that given Timespan. Out of the box, the string identifier is simply an IP of the user, but you can subclass ThrottlingHandler and override it with some other identification mechanism, such as a username.

The default implementation of throttling uses InMemoryThrottleStore, which persists the quota and hits count data in-process directly in memory, using a ConcurrentDictionary. If you want to change this, you have to implement the IThrottleStore interface shown in Listing 5-1. With this interface, it's possible to back API throttling with a caching server such as Redis or Windows Azure Cache, which is also a way to support throttling in situations when your API is distributed across different servers.

Listing 5-1. Definition of IThrottleStore Interface

```
public interface IThrottleStore
{
    bool TryGetValue(string key, out ThrottleEntry entry);
    void IncrementRequests(string key);
    void Rollover(string key);
    void Clear();
}
```

■ **Tip** It's a good idea to replace the ConcurrentDictionary at least with System.Runtime.Caching.MemoryCache, as it can automatically expire older entries.

ThrottlingHandler additionally injects two headers into the Web API response, RateLimit-Limit and RateLimit-Remaining, informing the client about his current API usage in a given timespan.

In case a quota has been exceeded, the handler will respond with HttpStatusCode.Conflict (status code 409). If the user cannot be identified, the response from the handler will be HttpStatusCode.Forbidden (status code 403).

The Code

To enable throttling in your API, you need to register the ThrottlingHandler against your HttpConfiguration. In the example shown in Listing 5-2, the rate limit per user is set to ten calls per minute, and the count is done per IP (which is the default behavior).

Listing 5-2. Basic ThrottlingHandler Setup

```
var throttlingHandler = new ThrottlingHandler(
    new InMemoryThrottleStore(),
    ip => 10,
```

```
        TimeSpan.FromMinutes(1),
        "Only ten requests per minute allowed")
config.MessageHandlers.Add(throttlingHandler);
```

To provide rate limiting based on a user identity, you need to override the GetUserIdentifier method. In the example from Listing 5-3, you reach into the RequestContext to fetch the Principal object associated with the current request, as that should give you the currently logged in user's username. In another case, you simply fallback to the base class, which is the IP-based rate limiting.

Listing 5-3. Throttling in the Context of a User

```
public class UserAwareThrottlingHandler : ThrottlingHandler
{
    public UserAwareThrottlingHandler(IThrottleStore store, Func<string, long>
maxRequestsForUserIdentifier, TimeSpan period, string message)
        : base(store, maxRequestsForUserIdentifier, period, message)
    {

    }

    protected override string GetUserIdentifier(HttpRequestMessage request)
    {
        var user = request.GetRequestContext().Principal;
        if (user != null)
        {
            return user.Identity.Name;
        }
        return base.GetUserIdentifier(request);
    }
}
```

You should now modify the throttling handler registration from Listing 5-2 to the one shown in Listing 5-4. You change the Func<string, long> that is used to convert a user identifier to a quota, so that it looks up the limit configuration for a user in your user data store (here a hypothetical IUserStore is used). If a user is not found, then you deal with an IP and fall back again to the default of ten calls per minute.

Listing 5-4. Registering a Throttling Handler That Varies the Rate Limit by User

```
var throttlingHandler = new UserAwareThrottlingHandler(
        new InMemoryThrottleStore(),
        identifier =>
            {
                var userStore = config.DependencyResolver.GetService(typeof (IUserStore));
                var user = userStore.FindByUsername(identifier);
                if (user != null)
                {
                    return user.RateLimit;
                }

                return 10;
            },
        TimeSpan.FromMinutes(1));
    config.MessageHandlers.Add(throttlingHandler);
```

5-2. Use Controllers from an External Assembly

Problem

You would like your Web API to use controllers that are not part of your ASP.NET Web API project assembly.

Solution

It is quite common, in order to keep the Web API project lean and focused, to create controllers for the API in an external library. This also allows you to reuse them across different projects.

To introduce your own custom logic responsible for locating the assemblies, ASP.NET Web API allows you to plug in a custom implementation of IAssembliesResolver. As a matter of convenience, instead of implementing the interface directly, you can also override the default implementation, DefaultAssembliesResolver. This solution is shown in Listing 5-5.

Listing 5-5. Including an External Library in the ASP.NET Web API Controller Lookup

```
public class CustomAssembliesResolver : DefaultAssembliesResolver
{
    public override ICollection<Assembly> GetAssemblies()
    {
        var baseAssemblies = base.GetAssemblies().ToList();
        var assemblies = new List<Assembly>(baseAssemblies) {typeof (HelloController).Assembly};

        return assemblies.Distinct().ToList();
    }
}
```

The resolver is registered against the HttpConfiguration just like any other service.

```
config.Services.Replace(typeof(IAssembliesResolver), new CustomAssembliesResolver());
```

How It Works

By default, ASP.NET Web API tries to find controllers by scanning all of the assemblies from the current AppDomain (Listing 5-6).

Listing 5-6. Default Implementation of IAssembliesResolver

```
public class DefaultAssembliesResolver : IAssembliesResolver
{
    public virtual ICollection<Assembly> GetAssemblies()
    {
        return AppDomain.CurrentDomain.GetAssemblies().ToList();
    }
}
```

When you are hosting on top of IIS, all of the assemblies located in the server's bin folder will be loaded into the AppDomain automatically by ASP.NET, so when you use web host for your Web API, including controllers from external libraries can be done by simply dropping those into the bin folder.

For self-hosted Web API solutions, things are a bit more interesting. In case your API project references the external library, it will be loaded into the AppDomain only if any code explicitly references it or if you do so by hand (i.e. through Assembly.LoadFrom method). As a result, when writing a custom resolver like the one in Listing 5-5, it's generally a good idea to include a Distinct call at the end to make sure you avoid double loading some assemblies or simply use the resolver as a place to make an explicit code reference to the external assembly.

ASP.NET Web API uses the IAssembliesResolver registered against HttpConfiguration (your custom one or DefaultAssembliesResolver) in an internal HttpControllerTypeCache type, which is used to cache the list of discovered controller Types. Afterwards, that cache is used for controller look ups, and IAssembliesResolver is not consulted anymore. As a consequence, setting a custom IAssembliesResolver in your HttpConfiguration should be done only at application startup; replacing it at runtime will not have any effect.

The Code

An alternative version to the code from Listing 5-6 is shown in Listing 5-7. In this case, a call to typeof(HelloController) is enough to force the container Assembly to be loaded into the AppDomain, and the base DefaultAssembliesResolver will pick the controllers from there.

Listing 5-7. Including an External Library in the ASP.NET Web API Controller Lookup

```
public class CustomAssembliesResolver : DefaultAssembliesResolver
{
    public override ICollection<Assembly> GetAssemblies()
    {
        //ensures the external Assembly is in the AppDomain by referencing from code
        var externalControllers = typeof(HelloController).Assembly);

        return base.GetAssemblies();
    }
}
```

On the other hand, if your controllers reside in an unreferenced DLL, you can still include them in the Web API lookup process, but you will have to load them manually, as shown in Listing 5-8. In this example, the UnreferencedExternalLibrary.dll is located in the same directory as the currently executing Web API host process.

Listing 5-8. Including Unreferenced Libraries in the Lookup Process

```
public class CustomAssembliesResolver : DefaultAssembliesResolver
{
    public override ICollection<Assembly> GetAssemblies()
    {
        var baseAssemblies = base.GetAssemblies().ToList();
        var assemblies = new List<Assembly>(baseAssemblies);

        var unreferencedAssembly = Assembly.LoadFrom(Path.Combine(Path.GetDirectoryName(Assembly.
        GetExecutingAssembly().Location), "UnreferencedExternalLibrary.dll"));
        assemblies.Add(unreferencedAssembly);

        return assemblies;
    }
}
```

5-3. Use Controller-Scoped Configuration

Problem

You want specific ASP.NET Web API HttpConfiguration settings to be applied only to selected controllers.

Solution

The most common scenario is to configure ASP.NET Web API settings globally, for the entire application, in the global HttpConfiguration object. However, ASP.NET Web API also supports controller-scoped configuration. The framework provides a sealed class called HttpControllerSettings that defines which settings can be overridden or provided on a controller level, rather than globally.

The controller-scoped configuration is applied through a custom attribute implementing an IControllerConfiguration (Listing 5-9), which exposes an Initialize method that the Web API pipeline can invoke to configure your controller.

Listing 5-9. Definition of IControllerConfiguration Interface

```
public interface IControllerConfiguration
{
    void Initialize(HttpControllerSettings controllerSettings, HttpControllerDescriptor
controllerDescriptor);
}
```

How It Works

The settings that can be customized on a per-controller basis are

- MediaTypeFormatters
- ParameterBinding rules
- Services

These are the properties exposed by HttpControllerSettings, as shown in Listing 5-10; the rest of the configuration is provided by the global HttpConfiguration, which is passed through the constructor.

Listing 5-10. Definition of HttpControllerSettings

```
public sealed class HttpControllerSettings
{
    public HttpControllerSettings(HttpConfiguration configuration);

    public MediaTypeFormatterCollection Formatters { get; }
    public ParameterBindingRulesCollection ParameterBindingRules { get; }
    public ServicesContainer Services { get; }
}
```

What happens under the hood is that upon instantiation of a controller, ASP.NET Web API creates a controller-scoped copy of the global HttpConfiguration. If a controller has any of the above mentioned settings specified on the controller level, they take precedence and are used; otherwise, the global settings remain unchanged.

The controller-level configuration has to be applied to a controller through a configuration attribute. As a result, you need to create a new attribute that implements IControllerConfiguration.

The main reason for doing this through an attribute is that it allows Web API to statically know about the configuration to be used prior to creating a new instance of the controller for a given request. This in turn makes it possible for ASP.NET Web API to cache and reuse the configuration and not re-create it for every single request (which would be the case if, for example, the controller configuration was done in a constructor instead of an attribute). This makes sense because controller configuration really only needs to be read once for a given controller type per application lifetime. As a result you get, obviously, much better overall performance of your API.

As far as the Web API pipeline is concerned, reading the configuration from the attributes happens inside a private method called InvokeAttributesOnControllerType in the initialization of an HttpControllerDescriptor for a given controller Type. This is shown in Listing 5-11. Note that multiple configurations are supported also, as well as inheritance of the configuration from the base controller.

Listing 5-11. Excerpt from Web API Source Code Responsible for Application of Controller-scoped Configuration

```
private static void InvokeAttributesOnControllerType(HttpControllerDescriptor controllerDescriptor,
Type type)
{
    Contract.Assert(controllerDescriptor != null);

    if (type == null)
    {
        return;
    }
    // Initialize base class before derived classes (same order as //ctors).
    InvokeAttributesOnControllerType(controllerDescriptor, //type.BaseType);

    // Check for attribute
    object[] attrs = type.GetCustomAttributes(inherit: false);
    foreach (object attr in attrs)
    {
        var controllerConfig = attr as IControllerConfiguration;
        if (controllerConfig != null)
        {
            var originalConfig = controllerDescriptor.Configuration;
            var controllerSettings = new HttpControllerSettings(originalConfig);
            controllerConfig.Initialize(controllerSettings, controllerDescriptor);
            controllerDescriptor.Configuration = HttpConfiguration.ApplyControllerSettings
            (controllerSettings, originalConfig);
        }
    }
}
```

The Code

Suppose you would like to have the ability to configure a controller in a way that it would only serve XML content and, at the same time, log all of its operations using a specific ITraceWriter. The attribute implementing IControllerConfiguration and providing this functionality is shown in Listing 5-12. You can now selectively apply it to the relevant controllers without affecting the configuration of any others.

Listing 5-12. An Example of a Controller-scoped Configuration

```
public class XmlOnlyAndTraceAttribute : Attribute, IControllerConfiguration
{
        public void Initialize(HttpControllerSettings controllerSettings,
                   HttpControllerDescriptor controllerDescriptor)
        {
               controllerSettings.Formatters.Clear();
               controllerSettings.Formatters.Add(new XmlMediaTypeFormatter());

               var traceWriter = new SystemDiagnosticsTraceWriter()
               {
                   MinimumLevel = TraceLevel.Info,
                   IsVerbose = false
               };

               controllerSettings.Services.Replace(typeof(ITraceWriter), traceWriter);
        }
}

[XmlOnlyAndTrace]
public class TestController : ApiController
{
        //class internals omitted for brevity
}
```

▓ **Note**   The SystemDiagnosticsTraceWriter used in the example comes from Microsoft.AspNet.WebApi.Tracing NuGet package. See Recipe 7-4 for more information on logging and tracing in ASP.NET Web API.

If you now fire up your Web API, the TestController will be logging its pipeline activities to the trace and only returning XML response. All other controllers will still be using the global settings provided via the regular HttpConfiguration, so content negotiation will be in play and no tracing will be happening.

As mentioned, the configuration attributes can be combined together. You could split the example from Listing 5-12 into two separate configuration attributes, a trace-specific one and XML specific one. This is shown in Listing 5-13.

Listing 5-13. Trace Configuration and XML Configuration as Two Separate Attributes

```
public class TraceAttribute : Attribute, IControllerConfiguration
{
    public void Initialize(HttpControllerSettings controllerSettings,
                        HttpControllerDescriptor controllerDescriptor)
    {
        var traceWriter = new SystemDiagnosticsTraceWriter()
            {
                MinimumLevel = TraceLevel.Info,
                IsVerbose = false
            };

        controllerSettings.Services.Replace(typeof(ITraceWriter), traceWriter);
    }
}
```

```
public class XmlOnlyAttribute : Attribute, IControllerConfiguration
{
    public void Initialize(HttpControllerSettings controllerSettings,
                           HttpControllerDescriptor controllerDescriptor)
    {
        controllerSettings.Formatters.Clear();
        controllerSettings.Formatters.Add(new XmlMediaTypeFormatter());
    }
}

    [XmlOnly, Trace]
    public class TestController : ApiController
    {
            //class internals omitted for brevity
    }
```

In this case, both the trace settings and the formatting settings are used by this specific controller. This provides a nice, clean mechanism of isolating individual pieces of configuration logic in relevant classes and combining them together wherever needed.

5-4. Validate Input with Action Filters

Problem

You would like to move the validation noise such as null checks or ModelState inspection out of your controllers into a centralized place.

Solution

ASP.NET Web API supports standard DataAnnotations-based validation with a ModelState, like ASP.NET MVC. You can implement common, repetitive validation tasks using ActionFilterAttributes. By using the aspect-oriented approach of filters for validation, you can write much cleaner and simpler code in your controllers, which can make your life much easier—both in the development period and in the long-term maintainability of your application.

In this recipe, you will create two filters, ModelNullCheckTypeAttribute and ValidateModelStateAttribute. They can then be applied to your actions to provide validation of ModelState and null inspection without the need to repeat that code inline in the action.

```
[ValidateModelState]
public void Post(Item item)

[CheckModelForNull]
public void Post([FromBody]string text)
```

You can even register the filters globally to avoid having to declare them each time; you do this against your HttpConfiguration, and as a result both of these filters will run on every request:

```
config.Filters.Add(new ModelNullCheckTypeAttribute());
config.Filters.Add(new ValidateModelStateAttribute());
```

How It Works

Filters are certainly familiar to developers with ASP.NET MVC experience. With filters, you can intercept the request just prior to the action execution and immediately after the execution completes. All these hooks make filters perfect for implementing generic, repetitive tasks such as (but not limited to)

- Authorization/authentication (see Recipe 10-1)

- Exception handling (see Recipe 7-1)

- Logging

- Validation

- Unit of work management

There are four filter types in ASP.NET Web API: action filters, exception filters, authorization filters, and authentication filters. This recipe focuses only on action filters.

All filters types can be applied at three scope levels:

- Action

- Controller

- Global

When the API pipeline executes a specific action, all applicable filters from all scopes are collected into groups, and the groups are executed in turns: first, all global filters, then all controller-level filters, and finally action-level filters. After the action gets executed, the filters get a chance to process the outgoing response in a reverse order.

The bare minimum you should do to write an action filter is to create a class implementing IActionFilter (shown in Listing 5-14). It exposes a single method called ExecuteActionFilterAsync, which you can use to hook in the pre- and post-processing logic for the action. However, the async nature of the interface is not very convenient to implement, so ASP.NET Web API provides a base ActionFilterAttribute class, which you can inherit from. It exposes both synchronous and asynchronous extension points for plugging in logic to be invoked before and after action execution. The outline of that class is shown in Listing 5-14 as well.

Listing 5-14. Definitions of IActionFilter Interface and the Abstract ActionFilterAttribute

```
public interface IActionFilter : IFilter
{
    Task<HttpResponseMessage> ExecuteActionFilterAsync(HttpActionContext actionContext,
    CancellationToken cancellationToken, Func<Task<HttpResponseMessage>>continuation);
}

public abstract class ActionFilterAttribute : FilterAttribute, IActionFilter
{
    public virtual void OnActionExecuting(HttpActionContext actionContext);
    public virtual void OnActionExecuted(HttpActionExecutedContext actionExecutedContext);
    public virtual Task OnActionExecutingAsync(HttpActionContext actionContext, CancellationToken
    cancellationToken);
    public virtual Task OnActionExecutedAsync(HttpActionExecutedContext actionExecutedContext,
    CancellationToken cancellationToken);
}
```

■ **Caution** Unfortunately, MVC filters are members of the `System.Web.Mvc.Filters` namespace, and Web API filters are members of the `System.Web.Http.Filters`, and these two types, even though very similar at first glance, cannot be used interchangeably when running Web API on top of ASP.NET runtime.

The Code

Let's look at implementing action filters that validate model state and ensure that the model submitted by the client is not `null`.

Validate Model State

One of the most common scenarios for validation is to inspect `ModelState`. It can become extremely tedious and troublesome to have to repeat the same check in every single operation dealing with some data input; just have a look at the example in Listing 5-15. The same `ModelState` check would have to be done in every other action that takes any complex input from the client.

Listing 5-15. An Example of Validating ModelState Inline in an Action

```
public class Item
{
    [Required]
    public string Name { get; set; }

    [MaxLength(3)]
    public string Code { get; set; }
}

public void Post(Item item)
{
    if (item != null)
    {
        if (!ModelState.IsValid)
        {
            throw new HttpResponseException(HttpStatusCode.BadRequest);
        }

        //do stuff
    }
}
```

You can easily fix the redundancy in your controllers with aspect-oriented programming, checking the state of the model, prior to the action, inside the `ActionFilter` (see Listing 5-16) and potentially rejecting the request from there if it doesn't meet your requirements, without allowing it to ever reach the action.

Listing 5-16. An Action Filter That Validates ModelState in a Generic Way

```
[AttributeUsage(AttributeTargets.Method, Inherited = true)]
public class ValidateModelStateAttribute : ActionFilterAttribute
{
    public override void OnActionExecuting(HttpActionContext actionContext)
    {
        if (!actionContext.ModelState.IsValid)
        {
            actionContext.Response = actionContext.Request.CreateErrorResponse(HttpStatusCode.
            BadRequest, actionContext.ModelState);
        }
    }
}
```

In the filter, using the HttpActionContext, you can get access to the current HttpRequestMessage and obtain the associated ModelState dictionary. If the state of that object is invalid, you return an error response with the status code 400 (bad request) back to the client, with the ModelState attached, as it will contain the errors from your DataAnnotations or any other validation logic built around IValidateableObject. This response can then be inspected by the client and appropriate corrective actions taken on its side.

You can now decorate the actions with the newly created filter. Suppose a client now tries to POST an invalid object. The API response in this case will be a 400 error code, along with an informative error message. This is shown in Listing 5-17.

Listing 5-17. Example Response Generated by the Action Filter After the Input from the Client was Invalid

```
HTTP/1.1 400 Bad Request
Content-Length: 188
Content-Type: application/json; charset=utf-8
Server: Microsoft-HTTPAPI/2.0
Date: Mon, 07 April 2014 22:19:50 GMT

{
        "Message":"The request is invalid.",
        "ModelState":{
                "item.Name":["The Name field is required."],
                "item.Code":["The field Code must be a string or array type with a maximum length of '3'."]
        }
}
```

Guarding Against Null

Another common usage scenario for action filters is eliminating null checks. This might mean that either the client sent an empty body or that the body of the request contained an unexpected payload that could not be correctly deserialized into a server-side model, and the MediaTypeFormatter handling the request passed null to the action. You can solve the problem by writing another filter, such as the one shown in Listing 5-18.

Listing 5-18. An Action Filter Catching Null Action Argument

```
[AttributeUsage(AttributeTargets.Method, Inherited = true)]
public class CheckModelForNullAttribute : ActionFilterAttribute
{
    public override void OnActionExecuting(HttpActionContext actionContext)
    {
     if (actionContext.ActionArguments.ContainsValue(null))
     {
         actionContext.Response = actionContext.Request.CreateErrorResponse(HttpStatusCode.BadRequest,
             string.Format("The argument cannot be null: {0}", string.Join(",",
             actionContext.ActionArguments.Where(i => i.Value == null).Select(i => i.Key))));
     }
    }
}
```

In this filter, you check the action arguments to find out whether any of them has been passed as null; if that's true, you reject the request with a 400 response too. You use LINQ to find out all null parameters, and then return this list to the client.

Notice that this attribute is inheritable (just like the previous one), so that they can be applied to any possible base controller, should you have one.

Now, to use it you simply decorate an action with the attribute and try sending a null value; such request will be rejected (Listing 5-19). As a result, you no longer have to perform a null check inside an action, as the model is guaranteed to be not null.

Listing 5-19. Example Response Generated by the Action Filter After the Input from the Client was Null

```
HTTP/1.1 400 Bad Request
Content-Length: 47
Content-Type: application/json; charset=utf-8
Server: Microsoft-HTTPAPI/2.0
Date: Mon, 06 May 2013 22:23:22 GMT

{"Message":"The argument cannot be null: text"}
```

It is important to emphasize that even if you use DataAnnotations and explicitly require certain fields on your model, like we did in Listing 5-15, ModelState will be considered valid if the entire model is null – as the framework's DataAnnotation validation engine will only recognize an error if some specific properties are missing or empty. This is exactly why you need to combine the two filters shown in this recipe to get full protection of the integrity of the requests coming to your API.

A final point in this recipe is that Web API **does not guarantee** the order in which the filters will be run! So you have to keep that in mind if you try to put some sequential functionality in there. You can also have a look at Recipes 5-8 and 5-9 to work around this issue.

5-5. Override Filters

Problem

You would like to override filters from a higher scope level at a lower scope level.

Solution

Since ASP.NET Web API 2, the framework ships with a set of override attributes, allowing you to ignore higher scoped filters wherever needed.

You can override all four types of filters:

- action filters (IActionFilters), with OverrideActionFiltersAttribute

- authentication filters (IAuthenticationFilters), with OverrideAuthenticationAttribute

- authorization filters (IAuthorizationFilters), with OverrideAuthorizationAttribute

- exception filters (IExceptionFilters), with OverrideExceptionAttribute

How It Works

When the base ApiController calls its ExecuteAsync method to execute an action on the controller for a given HTTP request, it will internally ask HttpActionDescriptor to provide a filter pipeline relevant for this request.

HttpActionDescriptor then returns an instance of an internal type FilterGrouping, which is responsible for selecting the filters available for that action. If any override is found, it determines which filters lie at a higher scope level and thus should be ignored. The FilterGrouping then exposes an array of four filter groups, one for each filter category of action, authorization, authentication, and exception filters.

Filters are then layered on top of one another using custom IHttpActionResult implementations. If Web API finds any action filters, it wraps the selected action (HttpActionDescriptor) with ActionFilterResult. If authorization filters are found, the previous IHttpActionResult is wrapped with AuthorizationFilterResult. Then, if authentication filters are present, the pipeline is further wrapped with AuthenticationFilterResult, and finally, if some exception filters are present, with ExceptionFilterResult.

This pipeline is executed sequentially, with one IHttpActionResult calling the inner nested IHttpActionResult, or breaking the processing pipeline if needed.

Unfortunately, filter overriding, while often convenient, is also quite limited. You are not able to override a specific filter by its Type name; that is, if you override action filters, the entire action filter pipeline from higher scope levels is going to be excluded from participating in the request processing.

The Code

Listing 5-20 shows a sample AuthorizeAttribute, which denies all unauthenticated users from accessing a resource it protects.

Listing 5-20. Definition of DenyAnonymousAttribute, Which Prevents Anonymous Users from Accessing Web API Actions

```
public class DenyAnonymousAttribute : AuthorizeAttribute
{
    public override void OnAuthorization(HttpActionContext actionContext)
    {
        if (actionContext.RequestContext.Principal == null)
        {
            actionContext.Response = new HttpResponseMessage(HttpStatusCode.Unauthorized);
        }
    }
}
```

▓ **Tip**   Chapter 10 is dedicated entirely to Web API security, and authorization filters are discussed in detail there.

If you register it globally, every endpoint of your API will be accessible only for authenticated clients.

But what if you want to open up a specific endpoint publicly? This is a perfect example of where filter overriding can come into play. Listing 5-21 shows a controller with an action that overrides controller/global authorization filters. In that listing, the GetAll action is still available only for authenticated users, while GetById can now be accessed by anyone.

Listing 5-21. A Sample Controller Utilizing OverrideAuthorizationAttribute

```
public class ItemController : ApiController
{
    [Route("item")]
    public HttpResponseMessage GetAll()
    {
        return Request.CreateResponse(HttpStatusCode.OK);
    }

    [OverrideAuthorization]
    [Route("item/{id:int}")]
    public HttpResponseMessage GetById(int id)
    {
        return Request.CreateResponse(HttpStatusCode.OK, id);
    }
}
```

5-6. Add Caching to ASP.NET Web API
Problem

You would like to improve the performance of your ASP.NET Web API service by adding caching of the responses.

Solution

ASP.NET Web API does not provide any out-of-the-box caching solution, such as OutputCache, which you might be familiar with from ASP.NET MVC. However, it is fairly easy to implement basic caching with ActionFilterAttributes, since they allow you to define pre- and post-action execution behavior. In the post-execution hook, you can cache the response of the action, while in the pre-execution, you can check whether the response has already been cached, and if so, respond with it immediately, rather than let the action execute.

In this recipe, you'll build a CacheAttribute that will allow you to define the length of caching on the server side, as well as on the client side (that will take effect as Cache-Control header).

```
[Cache(Client = 10, Server = 10)]
[Route("test")]
public HttpResponseMessage Get()
{
    //omitted for brevity
}
```

How It Works

There are a few things to remember when implementing caching for a Web API. First of all, RFC2616 defines that only GET and HEAD may be cacheable, so you have to make sure that the caching filters only kick in for those types of requests.

Secondly, you have to ensure that you do not interfere with content negotiation; since entities returned by your Web API can have different formats, you will need to cache each representation separately. Similarly, when retrieving an entity from the cache store, a relevant representation for a given request has to be used.

Finally, even though it's tempting to attempt to cache the response body as a string, it is safest to cache the byte array instead, since some actions may attempt to return binary data. It is also the best performing approach, as you can use that byte array directly as the raw response to be sent to the client without any unnecessary conversion.

A sample wrapper object around the body of the response (byte[]) and a content type (represented in ASP.NET Web API by MediaTypeHeaderValue instance), suitable for a Web API cache implementation, is shown in Listing 5-22.

Listing 5-22. A Wrapper Class for Response Byte array Content and Its Content Type

```
public class WebApiCacheItem
{
    public WebApiCacheItem(MediaTypeHeaderValue contentType, byte[] content)
    {
        Content = content;
        ContentType = contentType.MediaType;
    }

    public string ContentType { get; private set; }
    public byte[] Content { get; private set; }

    public bool IsValid()
    {
        return Content != null && ContentType != null;
    }
}
```

The Code

The entire code for CacheAttribute is shown in Listing 5-23. To keep things simple, MemoryCache is used as an in-process store for cached data. The attribute will expose two public properties: the duration (in seconds) of caching on the server side, and on the client side. Using public properties rather than fields is a common approach in attribute development in C#. The attribute decoration is then more verbose, allowing developers to provide values through the names of the public properties rather than through a constructor, which can often lead to ambiguity and worse readability.

Listing 5-23. A Caching Action Filter

```
public class CacheAttribute : ActionFilterAttribute
{
    private string _cachekey;
    private static readonly ObjectCache Cache = MemoryCache.Default;

    public int Server { get; set; }

    public int Client { get; set; }

    private bool IsCacheable(int property, HttpActionContext ac)
    {
        if (property <= 0)
        {
            return false;
        }

        if (ac.Request.Method == HttpMethod.Get || ac.Request.Method == HttpMethod.Head)
            return true;

        return false;
    }

    private CacheControlHeaderValue GetClientCache()
    {
        var cachecontrol = new CacheControlHeaderValue
        {
            MaxAge = TimeSpan.FromSeconds(Client),
            MustRevalidate = true
        };

        return cachecontrol;
    }

    public override void OnActionExecuting(HttpActionContext actionContext)
    {
        if (IsCacheable(Server, actionContext))
        {
            var accept = actionContext.Request.Headers.Accept.FirstOrDefault() ??
            new MediaTypeHeaderValue("application/json");
            _cachekey = string.Format("{0}|{1}", actionContext.Request.RequestUri.PathAndQuery, accept);
```

```
        var cachedResponseContent = Cache.Get(_cachekey) as WebApiCacheItem;
        if (cachedResponseContent == null || !cachedResponseContent.IsValid()) return;

        actionContext.Response = actionContext.Request.CreateResponse();
        actionContext.Response.Content = new ByteArrayContent(cachedResponseContent.Content);
        actionContext.Response.Content.Headers.ContentType = new MediaTypeHeaderValue
        (cachedResponseContent.ContentType);

        if (IsCacheable(Client, actionContext))
        {
            actionContext.Response.Headers.CacheControl = GetClientCache();
        }
    }
}

public async override Task OnActionExecutedAsync(HttpActionExecutedContext
actionExecutedContext, CancellationToken cancellationToken)
{
    if (!Cache.Contains(_cachekey))
    {
        var body = await actionExecutedContext.Response.Content.ReadAsByteArrayAsync();
        var cacheItem = new WebApiCacheItem(actionExecutedContext.Response.Content.Headers.
        ContentType, body);
        Cache.Add(_cachekey, cacheItem, DateTime.Now.AddSeconds(Server));
    }

    if (IsCacheable(Client, actionExecutedContext.ActionContext))
    {
        actionExecutedContext.ActionContext.Response.Headers.CacheControl = GetClientCache();
    }
}
```

It's important to emphasize that designing a complete caching framework is beyond the scope of this recipe, and several simplifications had to be made in this implementation. For a mature open source caching implementation, see Recipe 5-7.

Let's walk through the code quickly, starting with OnActionExecuting. If the request is cacheable, you will construct a cache key from the full URL used by the client (actionContext.Request.RequestUri.PathAndQuery) and the Accept header, representing the media type the client is interested in. In case there is no Accept header, application/json is used by default. This is a way to guarantee that you won't respond to a specific media type request with a wrong format.

■ **Tip**   Ideally, instead of trusting the Accept header from the client, you'd perform a manual content negotiation (discussed in Recipe 4-7) here to determine the real expected media type. The solution from Recipe 5-7 will use just that.

You then try to fetch the entry from the cache and, if something is found there, you use it to respond to the client with the appropriate Content-Type being set. Since the cached item stores content as byte[], you can conveniently use ByteArrayContent as the HttpContent on the HttpResponseMessage. Finally, the Cache-Control header is correctly set using CacheControlHeaderValue composed from the values defined when the CacheAttribute was used to decorate an action. Notice that when you respond with the cached response, the request will never hit the action.

On the opposite side of the spectrum, in the OnActionExecutedAsync method, so after the action completes, you check if the cache contains an entry already, and if it doesn't, you cache an instance of WebApiCacheItem using ReadAsByteArrayAsync method as a way to read the body of the response (HttpContent) to a byte array. Similarly as before, you also apply client-side caching headers.

■ **Note** Support for asynchronous overrides was only introduced on ActionFilterAttribute in Web API 2.1.

5-7. Use an Existing Caching Library
Problem
You want to add caching to your ASP.NET Web API but do not want to build the whole infrastructure by hand.

Solution
You can use the popular Strathweb.CacheOutput library, which can be installed from NuGet:

```
install-package Strathweb.CacheOutput.WebApi2
```

The library provides very similar functionality and behavior to OutputCacheAttribute from System.Web. You can use it to decorate your actions with a predefined caching strategy for both server and client.

How It Works
Internally, the library uses a similar approach to that discussed in Recipe 5-6, as it implements caching with action filters and stores the content of your responses as byte arrays that can be used later to quickly respond to the client. Moreover, since it is filter-based, there is no need to enable, register, or activate anything else; just decorating the actions with caching attribute is enough to get started.

In addition to caching your responses, CacheOutput library also supports flexible cache invalidation, which can be done in three ways:

- Using AutoInvalidateCacheOutputAttribute at the controller level
- Using InvalidateCacheOutputAttribute with an action name as argument, at the action level
- Manually inside the action body

By default, the library uses MemoryCache from System.Runtime.Caching to store your data in process. You can create custom providers by implementing the IApiOutputCache interface, shown in Listing 5-24.

Listing 5-24. Defintion of the IApiOutputCache Interface

```
public interface IApiOutputCache
{
    T Get<T>(string key) where T : class;
    object Get(string key);
    void Remove(string key);
    void RemoveStartsWith(string key);
    bool Contains(string key);
    void Add(string key, object o, DateTimeOffset expiration, string dependsOnKey = null);
}
```

You can register your new provider for CacheOutput through the ASP.NET Web API HttpConfiguration object, and replace the default in-memory implementation (this is shown in Listing 5-25). The provider can also be registered against an Inversion of Control resolver and as long as you use a Web API IoC adapter, it will be picked up from there. For more details on IoC and Web API, see Chapter 10.

Listing 5-25. Registration of a Custom IApiOutputCache

```
//instance
configuration.CacheOutputConfiguration().RegisterCacheOutputProvider(() => new MyCache());

//singleton
var cache = new MyCache();
configuration.CacheOutputConfiguration().RegisterCacheOutputProvider(() => cache);
```

There are already community-developed providers for Microsoft Azure Cache and MongoDB. An additional interesting customization is the ability to introduce your own cache key strategy by implementing an ICacheKeyGenerator.

CacheOutput does not support entire client-side RFC2616 HTTP Caching implementation, but it will issue Cache-Control headers (max-age) and does support ETags. If ClientTimeSpan on your action is a positive number, the client will be issued an ETag, which he can then use in an If-None-Match header of subsequent requests. The example is shown in Listing 5-26.

Listing 5-26. Sample Request to an Action Cached with CacheOutput, with a Response Containing an Etag, Followed by Another Request Involving the If-None-Match

```
//initial request
GET /api/item
Accept: application/json

Status Code: 200
Cache-Control: max-age=100
Content-Length: 5
Content-Type: application/json; charset=utf-8
Date: Wed, 15 Apr 2014 03:37:11 GMT
ETag: "515C29C2-04A4-4DD6-B38D-3513E52ABE8D"
Server: Microsoft-HTTPAPI/2.0
Body: "Hello"
```

```
//next request
GET /api/item
Accept: application/json
If-None-Match: "515C29C2-04A4-4DD6-B38D-3513E52ABE8D"

Status Code: 304
Cache-Control: max-age=100
Content-Length: 0
Date: Wed, 15 Apr 2014 03:37:19 GMT
Server: Microsoft-HTTPAPI/2.0
```

■ **Note** To learn more about all features of CacheOutput, head over to the project's readme at
https://github.com/filipw/AspNetWebApi-OutputCache.

The Code

Two sample actions using Strathweb.CacheOutput are shown in Listing 5-27. Both methods are cached for 1 minute on both the client and the server side. You can also specify, by passing in AnonymousOnly flag like the Get method does, that cache should only kick in for anonymous users. CacheOutput will then check the presence of the Principal object on the incoming HTTP requests.

Listing 5-27. Sample Usage of CacheOutput

```
[CacheOutput(ClientTimeSpan = 60, ServerTimeSpan = 60)]
[Route("test/{id:int}")]
public TestItem GetById(int id)
{
    Console.WriteLine("hitting get by id");
    var item = Items.FirstOrDefault(x => x.Id == id);
    if (item == null) throw new HttpResponseException(HttpStatusCode.NotFound);

    return item;
}

[CacheOutput(ClientTimeSpan = 60, ServerTimeSpan = 60, AnonymousOnly = true)]
[Route("test")]
public List<TestItem> Get()
{
    Console.WriteLine("hitting get");
    return Items;
}
```

Listing 5-28 shows two controllers taking advantage of the auto-invalidation capabilities and a third controller performing manual invalidation through an instance of cache obtained from HttpConfiguration.

Listing 5-28. Examples of Invalidating Cache with CacheOutput

```
[AutoInvalidateCacheOutput]
public class ItemController : ApiController
{
    [CacheOutput(ServerTimeSpan = 60)]
    public IEnumerable<Item> Get()
    {
        //omitted for brevity
    }

    public void Post(Item value)
    {
        //omitted for brevity
    }
}

public class ItemController : ApiController
{
    [CacheOutput(ClientTimeSpan = 50, ServerTimeSpan = 50)]
    public IEnumerable<Item> Get()
    {
        //omitted for brevity
    }

    [CacheOutput(ClientTimeSpan = 50, ServerTimeSpan = 50)]
    public IEnumerable<Thing> GetThings(int id)
    {
        //omitted for brevity
    }

    [InvalidateCacheOutput("Get")]
    public void Post(Team value)
    {
        //omitted for brevity
        //this invalidates Get action cache
    }
}

    public void Put(int id, Item value)
    {
        //do stuff, update resource etc.

        //now get cache instance
        var cache = Configuration.CacheOutputConfiguration().GetCacheOutputProvider(Request);

        //and invalidate cache for method "Get" of "ItemController"
    cache.RemoveStartsWith(Configuration.CacheOutputConfiguration().MakeBaseCachekey
((ItemController t) => t.Get()));
    }
```

In the first case, AutoInvalidateCacheOutputAttribute forces all GET responses to be invalidated as soon as any other HTTP method is invoked on that controller. In the second controller, InvalidateCacheOutputAttribute is applied on an action level, and can give you specific control over which particular cache should be invalidated – in this case it's invalidating the Get action cache. Finally, you can also invalidate manually inline, by calling CacheOutputConfiguration().GetCacheOutputProvider() on the current HttpConfiguration object from within the action context, as that will give you access to the cache instance.

5-8. Order Filter Execution with Custom Filters

Problem

You need to control the execution order of Web API filters.

Solution

In ASP.NET MVC, you can predefine the execution order of the filters applied globally to a controller or an action by using an Order property, which all filters have. Unfortunately, this functionality is not built into ASP.NET Web API, and the framework does not guarantee that filters will be executed in the order they were statically defined in the code. You can still provide this functionality yourself, by introducing a custom base attribute from which all filters will inherit and a custom IFilterProvider which will be used to order the filter pipeline for each request.

However, this mechanism will only work with the filters you own, since you'd have to inherit all of them from the common base class. Should you want to use third-party filters (i.e. from the WebApiContrib project), you are better suited looking at Recipe 5-9.

How It Works

When an ASP.NET Web API action is executed, an HttpActionDescriptor instance representing that action queries the registered IFilterProviders to obtain a collection of filters that should be applied to the current execution process. IFilterProvider is a very simple, single-method interface (see Listing 5-29) and a collection of such providers is registered against HttpConfiguration. Out of the box, ASE.NET Web API uses a separate provider for retrieving controller/action filters (ActionDescriptorFilterProvider) and a separate one to retrieve global filters (ConfigurationFilterProvider).

Listing 5-29. Definition of IFilterProvider Interface

```
public interface IFilterProvider
{
    IEnumerable<FilterInfo> GetFilters(HttpConfiguration configuration, HttpActionDescriptor
actionDescriptor);
}
```

All filters in the ASP.NET Web API implement IFilter interface and in all internal operations are represented by a FilterInfo class. FilterInfo contains an instance of IFilter and its scope information (global, controller, or action) depending on which level the filter is declared. All of these types are shown in Listing 5-30.

Listing 5-30. Definitions of IFilter, FilterInfo, and FilterScope

```
public interface IFilter
{
    bool AllowMultiple { get; }
}

public sealed class FilterInfo
{
    public FilterInfo(IFilter instance, FilterScope scope)
    {
        if (instance == null)
        {
            throw Error.ArgumentNull("instance");
        }

        Instance = instance;
        Scope = scope;
    }

    public IFilter Instance { get; private set; }

    public FilterScope Scope { get; private set; }
}

public enum FilterScope
{
    Global = 0,
    Controller = 10,
    Action = 20,
}
```

In order to implement custom ordering, you will have to create a custom `IFilterProvider`, as well as introduce a custom class mimicking the behavior of `FilterInfo`, acting as a wrapper for the filter instance and its scope information. Under ideal circumstances you would not have do that, but unfortunately the default `FilterInfo` used by ASP.NET Web API is sealed and cannot be extended.

The Code

The base filter needed to facilitate the functionality discussed in this recipe is shown in Listing 5-31. Notice that it inherits from `ActionFilterAttribute`, which also automatically means that it will work only with this filter family. If you want to support others (`AuthorizationFilterAttribute`, `AuthenticationFilterAttribute`, `ExceptionFilterAttribute`) you need to subclass them separately.

The base filter introduces the `Order` property, which you'll use to sort the filters and compare them against one another.

Listing 5-31. A Base OrderedActionFilterAttribute, a Prerequisite for Providing the Filter Ordering Functionality

```
public abstract class OrderedActionFilterAttribute : ActionFilterAttribute
{
    public int Order { get; set; }

    public OrderedActionFilterAttribute() : this(-1)
    {}

    public OrderedActionFilterAttribute(int order)
    {
        Order = order;
    }
}
```

The custom FilterInfo (Listing 5-32) will implement IComparable and you'll use it to compare filters against each other using the Order property.

Listing 5-32. Custom IFilterInfo Capable of Sorting OrderedActionFilterAttributes

```
public class CustomFilterInfo : IComparable
{
    public CustomFilterInfo(IFilter instance, FilterScope scope)
    {
        Instance = instance;
        Scope = scope;
        FilterInfo = new FilterInfo(Instance, Scope);
    }

    public CustomFilterInfo(FilterInfo filterInfo)
    {
        Instance = filterInfo.Instance;
        Scope = filterInfo.Scope;
        FilterInfo = filterInfo;
    }

    public IFilter Instance { get; set; }
    public FilterScope Scope { get; set; }
    public FilterInfo FilterInfo { get; set; }

    public int CompareTo(object obj)
    {
        if (obj is CustomFilterInfo)
        {
            var item = obj as CustomFilterInfo;

            if (item.Instance is OrderedActionFilterAttribute)
            {
                var itemAttribute = item.Instance as OrderedActionFilterAttribute;
                var thisAttribute = Instance as OrderedActionFilterAttribute;
```

```
                    if (thisAttribute != null)
                        return thisAttribute.Order.CompareTo(itemAttribute.Order);
                }
            }

        throw new ArgumentException("Object is of wrong type");
    }
}
```

CustomFilterInfo also publicly exposes the FilterInfo that it wraps, as you will need to unwrap it later.

The next step is to add a filter provider that will respect the Order property, such as the one shown in Listing 5-33. It has a single method called GetFilters, which uses the current HttpActionDescriptor and a relevant HttpConfiguration to produce a list of filters to be used within the given request processing.

Listing 5-33. Custom IFilterProvider Responsible for Retrieving the Filter Pipeline and Sorting It

```
public class OrderBasedFilterProvider : IFilterProvider
{
    public IEnumerable<FilterInfo> GetFilters(HttpConfiguration configuration, HttpActionDescriptor
    actionDescriptor)
    {
        if (configuration == null)
        {
            throw new ArgumentNullException("configuration");
        }

        if (actionDescriptor == null)
        {
            throw new ArgumentNullException("actionDescriptor");
        }

        var customActionFilters = actionDescriptor.GetFilters().Select(i => new CustomFilterInfo(i,
        FilterScope.Action));
        var customControllerFilters = actionDescriptor.ControllerDescriptor.GetFilters().Select(i =>
        new CustomFilterInfo(i, FilterScope.Controller));
        var customGlobalFilters = configuration.Filters.Select(i => new CustomFilterInfo(i));

        var result = (customControllerFilters.Concat(customActionFilters).
        Concat(customGlobalFilters)).OrderBy(i => i).Select(i => i.FilterInfo);
        return result;
    }
}
```

Action-scoped filters can be obtained from HttpActionDescriptor and controller-scoped filters can be obtained from HttpControllerDescriptor, which is available as a property on the HttpActionDescriptor. Finally, global filters are accessible via the HttpConfiguration object. All of the filters are temporarily wrapped in the CustomFilterInfo class to support sorting.

You are able to apply the regular LINQ OrderBy expression to the concatenated collection of filters, since it's a collection of CustomFilterInfo that implements IComparable and therefore can be sorted. Then, to conform to the requirement of the IFilterProvider interface, you project the result to FilterInfo, which is available as a public property on CustomFilterInfo.

It's important to note that even though the filters are now sorted, `HttpActionDescriptor` will still group them into the relevant scope groups of `Action`, `Controller`, and `Global` levels. This means that whatever sorting based on the `Order` property you have done will be applied within the group only, while the built-in ASP.NET Web API filter precedence will be preserved, and the filters will still be executed in the following group order:

1. Global

2. Controller

3. Action

If you need to apply sorting across different scopes, you can assign all of the filters to the same group (doesn't matter which) in the `CustomFilterInfo`, for example `Global`:

```
var customActionFilters = actionDescriptor.GetFilters().Select(i => new CustomFilterInfo(i,
FilterScope.Global));
var customControllerFilters = actionDescriptor.ControllerDescriptor.GetFilters().Select(i =>
new CustomFilterInfo(i, FilterScope. Global));
var customGlobalFilters = configuration.Filters.Select(i => new CustomFilterInfo(i));
```

In this case, since all of the filters are treated as global, they will be sorted amongst themselves using the `Order` property, and the default precedence of filter groups will not be applied anymore.

The usage of the solution is shown in Listing 5-34. Filters can now be ordered using an `Order` property, as long as they inherit from the common `OrderedActionFilterAttribute` and the `OrderBasedFilterProvider` is registered in the global configuration in place of the default `IFilterProviders`: `ActionDescriptorFilterProvider` (responsible for controller and action filters) and `ConfigurationFilterProvider` (responsible for global filters).

Listing 5-34. Sample Usage of the Ordering Mechanism and Its Registration Against HttpConfiguration

```
[MyFilter(Order = 3)]
[MyFilter(Order = 2)]
[MyFilter(Order = 1)]
public class TestController : ApiController
{
    [MyFilter(Order = 2)]
    [MyFilter(Order = 1)]
    [MyFilter(Order = 3)]
    public HttpResponseMessage Get()
    {
        //omitted for brevity
    }
}

config.Services.Add(typeof(IFilterProvider), new OrderBasedFilterProvider());
var providers = config.Services.GetFilterProviders();

var defaultprovider = providers.First(i => i is ActionDescriptorFilterProvider);
config.Services.Remove(typeof(IFilterProvider), defaultprovider);

var configprovider = providers.First(i => i is ConfigurationFilterProvider);
config.Services.Remove(typeof(IFilterProvider), configprovider);
```

5-9. Order Filter Execution Without Custom Filters

Problem

You want to be able to sort the filters in your Web API regardless of the base class they use.

Solution

Since the filters that are built into ASP.NET Web API do not have any ordering property, you'll have to provide instructions on how to order them in a different way. I already discussed one solution in Recipe 5-8; this is an alternative approach.

You can create a map (dictionary) of order priority and a filter Type, and store them in the HttpConfiguration of your Web API. You are then able to build a custom IFilterProvider that will extract the ordering mapping from the HttpConfiguration and order the filter pipeline accordingly.

How It Works

You can learn more about the Properties dictionary (Dictionary<string, object>) of HttpRequestMessage, which is suitable for per-request storage, in Recipe 5-12. Similarly, ASP.NET Web API provides a Properties dictionary (also a Dictionary<string, object>) on the HttpConfiguration class, which facilitates application-wide global storage, helping you to avoid global static containers and similar singleton constructs.

The other principles behind using a custom IFilterProvider are the same as in Recipe 5-8; you can sort the filters in your filter provider, and the HttpActionDescriptor is going to respect that.

The Code

Consider the setup shown in Listing 5-35; you add a Dictionary<Type, int> to the HttpConfiguration Properties under a predefined key, "FilterOrder". The number represents the order weight of the filter. The actual filter implementations used here are irrelevant (they are here for illustration reasons) but you ensure that LogAttribute is always executed first and CacheAttribute second.

Listing 5-35. Setting Up Filter Ordering Map in HttpConfiguration

```
config.Properties["FilterOrder"] = new Dictionary<Type, int>
{
    {typeof (LogAttribute), 1},
    {typeof (CacheAttribute), 2}
};
```

The filter provider, which is going to extract this information and reorder the filters accordingly, is shown in Listing 5-36. In case a filter is not found in the mapping, it gets a large ordering number (999), which effectively means it will be executed at the end, after the filters from the mapping.

Since the map can take in any Type, this is a technique you can use to order filters you do not own as well. Notice that, contrary to the example from Recipe 5-8, there is no need to introduce a customized FilterInfo anymore, since the ordering comes from outside of the filter instance now.

Listing 5-36. Implementation of MappingBasedFilterProvider

```
public class MappingBasedFilterProvider : IFilterProvider
{
    public IEnumerable<FilterInfo> GetFilters(HttpConfiguration configuration, HttpActionDescriptor
    actionDescriptor)
    {
        if (configuration == null)
        {
            throw new ArgumentNullException("configuration");
        }

        if (actionDescriptor == null)
        {
            throw new ArgumentNullException("actionDescriptor");
        }

        var actionFilters = actionDescriptor.GetFilters().Select(i => new FilterInfo(i,
        FilterScope.Action));
        var controllerFilters = actionDescriptor.ControllerDescriptor.GetFilters().Select(i =>
        new FilterInfo(i, FilterScope.Controller));;
        var globalFilters = configuration.Filters.Where(i => i.Scope == FilterScope.Global);

        var result = actionFilters.Concat(controllerFilters).Concat(globalFilters).Distinct().ToList();

        object filterMap;
        if (configuration.Properties.TryGetValue("FilterOrder", out filterMap))
        {
            var dictionaryFilterMap = filterMap as Dictionary<Type, int>;
            if (dictionaryFilterMap != null)
            {
                var orderedFilters = new List<KeyValuePair<FilterInfo, int>>();
                result.ForEach(x =>
                {
                    int position;
                    if (dictionaryFilterMap.TryGetValue(x.Instance.GetType(), out position))
                    {
                        orderedFilters.Add(new KeyValuePair<FilterInfo, int>(x, position));
                    }
                    else
                    {
                        orderedFilters.Add(new KeyValuePair<FilterInfo, int>(x, 999));
                    }
                });

                result = orderedFilters.OrderBy(x => x.Value).Select(x => x.Key).ToList();
            }
        }

        return result;
    }
}
```

The usage example is shown in Listing 5-37 and involves simply decorating the action/controller with the relevant attribute and replacing the default IFilterProviders with MappingBasedFilterProvider. In both the action and controller case, LogAttribute will be executed before CacheAttribute, while SomeOtherFilterAttribute, since it's not part of the map (don't forget to add the map from Listing 5-35), will be executed last.

Listing 5-37. Sample Usage and Registration of Filter Ordering with MappingBasedFilterProvider

```
[Cache]
[Log]
public class TestController : ApiController
{
    [SomeOtherFilter]
    [Cache]
    [Log]
    public HttpResponseMessage Get()
    {
        //omitted for brevity
    }
}

config.Services.Add(typeof(IFilterProvider), new MappingBasedFilterProvider());
var providers = config.Services.GetFilterProviders();

var defaultprovider = providers.First(i => i is ActionDescriptorFilterProvider);
config.Services.Remove(typeof(IFilterProvider), defaultprovider);

var configprovider = providers.First(i => i is ConfigurationFilterProvider);
config.Services.Remove(typeof(IFilterProvider), configprovider);
```

5-10. Customize Error Detail Policy
Problem

You would like to customize and control the verbosity of error messages returned by your ASP.NET Web API service.

Solution

The core setting that allows you to really easily control the verbosity of ASP.NET Web API errors (as well as your own exceptions thrown in a Web API application) is the IncludeErrorDetailPolicy enumeration. It's applied globally to the HttpConfiguration, typically at application startup (you can also change it at runtime, but the new value will still apply globally to all requests) and can take one of the following values:

- IncludeErrorDetailPolicy.Default

- IncludeErrorDetailPolicy.LocalOnly

- IncludeErrorDetailPolicy.Always

- IncludeErrorDetailPolicy.Never

How It Works

IncludeErrorDetailPolicy is a property on HttpConfiguration (see Listing 5-38), so in order to globally configure your Web API error detail level, you can do it there.

Listing 5-38. Definition of HttpConfiguration

```
public class HttpConfiguration : IDisposable
{
    public HttpConfiguration();
    public HttpConfiguration(HttpRouteCollection routes);

    public IDependencyResolver DependencyResolver { get; set; }
    public HttpFilterCollection Filters { get; }
    public MediaTypeFormatterCollection Formatters { get; }
    public IncludeErrorDetailPolicy IncludeErrorDetailPolicy { get; set; }
    public Action<HttpConfiguration> Initializer { get; set; }
    public Collection<DelegatingHandler> MessageHandlers { get; }
    public ParameterBindingRulesCollection ParameterBindingRules { get; internal set; }
    public ConcurrentDictionary<object, object> Properties { get; }
    public HttpRouteCollection Routes { get; }
    public ServicesContainer Services { get; internal set; }
    public string VirtualPathRoot { get; }
    public void Dispose();
    protected virtual void Dispose(bool disposing);
}
```

Setting it to IncludeErrorDetailPolicy.LocalOnly implies that error details are only shown by ASP.NET Web API when requests originate from localhost or 127.0.0.1. A sample Web API error without any details would look like this:

```
{
    "Message": "No HTTP resource was found that matches the request URI 'http://localhost/api/
myresource'."
}
```

The same error, for local requests, would contain a details property, like so:

```
{
    "Message": "No HTTP resource was found that matches the request URI 'http://localhost/api/
myresource'.",
    "MessageDetail": "No type was found that matches the controller named 'myresource'."
}
```

If the error is produced by the user, not by ASP.NET Web API internal processing pipeline, you'd additionally get a stack trace.

For IncludeErrorDetailPolicy.Always, every single request gets maximum error details in response. This is particularly useful during development (as you'd also get stack traces), especially when the development doesn't happen on localhost but rather on a remote IP, or even for QA testing, but should definitely be avoided in live environments.

IncludeErrorDetailPolicy.Default is the default mode of operation for Web API, and if you don't explicitly reset this value, this is how Web API will run. In practice, it means that if you are self-hosting, the error detail policy will be treated as IncludeErrorDetailPolicy.LocalOnly. If you are web-hosting, it will behave the same, unless you have an explicit <customErrors /> section definition in the web.config file. Then, depending on whether <customErrors /> has the value of on or off, your IncludeErrorDetailPolicy will be treated as Always or Never.

It's quite important to remember that <customErrors /> will always take higher priority; this may save you some headaches if you find out that the error detail policy is behaving differently than it should according to the value set in HttpConfiguration.

IncludeErrorDetailPolicy.Never simply means that Web API will never surface any error details at all, regardless of where the request originates (locally or remotely).

The Code

Since IncludeErrorDetailPolicy is an HttpConfiguration property, it automatically applies globally to all requests. This is a very straightforward setup performed at your app startup.

```
httpConfiguration.IncludeErrorDetailPolicy = IncludeErrorDetailPolicy.Always;
```

This also means that if you wish to be able to modify its value on a per-request basis, simply walking up to the configuration object and modifying it at runtime is not a solution. The reason is that the new, changed value will still be global and will then be applied to all subsequent requests too.

To change the error detail level at runtime for a single request, you should instead set the IncludeErrorDetail value of the RequestContext, which is available on each HttpRequestMessage.

By setting it to true, you can force Web API to operate in the IncludeErrorDetailPolicy.Always mode for the lifetime of this given request, overriding any global settings. You can do that in the MessageHandler that will run at the entry point to the pipeline, such as the one shown in Listing 5-39.

Listing 5-39. A Message Handler Modifying the Error Detail Policy at Runtime on a Per Request Basis

```
public class PolicySetterHandler : DelegatingHandler
{
    protected override Task<HttpResponseMessage> SendAsync(
        HttpRequestMessage request, CancellationToken cancellationToken)
    {
        if (SOME_CONDITION)
        {
            request.GetRequestContext().IncludeErrorDetail = true;
        }
        else
        {
            request.GetRequestContext().IncludeErrorDetail = false;
        }
        return base.SendAsync(request, cancellationToken);
    }
}

config.MessageHandlers.Add(new PolicySetterHandler());
```

The condition could be anything you wish to diversify the error detail policy by, such as a user role, whitelisted IPs, and so on. Any exception you'd now throw yourself, or Web API would throw for you, will be returned to the client with error details based on that condition.

5-11. Return HTML from ASP.NET Web API

Problem

You would like to serve HTML pages from ASP.NET Web API.

Solution

There are three possible solutions to this problem, and each of the option has relevant application scenarios:

- Create a static HTML page and serve it through IIS (if you are web hosting), through OWIN static file middleware (if you are OWIN hosting), or as `StringContent` from a Web API controller (any other case).

- Treat HTML (`text/html`) as any another media type and serve the data using an HTML `MediaTypeFormatter`.

- Bypass content negotiation (which is discussed in Recipe 4-8) and serve the HTML response directly as an `HttpResponseMessage` or through a custom `IHttpActionResult`.

How It Works

In the first option you are only dealing with static files, so the option would be best for you if your usage scenario is a very simple one, such as serving some pre-generated documentation, readme files, and other documents that do not need to be processed on the server side.

The second option was briefly mentioned in Recipe 4-2. WebApiContrib contains two formatters that can be added to your Web API: `WebApiContrib.Formatting.Html`, for basic HTML and `WebApiContrib.Formatting.Razor`, for supporting Razor views. With this solution you are able to treat `text/html` on equal terms with other media types and be part of regular content negotiation. This can be extremely valuable, as it allows you to serve the same data not only in all the formats that your Web API might normally support (JSON, XML) but also represented in a nicely formatted HTML.

Finally, if you have some functionality and data that does not have a valid representation in formats other than HTML, such as login forms or heavily dynamic pages, you can designate specific controllers to be "HTML-controllers" and have them bypass any content negotiation. The best way to achieve that is to write a custom `IHttpActionResult` that will support Razor.

The Code

Let's look at code examples for these three solutions.

Static Files

When your API is running on IIS, it will automatically pick up any static HTML files, so there isn't anything special you need to do.

Things are more interesting with OWIN. Project Katana provides a very useful static files middleware component which can be added to your OWIN pipeline: `Microsoft.Owin.StaticFiles` (it's available on NuGet under that name too). The following example shows this particular middleware registered alongside Web API (for more on OWIN hosting Web API, see Recipe 2-2). The registration of this handler is shown in Listing 5-40.

Listing 5-40. Setting Up an OWIN Static Files Handler for a "web" Folder

```
public class Startup
{
    public void Configuration(IAppBuilder appBuilder)
    {
        var staticFilesDir = Path.Combine(Path.GetDirectoryName(Assembly.GetExecutingAssembly().
        Location), "web");
        var config = new HttpConfiguration();
        config.Routes.MapHttpRoute(
            name: "DefaultApi",
            routeTemplate: "api/{controller}/{id}",
            defaults: new { id = RouteParameter.Optional }
        );

        appBuilder.UseStaticFiles(staticFilesDir);
        appBuilder.UseWebApi(config);
    }
}
```

Alternatively, if you are hosting Web API using the built-in WCF-based Web API self-host engine, you can pick up the file by hand and serve to the user as a simple StringContent or StreamContent (subclasses of HttpContent), as shown in Listing 5-41. You can learn more about serving binary data and StreamContent from Recipe 4-10.

Listing 5-41. An ASP.NET Web API Controller Serving HTML as String Content

```
public class HtmlController : ApiController
{
    public HttpResponseMessage Get(string filename)
    {
        var response = new HttpResponseMessage
        {
            Content = new StreamContent(File.Open(AppDomain.CurrentDomain.BaseDirectory + "/files/"
            + filename, FileMode.Open))
        };
        response.Content.Headers.ContentType = new MediaTypeHeaderValue("text/html");
        return response;
    }
}
```

The controller grabs the local file from the files directory and writes it as a Stream directly to the response message. Alternatively, all the contents of the HTML file could have been read and StringContent used as the body of the response instead. One thing to note here, since in self-host you used AppDomain.CurrentDomain.BaseDirectory to determine the location on the disk, the location of your files folder will be relative to the DLL of the self-hosted service. In this case, the assumption has been that the files in the files folder are configured as Copy Always and Content in the Build actions for that file.

On more thing required here is the route that will provide the filename parameter.

```
config.Routes.MapHttpRoute("HTML", "files/{filename}", new { controller = "Html" });
```

You can now request static HTML pages from your self-hosted server accordingly.

```
GET /files/test.html
```

HTML via MediaTypeFormater

Once you install the WebApiContrib's `WebApiContrib.Formatting.Razor` from NuGet, registering it in your Web API boils down to a single line of code, which will allow HTML to be a fully-fledged member of the content negotiation process.

```
config.Formatters.Add(new RazorViewFormatter());
```

The above registration uses the default settings, which can obviously be tweaked; the constructor takes the following three configuration parameters:

- The root folder containing the view files; defaults to ~/Views

- An instance of `IViewLocator`; defaults to `RazorViewLocator`

- An instance of `IViewParser`; defaults to `RazorViewParser`

By modifying those you are able to change the logic used to determine which view should be used and how they are processed (for example you can arbitrarily inject your custom layout to all views and so on).

The default view location mechanism will expect a view with the same name as the name of the return type from an action. An example is shown in Listing 5-42.

Listing 5-42. A Regular ASP.NET Web API Action and a Corresponding Razor View for the tex/html Format

```
//action
public Item Get(int id)
{
    return new Item {Id = id, Name = "Filip"};
}

//Item.cshtml
@model Apress.Recipes.WebApi.Controllers.Item
<!DOCTYPE html>

<html>
<head>
    <meta name="viewport" content="width=device-width" />
    <title>Item</title>
</head>
    <body>
            <h1>@Model.Id</h1>
            <h2>@Model.Name</h2>
    </body>
</html>
```

This also means that when you are returning collections, you would ideally wrap them in a view model, rather than returning a list directly. This is shown in Listing 5-43.

Listing 5-43. Returing a Collection of Items with the HTML Formatter in Use

```
//view model
public class Items
{
    public IEnumerable<Item> Collection { get; set; }
}

//action
public Items Get()
{
    var list = new List<Item>
    {
        new Item {Id = 1, Name = "Filip"},
        new Item {Id = 2, Name = "Not Filip"}
    };

    return new Items {Collection = list};
}

//Items.cshtml
@model Apress.Recipes.WebApi.Controllers.Items
<!DOCTYPE html>

<html>
<head>
    <meta name="viewport" content="width=device-width" />
    <title>Item</title>
</head>
    <body>
        @foreach (var item in Model.Collection)
        {
            <h1>@item.Id</h1>
            <h2>@item.Name</h2>
        }
    </body>
</html>
```

In each case, the HTML representation is served to the client only when he requests a text/html, application/xhtml, or application/xhtml+xml media type. In other circumstances, you still get the resource in a relevant content negotiated format (i.e. JSON).

The formatter additionally allows you to locate views through a global map or attributes on the DTOs. Documentation with examples can be found under https://github.com/WebApiContrib/WebApiContrib.Formatting.Razor.

HTML via IHttpActionResult

Finally, if you want to bypass content negotiation, but you still want to use the full power of dynamic Razor-backed HTML, you can easily create a custom IHttpActionResult to serve HTML content. To do that, you need to add RazorEngine package from NuGet. The rest is quite simple: I discussed IHttpActionResult in Chapter 4. The HtmlActionResult is shown in Listing 5-44.

Listing 5-44. An HTML Implementation of IHttpActionResult

```
public class HtmlActionResult : IHttpActionResult
{
    private readonly string _view;
    private readonly dynamic _model;

    public HtmlActionResult(string viewName, dynamic model)
    {
        _view = LoadView(viewName);
        _model = model;
    }

    public Task<HttpResponseMessage> ExecuteAsync(CancellationToken cancellationToken)
    {
        var response = new HttpResponseMessage(HttpStatusCode.OK);
        var parsedView = RazorEngine.Razor.Parse(_view, _model);
        response.Content = new StringContent(parsedView);
        response.Content.Headers.ContentType = new MediaTypeHeaderValue("text/html");
        return Task.FromResult(response);
    }

    private static string LoadView(string name)
    {
        var view = File.ReadAllText(Path.Combine(AppDomain.CurrentDomain.BaseDirectory, "views",
        name + ".cshtml"));
        return view;
    }
}
```

The code here loads the view from a predefined path, uses RazorEngine to parse it, and constructs an instance of HttpResponseMessage using StringContent and the relevant text/html content type.

Now you can use the identical Items.cshtml view as before, and just modify the controller slightly, in a way shown in Listing 5-45. Similarly as before, the template Razor file has to be configured as Copy Always and Content in the Build Actions, otherwise it would not be copied to the output folder (AppDomain.CurrentDomain.BaseDirectory).

Listing 5-45. Modified Action Returning Items, This Time Through HtmlActionResult

```
public IHttpActionResult Get()
{
    var list = new List<Item>
    {
        new Item {Id = 1, Name = "Filip"},
        new Item {Id = 2, Name = "Not Filip"}
    };

    return new HtmlActionResult {"Items", new Items { Collection = list }};
}
```

5-12. Store Objects for the Duration of HTTP Request

Problem

You need to store some objects in a commonly accessible place for the duration of the HTTP request.

Solution

There are three primary ways of supporting per request storage in ASP.NET Web API.

- If you are using a web host with an ASP.NET runtime available to you, you can always reach to the traditional HttpContext.Current.Items dictionary. This is a not very elegant solution but it's often the simplest and quickest to implement.

- The second option is to use the Properties dictionary on the current HttpRequestMessage. It's a generic store for all kinds of objects that's disposed of together with the HttpRequestMessage.

- Finally, ASP.NET Web API exposes an extension method called GetCorrelationId that gets an ID of a given HttpRequestMessage. You can use that ID to store request-specific information in some external storage.

How It Works

Since the current request is available in almost every single place in the ASP.NET Web API pipeline (controllers, filters, message handlers, formatters), you will always be able to quite easily extract the information you stored in its Properties, which is a Dictionary<string, object>.

The Properties dictionary is initialized at the very beginning of the request lifetime with some basic contextual information about that request. ASP.NET Web API itself uses this dictionary to store all kinds of interesting information, such as a flag whether the request is local, information about the ErrorDetail policy (Recipe 5-10) for the given request and even a reference to the relevant context of the underlying host (HttpContext, OwinContext, or OWIN environment dictionary). This brings us back to the initial option of using HttpContext; to improve the testability of your methods you can avoid calling HttpContext directly and try to extract it from the request's Properties instead.

```
var httpContext = Request.Properties["MS_HttpContext"] as HttpContextBase;
```

Similarly, you can access the IOwinContext if you are hosting using Project Katana.

```
var owinContext = Request.Properties["MS_OwinContext"] as IOwinContext;
var owinEnvironment = Request.Properties["MS_OwinEnvironment"] as IDictionary<string, object>;
```

ASP.NET Web API provides a number strongly typed keys through the HttpPropertyKeys class (Listing 5-46) to access the information it stores there. The comments in the class come directly from the ASP.NET Web API source code and provide a description of what a given key is used for.

Listing 5-46. Definition of HttpPropertyKeys

```
public static class HttpPropertyKeys
{
    /// Provides a key for the HttpConfiguration associated with this ///request.
    public static readonly string HttpConfigurationKey = "MS_HttpConfiguration";

    /// Provides a key for the IHttpRouteData associated with this request.
    public static readonly string HttpRouteDataKey = "MS_HttpRouteData";

    /// Provides a key for the HttpActionDescriptor associated with this ///request.
    public static readonly string HttpActionDescriptorKey = "MS_HttpActionDescriptor";

    /// Provides a key for the current SynchronizationContext stored in ///HttpRequestMessage.Properties
    /// If SynchronizationContext.Current is null then no context is ///stored.
    public static readonly string SynchronizationContextKey = "MS_SynchronizationContext";

    /// Provides a key for the collection of resources that should be ///disposed when a request is disposed.
    public static readonly string DisposableRequestResourcesKey = "MS_DisposableRequestResources";

    /// Provides a key for the dependency scope for this request.
    public static readonly string DependencyScope = "MS_DependencyScope";

    /// Provides a key for the client certificate for this request.
    public static readonly string ClientCertificateKey = "MS_ClientCertificate";

    /// Provides a key for a delegate which can retrieve the client ///certificate for this request.
    public static readonly string RetrieveClientCertificateDelegateKey = "MS_
RetrieveClientCertificateDelegate";

    /// Provides a key for the HttpRequestContext for this request.
    public static readonly string RequestContextKey = "MS_RequestContext";

    /// Provides a key for the Guid stored in ///HttpRequestMessage.Properties.
    /// This is the correlation id for that request.
    /// </summary>
    public static readonly string RequestCorrelationKey = "MS_RequestId";

    /// Provides a key that indicates whether the request originates from a ///local address.
    public static readonly string IsLocalKey = "MS_IsLocal";

    /// Provides a key that indicates whether the request failed to match a ///route.
    public static readonly string NoRouteMatched = "MS_NoRouteMatched";

    /// Provides a key that indicates whether error details are to be ///included in the response
    for this HTTP request.
    public static readonly string IncludeErrorDetailKey = "MS_IncludeErrorDetail";

    /// Provides a key for the parsed query string stored in ///HttpRequestMessage.Properties.
    public static readonly string RequestQueryNameValuePairsKey = "MS_QueryNameValuePairs";

    /// Provides a key that indicates whether the request is a batch ///request.
    public static readonly string IsBatchRequest = "MS_BatchRequest";
}
```

At this point you will probably not be surprised to learn that the GetCorrelationId extension method mentioned before, actually also uses the Properties dictionary to store the ID of the request (RequestCorrelationKey). The source code for that method is shown in Listing 5-47 and as you can see, it tries to extract the request-specific Guid from the Properties. If it's not found, it will be created, persisted in the dictionary, and returned so that the next time you reach for it, it will already be available.

Listing 5-47. Definition of GetCorrelationId Method

```
public static Guid GetCorrelationId(this HttpRequestMessage request)
{
    if (request == null)
    {
        throw Error.ArgumentNull("request");
    }

    Guid correlationId;
    if (!request.Properties.TryGetValue<Guid>(HttpPropertyKeys.RequestCorrelationKey, out
    correlationId))
    {
        correlationId = Trace.CorrelationManager.ActivityId;
        if (correlationId == Guid.Empty)
        {
correlationId = Guid.NewGuid();
        }

        request.Properties.Add(HttpPropertyKeys.RequestCorrelationKey, correlationId);
    }

    return correlationId;
}
```

The Code

Listing 5-48 introduces two generic helper methods that allow you to add and retrieve objects to the current HttpRequestMessage in an easy way from any place in your Web API pipeline. It uses the underlying Properties dictionary as the storage.

Listing 5-48. Extensions to Work with HttpRequestMessage Properties

```
public static class HttpRequestMessageExtensions
{
    public static void Add(this HttpRequestMessage request, string key, object o)
    {
        request.Properties[key] = o;
    }
```

```
    public static T Get<T>(this HttpRequestMessage request, string key)
    {
        object result;
        if (request.Properties.TryGetValue(key, out result))
        {
            if (result is T)
            {
                return (T) result;
            }
            try
            {
                return (T)Convert.ChangeType(result, typeof (T));
            }
            catch (InvalidCastException) {}
        }

        return default(T);
    }
}
```

Next, let's look at an example of working with the correlation ID. Listing 5-49 shows a sample global storage. The implementation details are not important; it might just as well be cache, document database, traditional database, or anything else.

Listing 5-49. A Sample Globally-Accessible Storage Container

```
public static class Global
{
    static Global()
    {
        Storage = new ConcurrentDictionary<string, object>();
    }

    public static ConcurrentDictionary<string, object> Storage { get; set; }
}
```

You can now create a message handler wrapping your entire ASP.NET Web API processing pipeline (remember that message handlers are executed first and last in the pipeline) like the one shown in Listing 5-50.

Listing 5-50. A Demo Handler Injecting the Correlation ID and the HttpRequestMessage into a Global Container for Later Use

```
public class CorrelationHandler : DelegatingHandler
{
    protected async override Task<HttpResponseMessage> SendAsync(HttpRequestMessage request,
    CancellationToken cancellationToken)
    {
        var reqId = request.GetCorrelationId().ToString();
        if (Global.Storage.TryAdd(reqId, request))
        {
```

```
            var result = await base.SendAsync(request, cancellationToken);

            object req;
            Global.Storage.TryRemove(reqId, out req);
            return result;
        }

        return await base.SendAsync(request, cancellationToken);
    }
}
```

The handler grabs a correlation ID of a request and puts the entire HttpRequestMessage as a reference in the global dictionary you previously created. Now, if you want to reach into the current request from some of your services, you can do so through that ID.

Granted, you will still need to pass around that ID, but that's much easier than passing around the entire HttpRequestMessage. To avoid memory leak, the request is removed from the storage at the end of the pipeline.

CHAPTER 6

Embrace HTTP with ASP.NET Web API

This chapter discusses some of the HTTP concepts that have traditionally been neglected or were difficult to work with in ASP.NET, but are now easy to implement with ASP.NET Web API. By taking advantage of some of them you can immediately benefit by having a more flexible, client-friendly, and maintainable application.

You will learn how to do the following:

- Work with `HttpRequestMessage` (Recipe 6-1)

- Support partial GET requests (Recipe 6-2)

- Support less common HTTP verbs such as HEAD and PATCH (Recipes 6-3 and 6-4)

- Introduce HTTP batching (Recipe 6-5)

- Enable automatic 406 response from content negotiation (Recipe 6-6)

- Implement API versioning (Recipes 6-7 and 6-8)

- Use custom `HttpContent` (Recipe 6-9)

6-1. Work Directly with HttpRequestMessage
Problem

You would like to work directly with `HttpRequestMessage` in your actions.

Solution

The current `HttpRequestMessage` is always available as a public `Request` property on the base controller (`ApiController`), and it can always be accessed through it.

```
public HttpResponseMessage Post()
{
    //access Request here
}
```

Alternatively, instead of using custom models as action parameters, with the intent of the Web API pipeline binding them for you, you can use the raw `HttpRequestMessage`.

```
public HttpResponseMessage Post(HttpRequestMessage request)
{
    //access request here
}
```

Some might argue the latter approach is visually more compelling as the action is explicit about its dependencies, rather than relying on a hidden property.

How It Works

The Web API pipeline, specifically HttpControllerDispatcher, is responsible for creating an HttpControllerContext for a controller selected to handle the incoming HTTP request. That object contains a public property called Request, which in turn is surfaced by ApiController (see Listing 6-1).

The setter on the Request property actually internally performs a bunch of initialization work, which allows you to easily use that in your unit tests, in case your action uses the HttpRequestMessage directly.

Listing 6-1. Definition of the Request Property on ApiController

```
public HttpRequestMessage Request
{
    get
    {
        return ControllerContext.Request;
    }
    set
    {
        if (value == null)
        {
            throw Error.PropertyNull();
        }

        HttpRequestContext contextOnRequest = value.GetRequestContext();
        HttpRequestContext contextOnController = RequestContext;

        if (contextOnRequest != null && contextOnRequest != contextOnController)
        {
            throw new InvalidOperationException(SRResources.RequestContextConflict);
        }

        ControllerContext.Request = value;
        value.SetRequestContext(contextOnController);

        RequestBackedHttpRequestContext requestBackedContext =
            contextOnController as RequestBackedHttpRequestContext;

        if (requestBackedContext != null)
        {
            requestBackedContext.Request = value;
        }
    }
}
```

On the other hand, if you were to use an HttpRequestMessage as a parameter for your action, the default IActionValueBinder would select HttpRequestParameterBinding to handle the binding.

Not surprisingly, the end result would be the same as accessing Request directly off ApiController because HttpRequestParameterBinding also uses HttpControllerContext to hydrate your action's argument (as shown in Listing 6-2).

Listing 6-2. Definition of HttpRequestParameterBinding

```
public class HttpRequestParameterBinding : HttpParameterBinding
{
    public HttpRequestParameterBinding(HttpParameterDescriptor descriptor)
        : base(descriptor)
    {
    }

    public override Task ExecuteBindingAsync(ModelMetadataProvider metadataProvider,
    HttpActionContext actionContext, CancellationToken cancellationToken)
    {
        string name = Descriptor.ParameterName;
        HttpRequestMessage request = actionContext.ControllerContext.Request;
        actionContext.ActionArguments.Add(name, request);

        return TaskHelpers.Completed();
    }
}
```

The Code

The example in Listing 6-3 shows both approaches to dealing with HttpRequestMessage. In each case, you can easily access all the context and header information, as well as read and process the body of the request. Notice that your actions can also combine the regular URI parameter binding with HttpRequestMessage binding.

Listing 6-3. A Sample Controller Working with HttpRequestMessage in Different Ways

```
public class TestController : ApiController
{
    [Route("test/{id:int}")]
    public string Get(int id, HttpRequestMessage req)
    {
        return id + " " + req.RequestUri;
    }

    [Route("test/{text:alpha}")]
    public string Get(string text)
    {
        return text + " " + Request.RequestUri;
    }
}
```

173

```
    [Route("testA")]
    public async Task<TestItem> Post(HttpRequestMessage req)
    {
        return await req.Content.ReadAsAsync<TestItem>();
    }

    [Route("testB")]
    public async Task<TestItem> Post()
    {
        return await Request.Content.ReadAsAsync<TestItem>();
    }
}
```

HTTPREQUESTMESSAGE

HttpRequestMessage, as part of the new HTTP object model in .NET (System.Net.Http), provides a very rich, strongly typed abstraction over HTTP. This helps you enforce compile-time checks on different HTTP-bound operations such as parsing specific header types.

```
public class HttpRequestMessage : IDisposable
{
    public HttpRequestMessage(HttpMethod method, String requestUri);
    public HttpRequestMessage(HttpMethod method, Uri requestUri);
    public HttpRequestMessage();

    public HttpContent Content { get; set; }
    public HttpRequestHeaders Headers { get; }
    public HttpMethod Method { get; set; }
    public IDictionary<String,Object> Properties { get; }
    public Uri RequestUri { get; set; }
    public Version Version { get; set; }

    protected virtual void Dispose(Boolean disposing);

    public override String ToString();
    public void Dispose();
}
```

You can read more about HttpRequestMessage at MSDN http://msdn.microsoft.com/en-us/library/system.net.http.httprequestmessage(v=vs.110).aspx.

6-2. Support Partial GET

Problem

You'd like to support partial GET in your API, using the combination of Range, Accept-Ranges, and Content-Range headers.

Solution

System.Net.Http makes it quite easy to handle range requests, as all of the headers are strongly typed. To support partial GETs, you will need to manually inspect the Range header in your action, and respond accordingly—either with the entire resource or a subset of it.

```
public HttpResponseMessage Get()
{
    var rangeHeader = Request.Headers.Range;
    //process rangeHeader
}
```

How It Works

The idea behind range requests is that the client can request a subset of a resource, rather than an entire resource.

On the request side, the RangeHeaderValue contains the Unit relevant for the given resource and a collection of RangeItemHeaderValues, each of which wraps the From and To values that the client wishes to retrieve from the API. The definitions of those can be seen in Listing 6-4.

Listing 6-4. RangeHeaderValue and RangeItemHeaderValue Definitons

```
public class RangeHeaderValue : ICloneable
{
    public RangeHeaderValue();
    public RangeHeaderValue(long? from, long? to);

    public ICollection<RangeItemHeaderValue> Ranges { get; }
    public string Unit { get; set; }

    public static RangeHeaderValue Parse(string input);
    public static bool TryParse(string input, out RangeHeaderValue parsedValue);
}

public class RangeItemHeaderValue : ICloneable
{
    public RangeItemHeaderValue(long? from, long? to);

    public long? From { get; }
    public long? To { get; }
}
```

On the response side, ContentRangeHeaderValue wraps all of that information in a single header (Listing 6-5).

Listing 6-5. ContentRangeHeaderValue Definiton

```
public class ContentRangeHeaderValue : ICloneable
{
    public ContentRangeHeaderValue(long length);
    public ContentRangeHeaderValue(long from, long to);
    public ContentRangeHeaderValue(long from, long to, long length);

    public bool HasLength { get; }
    public bool HasRange { get; }
    public long? Length { get; }
    public long? To { get; }
    public string Unit { get; set; }

    public static ContentRangeHeaderValue Parse(string input);
    public static bool TryParse(string input, out ContentRangeHeaderValue parsedValue);
}
```

The request for partial content should contain an Accept-Range header, indicating at least start position or end position. In the HTTP specification, bytes were chosen as the default unit; however, custom units can be used too. As a result, you can use partial GETs as a viable alternative for paging and query string/route-based parameters, an example of which can be seen in Listing 6-6.

Listing 6-6. Sample GET Request for a Specific Range

```
GET http://localhost:9000/items  HTTP/1.1
Accept: application/json
Range: Item=2-4
```

If the request is fulfilled as a partial one, the returned HttpResponseMessage should contain a status code of 206 (HttpStatusCode.PartialContent). Additionally, the Content-Range header should be set on the response, informing the client what range is being returned and the total length of the resource. A sample partial response is shown in Listing 6-7.

Listing 6-7. Sample 206 Response with a Specific Range

```
206 Partial Content
Accept-Ranges: Item
Date: Tue, 04 Mar 2014 19:23:55 GMT
Server: Microsoft-HTTPAPI/2.0
Content-Length: 74
Content-Range: Item 2-4/4
Content-Type: application/json; charset=utf-8
[{"Id":2,"Text":"World"},{"Id":3,"Text":"Goodbye"},{"Id":4,"Text":"Hell"}]
```

The Code

The controller shown in Listing 6-8 contains a basic example of a Web API endpoint exposing a collection of resources. Let's modify this sample to support partial GETs.

Listing 6-8. Sample GET Controller

```
public class ItemController : ApiController
{
    private static List<Item> _items = new List<Item>
    {
        new Item {Id = 1, Text = "Hello"},
        new Item {Id = 2, Text = "World"},
        new Item {Id = 3, Text = "Goodbye"},
        new Item {Id = 4, Text = "Hell"}
    };

    [Route("items")]
    public HttpResponseMessage Get()
    {
        var response = Request.CreateResponse(HttpStatusCode.OK, _items);
        return response;
    }
}
```

Since the resource in question is a collection, you can introduce a custom range Unit representing an individual element of that collection. In this particular example, that would be an Item entity, so it could be called "Item" too (recall that the "x-" prefix is deprecated). The partial GET support can be easily used here to navigate back and forth between the collection's members, in a typical pagination manner.

To achieve that, you have to look at a few things:

- The Range header has to be present.

- The Unit contained in that Range header has to be equal to the custom unit supported by the HTTP endpoint.

- The Range definition inside the Range header has to make sense. In other words, it can't be out of bounds of the collection size at both the start and end, and at least one of the values (From or To) has to be provided by the client.

With this knowledge, you can go ahead and modify the original action with specific behavior that will be processed if all of the above conditions are satisfied (Listing 6-9). You can use the Range header information to determine the LINQ Skip and Take parameters for the original collection and to construct a 206 Partial Content response based on that. Additionally, this filtering information should be added to the Content-Range header of the response, along with the overall collection length.

Listing 6-9. Extending the Original GET Action with PartialContent Support

```
public HttpResponseMessage Get()
{
    var rangeHeader = Request.Headers.Range;
    if (rangeHeader != null && rangeHeader.Unit == "Item" && rangeHeader.Ranges != null)
    {
        var rangeValue = rangeHeader.Ranges.FirstOrDefault();
        if (rangeValue != null)
        {
            if ((!rangeValue.From.HasValue && !rangeValue.To.HasValue) ||
                rangeValue.From > _items.Count || rangeValue.To > _items.Count)
                throw new HttpResponseException(HttpStatusCode.BadRequest);
```

```
        var skip = (rangeValue.From ?? 0);
        var take = (rangeValue.To ?? _items.Count) - rangeValue.From + 1;

        var partialRes = Request.CreateResponse(HttpStatusCode.PartialContent,
            _items.Skip((int) skip - 1).Take((int) take));
        partialRes.Headers.AcceptRanges.Add("Item");
        partialRes.Content.Headers.ContentRange = new ContentRangeHeaderValue(skip,
            rangeValue.To ?? _items.Count, _items.Count) {Unit = "Item"};

        return partialRes;
    }
}

var response = Request.CreateResponse(HttpStatusCode.OK, _items);
response.Headers.AcceptRanges.Add("Item");
return response;
}
```

Finally, notice how in both cases (full response and partial response) you should add the Accept-Ranges header entry to the response. This is a hint to the client what Unit you are expecting.

SUPPORTING PARTIAL GET WITH BYTES

If you would like the client to be able to specify which bytes of your resource he should get, Web API offers a custom HttpContent that is of great help: ByteRangeStreamContent. Its constructor takes in a Stream representing the object you'd like to return from the API and a raw RangeHeaderValue. Internally, it will figure out which bytes exactly should be part of the response, and the necessary Content headers will also be set for you.

```
var partialResponse = Request.CreateResponse(HttpStatusCode.PartialContent);
partialResponse.Content = new ByteRangeStreamContent(stream, Request.Headers.Range,
"application/json");
return partialResponse;
```

For more information on custom HttpContent, see Recipe 6-9.

6-3. Support the HEAD Verb

Problem

You would like to add support for the HEAD verb in your Web API service. HEAD requests are often used to determine the size of the resource prior to requesting it (i.e. to provide a loading progress) or to simply ping an HTTP endpoint.

Solution

ASP.NET Web API provides AcceptVerbsAttribute, which you can use to annotate an action as supporting HTTP verbs other than those inferred from the Web API convention.

However, support for the HEAD verb is inconsistent across different Web API hosts, so the safest solution is to roll out a custom MessageHandler-based solution, which will convert each HEAD request into a GET, let it execute as a regular GET, and strip away the body of the response as it leaves your Web API.

STRONGLY TYPED HTTP VERB ATTRIBUTES

Aside from `AcceptVerbsAttribute`, which lets you pass in HTTP verbs as strings, ASP.NET Web API also provides strongly typed attributes for the core HTTP methods:

- `HttpGetAttribute`
- `HttpPostAttribute`
- `HttpPutAttribute`
- `HttpDeleteAttribute`
- `HttpHeadAttribute`
- `HttpPatchAttribute`
- `HttpOptionsAttribute`

However, from a functionality perspective, there is no difference between them; both `AcceptVerbsAttribute` and the dedicated method attributes implement `IActionHttpMethodProvider`, which is used to hint to the ASP.NET Web API pipeline which HTTP verb an action should respond to.

How It Works

The HEAD verb is defined in RFC 2616, section 9.4, which states the following:

> *The HEAD method is identical to GET except that the server MUST NOT return a message-body in the response. The metainformation contained in the HTTP headers in response to a HEAD request SHOULD be identical to the information sent in response to a GET request. This method can be used for obtaining metainformation about the entity implied by the request without transferring the entity-body itself.*

Hypertext Transfer Protocol -- HTTP/1.1
RFC 2616 Fielding, et al.

In other words, the behavior of HEAD is supposed to be exactly like GET but without returning the response body. All the other headers should be present, including the `Content-Length` header.

You could normally expect to force ASP.NET Web API to support HEAD using the following setup:

```
public class TestController : ApiController
{
    [Route("test")]
    [AcceptVerbs("GET","HEAD")]
    public string Get()
    {
        return "Hello";
    }
}
```

Unfortunately, as mentioned before, support for HEAD in ASP.NET Web API is, at the time of writing (ASP.NET Web API 2.1), rather spotty, and this is how the above controller would behave under different hosts:

- Web host: HEAD will work correctly.

- Self-host: HEAD request will be responded to with a 200 status code but Content-Length will always be 0.

- Own host (project Katana): HEAD will not work, and no response from server will be returned.

So unless you are exclusively on a web host, a simple and reliable solution is to rely on the ASP.NET Web API MessageHandler pipeline. Message handlers form a so-called "Russian doll" pipeline in Web API, as they execute one after another as the request flows into the system, and in the opposite order as the response is sent out the system.

This processing pipeline is very powerful, as its design allows you to register any number of handlers, responsible for addressing all kinds of cross-cutting concerns, such as authentication or logging. Using the same methodology, in this particular recipe, you will be able to intercept a HEAD request on its way into your API, swap the HTTP verb on the request with a GET, and let it execute as if it were a regular GET. As the response is sent out, the handler will have a chance to process it, and that's when it can remove the body from the response to conform to the standards defined in RFC 2616.

As the base class to be used for Web API message handlers, DelegatingHandler exposes a single method to override and call (Listing 6-10).

Listing 6-10. Definition of the DelegatingHandler

```
public abstract class DelegatingHandler : HttpMessageHandler
{
    public HttpMessageHandler InnerHandler { get; set; }

    protected internal override Task<HttpResponseMessage> SendAsync(
        HttpRequestMessage request,
        CancellationToken cancellationToken
    )
}
```

When a handler wants to hand off the incoming request to the next member of the processing pipeline—which it normally should, unless it wants to break the pipeline and respond to the client immediately—it should call the base.SendAsync method. By awaiting the output of this call to base, it's also able to get a hold of the outgoing HttpResponseMessage and process that.

The Code

The message handler shown in Listing 6-11 provides the core functionality discussed in this recipe. The highlighted bit of code is where the response is being grabbed on its way from the Web API.

Listing 6-11. Handler Responsible for Adding Support for the HEAD Verb

```
public class HeadHandler : DelegatingHandler
{
    protected override async Task<HttpResponseMessage> SendAsync(HttpRequestMessage request, System.
    Threading.CancellationToken cancellationToken)
    {
```

```
        if (request.Method == HttpMethod.Head)
        {
            request.Method = HttpMethod.Get;
            request.Properties.Add("HeadMarker", true);
        }

        var response = await base.SendAsync(request, cancellationToken);

        object isHead;
        response.RequestMessage.Properties.TryGetValue("HeadMarker", out isHead);

        if (response.IsSuccessStatusCode && isHead != null && ((bool)isHead))
        {
            var oldContent = await response.Content.ReadAsByteArrayAsync();
            var content = new StringContent(string.Empty);
            content.Headers.Clear();

            foreach (var header in response.Content.Headers)
            {
                content.Headers.Add(header.Key, header.Value);
            }

            content.Headers.ContentLength = oldContent.Length;
            response.Content = content;
        }

        return response;
    }
}
```

In case of a successful response, the content of the response is swapped with an empty `StringContent`. Additionally, all content headers are copied over and the `Content-Length` header of the new response content is set to be equal to the original one. If `IsSuccessStatusCode` returns `false`, it means that the server returned one of the 4xx or 5xx codes, and at that point you should not purge the body of the response.

You can now register the message handler against the `MessageHandlers` collection of your `HttpConfiguration` object. The order in which they are registered is important; in the spirit of the "Russian doll" model, the first message handler will process the request first and the response last, and so on.

```
var config = new HttpConfiguration();
config.MessageHandlers.Add(new HeadHandler());
```

With this in place, there is no need for any additional attribute decoration at action level.

▨ **Tip**   Because HEAD requests execute as normal GET requests, it's common to combine such actions with some sort of server-side caching to avoid incurring performance penalties.

6-4. Support the PATCH Verb

Problem

You would like to support partial updates in your ASP.NET Web API application using the PATCH HTTP verb.

Solution

PATCH is supported by ASP.NET Web API out of the box using verb-based dispatching. As a result, it's enough to add a Patch method or any other method decorated with an [HttpPatch] or [AcceptVerbs("PATCH")] attribute, and you will have Web API correctly route the client's request there.

However, since PATCH is responsible for partial updates of your resources, it's interesting to dissect how this process may be performed. There are three primary ways:

- Manual updates
- Use the Delta<T>, which is part of the Microsoft.AspNet.WebApi.OData (OData Version 3.0) or Microsoft.AspNet.OData (OData Version 4.0) package
- Roll out a custom reflection-based solution

How It Works

PATCH is defined in RFC 5789. It allows your client to perform partial updates on an HTTP resource.

> *The PATCH method requests that a set of changes described in the request entity be applied to the resource identified by the Request-URI. The set of changes is represented in a format called a "patch document" identified by a media type.*
>
> Internet Engineering Task Force (IETF)
> Request for Comments: 5789

It's also semantically different to PUT, which is intended to update the whole entity. Again, this is clearly stated in RFC 5789.

> *The PUT method is already defined to overwrite a resource with a complete new body, and cannot be reused to do partial changes. Otherwise, proxies and caches, and even clients and servers, may get confused as to the result of the operation.*
>
> Internet Engineering Task Force (IETF)
> Request for Comments: 5789

The Microsoft.AspNet.WebApi.OData and Microsoft.AspNet.OData NuGet packages introduce Delta<T>, a dynamic proxy object that can wrap any of your models. While it was developed for and intended to be used with OData only (and ODataMediaTypeFormatter), it can also be used with JsonMediaTypeFormatter (not XmlMediaTypeFormatter, though). Delta<T> uses dynamically compiled expressions trees to provide property getters and setters, and correctly update the properties of your model (represented by the T).

Supporting PATCH through reflection boils down to creating a custom helper that will iterate through all the properties of the model and try to update them according to the client's request. There are certainly many ways to approach this; one approach is shown in the next section.

The Code

Let's go through all of the potential options for supporting PATCH in your APIs. The controller used in all of the examples in this recipe will look like the one shown in Listing 6-12. For simplicity, a static list will be used as a data source..

Listing 6-12. Sample Controller Supporting PATCH

```
public class ItemController : ApiController
{
    private static readonly List<Item> _items = new List<Item>
    {
        new Item {Id = 1, Name = "Filip", Country = "Switzerland"},
        new Item {Id = 2, Name = "Felix", Country = "Canada"},
        new Item {Id = 3, Name = "Michal", Country = "Poland"}
    };

    public Item Patch(int id, Item newItem)
    {
        //different for each approach
    }
}
```

Manual Updates

This method is the one used most often because it's the easiest to implement. You need to create a Patch action accepting your model and simply update all of the properties of the target resource by hand, as shown in Listing 6-13.

Listing 6-13. Traditional, Manual Way of Supporting PATCH

```
[Route("traditional/{id:int}")]
public Item Patch(int id, Item newItem)
{
    var item = _items.FirstOrDefault(x => x.Id == id);
    if (item == null) throw new HttpResponseException(HttpStatusCode.NotFound);

    if (newItem.Name != null)
        item.Name = newItem.Name;

    if (newItem.Country != null)
        item.Country = newItem.Country;
    return item;
}
```

Of course, this approach has a number of issues. For example, the client might submit only a handful of properties of the model, leaving the rest of them null. Therefore, ideally, you should only use the non-null ones to update the target resource. On the other hand, this poses a challenge if you want to allow the client to nullify some of the properties. Moreover, such an approach forces your model to use only reference types as properties (all value types should become nullable).

Using Delta<T>

Listing 6-14 shows Delta<T> in use. You will need to tweak your PATCH method to take Delta<T> as an input instead of just using your model. Then, to perform a patch update over an existing resource, you call the PATCH method exposed by the Delta<T> proxy and pass in an instance of that object that should be updated. In this example, you have no DB to persist in, but you should then proceed to save the original object in the DB, as its state has been modified to reflect the updates requested by the client.

Listing 6-14. Using Delta<T> in a Patch Action

```
[Route("delta/{id:int}")]
public Item Patch(int id, Delta<Item> newItem)
{
    var item = _items.FirstOrDefault(x => x.Id == id);
    if (item == null) throw new HttpResponseException(HttpStatusCode.NotFound);

    newItem.Patch(item);
    //item instance is now updated

    return item;
}
```

Usage from the client side is very simple; you just use the original model to send the HTTP request. The example, utilizing HttpClient, is shown in Listing 6-15.

Listing 6-15. PATCH Request Using Delta<T>

```
var item = new Item()
        {
            Id = 1,
            Country = "Scotland"
        };
        var client = new HttpClient();
        var msg = new HttpRequestMessage(new HttpMethod("PATCH"), address + "delta/1")
        {
        Content = new ObjectContent(typeof (Item), item, new JsonMediaTypeFormatter())
        };

var response = await client.SendAsync(msg);
```

Using Reflection

As mentioned already, there are a number of approaches that could be taken to support reflection-based PATCH. Listing 6-16 shows one way of doing it. You will need to change the Patch action to take in an IEnumerable<KeyValuePair<string, object>> instead of your model.

Listing 6-16. Using a Reflection-based Solution in a Patch Action

```
[Route("custom/{id:int}")]
public Item Patch(int id, IEnumerable<KeyValuePair<string, object>>updateProperties)
{
    var item = _items.FirstOrDefault(x => x.Id == id);
    if (item == null) throw new HttpResponseException(HttpStatusCode.NotFound);
```

```
    foreach (var property in updateProperties)
    {
        //update all properties with reflection
    }

    return item;
}
```

You are forcing the client to submit a list of KeyValuePairs representing a property to be updated and a new value to be set. To facilitate that, let's build a helper class (Listing 6-17) that will take in an instance of a model, a property by name, and a new value, and will be able to use reflection to update the model correctly.

Listing 6-17. A Helper Class Using Reflection to Update the Relevant Property on the Model

```
public static class Updater
{
    public static void Patch<T>(T obj, string propertyName, object value)
    {
        if (value is Int64)
            value = Convert.ToInt32(value);

        var propertyInfo = obj.GetType().GetProperty(propertyName, BindingFlags.IgnoreCase |
        BindingFlags.Public | BindingFlags.Instance);
        if (propertyInfo == null)
            throw new ArgumentException("Property cannot be updated.");

        if (!propertyInfo.CanRead || (typeof(IEnumerable).IsAssignableFrom(propertyInfo.
        PropertyType) && propertyInfo.PropertyType != typeof(string)))
            throw new ArgumentException("Property cannot be updated.");

        SetValue(obj, value, propertyInfo);
    }

    private static void SetValue(object o, object value, PropertyInfo propertyInfo)
    {
        if (propertyInfo.PropertyType.IsEnum)
        {
            propertyInfo.SetValue(o, Convert.ToInt32(value));
        }
        else if (propertyInfo.PropertyType.IsNumericType())
        {
            propertyInfo.SetValue(o, Convert.ChangeType(value, propertyInfo.PropertyType));
        }
        else if (propertyInfo.PropertyType == typeof(Guid) || propertyInfo.PropertyType == typeof(Guid?))
        {
            Guid g;
            if (Guid.TryParse((string)value, out g))
            {
                propertyInfo.SetValue(o, g);
            }
```

```
        else
        {
            throw new InvalidOperationException("Cannot use non Guid value on a Guid property!");
        }
    }
    else
    {
        propertyInfo.SetValue(o, value);
    }
    }
}
}
```

The highlighted bits of code show different potential paths for setting the new property value. This is a simple example. Depending on the types of properties on your model, you will hit a fair share of edge cases and will have to handle all kinds of errors, but the gist is very clear.

You may now update the controller's action to use the Updater helper class.

```
foreach (var property in updateProperties)
{
    Updater.Patch(item, property.Key, property.Value);
}
```

The client can now use this PATCH endpoint to easily update the resources in your API. Listing 6-18 shows a sample request made from HttpClient.

Listing 6-18. Sample Request to a Reflection-Based Patch Action

```
var postData = new List<KeyValuePair<string, object>>
{
    new KeyValuePair<string, object>("Country", "Finland"),
    new KeyValuePair<string, object >("Name", "Sami")
};
var msgTwo = new HttpRequestMessage(new HttpMethod("PATCH"), address + "custom/2")
{
    Content = new ObjectContent(typeof(IEnumerable<KeyValuePair<string,object>>), postData, new
    JsonMediaTypeFormatter())
};
var responseTwo = await client.SendAsync(msgTwo);
```

6-5. Support Batching of HTTP Requests
Problem

You would like to save on the number of HTTP requests between your client and the server, and are looking for a mechanism allowing you to batch the HTTP calls to your Web API service.

Solution

To facilitate batching, you need to declare a dedicated batching route that will be the entry point for the client to call. From there, each of the batched requests will be dispatched throughout your Web API pipeline as if it was a regular incoming HttpRequestMessage.

To dedicate a route as a batch entry route, you have to use a `MapHttpBatchRoute` extension method.

```
config.Routes.MapHttpBatchRoute("WebApiBatch", "api/batch",
    new DefaultHttpBatchHandler(new HttpServer(config, new HttpRoutingDispatcher(config))));
```

You can now post batch messages to your Web API using the multipart request format shown in Listing 6-19.

Listing 6-19. Sample Batching HTTP Request

```
POST http://localhost:9000//api/batch' HTTP 1.1
Content-Type: multipart/mixed; boundary="44503acf-0fe0-40ab-90ca-c431e69c72de"

--44503acf-0fe0-40ab-90ca-c431e69c72de
Content-Type: application/http; msgtype=request

POST /api/items HTTP 1.1
Content-Type: application /json; charset=utf-8
{"Id": 1, "Name":"Filip", "Country": "Switzerland"}

--44503acf-0fe0-40ab-90ca-c431e69c72de
Content-Type: application/http; msgtype=request

POST /api/items HTTP 1.1
Content-Type: application /json; charset=utf-8
{"Id": 2, "Name":"Felix", "Country": "Canada"}

--44503acf-0fe0-40ab-90ca-c431e69c72de
Content-Type: application/http; msgtype=request

GET /api/items HTTP 1.1
Accept: application /json
--44503acf-0fe0-40ab-90ca-c431e69c72de
```

In Listing 6-19, the request creates two resources and then retrieves a list of them, all in one HTTP trip.

How It Works

ASP.NET Web API supports request batching since version 2.1 of the framework. The batch itself is just a `multipart/mixed` HTTP request, except each individual part's content type is set to be `application/http; msgtype=request` media type. Conversely, the response is also multipart, and each part of the response is `application/http; msgtype=response`.

When mapping the batch route, Web API creates a route with a dedicated per-route message handler attached to it (see Chapter 3 for more details on route specific handlers). In the batching case, the handler is derived from the abstract `HttpBatchHandler`; Web API uses different implementations for regular Web API endpoints (`DefaultHttpBatchHandler`) and for OData ones (`DefaultODataBatchHandler`). You can also provide your own custom implementation in the case that you want to customize some of the default behaviors.

The handler will extract all requests from the multipart request and dispatch them in process through the Web API pipeline sequentially. It also composes a list of `HttpResponseMessages`, which—once everything is processed—will be converted to a multipart response and sent back to client. The principle of in-process request dispatching is the same as Web API's in-memory hosting, which is described in detail in Recipe 11-7.

If you don't care about execution order, you can speed things up by setting a NonSequential flag on the DefaultHttpBatchHandler.

```
config.Routes.MapHttpBatchRoute("WebApiBatch", "api/batch",
                new DefaultHttpBatchHandler(new HttpServer(config, new
HttpRoutingDispatcher(config)))) { ExecutionOrder = BatchExecutionOrder.NonSequential });
```

The Code

The batching support is easily enabled with the route registration:

```
config.Routes.MapHttpBatchRoute("WebApiBatch", "api/batch",
    new DefaultHttpBatchHandler(new HttpServer(config, new HttpRoutingDispatcher(config))));
```

With that in place all you need to do is adhere to the standards of sending a mixed/multipart request. Listing 6-20 shows a sample done using HttpClient.

Listing 6-20. A Sample Request from a .NET HttpClient to a Batching Web API Endpoint

```
var client = new HttpClient();
var batchContent = new MultipartContent("mixed")
{
    new HttpMessageContent(new HttpRequestMessage(HttpMethod.Post, address + "/api/items")
    {
        Content = new ObjectContent(typeof (Item),
                new Item {Country = "Switzerland", Id = 1, Name = "Filip"},
                new JsonMediaTypeFormatter())
    }),

    new HttpMessageContent(new HttpRequestMessage(HttpMethod.Post, address + "/api/items")
    {
        Content =
            new ObjectContent(typeof (Item), new Item {Country = "Canada", Id = 2, Name = "Felix"},
                new JsonMediaTypeFormatter())
    }),

    new HttpMessageContent(new HttpRequestMessage(HttpMethod.Get, address + "/api/items"))
};

var batchRequest = new HttpRequestMessage(HttpMethod.Post, address + "/api/batch")
{
    Content = batchContent
};

var batchResponse = await client.SendAsync(batchRequest);
var provider = await batchResponse.Content.ReadAsMultipartAsync();
foreach (var content in provider.Contents)
{
    var response = await content.ReadAsHttpResponseMessageAsync();
    //process response
}
```

A new `MultipartContent` is constructed and then populated with individual `HttpMessageContent` instances representing separate `HttpRequestMessages` that will be dispatched into the Web API. If you take this request and send it to the server, it will produce the response shown in Listing 6-21.

Listing 6-21. Sample Response from a Batch-Friendly Endpoint

```
HTTP/1.1  200 OK
Content-Type: multipart/mixed; boundary="1e075dc8-aea8-48b0-9df9-12e8a961016a"
Content-Length: 536


--1e075dc8-aea8-48b0-9df9-12e8a961016a
Content-Type: application/http; msgtype=response
HTTP/1.1 204 No Content

--1e075dc8-aea8-48b0-9df9-12e8a961016a
Content-Type: application/http; msgtype=response
HTTP/1.1 204 No Content

--1e075dc8-aea8-48b0-9df9-12e8a961016a
Content-Type: application/http; msgtype=response
HTTP/1.1 200 OK


Content-Type: application/json; charset=utf-8
[{"Id": 1, "Name":"Filip", "Country": "Switzerland"}, {"Id": 2, "Name":"Felix", "Country":
"Canada"}]


--1e075dc8-aea8-48b0-9df9-12e8a961016a
```

6-6. Automatic HTTP 406/Not Acceptable Server Responses
Problem

By default, if the client asks for a media type that your ASP.NET Web API service doesn't support, the framework will respond with the first available formatter (usually JSON, `application/json`). You would like to change this behavior, so that in cases when a proper media type cannot be served, your Web API application automatically issues a 406 HTTP status code (Not Acceptable) instead.

Solution

You can enable this feature by appropriately modifying the `DefaultContentNegotiator`, the out-of-the-box implementation of the content negotiating mechanism (`IContentNegotiator`), which has a built in option of issuing 406 responses automatically.

How It Works

As discussed in Chapter 4, ASP.NET Web API will go through a series of steps when trying to determine a relevant formatter for a given HTTP request. As soon as a match is found, the result yields, and no further processing is done. This gives the developers a chance to declare their rules at different precedence levels.

The steps are the following:

- Trying to match the MediaTypeMappings (see Recipe 4-9).

- Inspecting the client's Accept header.

- Inspecting the client's Content-Type header.

- Checking whether serialization with any formatter (in the order they are registered) is possible.

If the content negotiation process does not yield any relevant formatter, then the Web API will issue a 406 Not Acceptable response to the client. However, this will never happen out of the box because, at worst, the JSON formatter will match any kind of request. As mentioned, you can alter this behavior by tweaking DefaultContentNegotiator, which has a designated constructor to achieve that result.

The Code

DefaultContentNegotiator has a constructor parameter that allows you to instruct it to skip checking on the last rule (trying to determine if the serialization is possible) and issue a 406 response immediately.

You can swap the registered IContentNegotiator with its modified version on your HttpConfiguration object.

```
var negotiator = new DefaultContentNegotiator(excludeMatchOnTypeOnly: true);
httpConfiguration.Services.Replace(typeof(IContentNegotiator), negotiator);
```

As a result, making an HTTP request, which expects an unsupported media type, will receive an automatic 406 Not Acceptable HTTP response, such as the one shown in Listing 6-22.

Listing 6-22. Request for an Unsupported Media Type and a 406 Response

```
GET http://localhost:999/api/values HTTP/1.1
User-Agent: Fiddler
Accept: text/plain
Host: localhost:999

HTTP/1.1 406 Not Acceptable
Content-Length: 0
Server: Microsoft-HTTPAPI/2.0
Date: Sun, 5 January 2014 13:31:45 GMT
```

6-7. Implement Versioning of a Web API with Centralized Routes

Problem

Your ASP.NET Web API application is usingCentralized routing and you would like to support versioning of your API resources/endpoints.

Solution

There are three primary ways of versioning a REST API:

- URI-based versioning

```
GET /api/Items HTTP 1.1
GET /api/v2/Items HTTP 1.1
```

- Header-based versioning

```
GET /api/Items HTTP 1.1
```

```
GET /api/Items HTTP 1.1
ApiVersion: 2
```

- Media type-based versioning

```
GET /api/Items HTTP 1.1
Accept: application/vnd.apress.recipes.webapi+json
```

```
GET /api/Items HTTP 1.1
Accept: application/vnd.apress.recipes.webapi-v2+json
```

URI-based versioning can be achieved using a customized routing definition. The latter two methods, header and accept-based versioning, can be supported using a custom IHttpControllerSelector.

How It Works

IHttpControllerSelector is responsible for taking in a request and finding a relevant controller to handle this request. The default implementation, DefaultHttpControllerSelector, gives precedence to attribute routing, and in case a matching controller can be found by inspecting routes registered with attribute routing, that particular controller is used.

If no match is found via attribute routing, DefaultHttpControllerSelector proceeds to try to obtain a controller name from the request (normally from RouteData). Then the string name of the controller is used to find a matching controller Type in the internal cache of controllers that it maintains. This GetControllerName method is virtual and provides excellent extensibility points for supporting versioning.

───

■ **Note**   The internals of routing in ASP.NET Web API are discussed in detail in Chapter 3.

───

The Code

In this section, you'll have a look at supporting different types of versioning for centralized routes. But before you do that, let's define some sample models and controllers, representing different versions of your API (Listing 6-23). You'll then use them throughout all of the examples.

Listing 6-23. Sample Models Representing Different Versions of Resources

```
public class Item
{
    public int Id { get; set; }

    public string Name { get; set; }

    public string Country { get; set; }
}

public class SuperItem : Item
{
    public double Price { get; set; }
}
```

Item is the basic version 1 resource, whereas SuperItem will be used in version 2 of your API. For simplicity of illustration, the sample controllers (Listing 6-24) will only have a single GET method, as all the other action will behave identically.

Listing 6-24. Sample Controllers Representing Different Versions of HTTP Endpoints

```
public class ItemsV2Controller : ApiController
{
    public SuperItem Get(int id)
    {
        return new SuperItem { Id = id, Name = "Xbox One", Country = "USA", Price = 529.99 };
    }
}

public class ItemsController : ApiController
{
    public Item Get(int id)
    {
        return new Item { Id = id, Name = "PS4", Country = "Japan"};
    }
}
```

In all of the cases, you'll resort to a custom IHttpControllerSelector. Creating a controller selector that will respect the version is actually very easy, as long as you can find the version correctly. A VersionAwareControllerSelector can be found in Listing 6-25.

Listing 6-25. Customized IHttpControllerSelector That Takes Versioning into Account

```
public class VersionAwareControllerSelector : DefaultHttpControllerSelector
{
    public VersionAwareControllerSelector(HttpConfiguration configuration) : base(configuration) { }

    public override string GetControllerName(HttpRequestMessage request)
    {
        var controllerName = base.GetControllerName(request);
        var version = ??? //find the version somehow!
```

```
    if (version > 0)
    {
        return GetVersionedControllerName(request, controllerName, version);
    }

    return controllerName;
}

private string GetVersionedControllerName(HttpRequestMessage request, string baseControllerName,
int version)
{
    var versionControllerName = string.Format("{0}v{1}", baseControllerName, version);
    HttpControllerDescriptor descriptor;
    if (GetControllerMapping().TryGetValue(versionControllerName, out descriptor))
    {
        return versionControllerName;
    }

    throw new HttpResponseException(request.CreateErrorResponse(
            HttpStatusCode.NotFound,
            String.Format("No HTTP resource was found that matches the URI {0} and version number {1}",
                request.RequestUri, version)));
    }
}
```

Instead of implementing the interface directly, you can inherit from `DefaultHttpControllerSelector`, since it has all the necessary logic and caching already, and exposes the methods necessary to support versioning as virtual members. The idea here is very simple: when the controller selector finds a controller, you'll try to pick a version from the `HttpRequestMessage` from URI or headers, and if you find it, the selector will try to find a versioned controller through a convention—named the same but with a `V{number}` suffix—and use that one instead.

URI-Based Versioning

In order to provide correct routing to specific version of the controller, you may define a relevant route for each of the versions.

```
config.Routes.MapHttpRoute("ItemsV2", "v2/items/{id}", new { controller = "ItemsV2",
id = RouteParameter.Optional });
config.Routes.MapHttpRoute("Items", "items/{id}", new { controller = "Items",
id = RouteParameter.Optional });
config.Routes.MapHttpRoute("default", "{controller}/{id}", new { id = RouteParameter.Optional });
```

In this case, a very specific template is provided to match the URI and use the relevant version of the controller based on that. Of course, this is hardly optimal since you'd have to maintain a lot of routes by hand.

An alternative solution is to create a generic route that contains a version parameter.

```
config.Routes.MapHttpRoute("defaultVersioned", "v{version}/{controller}/{id}", new
{ id = RouteParameter.Optional }, new { version = @"\d+" });
config.Routes.MapHttpRoute("default", "{controller}/{id}", new { id = RouteParameter.Optional });
```

It can coexist along the default unversioned route because the version parameter is constrained (using regular expression constraint) to be a number and to be preceded by a "v" so this route will match only very specific request URIs.

This alone will not work yet; you will have to somehow hint to Web API how it should use the route parameter representing a version to switch from the default controller to a versioned one. This can be achieved by implementing a custom IHttpControllerSelector.

But before doing that, let's create a helper class called VersionFinder, which you will use in this recipe (and also the next one) to pull out version information from an HttpRequestMessage. It's shown in Listing 6-26.

Listing 6-26. VersionFinder, Responsible for Looking Up a Version in HttpRequestMessage

```
public class VersionFinder
{
    private static bool NeedsUriVersioning(HttpRequestMessage request, out string version)
    {
        var routeData = request.GetRouteData();
        if (routeData != null)
        {
            object versionFromRoute;
            if (routeData.Values.TryGetValue("version", out versionFromRoute))
            {
                version = versionFromRoute as string;
                if (!string.IsNullOrWhiteSpace(version))
                {
                    return true;
                }
            }
        }

        version = null;
        return false;
    }

    private static int VersionToInt(string versionString)
    {
        int version;
        if (string.IsNullOrEmpty(versionString) || !int.TryParse(versionString, out version))
            return 0;

        return version;
    }

    public int GetVersionFromRequest(HttpRequestMessage request)
    {
        string version;
        if (NeedsUriVersioning(request, out version))
        {
            return VersionToInt(version);
        }

        return 0;
    }
}
```

The class exposes a single method, GetVersionFromRequest, which can be used to obtain a version from the client's request. You'll keep on extending it, but for now it only checks the URI and tries to pull out a version from RouteData (according to the route template you just defined moments ago). If a version is found, the number of the version is returned; otherwise, it is 0.

You can now update the VersionAwareControllerSelector to use the VersionFinder; see Listing 6-27.

Listing 6-27. Updated GetControllerName on the Custom Controller Selector, Using VersionFinder

```
public override string GetControllerName(HttpRequestMessage request)
{
    var controllerName = base.GetControllerName(request);
    var versionFinder = new VersionFinder();
    var version = versionFinder.GetVersionFromRequest(request);

    if (version > 0)
    {
        return GetVersionedControllerName(request, controllerName, version);
    }

    return controllerName;
}
```

One final thing is to register the selector as the one to be used by your API.

```
config.Services.Replace(typeof(IHttpControllerSelector), new VersionAwareControllerSelector(config));
```

And that's all; you can now make requests such as

```
GET /api/Items HTTP 1.1
GET /api/v2/Items HTTP 1.1
```

and they will be routed properly to ItemsController and ItemsV2Controller.

Header-Based Versioning

In the previous example, with classes like VersionAwareControllerSelector and VersionFinder, you laid the groundwork for the entire versioning infrastructure. Supporting different versioning mechanisms is therefore actually extremely easy.

In order to allow your API to work with a relevant version header, say ApiVersion in this case, it's just a matter of extending the VersionFinder to look into the headers, instead of just the URI. There is no need to change anything anymore in the VersionAwareControllerSelector. The method shown in Listing 6-28 should be added to VersionFinder, and GetVersionFromRequest should be updated accordingly.

Listing 6-28. Updated VersionFinder, Supporting Header-Based Versioning

```
private static bool NeedsHeaderVersioning(HttpRequestMessage request, out string version)
{
    if (request.Headers.Contains("ApiVersion"))
    {
        version = request.Headers.GetValues("ApiVersion").FirstOrDefault();
        if (version != null)
```

```
        {
            return true;
        }
    }

    version = null;
    return false;
}

public int GetVersionFromRequest(HttpRequestMessage request)
{
    string version;
    if (NeedsUriVersioning(request, out version))
    {
        return VersionToInt(version);
    }

    if (NeedsHeaderVersioning(request, out version))
    {
        return VersionToInt(version);
    }

    return 0;
}
```

And that's it. This small tweak now allows your API to support the following requests:

```
GET /api/Items HTTP 1.1

GET /api/Items HTTP 1.1
ApiVersion: 2
```

Media Type-Based Versioning

Versioning based on media types is a very powerful mechanism, as it allows you to decouple versioning of the resource from both the versioning of the format and the protocol that it uses.

To support it in Web API, all you need to do, similar to the previous example, is just extend your VersionFinder to look into the Accept header and try to extract the version number from there. This is shown in Listing 6-29.

Listing 6-29. Updated VersionFinder, Supporting Accept-Based Versioning

```
private static bool NeedsAcceptVersioning(HttpRequestMessage request, out string version)
{
    if (request.Headers.Accept.Any())
    {
        var acceptHeaderVersion =
            request.Headers.Accept.FirstOrDefault(x => x.MediaType.Contains("vnd.apress.recipes.
webapi"));
        if (acceptHeaderVersion != null && acceptHeaderVersion.MediaType.Contains("-v") &&
            acceptHeaderVersion.MediaType.Contains("+"))
        {
```

```
                version = acceptHeaderVersion.MediaType.Between("-v", "+");
                return true;
            }
        }

        version = null;
        return false;
    }

    public int GetVersionFromRequest(HttpRequestMessage request)
    {
        string version;
        if (NeedsUriVersioning(request, out version))
        {
            return VersionToInt(version);
        }

        if (NeedsAcceptVersioning(request, out version))
        {
            return VersionToInt(version);
        }

        if (NeedsHeaderVersioning(request, out version))
        {
            return VersionToInt(version);
        }

        return 0;
    }
```

With this change in place, your API will now extract a version out of the media type, but only in cases when such an operation is possible. This allows you to respond with a relevant version to the following requests:

```
GET /api/Items HTTP 1.1
Accept: application/vnd.apress.recipes.webapi+json

GET /api/Items HTTP 1.1
Accept: application/vnd.apress.recipes.webapi-v2+json
```

Notice that in this final version of the VersionFinder, you have all three versioning mechanisms working side by side, and you can change the precedence by shuffling around the checks inside the GetVersionFromRequest method.

6-8. Implement Versioning of a Web API with Attribute Routing
Problem

Your Web API application is using attribute routing and you would like to support versioning of your API resources/endpoints.

Solution

The core API versioning possibilities were mentioned in Recipe 6-7. All of them can be supported with attribute routing.

- URI-based versioning: Already supported through the nature of attribute routing; it's just a matter of defining a correct route template on the relevant controller.

- Header-based versioning: Through a custom RouteFactoryAttribute.

- Media type-based versioning: Also through a custom RouteFactoryAttribute.

To cover all of these scenarios, and to follow the convention from Recipe 6-7, such a v{number} controller can be decorated with routing attributes in the manner shown in the following code snippet, where VersionedRoute is a custom implementation of RouteFactoryAttribute able to recognize the relevant version:

```
public class ItemsV2Controller : ApiController
{
    [VersionedRoute("items/{id:int}", Version = 2)]
    [Route("v2/items/{id:int}")]
    public HttpResponseMessage Get(int id)
    {
        // omitted for brevity
    }
}
```

How It Works

The DefaultHttpControllerSelector will give attribute routing priority. It will try to match the incoming request with attribute routes by calling the internal GetDirectRouteCandidates on the HttpRouteData. If nothing is found, the selector goes on to the process of looking up matches among the traditional routes registered by hand.

RouteFactoryAttribute is a convenience abstract class implementing IDirectRouteFactory (Listing 6-30). By implementing this interface or extending RouteFactoryAttribute, you are able to extend the attribute routing mechanism, providing, for example, custom constraints (the default RouteAttribute also implements it).

Listing 6-30. Definition of IDirectRouteFactory

```
public interface IDirectRouteFactory
{
    RouteEntry CreateRoute(DirectRouteFactoryContext context);
}
```

The Code

The approach to versioning with attribute routing is similar to that from Recipe 6-7; however, there is no IHttpControllerSelector in play. You'll still use VersionFinder in the exact same format as in Recipe 6-7 to extract a version number from the incoming HttprequestMessage.

Let's declare the following test controllers and incorporate the versioning support in a way that ItemsV2Controller is the version 2 of ItemsController. The models used here were also defined in Recipe 6-7.

Listing 6-31. Sample Controller Using Attribute Routing and its v2 Version

```
public class ItemsController : ApiController
{
    [Route("items/{id:int}")]
    public Item Get(int id)
    {
        return new Item { Id = id, Name = "PS4", Country = "Japan"};
    }
}

public class ItemsV2Controller : ApiController
{
    [???] //see examples in this recipe
    public SuperItem Get(int id)
    {
        return new SuperItem { Id = id, Name = "Xbox One", Country = "USA", Price = 529.99 };
    }
}
```

URI-Based Versioning

Route declaration directly on the controller or action is the very nature of attribute routing. Therefore, supporting a v{next} route is as simple as decorating the v{next} controller with the appropriate RouteAttribute. This is shown in Listing 6-32.

Listing 6-32. Supporting URI-Based Versioning with Attribute Routing

```
public class ItemsV2Controller : ApiController
{
    [Route("v2/items/{id:int}")]
    public SuperItem Get(int id)
    {
        //omitted for brevity
    }
}
```

This does not collide with the original route and enables the client to call both of the following endpoints without any extra setup:

```
GET /api/Items HTTP 1.1
GET /api/v2/Items HTTP 1.1
```

Header-Based and Media Type-Based Versioning

The only difference between header-based and media-based versions is how the version is obtained from the HttpRequestMessage (in the former case from ApiVersion header, in the latter from the Accept header), and since this has already been handled by VersionFinder (again, see Recipe 6-8 for details) all that's left to do to incorporate support for attribute routing is to create a custom VersionConstraint (IHttpRouteConstraint) and a RouteFactoryAttribute that will respect that version constraint (see Listing 6-33).

Listing 6-33. Definition of the VersionConstraint, a Custom IHttpRouteConstraint Recognizing API Versions

```
public class VersionConstraint : IHttpRouteConstraint
{
    private readonly int _version;

    public VersionConstraint(int version)
    {
        _version = version;
    }

    public bool Match(HttpRequestMessage request, IHttpRoute route, string parameterName,
        IDictionary<string, object> values, HttpRouteDirection routeDirection)
    {
        var versionFinder = new VersionFinder();
        var version = versionFinder.GetVersionFromRequest(request);
        return _version == version;
    }
}
```

The VersionConstraint instance is specific to a given version number. This will be provided by the developer annotating his API endpoint. In the Match method, you look into the VersionFinder and try to compare the version extracted from the request with the one set on the constraint. The match is represented by trying to equate both of those values.

The new route attribute is shown in Listing 6-34. It will take a version as a parameter, and constrain the route using the VersionConstraint. Since the default value of int is 0, if it's not set, the constraint will use version 0, which matches the default response of VersionFinder (recall that if it doesn't find a version in the HttpRequestMessage, it will return 0 too).

Listing 6-34. Definition of VersionedRouteAttribute

```
public class VersionedRouteAttribute : RouteFactoryAttribute
{
    public VersionedRouteAttribute(string template) : base(template)
    {
        Order = -1;
    }

    public int Version { get; set; }

    public override IDictionary<string, object> Constraints
    {
        get
        {
            return new HttpRouteValueDictionary
            {
                {"", new VersionConstraint(Version)}
            };
        }
    }
}
```

With these bits in place, you may now decorate your controllers with the new VersionedRouteAttribute, instead of the default RouteAttribute. On the other hand, they are not mutually exclusive, and you can use them together as well, like in Listing 6-35.

Listing 6-35. Versioned Controllers Decorated with Version-Aware VersionedRouteAttribute

```
public class ItemsController : ApiController
{
    [VersionedRoute("items/{id:int}")] //version = 0, so default
    public Item Get(int id)
    {
        return new Item { Id = id, Name = "PS4", Country = "Japan"};
    }
}

public class ItemsV2Controller : ApiController
{
    [VersionedRoute("items/{id:int}", Version = 2)]
    [Route("v2/items/{id:int}")]
    public SuperItem Get(int id)
    {
        return new SuperItem { Id = id, Name = "Xbox One", Country = "USA", Price = 529.99 };
    }
}
```

This setup allows you to easily support all of the following versioned API calls:

```
GET /api/Items HTTP 1.1

GET /api/Items HTTP 1.1
ApiVersion: 2

GET /api/Items HTTP 1.1
Accept: application/vnd.apress.recipes.webapi+json

GET /api/Items HTTP 1.1
Accept: application/vnd.apress.recipes.webapi-v2+json
```

6-9. Use Custom HTTP Content

Problem

You previously implemented a custom MediaTypeFormatter, but would now like to move closer to the core System.Net.Http HTTP abstractions when handling HTTP requests in your Web API application.

Solution

You can build a custom HttpContent implementation, which could be a wrapper for any specific media type you wish. This is a very powerful technique as it allows you to package the media type into very clean, reusable logic (potentially even in custom formatters), which can be used both on the server and the .NET client side.

Building custom content means extending the base HttpContent class and implementing, at the very least, its two abstract methods, as highlighted in Listing 6-36.

Listing 6-36. Definition of the Abstract HttpContent

```
public abstract class HttpContent : IDisposable
{
    protected HttpContent();
    public HttpContentHeaders Headers { get; }
    public Task CopyToAsync(Stream stream);
    public Task CopyToAsync(Stream stream, TransportContext context);
    protected virtual Task<Stream> CreateContentReadStreamAsync();
    public void Dispose();
    protected virtual void Dispose(bool disposing);
    public Task LoadIntoBufferAsync();
    public Task LoadIntoBufferAsync(long maxBufferSize);
    public Task<byte[]> ReadAsByteArrayAsync();
    public Task<Stream> ReadAsStreamAsync();
    public Task<string> ReadAsStringAsync();
    protected abstract Task SerializeToStreamAsync(Stream stream, TransportContext context);
    protected internal abstract bool TryComputeLength(out long length);
}
```

You can then follow up by writing useful extension methods for both HttpClient and HttpContent, responsible for sending the custom content over the network, and for reading it into the relevant target format.

How It Works

SerializeToStreamAsync is responsible for writing the object contained by the HttpContent to the response or request Stream (depending on the type of message being constructed).

TryComputeLength is used to provide the Content-Length header of the body of the HTTP message; to support that in a custom content implementation, you can simply return the length of the Stream representing the object you are wrapping in the HttpContent. However, the method itself does not have to return a valid content length in every case (hence the Try prefix). You might set it to 0 and return false if you wish to operate in *chunked transfer encoding* or in general are dealing with streamed resources of unknown length.

The Code

Let's have a look at building a custom HttpContent implementation for protocol buffers, using protobuf-net. The idea is very simple: in the constructor you can pass in a model to be serialized into the appropriate format and saved into a MemoryStream. Then, in the SerializeToStreamAsync you can simply copy the saved Stream into the HTTP message Stream, which will be passed into the method, as shown in Listing 6-37.

Listing 6-37. Definition of the Custom ProtoBufContent

```
public class ProtoBufContent : HttpContent
{
    private readonly MemoryStream _stream;

    public ProtoBufContent(object model)
    {
        _stream = new MemoryStream();
```

```
    Serializer.Serialize(_stream, model);
    _stream.Position = 0;
    Headers.ContentType = new MediaTypeHeaderValue("application/x-protobuf");
}

protected override Task SerializeToStreamAsync(Stream stream, TransportContext context)
{
    return _stream.CopyToAsync(stream);
}

protected override bool TryComputeLength(out long length)
{
    if (!_stream.CanSeek)
    {
        length = 0;
        return false;
    }

    length = _stream.Length;
    return true;
}

protected override void Dispose(bool disposing)
{
    _stream.Dispose();
}
}
```

Using the new custom content is as easy as setting it as part of either HttpRequestMessage or HttpResponseMessage (see Listing 6-38). Obviously, if you do that from the controller, you are also going to bypass the ASP.NET Web API content negotiation process.

Listing 6-38. Using the ProtoBufContent in a Controller

```
public HttpResponseMessage Get()
{
    var item = new Item
    {
        Id = 1,
        Name = "Filip"
    };

    return new HttpResponseMessage(HttpStatusCode.OK)
    {
        Content = new ProtoBufContent(item)
    };
}
```

To further simplify the process of dealing with protocol buffers, you can now provide convenient extension methods for the base HttpContent class and for HttpClient, which will enhance the ProtobufContent operations. They are shown in Listing 6-39.

Listing 6-39. Definitions of the ProtoBufContent-Aware Extensions Methods for HttpContent and HttpClient

```
public static class HttpContentExtensions
{
    public static async Task<T> ReadAsProtoBuf<T>(this HttpContent content)
    {
        return Serializer.Deserialize<T>(await content.ReadAsStreamAsync());
    }
}

public static class HttpClientExtensions
{
    public static async Task<HttpResponseMessage> PostAsProtoBufAsync<T>(this HttpClient client,
    string address, T obj)
    {
        return await client.PostAsync(address, new ProtoBufContent(obj));
    }
}
```

With the HttpContent extension, you can quickly deserialize the response into a statically typed predefined object. On the other hand, by using the HttpClient extensions, you can provide quick and easy access to performing core HTTP operations, such as POST or GET, using the custom HttpContent. Those operations are shown in Listing 6-40.

Listing 6-40. Using the ProtoBufContent-Aware Extensions Methods for HttpContent and HttpClient

```
//HttpContent extension
var item = await Request.Content.ReadAsProtoBuf<Item>();

//HttpClient extension
var itemToSend = new Item {Id = 10, Name = "Filip"};
var response = await client.PostAsProtoBufAsync(address, itemToSend);
```

■ ■ ■

CHAPTER 7

Exceptions, Troubleshooting, and Documenting

This chapter covers dealing with exceptions in ASP.NET Web API, debugging issues with ASP.NET Web API tracers, and documenting your API endpoints with the ASP.NET Web API Help Page library.

You will learn how to do the following:

- Handle and log exceptions (Recipes 7-1, 7-2, and 7-3)

- Use Web API tracers (Recipes 7-4, 7-5, and 7-6)

- Write a custom Web API tracer (Recipe 7-7)

- Add a Web API help page (Recipe 7-8)

- Customize a Web API help page (Recipes 7-9, 7-10, and 7-11)

7-1. Handle Exceptions with Filters
Problem

You need a simple mechanism for handling exceptions that might occur in your controllers' actions.

Solution

It is common to deal with cross-cutting concerns through the use of filters. You can subclass an `ExceptionFilterAttribute` and apply it selectively to a specific scope of your API:

- Individual actions (action level)

- All actions within a controller (controller level)

- All actions in the API (global level)

While ASP.NET Web API provides a way of handling all errors globally (see Recipe 7-2), it is still quite useful to be able to target specific actions with relevant exception handling mechanisms, rather than relying only on the global one.

How It Works

In ASP.NET Web API, the exception filters will catch all of the errors that happen inside an action, as well as those from inside any action filter, except for authorization and authentication exceptions as they are located higher in the execution pipeline.

When `ApiController` executes a Web API action guarded by an exception filter, instead of invoking it directly, it wraps it in an `ExceptionFilterResult` (a special implementation of `IHttpActionResult`). The `ExceptionFilterResult` captures all exceptions and then respects the error handling logic defined in the appropriate exception filters by passing the captured exception to them for processing.

`ExceptionFilterAttribute` implements an `IExceptionFilter` interface, and while you might go ahead and implement your logic around the latter, the attribute version is a much easier starting point. See Listing 7-1.

Listing 7-1. IExceptionFilter Interface Defintion

```
public interface IExceptionFilter : IFilter
{
    Task ExecuteExceptionFilterAsync(HttpActionExecutedContext actionExecutedContext,
    CancellationToken cancellationToken);
}
```

The attribute exposes two core methods to override, for both synchronous and asynchronous exception handling. See Listing 7-2.

Listing 7-2. Base Abstract ExceptionFilterAttribute Defintion

```
public abstract class ExceptionFilterAttribute : FilterAttribute, IExceptionFilter
{
    public virtual void OnException(HttpActionExecutedContext actionExecutedContext)
    {}

    public virtual Task OnExceptionAsync(HttpActionExecutedContext actionExecutedContext,
    CancellationToken cancellationToken)
    {}
}
```

The Code

Consider an example of a custom exception that is raised by your application whenever a specific resource has been permanently deleted. You can use the filter shown in Listing 7-3 to handle it.

Listing 7-3. A Sample ExceptionFilterAttribute

```
public class ResourceRemovedException : Exception { }

public class ResourceRemovedAttribute : ExceptionFilterAttribute
{
    public override void OnException(HttpActionExecutedContext actionExecutedContext)
    {
        if (actionExecutedContext.Exception is ResourceRemovedException)
        {
            actionExecutedContext.Response = new HttpResponseMessage(HttpStatusCode.Gone);
        }
    }
}
```

The custom filter will catch the exception and convert it into a response that is handy for the client, the HTTP 410 Gone response.

```
[ResourceRemoved]
public HttpResponseMessage Get(int id)
{
  //some service accessed here throws ResourceRemovedException
}
```

Since exception handling can also be done asynchronously, you are able to take advantage of the APIs that are remote or expensive to call in a much easier way, without blocking a thread. For example, you could have some application-wide logging that allows you to log to a database in an asynchronous manner, as shown in Listing 7-4.

Listing 7-4. Async Call Done from Inside the Exception Filter

```
public class ResourceRemovedAttribute : ExceptionFilterAttribute
{
    public async override Task OnExceptionAsync(HttpActionExecutedContext actionExecutedContext)
    {
        if (actionExecutedContext.Exception is ResourceRemovedException)
        {
            actionExecutedContext.Response = new HttpResponseMessage(HttpStatusCode.Gone);
            await MyLogging.LogToDbAsync(actionExecutedContext.Exception); //example async call
        }
    }
}
```

7-2. Handle Exceptions Globally
Problem

You want to have a single place to handle all ASP.NET Web API exceptions, similar to an ASP.NET Application_Error event, except Web API-specific. It should also be compatible with all types of Web API hosts.

Solution

Since version 2.1, ASP.NET Web API exposes a very convenient mechanism for handling exceptions globally: IExceptionHandler. It allows you to catch exceptions from almost everywhere within the API:

- Action execution
- Controller initialization
- All filters (even exceptions thrown by exception filters)
- Some MessageHandlers
- Routing exceptions
- In some cases, MediaTypeFormatter exceptions

How It Works

IExceptionHandler, shown in Listing 7-5, exposes only a single method to implement, but like most Web API services, it's much easier to work off the base abstract implementations instead (see Listing 7-6).

Listing 7-5. The Defintion of the IExceptionHandler Interface

```
public interface IExceptionHandler
{
    Task HandleAsync(ExceptionHandlerContext context, CancellationToken cancellationToken);
}
```

Listing 7-6. Outline of the Abstract ExceptionHandler Which Should Be Used as a Base for Custom Handlers

```
public class ExceptionHandler : IExceptionHandler
{
    public virtual void Handle(ExceptionHandlerContext context)
    {
      //can be overriden
    }

    public virtual Task HandleAsync(ExceptionHandlerContext context, CancellationToken
    cancellationToken)
    {
      //can be overriden
    }

    public virtual bool ShouldHandle(ExceptionHandlerContext context)
    {
      //can be overriden
    }
}
```

You are able to override the method responsible for handling the occurring exception and the base class actually exposes the way to do it in both a synchronous and asynchronous way.

The Web API exception handling pipeline supports a single handler only. The exception details are exposed to the handler through `ExceptionHandlerContext`. It exposes an `ExceptionContext` property, which, through its own public properties, provides some key exception information such as `HttpActionContext`, `HttpRequestContext`, `HttpRequestMessage`, `HttpResponseMessage`, or the actual exception. Those can be used to log or handle the exception state of your Web API application appropriately.

BEWARE OF THE EXCEPTIONCONTEXT

Because the exception can be raised from different places in the Web API pipeline, there is no guarantee that some of the properties on the `ExceptionContext` will not be `null`.

For example, an exception raised by a `MessageHandler` will not have an `HttpActionContext`. This has to be kept in mind when you develop custom handler or logger (Recipe 7-3).

The Code

A sample of a customized `ExceptionHandler` is shown in Listing 7-8. Imagine that you want to intercept an unhandled exception, create an exception ID so that your support staff can identify the exception later, and issue your client a content-negotiated response with some generic information about the error, as well as the attached exception ID (a model for that is shown in Listing 7-7).

Listing 7-7. An Example of a DTO Wrapper Class Used for the Publicly Available Application Error Information

```
public class ErrorData
{
    public string Message { get; set; }
    public DateTime DateTime { get; set; }
    public Uri RequestUri { get; set; }
    public Guid ErrorId { get; set; }
}
```

The `ExceptionHandler` should be capable of returning a content-negotiated response; therefore it will use the `CreateResponse` extension method off the `HttpRequestMessage` (for more on this, see Recipe 4-3). You instruct the Web API pipeline to use a specific response by setting the `Result` property (which should be an instance of `IHttpActionResult`) on the `ExceptionHandlerContext`. Registration of the custom handler happens against `HttpConfiguration`.

Listing 7-8. An Implementation of a Sample ExceptionHandler

```
public class ContentNegotiatedExceptionHandler : ExceptionHandler
{
    public override void Handle(ExceptionHandlerContext context)
    {
        var metadata = new ErrorData
        {
            Message = "An unexpected error occurred! Please use the ticket ID to contact support",
            DateTime = DateTime.Now,
            RequestUri = context.Request.RequestUri,
            ErrorId = Guid.NewGuid()
        };
```

```
        //log the metadata.ErrorId and the correlated Exception info to your DB/logs
        //or, if you have IExceptionLogger (recipe 7-3), it will already have been logged
      //omitted here for brevity
        var response = context.Request.CreateResponse(HttpStatusCode.InternalServerError, metadata);
        context.Result = new ResponseMessageResult(response);
    }
}
```

ResponseMessageResult is an IHttpActionResult implementation, which doesn't do anything except forward an existing HttpResponseMessage instance directly to the client. It is a convenient helper in situations like the one in Listing 7-8, where you have an instance of HttpResponseMessage that you'd like to send to the client, but the framework expects an IHttpActionResult instead.

Registration of the handler is extremely simple; it only takes a single line of replacing the default IExceptionHandler (the default one is a null-pattern implementation, so it does nothing).

```
config.Services.Replace(typeof(IExceptionHandler), new ContentNegotiatedExceptionHandler());
```

As a result, the client who encounters an exception on its request will get a content-negotiated response that will contain all the relevant metadata you want it to receive, as shown in Listing 7-9.

Listing 7-9. A Sample Response from the ExceptionHandler Built in this Chapter

```
Status: 500 Internal Server Error
{
    Message: "An unexpected error occurred! Please use the ticket ID to contact support",
    DateTime: "2014-01-19T14:07:49.0218346+01:00",
    RequestUri: "http://localhost:999/api/my",
    ErrorId: "3e6530ce-7530-40e9-8ec7-0aa60d0ed756"
}
```

7-3. Log Exceptions Globally
Problem

You would like to be able to log all of the exceptions happening in your Web API application, regardless of whether IExceptionHandler is able to handle them or not.

Solution

Alongside IExceptionHandler (Recipe 7-2), ASP.NET Web API, since version 2.1, provides a second exception-related interface: IExceptionLogger. Its only role is to log exceptions rather than handle them. By implementing a custom IExceptionLogger you are able to centralize all exception logging in a single place, as well as log those of the exceptions that are normally uncatchable by IExceptionHandler.

How It Works

While both IExceptionLogger and IExceptionHandler seem similar at first glance, there is a clear difference between the two. The former only supports logging an exception, while the latter allows you to respond with a specific error response.

There are some situations where you may want to only log a response, and let the default Web API pipeline respond to the client. Furthermore, it is also possible that an exception is thrown at the time when a response to the client has already be sent; a good example might be a MediaTypeFormatter error while streaming a response body to the client, after the headers have already been sent. At that point, the only thing left to do is to log the error.

Just like IExceptionHandler, IExceptionLogger constitutes a single method to implement (Listing 7-10). In addition to that, the framework ships with an abstract base called ExceptionLogger which makes it easier to create custom implementations (Listing 7-11).

Listing 7-10. Definition of the IExceptionLogger Interface

```
public interface IExceptionLogger
{
    Task LogAsync(ExceptionLoggerContext context, CancellationToken cancellationToken);
}
```

Listing 7-11. Outline of the Abstract ExceptionLogger Which Should Be Used as a Base for Custom Loggers

```
public abstract class ExceptionLogger : IExceptionLogger
{
    public virtual Task LogAsync(ExceptionLoggerContext context, CancellationToken
    cancellationToken)
    {
      //can be overriden
    }

    public virtual void Log(ExceptionLoggerContext context)
    {
      //can be overriden
    }

    public virtual bool ShouldLog(ExceptionLoggerContext context)
    {
      //can be overriden
    }
}
```

Contrary to exception handlers, of which only a single one can be registered against your application, Web API supports multiple loggers. Each logger can make its own decision about participating in the logging process through the ShouldLog method. Exception details are exposed to the logger through ExceptionLoggerContext. It exposes an ExceptionContext property, which is the same as in the ExceptionHandler case (see Recipe 7-2).

The Code

A custom logger is extremely easy to implement. The example in Listing 7-11 creates one that is NLog-based. NLog is a popular logging framework for .NET and can be installed from NuGet:

```
install-package NLog
```

NLog can be used to write to a number of different logging targets such as log files, database, email, or an event log. It exposes its Logger instance through a static method called LogManager.GetCurrentClassLogger, which will be used in this recipe to build a custom IExceptionLogger (Listing 7-12).

Listing 7-12. Implementation of IExceptionLogger Wrapped Around NLog

```
public class NLogExceptionLogger : ExceptionLogger
{
    private static readonly Logger Nlog = LogManager.GetCurrentClassLogger();
    public override void Log(ExceptionLoggerContext context)
    {
        Nlog.LogException(LogLevel.Error, RequestToString(context.Request), context.Exception);
    }

    private static string RequestToString(HttpRequestMessage request)
    {
        var message = new StringBuilder();
        if (request.Method != null)
            message.Append(request.Method);

        if (request.RequestUri != null)
            message.Append(" ").Append(request.RequestUri);

        return message.ToString();
    }
}
```

The logger simply grabs the ExceptionLoggerContext, produces some basic info based on the request (HttpRequestMessage and exception properties are never null in the pipeline), and passes it, along with the exception, to NLog.

Let's consider an NLog configuration, such as the one shown in Listing 7-13, which logs to EventLog.

Listing 7-13. Sample NLog Configuration Responsible for Writing to EventLog

```
<configuration>
  <configSections>
    <section name="nlog" type="NLog.Config.ConfigSectionHandler, NLog"/>
  </configSections>
    <startup>
        <supportedRuntime version="v4.0" sku=".NETFramework,Version=v4.5" />
    </startup>
  <nlog xmlns:xsi="http://www.w3.org/2001/XMLSchema-instance">
    <targets>
      <target name="eventlog" xsi:type="EventLog" layout="${message} ${exception:format=tostring}"
log="Application" source="My Web API Application" />
    </targets>
    <rules>
      <logger name="*" minlevel="Trace" writeTo="eventlog" />
    </rules>
  </nlog>
</configuration>
```

Any exception thrown from the ASP.NET Web API pipeline will be logged in the Event Log with all the necessary details, as long as the logger is registered in the HttpConfiguration. See Listing 7-14 for an example of such a log entry.

Notice that you *add* a new logger instead of *replacing* any existing one, since multiple loggers are supported. You could keep adding different ones (responsible for writing to different output targets) here.

Registration is done like any other Web API service registration.

```
httpConfiguration.Services.Add(typeof(IExceptionLogger), new NLogExceptionLogger());
```

Listing 7-14. Sample Error Entry from the Event Log

```
GET http://localhost:999/api/my System.InvalidOperationException: unable to cast string "hello" into
int
   at Apress.Recipes.WebApi.SelfHost.MyController.Get(IEnumerable`1 numbers) in d:\Dropbox\apress\
code\Apress.Recipes.WebApi.SelfHost\Apress.Recipes.WebApi.SelfHost\Program.cs:line 85
   at lambda_method(Closure , Object , Object[] )
   at System.Web.Http.Controllers.ReflectedHttpActionDescriptor.ActionExecutor.<>c__DisplayClass10.<
GetExecutor>b__9(Object instance, Object[] methodParameters)
   at System.Web.Http.Controllers.ReflectedHttpActionDescriptor.ActionExecutor.Execute(Object
instance, Object[] arguments)
   at System.Web.Http.Controllers.ReflectedHttpActionDescriptor.ExecuteAsync(HttpControllerContext
controllerContext, IDictionary`2 arguments, CancellationToken cancellationToken)
```

■ **Tip**   The WebApiContrib project contains a very interesting package, WebApiContrib.Logging.Raygun, which is an IExceptionLogger built to support the raygun.io error management service.

7-4. Add a Tracer
Problem

To troubleshoot a problem in your Web API application, you would like to inspect exactly what is happening internally in the request pipeline on each HTTP call.

Solution

ASP.NET Web API provides a very handy tracing mechanism wrapped around a public interface called ITraceWriter, which logs all internal operations of the Web API throughout its entire processing pipeline. The Web API team ships a very basic implementation called SystemDiagnosticsTraceWriter, which writes its output to System. Diagnostics.Trace.

■ **Note**   SystemDiagnosticsTraceWriter is not part of the core Web API. You have to pull down that package from NuGet: Microsoft.AspNet.WebApi.TraceWriter.

How It Works

ITraceWriter is extremely simple and consists of just a single method (see Listing 7-15), responsible for writing a TraceRecord to any output at the appropriate TraceLevel. It always has access to the current HTTP request message, too.

Listing 7-15. Definition of the ITraceWriter Interface

```
public interface ITraceWriter
{
    void Trace(HttpRequestMessage request, string category, TraceLevel level,
    Action<TraceRecord> traceAction) {}
}
```

Trace creates a new TraceRecord off a current HTTP request, with a specific TraceLevel (which is an enumeration). It is then up to the developer to deal with it; in the case of the default implementation, it outputs the record to System.Diagnostics.Trace.

The trace levels used by Web API are the following:

- TraceLevel.Info
- TraceLevel.Debug
- TraceLevel.Error
- TraceLevel.Fatal
- TraceLevel.Warn

The Code

To enable tracing in your ASP.NET Web API service, you can simply walk up to your Web API configuration and register TraceWriter against it. You can do it like you would register any other service, or through an extension method that the package provides. This is shown in Listing 7-16.

Listing 7-16. Registration of ITraceWriter

```
//regular registration
httpConfiguration.Services.Replace(typeof(ITraceWriter), new SystemDiagnosticsTraceWriter());

//through an extension method
httpConfiguration.EnableSystemDiagnosticsTracing();
```

In the first case, the tracer can also be configured in terms of verbosity and detail level, while the extension method automatically sets it to TraceLevel.Info.

```
httpConfiguration.Services.Replace(typeof(ITraceWriter), new SystemDiagnosticsTraceWriter() {
TraceLevel = TraceLevel.Error } );
```

From that point on, all ASP.NET Web API internal activities are logged to the Trace output.

7-5. Use an External Tracer

Problem

You are using a popular logging framework (such as NLog or log4net) and would like the ASP.NET Web API tracing output to be redirected to it.

Solution

You need to add an adapter between the logging framework of your choice and the `ITraceWriter`. However, the good news is that there is no need to reinvent the wheel, as the WebApiContrib project already provides a handful of logging solutions which are ready to be used:

- `WebApiContrib.Tracing.Log4Net`
- `WebApiContrib.Tracing.Nlog`

How It Works

Similarly to the default `TraceWriter` example, the authors of these adapters utilize custom `ITraceWriter` implementations to translate the `TraceRecord` to a log message understandable by the relevant logging framework. Additionally, the ASP.NET Web API log levels have to be mapped to the corresponding framework log levels.

The Code

All WebApiContrib packages are available on NuGet, so adding them to your API solution is as simple as running the NuGet installation:

```
install-package WebApiContrib.Tracing.Nlog
install-package WebApiContrib.Tracing.Log4Net
```

Enabling the custom tracers is done in the same way as registering the default `TraceWriter`. For example, NLog is enabled like so:

```
httpConfiguration.Services.Replace(typeof(ITraceWriter), new NlogTraceWriter());
```

When ASP.NET Web API runs now, it will log all of its operations to the NLog output. These include things like controller dispatching, action selection, filter execution, content negotiation, and formatting.

■ **Note** Remember that this relies on NLog being properly configured in your application already.

You would normally configure NLog in the root configuration file of your application, such as `web.config` for Web-based API and `app.config` for self-hosted API. The intent here isn't to go into details about NLog's capabilities (which are actually extremely vast), but config examples might look something like Listings 7-17 and 7-18.

Listing 7-17. An NLog ConfigSection for Your Application's Configuration File

```
<section name="nlog" type="NLog.Config.ConfigSectionHandler, NLog"/>
```

The actual configuration is in Listing 7-18.

Listing 7-18. A Sample NLog Configuration Directing All Output to a Text File

```
<nlog xmlns:xsi="http://www.w3.org/2001/XMLSchema-instance">
<targets>
    <target name="logfile" xsi:type="File" fileName="${basedir}/${date:format=yyyy-MM-dd}-webapi.log" />
</targets>
<rules>
    <logger name="*" minlevel="Trace" writeTo="logfile" />
</rules>
</nlog>
```

7-6. Call the Tracer Manually
Problem

You are already using an ASP.NET Web API tracer in your application. However, instead of just having the Web API pipeline log its internal messages to it, you would like to write your own custom log entries there as well.

Solution

ASP.NET Web API allows you to always grab an instance of the registered tracer through the global HttpConfiguration object and use it as your own logging mechanism. This results in a coherent logging experience and saves you the hassle of having to manually inject (and manage) a custom logger into different parts of your Web API application.

To grab an instance of a tracer, you simply need to retrieve it from the current HttpConfiguration:

```
var tracer = httpConfiguration.Services.GetTraceWriter();
```

The registered ITraceWriter can also be obtained off a current HttpRequestMessage (since the request always has access to HttpConfiguration) at any point in the Web API pipeline.

```
var tracer = request.GetConfiguration().Services.GetTraceWriter();
```

Since, as shown, the tracer is available throughout the life cycle of the HTTP request, you can get a hold of it in all key Web API artifacts (filters, message handlers, formatters, or controllers).

Interestingly, even in situations where you don't have access to the current HttpRequestMessage (e.g. in your custom services), when running a web-hosted Web API, you can still obtain an instance of the logger through the static global GlobalConfiguration object if you are using the web host. This isn't necessarily the best practice, but might come in handy at times.

```
var tracer = GlobalConfiguration.Configuration.Services.GetTraceWriter();
```

How It Works

Custom trace messages will appear in between the internal Web API trace messages; if you registered some external provider as your ITraceWriter (i.e. NLog), obviously the custom messages will also be written there.

What's critical for debugging purposes is that you will also see the messages in the correct chronological context, which can often help you identify whether things like model binding or formatting have already run or not.

The Code

As an example, say you want to always grab the tracer in the controller's constructor, and then use it in whichever action you want. This is shown in Listing 7-19.

Listing 7-19. A Sample Controller Calling the Currently Registered Tracer by Hand

```
public class DemoController : ApiController
    {
    private readonly ITraceWriter _tracer;

    public DemoController()
    {
        _tracer = Request.GetConfiguration().Services.GetTraceWriter();
    }

    public HttpResponseMessage Get()
    {
    _tracer.Info(Request, this.ControllerContext.ControllerDescriptor.ControllerType.FullName,
    "I'm inside Get method!");

    return new HttpResponseMessage();
    }
}
```

If you recall from previous recipes, ITraceWriter is a simple interface with just one method, which makes advanced usage scenarios rather difficult.

To solve this, and to simplify your work with the tracer, once you get hold of the current instance, you can use one of the many extensions methods the framework provides. These are shown in Listing 7-20.

Listing 7-20. A Wide Range of Helper Extension Methods You Can Call on the Tracer

```
public static void Debug(this ITraceWriter traceWriter, HttpRequestMessage request, string category,
string messageFormat, params object[] messageArguments)
public static void Debug(this ITraceWriter traceWriter, HttpRequestMessage request, string category,
Exception exception)
public static void Debug(this ITraceWriter traceWriter, HttpRequestMessage request, string category,
Exception exception, string messageFormat, params object[] messageArguments)

public static void Error(this ITraceWriter traceWriter, HttpRequestMessage request, string category,
string messageFormat, params object[] messageArguments)
public static void Error(this ITraceWriter traceWriter, HttpRequestMessage request, string category,
Exception exception)
public static void Error(this ITraceWriter traceWriter, HttpRequestMessage request, string category,
Exception exception, string messageFormat, params object[] messageArguments)
```

```
public static void Fatal(this ITraceWriter traceWriter, HttpRequestMessage request, string category,
string messageFormat, params object[] messageArguments)
public static void Fatal(this ITraceWriter traceWriter, HttpRequestMessage request, string category,
Exception exception)
public static void Fatal(this ITraceWriter traceWriter, HttpRequestMessage request, string category,
Exception exception, string messageFormat, params object[] messageArguments)

public static void Info(this ITraceWriter traceWriter, HttpRequestMessage request, string category,
string messageFormat, params object[] messageArguments)
public static void Info(this ITraceWriter traceWriter, HttpRequestMessage request, string category,
Exception exception)
public static void Info(this ITraceWriter traceWriter, HttpRequestMessage request, string category,
Exception exception, string messageFormat, params object[] messageArguments)

public static void Trace(this ITraceWriter traceWriter, HttpRequestMessage request, string category,
TraceLevel level, Exception exception)
public static void Trace(this ITraceWriter traceWriter, HttpRequestMessage request, string category,
TraceLevel level, Exception exception, string messageFormat, params object[]
public static void Trace(this ITraceWriter traceWriter, HttpRequestMessage request, string category,
TraceLevel level, string messageFormat, params object[] messageArguments)

public static void Warn(this ITraceWriter traceWriter, HttpRequestMessage request, string category,
string messageFormat, params object[] messageArguments)
public static void Warn(this ITraceWriter traceWriter, HttpRequestMessage request, string category,
Exception exception)
public static void Warn(this ITraceWriter traceWriter, HttpRequestMessage request, string category,
Exception exception, string messageFormat, params object[] messageArguments)
```

All in all, the modularity of ASP.NET Web API makes it easy to replace its parts, and ITraceWriter is a great example of that. As a result, you get very fine-grained control over your tracing and debugging mechanisms, without the need to reinvent the wheel.

7-7. Write a Real-Time Tracer
Problem

For development/monitoring purposes, you would like to have a real-time tracer that pushes all information from ITraceWriter to you as the requests flow into your API. In addition, you still want to log to your default trace provider.

Solution

You can add the real-time aspect to the tracing in your ASP.NET Web API by implementing a custom ITraceWriter based on an ASP.NET SignalR hub. This allows you to facilitate a very fundamental requirement of any good tracing implementation: immediate feedback, with the real-time aspect of SignalR. Furthermore, you can use this tracer as a wrapper around your default one (say, an NLog-based one), and push the log messages to both tracers.

How It Works

While you are able to have only one trace writer registered in ASP.NET Web API, you can always wrap one tracer with another. ASP.NET SignalR real-time communication framework is great for pushing messages to the connected client in real time. Remember that you do not want to lose any log output (imagine that the client disconnects).

The easiest way to go about this is to wrap any existing trace implementation with a SignalR-based tracer. Effectively you end up with two ITraceWriters, one embedded into the other and calling it.

This very simple idea allows you to nicely separate the real-time aspect of the tracer from its core trace output. This also allows you to control the real-time functionality at runtime, switching it on or off when needed.

The Code

The prerequisite will be to install ASP.NET SignalR from NuGet. The package will be different based on your host environment.

```
Install-Package Microsoft.AspNet.SignalR          // web host
Install-Package Microsoft.AspNet.SignalR.SelfHost // self host or OWIN
```

Before anything else, you will need to add the Katana (OWIN) Startup class, since SignalR is OWIN only. If you are not on a web host, you will additionally need to add the WebApp.Start block (see Listing 7-21).

Listing 7-21. A Bare Minimum Startup Setup for SignalR

```
class Startup
{
    public void Configuration(IAppBuilder app)
    {
        app.MapSignalR();
    }
}

//for self-host
static void Main(string[] args)
{
    string url = "http://localhost:8080";
    using (WebApp.Start(url))
    {
        Console.WriteLine("Server running on {0}", url);
        Console.ReadLine();
    }
}
}
```

If you recall, to create a Web API tracer you need to implement the ITraceWriter interface, which consists of a single method. In the SignalR case it will look like in Listing 7-22.

Listing 7-22. An Implementation of the Trace Method for the Real-Time Tracer

```
public void Trace(HttpRequestMessage request, string category, TraceLevel level, Action<TraceRecord>
traceAction)
{
    if (level != TraceLevel.Off && !string.IsNullOrWhiteSpace(_hubname))
    {
        var record = new TraceRecord(request, category, level);
        _hub.Value.Clients.All.logMessage(ComposeMessage(record));
        _traceWriter.Trace(request, category, level, traceAction);
    }
}
```

As discussed before, you can compose the tracer from two layers. The outer (this one) will be notifying the subscribers about trace events in real time. The inner (represented by the _traceWriter field) will pass the trace context to the regular tracer, which might log to anywhere, such as a text file or event log, as it could be any ITraceWriter implementation.

The message is composed using a private method ComposeMessage which is not really interesting from the bigger perspective of this implementation, as all it does is just concatenated strings; however, for the sake of documentation let's look at it. See Listing 7-23.

Listing 7-23. A Helper Method Creating a String with Log Message from TraceRecord

```
private static string ComposeMessage(TraceRecord record)
{
    var message = new StringBuilder();

    if (record.Request != null)
    {
        if (record.Request.Method != null)
            message.Append(record.Request.Method);

        if (record.Request.RequestUri != null)
            message.Append(" ").Append(record.Request.RequestUri);
    }

    if (!string.IsNullOrWhiteSpace(record.Category))
        message.Append(" ").Append(record.Category);

    if (!string.IsNullOrWhiteSpace(record.Operator))
        message.Append(" ").Append(record.Operator).Append(" ").Append(record.Operation);

    if (!string.IsNullOrWhiteSpace(record.Message))
        message.Append(" ").Append(record.Message);

    if (record.Exception != null && !string.IsNullOrWhiteSpace(record.Exception.GetBaseException().
        Message))
        message.Append(" ").Append(record.Exception.GetBaseException().Message);

    return message.ToString();
}
```

Of course, the private variables that Trace method relies on (_hubname, _hub, and _traceWriter) have to come from somewhere, usually from the constructor, so add them too. This is shown in Listing 7-24.

Listing 7-24. The Class Representing the Real-Time SignalR Tracer

```
public class SignalRTraceWrapper : ITraceWriter
{
    private readonly ITraceWriter _traceWriter;
    private readonly Lazy<IHubContext> _hub = new Lazy<IHubContext>(() => GlobalHost.
ConnectionManager.GetHubContext(_hubname));
    private static string _hubname = "trace";

    public SignalRTraceWrapper(ITraceWriter traceWriter, string hubname)
    {
        _traceWriter = traceWriter;
        _hubname = hubname;
    }


    //rest omitted for brevity
}
```

The inner trace writer gets passed into SignalR tracer so that you can use it whenever the Trace method gets invoked. Additionally, you pass in a hub name (indicating the destination to which SignalR should broadcast the log), which is a static field (I'll explain soon) with a default value of trace.

The hub context is a Lazy<T> and gets resolved to a proper hub context whenever the Trace method is first called. You'll expand on this technique further in Recipe 8-6, but for now this approach is sufficient.

You can now register the trace writer against your Web API configuration. For example,

```
config.Services.Replace(typeof(ITraceWriter), new SignalRTraceWrapper(new NlogTraceWriter(), "myLog"));
```

This will register NLogTraceWriter (see Recipe 7-5 for more information about NLog-based trace writer) as the inner tracer (for real, concrete logging) and the myLog hub will be registered as the destination for the SignalR real-time log.

The final piece is the possibility to switch the real-time aspect of the tracer (the SignalR part) on and off. Actually that is why you made the _hubname private variable static. This allows you to add in the switch as shown in Listing 7-25.

Listing 7-25. The Switch Methods That Will Allow You to Switch the Real-Time Functionality On and Off

```
public static void Enable(string hubname)
{
    _hubname = hubname;
}

public static void Disable()
{
    _hubname = null;
}
```

If you recall, the log would execute if the following condition was met:

```
if (level != TraceLevel.Off && !string.IsNullOrWhiteSpace(_hubname))
{
    //do stuff
}
```

So, if you nullify the _hubname, it will switch off logging. However, you probably don't want to switch off the inner tracer, just the SignalR real-time bits, so you should rewrite the condition as shown in Listing 7-26.

Listing 7-26. New Tracing Conditions Facilitating On and Off Switches for the Real-Time Tracing

```
if (level != TraceLevel.Off)
{
    var record = new TraceRecord(request, category, level);
    if (!string.IsNullOrWhiteSpace(_hubname))
        _hub.Value.Clients.All.logMessage(ComposeMessage(record));

    _traceWriter.Trace(request, category, level, traceAction);
}
```

As a result, you have a nice real-time wrapper for any trace writer. You could now control its behavior with `Enable` and `Disable` methods. You can also switch the output hub name as you wish.

```
SignalRTraceWrapper.Enable("traceHub");
SignalRTraceWrapper.Disable();
```

To be able to instantiate the tracer correctly, you just need a SignalR hub now; one without any extra customizations will do, as long as you give it a name that you can later use inline with the tracer registration.

```
[HubName("trace")]
public class TraceHub : Hub
{ }
```

The registration is done in a familiar fashion, except you have to pass in the inner tracer too. In this example, it will be an NLog one and a hub name.

```
config.Services.Replace(typeof(ITraceWriter), new SignalRTraceWrapper(new NlogTraceWriter(), "trace"));
```

Now the last thing to do is to create some sort of an admin client that can listen to the messages broadcasted by the SignalR hub and display the relevant info. Listing 7-27 shows a basic JS implementation (an HTML page), which will display all logs in real time. Obviously, at the same time, NLog will do its logging job on the side.

■ **Note**   The source code for this chapter uses a helper controller to serve that HTML page, but this is normally required only if you are not using a web server capable of hosting static files.

Listing 7-27. JS/HTML Client Listening for the Real-Time Tracer

```
<!DOCTYPE html>
<html xmlns="http://www.w3.org/1999/xhtml">
<head>
    <title>Real time Web API Trace</title>
</head>
<body>
    <ul id="messages"></ul>
</body>

<script type="text/javascript" src="http://ajax.aspnetcdn.com/ajax/jquery/jquery-1.9.0.js"></script>
<script type="text/javascript" src="http://ajax.aspnetcdn.com/ajax/signalr/jquery.signalr-2.0.2.min.js"></script>
<script type="text/javascript" src="http://localhost:9000/signalr/hubs"></script>

<script type="text/javascript">
    $(function () {
        hub = $.connection.trace;
        hub.client.logMessage = function (data) {
            $('#messages').prepend('<li>' + data + '</li>');
        };

        $.connection.hub.start();
    });
</script>
</html>
```

7-8. Create a Documentation Page for ASP.NET Web API

Problem

You would like your ASP.NET Web API to expose an overview page with information about all of your endpoints.

Solution

While such documentation could possibly be created by hand, ASP.NET Web API makes it trivially easy to generate an API help page. In fact, the help page is already bundled in the default MVC (with Web API) or pure Web API project templates in Visual Studio.

If you self-host or host on OWIN, or simply added Web API to your project by hand, you can always add the help page functionality through an external library available on NuGet:

```
Install-Package Microsoft.AspNet.WebApi.HelpPage
```

How It Works

The help page functionality takes advantage of the IApiExplorer (and its default implementation, ApiExplorer), which is a service that's part of the core Web API. It exposes metadata information about every single endpoint of the API through an ApiDescription object.

■ **Note** ApiExplorer considers every variation of an HTTP method and an action (if a single action supports multiple methods) as a separate API endpoint, and provides a unique ApiDescription for each.

While the ASP.NET Web API help page is heavily customizable, there is nothing stopping you from implementing a completely custom API documentation solution based on ApiExplorer directly (in fact, you may even expose that documentation as its own separate API!).

The Code

After installation, ASP.NET Web API will generate the help page under Areas ➤ HelpPage and, through HelpPageAreaRegistration shown in Listing 7-28, register a default route enabling access to the help page.

Listing 7-28. Default Help Page Area Registration and Route Setup

```
public class HelpPageAreaRegistration : AreaRegistration
{
    public override string AreaName
    {
        get
        {
            return "HelpPage";
        }
    }

    public override void RegisterArea(AreaRegistrationContext context)
    {
        context.MapRoute(
            "HelpPage_Default",
            "Help/{action}/{apiId}",
            new { controller = "Help", action = "Index", apiId = UrlParameter.Optional });

        HelpPageConfig.Register(GlobalConfiguration.Configuration);
    }
}
```

That class is also the place to go for any help page routing changes. Depending on the type of customization you would like to perform, a couple of other classes can be modified too.

- HelpController: The help page initialization, creation, and access rights.

- HelpPageApiModel: The model used to generate the help page.

- HelpPageSampleGenerator: Responsible for generating the samples.

- HelpPageConfig: Provides general configuration settings for the help page functionality. Out of the box it doesn't do anything, but it ships with predefined code snippets which can be commented out, allowing you to set DocumentationProvider or control sample objects.

- /Views/Help/Index.cshtml: The main view rendering the landing page.

- /Views/Help/Api.cshtml: The detailed view of an individual API endpoint.

- /Views/Help/DisplayTemplates/*: Views used for individual samples, based on sample type.

Since all API information is fed into the help page through `ApiExplorer`, the framework provides you with an `ApiExplorerSettingsAttribute`, which you can use to hide a specific action or entire controller from being visible to the help page (Listing 7-29).

Listing 7-29. Example of Hiding an Entire Controller and a Single Action from a Web API Help Page

```
[ApiExplorerSettings(IgnoreApi = true)]
public class ValuesController : ApiController
{
    //omitted for brevity
}

[ApiExplorerSettings(IgnoreApi = true)]
public IEnumerable<string> Get()
{
    return new string[] { "value1", "value2" };
}
```

ASP.NET WEB API HELP PAGE OUTSIDE OF ASP.NET AND IIS

The Web API Help Page uses an MVC controller and Razor templates to provide its functionality. As such, it will only work in web-hosted scenarios.

It is, however, relatively easy to adapt the help page to work on a self-host or under an OWIN host. You would have to replace the `HelpController` with an `ApiController` capable of serving HTML with Razor views. Have a look at Recipe 5-11 to see an example.

7-9. Add Custom Samples to ASP.NET Web API Help Page

Problem

You would like the ASP.NET Web API help page to display a sample response for a media type not supported by Web API out of the box.

Solution

If your new media type is a text-based one (such as `text/rss` or `text/csv`), the Web API help page will automatically display a sample using its own set of dummy data. You can still provide a specific sample response using `HelpPageConfig` and its `SetSampleResponse` or `SetSampleForMediaType` methods.

If your media type is not text-based (such as `text/pdf` or `application/bson`), the Web API help page will skip it. To support such media types in the help page, you need to do the following steps:

- Add a custom presentation model that will contain the sample.

- Add a custom view responsible for rendering the sample.

- Hook those up into the help page also using the same `SetSampleResponse` or `SetSampleForMediaType` methods mentioned before.

In that case, since you control both the model and the display template, you are free to present the sample on the help page exactly the way you wish; in other words, you can render a PDF or image, or embed a video.

How It Works

ASP.NET Web API Help Page makes it really easy to add support for additional help page samples. In fact, it will try its best to automatically generate them for you by inspecting the `Formatters` collection of your `HttpConfiguration` object and trying to pick up all the media types supported by your API. It will then invoke the relevant `MediaTypeFormatter` on the dummy data, and show the sample as a `TextSample` on the help page. This will normally cover all text-based scenarios.

In all other cases, or if you simply want to have full control over how the sample is presented, you need to create a custom presentation model and add a view with the exact same name to the `DisplayTemplates` folder. Web API will pick it up from there automatically.

The Code

For text-based formats, while ASP.NET Web API can generate the samples itself, `HelpPageConfig` lets you replace the default samples with your own custom ones, either globally (`SetSampleForMediaType`) or per action (`SetSampleResponse`).

For example, in Listing 7-30 you set an arbitrary RSS string as a sample for `ValuesController` and its `Get` action for the `text/rss` media type.

Listing 7-30. Setting a Custom RSS Sample for a Specific Controller

```
var rss = @"<?xml version=""1.0"" encoding=""UTF-8"" ?>
    <rss version=""2.0"">
    <channel>
     <title>Title</title>
     <description>Desc</description>
     <link>http://www.test.com</link>
     <pubDate>Tue, 21 Jan 2014 18:45:00 +0000 </pubDate>

     <item>
      <title>Item</title>
      <description>Desc</description>
      <link>http://www.test.com/1</link>
      <pubDate>Tue, 21 Jan 2014 18:45:00 +0000 </pubDate>
     </item>

    </channel>
    </rss>";
config.SetSampleResponse(rss, new MediaTypeHeaderValue("text/rss"), "Values", "Get" );
```

A good case study for adding support for non-text formats could be BSON. The `BsonMediaTypeFormatter` ships together with Web API; however, out of the box the help page does not support it, displaying only a link to the BSON spec instead, which is shown in Listing 7-31.

Listing 7-31. Default Behavior of ASP.NET Web API Help Page for BSON Formatter

```
config.SetSampleForMediaType(
    new TextSample("Binary JSON content. See http://bsonspec.org for details."),
    new MediaTypeHeaderValue("application/bson"));
```

Since BSON is a binary format, you can display the raw bytes it produces, converted into HEX instead. To extend the help page with this type of sample, you need a new sample model and a view. The model (Listing 7-32) will hold the bytes while the view will use `x.ToString("X2")` to convert them to hexadecimal format.

Listing 7-32. ByteSample.cs and DisplayTemplates/ByteSample.cshtml

```
public class ByteSample
{
    public byte[] Bytes { get; set; }
}

@model ByteSample

<pre class="wrapped">
    @string.Concat(Model.Bytes.Select(x => x.ToString("X2")));
</pre>
```

As in the other cases, the sample itself is set in the `HelpPageConfig`. In this case, that would grab the `BsonMediaTypeFormatter` and use it to serialize a sample string. This is shown in Listing 7-33 and the output produced by such a customized help page can be seen in Figure 7-1.

Listing 7-33. Setting the Sample BSON Response

```
var bsonFormatter = new BsonMediaTypeFormatter();
byte[] bson;
using (var s = new MemoryStream())
{
    bsonFormatter.WriteToStream(typeof(string), "Hello world", s, Encoding.UTF8);
    bson = s.ToArray();
}
config.SetSampleForMediaType(
    new ByteSample {Bytes = bson},
    new MediaTypeHeaderValue("application/bson"));
```

Figure 7-1. *Output from the customized help page*

As a result, your help page can now produce the output shown in Figure 7-1.

7-10. Add Filters Information to ASP.NET Web API Help Page

Problem

You have some action filters on your ASP.NET Web API actions, such as providing authorization functionality or caching. You would like the filters to be taken into account by the ASP.NET Web API help page.

Solution

You have to extend `HelpPageApiModel` with additional properties, such as:

- `public bool RequiresAuthorization { get; set; }`
- `public bool IsCached { get; set; }`

The `HelpPageConfigurationExtensions` class contains a private method called `GenerateApiModel`. That method generates the help page model, which represents an API action. Since the Web API help page is added to your project as raw source code, there is nothing preventing you from modifying this method, reading the `FilterAttributes` from inside it, and setting the relevant information on the newly extended `HelpPageApiModel`. Finally, `HelpPageApiModel.cshtml`, which is responsible for presenting the data to the user, should be modified to properly display information from the extra properties.

How It Works

When you arrive at an API page, the Api action, shown in Listing 7-34, of the HelpController is invoked.

Listing 7-34. Action Responsible for Rendering API Endpoint Details

```
public ActionResult Api(string apiId)
{
    if (!String.IsNullOrEmpty(apiId))
    {
        HelpPageApiModel apiModel = Configuration.GetHelpPageApiModel(apiId);
        if (apiModel != null)
        {
            return View(apiModel);
        }
    }

    return View(ErrorViewName);
}
```

The GetHelpPageApiModel method will be used to create the model for the given API endpoint (represented by apiId). That public method will in turn call the private GenerateApiModel just mentioned. The GenerateApiModel method has access to the ApiDescription object, which exposes an ActionDescriptor relevant for the given action. ActionDescriptor can be used to obtain all Filters applied to an action and set them on the model.

What's important is that ActionDescriptor, through its GetFilterPipeline method, allows you to look at the **entire** filter pipeline, which will pick up action filters not only applied directly to the action, but at the controller or at the global level too.

The Code

Consider the sample setup shown in Listing 7-35, a simple controller with two filters applied, a built-in AuthorizationFilterAttribute and a custom CachedFilterAttribute (its implementation details are completely irrelevant for this discussion).

Listing 7-35. A Sample Controller with Two Filters

```
[Authorize]
public class MyController : ApiController
{
    public string Get()
    {
        return "Hello world";
    }

    [Cached]
    public string Get(int id)
    {
        return "Hello world " + id;
    }
}
```

You are able to check against the presence of both Authorize and Cached in the GenerateApiModel quite easily (Listing 7-36) using the techniques already mentioned in the solution part of this recipe.

Listing 7-36. Finding Out If a Filter Pipeline Contains a Specific Filter

```
if (apiDescription.ActionDescriptor.GetFilterPipeline().Any(x => x.Instance is
IAuthorizationFilter))
                apiModel.RequiresAuthorization = true;

if (apiDescription.ActionDescriptor.GetFilterPipeline().Any(x => x.Instance is CachedAttribute))
                apiModel.IsCached = true;
```

CATERING FOR ALLOWANONYMOUS

If you would like to verify that your action isn't subject to the [AllowAnonymous] attribute, you have to apply an additional check. apiDescription.ActionDescriptor.GetCustomAttributes<AllowAnonymousAttribute>(). Any() && apiDescription.ActionDescriptor.ControllerDescriptor.GetCustomAttributes<AllowAnonymousAttribute>().Any()

This is because [AllowAnonymous] is only a decorator attribute and is not part of the filter pipeline, so you have to check for its presence on both the action and controller level using GetCustomAttributes directly.

As a final step, you need to tweak the HelpPageApiModel.cshtml to display information about the filters (Listing 7-37).

Listing 7-37. Relevant Razor Code Displaying Info About the Filters

```
<h2>Response Information</h2>

<h3>Resource Description</h3>

<p>@description.ResponseDescription.Documentation</p>

@if (Model.RequiresAuthorization)
{
    <h3>Requires Authorization.</h3>
}

@if (Model.IsCached)
{
    <h3>Caching Enabled.</h3>
}
```

7-11. Support Data Annotations in ASP.NET Web API Help Page

Problem

You would like the ASP.NET Web API help page to display information about data annotations you used in your models (DTOs) to notify the client what is required and which property will be validated in which way.

Solution

The ASP.NET Web API help page supports the most common data annotations out of the box, and the restrictions imposed by them on your models are displayed automatically. However, it's also very easy to add support for additional or completely custom data annotations, as well as to tweak the messages of the already supported ones.

To do that, you have to add those additional annotation attributes to the `ModelDescriptionGenerator` class and its private `AnnotationTextGenerator` dictionary, which is used by the help page in the generation process.

How It Works

The ASP.NET Web API help page uses the `GetOrCreateModelDescription` method on the `ModelDescriptionGenerator` class to generate a description of the parameters of your Web API actions. Depending on the parameter type, the result is one of the classes derived from an abstract `ModelDescription`:

- `ComplexTypeModelDescription`
- `SimpleTypeModelDescription`
- `CollectionModelDescription`
- `DictionaryModelDescription`
- `EnumTypeModelDescription`
- `KeyValuePairModelDescription`

If the model type happens to be a complex type indeed, `ComplexTypeModelDescription` is used, and the `AnnotationTextGenerator` dictionary is checked to provide descriptions for the supported annotations.

Out of the box, the following annotations are supported:

- `RequiredAttribute`
- `RangeAttribute`
- `MaxLengthAttribute`
- `MinLengthAttribute`
- `StringLengthAttribute`
- `DataTypeAttribute`
- `RegularExpressionAttribute`

Whenever you arrive at a help page documenting an API resource, the relevant `ModelDescription` will be generated. For complex types, the view `ComplexTypeModelDescription.cshtml` will be selected, which in turn will use `Parameters.cshtml` to render annotation information. If you want to tweak the look and feel of the annotations presentation, this is the place to go.

The Code

Consider an example of CompareAttribute and EmailAddressAttribute (both introduced into System. ComponentModel.DataAnnotations in .NET 4.5), which are not supported by the help page by default.

CompareAttribute is used to compare two properties on the model against each other (such as Password and RepeatPassword), while EmailAddressAttribute is used to ensure a valid email address. To support them in your help page, all you need are two additional entries in the aforementioned AnnotationTextGenerator dictionary, which is shown in Listing 7-38.

Listing 7-38. AnnotationTextGenerator Dictionary with a Custom Entry Added at the End

```
private readonly IDictionary<Type, Func<object, string>>AnnotationTextGenerator = new
Dictionary<Type, Func<object, string>>
        {
            { typeof(RequiredAttribute), a => "Required" },
            { typeof(RangeAttribute), a =>
                {
                    RangeAttribute range = (RangeAttribute)a;
                    return String.Format(CultureInfo.CurrentCulture, "Range: inclusive between {0}
                    and {1}", range.Minimum, range.Maximum);
                }
            },
            { typeof(MaxLengthAttribute), a =>
                {
                    MaxLengthAttribute maxLength = (MaxLengthAttribute)a;
                    return String.Format(CultureInfo.CurrentCulture, "Max length: {0}",
                    maxLength.Length);
                }
            },
            { typeof(MinLengthAttribute), a =>
                {
                    MinLengthAttribute minLength = (MinLengthAttribute)a;
                    return String.Format(CultureInfo.CurrentCulture, "Min length: {0}",
                    minLength.Length);
                }
            },
            { typeof(StringLengthAttribute), a =>
                {
                    StringLengthAttribute strLength = (StringLengthAttribute)a;
                    return String.Format(CultureInfo.CurrentCulture, "String length: inclusive
                    between {0} and {1}", strLength.MinimumLength, strLength.MaximumLength);
                }
            },
            { typeof(DataTypeAttribute), a =>
                {
                    DataTypeAttribute dataType = (DataTypeAttribute)a;
                    return String.Format(CultureInfo.CurrentCulture, "Data type: {0}",
                    dataType.CustomDataType ?? dataType.DataType.ToString());
                }
            },
```

```
            { typeof(RegularExpressionAttribute), a =>
                {
                    RegularExpressionAttribute regularExpression = (RegularExpressionAttribute)a;
                    return String.Format(CultureInfo.CurrentCulture, "Matching regular expression
                    pattern: {0}", regularExpression.Pattern);
                }
            },
            { typeof(CompareAttribute), a =>
                {
                    CompareAttribute  compare = (CompareAttribute)a;
                    return String.Format(CultureInfo.CurrentCulture, "Must match: {0}",
                    compare. OtherProperty);
                }
            },
            { typeof(EmailAddressAttribute), a => "Must be a valid email" }
        };
}
```

With this change in place, the help page will now display a "Must match" note beside each of the properties that are subject to comparison and a "Must be a valid email" note beside each email-type property, as seen in Figure 7-2.

POST api/Test

Request Information

URI Parameters

None.

Body Parameters

UserData

Name	Description	Type	Additional information
Username		string	Required
Email		string	Must be a valid email Must match: RepeatEmail
RepeatEmail		string	Must be a valid email Must match: Email

Figure 7-2. *Custom Annotations Shown in the Help Page*

■ **Note**   If you use data annotations that are not supported by the help page, the generator will simply ignore them and the help page will display None in the Additional information column.

CHAPTER 8

Cross Domain and Push Communication

In this chapter, you'll explore how to overcome browser restrictions when it comes to crossing the origin boundaries in AJAX communication. Moreover, since all modern web applications need to have a flavor of real-time to them, you'll look at how you can facilitate push communication from the Web API to the client and how to integrate real-time duplex communication between the client and your Web API application.

You will learn how to do the following:

- Use JSONP and CORS for cross-origin communication (Recipes 8-1, 8-2, and 8-3)

- Support streaming and pushing data from Web API with PushStreamContent (Recipe 8-4)

- Support server-sent events and the text/eventstream media type (Recipe 8-5)

- Integrate SignalR and use web sockets with Web API (Recipes 8-6 and 8-7)

8-1. Use JSONP in ASP.NET Web API

Problem

You need to support cross-domain GET requests and would like to add JSONP support to your API.

Solution

WebApiContrib already has a JsonpMediaTypeFormatter, so adding it to your Web API application is as easy as installing it from NuGet and enabling it in your HttpConfiguration.

```
Install-package WebApiContrib.Formatting.Jsonp
```

The WebApiContrib implementation requires you to pass an instance of a regular JSON formatter, as it will be used for JSON serialization of the JSONP responses. It also ships with JsonpQueryStringMapping (see Recipe 4-9 for more information about mappings), ensuring that JSONP only kicks in when a "callback" parameter is passed by the client.

```
var jsonpFormatter = new JsonpMediaTypeFormatter(config.Formatters.JsonFormatter);
httpConfiguration.Formatters.Insert(0, jsonpFormatter);
```

How It Works

The solution presented here relies on a custom `MediaTypeFormatter`, which is only going to handle GET requests that have a `QueryString` "callback" parameter included with them. Then, the body of the request gets wrapped in the brackets, with the callback parameter value in front of it to adhere to the JSONP standard.

Many popular client-side libraries such as jQuery or AngularJS support JSONP out of the box and, as long as you use their correct API methods, they will generate the request with the relevant callback parameter for you.

On the Web API side, by using a custom formatter which is able to handle the callback, you can then respond in the appropriate format, as shown in Listing 8-1.

Listing 8-1. Sample JSONP Request and Response Originated from jQuery

```
GET api.domain.com/books?callback=jQuery210002522223792038858_1394613576462&_=1394613576463 HTTP/1.1
Referer: http://main.domain.com

HTTP/1.1 200 OK
Content-Length: 395
Content-Type: text/javascript; charset=utf-8
jQuery210002522223792038858_1394613576462([
{"Id":1,"Author":"John Robb","Title":"Punk Rock: An Oral History"},
{"Id":2,"Author":"Daniel Mohl","Title":"Building Web, Cloud, and Mobile Solutions with F#"},
{"Id":3,"Author":"Steve Clarke","Title":"100 Things Blue Jays Fans Should Know & Do Before
They Die"}]);
```

How exactly was this response produced? In the `MediaTypeFormatter` responsible for JSONP handling, inside the `WriteToStreamAsync` method, the body of the response is wrapped in the value of the callback parameter and the brackets, as shown in Listing 8-2; it's a simplified version of the code present in the WebApiContrib implementation. As you can see, the core job of the formatter is to inject the callback into the response, and then delegate the actual serialization process to the default `JsonMediaTypeFormatter`.

Listing 8-2. A Basic Example of WriteToStreamAsync for JSONP Formatter

```
public override async Task WriteToStreamAsync(Type type, object value, Stream stream, HttpContent
content, TransportContext transportContext)
{
    var encoding = SelectCharacterEncoding(content.Headers);
    using (var writer = new StreamWriter(stream, encoding, 4096, true))
    {
        writer.Write(_callback + "(");
        writer.Flush();
        await _jsonMediaTypeFormatter.WriteToStreamAsync(type, value, stream, content, transportContext);
        writer.Write(");");
        writer.Flush();
    }
}
```

■ **Tip**   Due to the limitations of JSONP (GET-support only), using CORS for cross-domain requests instead (Recipes 8-2 and 8-3) will give you much more flexibility. JSONP should be used if you need to support old browsers, such as IE7, which do not have CORS support.

The Code

Let's look at a complete example (Listing 8-3) of adding support for JSONP in your Web API. In the API, you'll use a sample controller and a model representing book resources, and you'll call this controller from a different domain. To avoid unnecessary complexity, an in-memory list represents the data store.

Listing 8-3. A Sample Model and a Controller That Will Support JSONP

```
public class Book
{
    public int Id { get; set; }
    public string Author { get; set; }
    public string Title { get; set; }
}

public class BooksController : ApiController
{
    private static List<Book> _books = new List<Book>
    {
        new Book {Id = 1, Author = "John Robb", Title = "Punk Rock: An Oral History"},
        new Book {Id = 2, Author = "Daniel Mohl", Title = "Building Web, Cloud, and Mobile
                   Solutions with F#"},
        new Book {Id = 3, Author = "Steve Clarke", Title = "100 Things Blue Jays Fans Should
                   Know & Do Before They Die"},
        new Book {Id = 4, Author = "Mark Frank", Title = "Cuban Revelations: Behind the Scenes
                   in Havana "}
    };

    [Route("books")]
    public IEnumerable<Book> GetAll()
    {
        return _books;
    }
}
```

The configuration process is very simple and you have already looked at it before, but it's shown here again in Listing 8-4. What's important to note is that JsonpMediaTypeFormatter takes a second parameter in its constructor, allowing you to provide a name for the callback parameter. It defaults to "callback", but should you need to support a different one, you can do that too.

Listing 8-4. Enabling the JSONP Formatter in Your HttpConfiguration

```
var config = new HttpConfiguration();
config.MapHttpAttributeRoutes();

var jsonpFormatter = new JsonpMediaTypeFormatter(config.Formatters.JsonFormatter);
config.Formatters.Insert(0, jsonpFormatter);
```

Now, on the client side, you'll create a brand new web application, which will sit on a different domain, subdomain, or port from your API because a difference in any one of those will make browsers treat the request as cross domain. In this application, you will add some HTML and a request for a book list in a JSONP format. This is shown in Listing 8-5.

Listing 8-5. A Sample Application Using Bootstrap, KnockoutJS, and jQuery, Making a JSONP Request to the Web API

```html
<html lang="en">
<head>
    <title></title>
    <link href="Content/bootstrap.css" rel="stylesheet" />
    <link href="Content/bootstrap-theme.css" rel="stylesheet" />

    <script src="Scripts/jquery-2.1.0.js"></script>
    <script src="Scripts/knockout-3.1.0.js"></script>
    <script src="Scripts/bootstrap.js"></script>

    <script type="text/javascript">
        $(document).ready(function () {
            var vm = new Apress.Books();
            ko.applyBindings(vm);
            vm.loadBooks();
        });

        var Apress = Apress || {};
        Apress.Books = function () {
            var self = this;

            self.books = ko.observableArray([]);

            self.loadBooks = function () {
                $.ajax("http://localhost:9000/books", {
                        dataType: 'jsonp'
                    })
                    .done(function (data) {
                        $.each(data, function (idx, item) {
                            self.books.push(item);
                        });
                    })
                    .fail(function (xhr, status, error) {
                        alert(status);
                    });
            };
        };
    </script>
</head>
<body>
    <div class="container">
        <ul data-bind="foreach: books, visible: books().length > 0">
            <li>
                <h3 data-bind="text: Title"></h3>
                <small data-bind="text: Author"></small>
            </li>
        </ul>
    </div>
</body>
</html>
```

If the request is sent from jQuery without the dataType: 'jsonp', you'll see an error; in other cases, the request will succeed, and the view will be correctly populated with the list of books. Likewise, since JSONP is GET-only, all HTTP methods other than GET will be blocked by the browser.

8-2. Use CORS in ASP.NET Web API

Problem

You would like to enable CORS (cross-origin resource sharing) support in your Web API service.

Solution

ASP.NET Web API introduced support for CORS in version 2 of the framework, as a community contribution from Brock Allen. It shipped not as part of the core Web API, but as an additional package which you can install from NuGet.

```
Install-package Microsoft.AspNet.WebApi.Cors
```

To enable CORS, you need call the `EnableCors` extension method against your Web API `HttpConfiguration`.

```
httpConfiguration.EnableCors();
```

However, this alone doesn't introduce any specific CORS rules yet; it merely activates the infrastructure required by the CORS components. Afterwards, to support CORS in individual actions or controllers, you have to decorate them with an `EnableCorsAttribute`, which is applicable to both methods and classes.

```
[EnableCors(origins: "http://allowed.origin.ch", headers: "*", methods:"GET ")]
public class BooksController : ApiController {}
```

Alternatively, you can provide a specific global policy by passing an attribute instance to the `EnableCors` method.

```
httpConfiguration.EnableCors(new EnableCorsAttribute(origins: "http://allowed.origin.ch",
headers: "*", methods:"GET "));
```

■ **Note** `EnableCorsAttribute` takes several strings in its constructor. The examples here use named parameters for readability but they can easily be omitted too.

How It Works

CORS is a W3C specification that allows a JavaScript client (browser) and a server to agree on relaxing the same-origin policy in their bilateral communication. CORS is enforced and supported by all modern browsers, but needs to be explicitly supported on the server side.

User agents commonly apply same-origin restrictions to network requests. These restrictions prevent a client-side Web application running from one origin from obtaining data retrieved from another origin, and also limit unsafe HTTP requests that can be automatically launched toward destinations that differ from the running application's origin. In user agents that follow this pattern, network requests typically include user credentials with cross-origin requests, including HTTP authentication and cookie information.

Cross-Origin Resource Sharing specification
www.w3.org/TR/cors/

■ **Tip**   Contrary to the situation with JSONP, CORS can be used with all HTTP verbs, not just GET.

In the Web API implementation, under the hood, the EnableCors method registers a CorsMessageHandler in the Web API execution pipeline. It also marks the request as being CORS-enabled by adding an MS_CorsEnabledKey key to the request's properties dictionary with a value true.

Every request coming into the system will have to flow through this handler, which will compare the request's contextual information, such as origin and HTTP method with the CORS settings defined, by default looking them up in the attributes, or, in case a custom provider or custom provider factory are registered, through them. It will then emit the appropriate CORS response headers.

CorsMessageHandler will also handle preflight requests should the browser send any. Preflight requests are sent by browsers for non-trivial HTTP calls and use the HTTP OPTIONS verb call. They are effectively a handshake calls to obtain permissions from the server. Successful response to a preflight request is the followed by the regular AJAX call.

A sample preflight request and response are shown in Listing 8-6.

Listing 8-6. Sample Preflight Request and Response

```
OPTIONS http://localhost:9000/books HTTP/1.1
Access-Control-Request-Method: POST
Origin: http://localhost:43641
Access-Control-Request-Headers: content-type
Accept: application/josn

HTTP/1.1 200 OK
Access-Control-Allow-Origin: http://localhost:43641
Access-Control-Allow-Methods: GET,POST,
Access-Control-Allow-Headers: Content-Type
```

Interestingly, CORS support also integrates very well into Web API's tracing infrastructure, so if you use an implementation of ITraceWriter (discussed in Chapter 7), you'll see the relevant CORS information showing up there too: the CORS policy provider selection, the policy selection process, and finally, the result and validity of the response.

The Code

To see an example of CORS in action, let's extend the BookController example used in Recipe 8-1. If you read it, you will already be familiar with the structure, but it's shown again in Listing 8-7 along with some extra actions. You'll throw away JSONP and use CORS instead; and since CORS supports every HTTP method, you can add some of the more complicated functionality such as the ability to POST a new book from the client.

Listing 8-7. A Sample Model and a Controller That Will Support CORS

```
public class Book
{
    public int Id { get; set; }
    public string Author { get; set; }
    public string Title { get; set; }
}

public class BooksController : ApiController
{
    private static List<Book> _books = new List<Book>
    {
        new Book {Id = 1, Author = "John Robb", Title = "Punk Rock: An Oral History"},
        new Book {Id = 2, Author = "Daniel Mohl", Title = "Building Web, Cloud, and Mobile Solutions
                with F#"},
        new Book {Id = 3, Author = "Steve Clarke", Title = "100 Things Blue Jays Fans Should Know &
                Do Before They Die"},
        new Book {Id = 4, Author = "Mark Frank", Title = "Cuban Revelations: Behind the Scenes in
                Havana "}
    };

    [Route("books")]
    public IEnumerable<Book> GetAll()
    {
        return _books;
    }

    [Route("books/{id:int}", Name = "GetBookById")]
    public Book GetById(int id)
    {
        return _books.FirstOrDefault(x => x.Id == id);
    }

    [Route("books")]
    public IHttpActionResult Post(Book book)
    {
        book.Id = _books.Last() != null ? _books.Last().Id + 1 : 1;
        _books.Add(book);
        return CreatedAtRoute("GetBookById", new {id = book.Id}, book);
    }
}
```

The HTML and JavaScript allowing the user to add new books is shown in Listing 8-8. As you can see, the sendBook function is performing a typical POST request, just as if you weren't crossing the origin boundaries. In other words, the developer does not have to do anything, as all the responsibility of making this work lies on the browser and the server.

Listing 8-8. A Sample Application Using Bootstrap, KnockoutJS, and jQuery, Making a CORS Requests to the Web API

```html
<html lang="en">
<head>
    <title></title>
    <link href="Content/bootstrap.css" rel="stylesheet" />
    <link href="Content/bootstrap-theme.css" rel="stylesheet" />

    <script src="Scripts/jquery-2.1.0.js"></script>
    <script src="Scripts/knockout-3.1.0.js"></script>
    <script src="Scripts/bootstrap.js"></script>

    <script type="text/javascript">
        $(document).ready(function () {
            var vm = new Apress.Books();
            ko.applyBindings(vm);
            vm.loadBooks();
        });

        var Apress = Apress || {};
        Apress.Books = function () {
            var self = this;

            self.books = ko.observableArray([]);

            self.loadBooks = function () {
                $.ajax("http://localhost:9000/books")
                    .done(function (data) {
                        $.each(data, function (idx, item) {
                            self.books.push(item);
                        });
                    })
                    .fail(function (xhr, status, error) {
                        alert(status);
                    });
            };

            self.sendBook = function() {
                $.ajax("http://localhost:9000/books", {
                    type: "POST",
                    contentType: "application/json",
                    dataType: 'json',
                    data: JSON.stringify({Title: self.newBook.Title(), Author: self.newBook.Author()})
                })
                    .done(function (data) {
                        self.books.push(data);
                    })
                    .fail(function (xhr, status, error) {
                        alert(status);
                    });
            };
        };
    </script>
</head>
```

```
<body>
    <div class="container">
        <ul data-bind="foreach: books, visible: books().length > 0">
            <li>
                <h3 data-bind="text: Title"></h3>
                <small data-bind="text: Author"></small>
            </li>
        </ul>
        <div class="input-group">
            <input type="text" class="form-control" placeholder="Title"
            data-bind="value: newBook.Title" />
            <input type="text" class="form-control" placeholder="Author"
            data-bind="value: newBook.Author" />
            <button type="button" class="btn btn-default" data-bind="click: sendBook">Send</button>
        </div>
    </div>
</body>
</html>
```

Now all that's required on the server side is to initialize the CORS support at application startup and decorate the BooksController with EnableCorsAttribute. This is shown in Listing 8-9.

Listing 8-9. Applying CORS to the Web API in the Configuration and to the BooksController

```
var config = new HttpConfiguration();
config.MapHttpAttributeRoutes();
config.EnableCors();
```

```
[EnableCors(origins: "http://localhost:43641/", headers: "*", methods:"GET,POST")]
public class BooksController : ApiController {}
```

8-3. Create Custom CORS Policies
Problem

You want to avoid hardcoding CORS policy information into the attributes and would like to use a more flexible solution, allowing you to modify the CORS policies without having to recompile the whole application.

Solution

ASP.NET Web API allows you to create custom CORS policies, which you can then use instead of the EnableCorsAttribute. To do that, you need to create a class derived from a standard .NET Attribute (so that it can be applied as an attribute) and implement an ICorsPolicyProvider interface.

How It Works

In your implementation of ICorsPolicyProvider (interface shown in Listing 8-10), you may load the CORS settings, such as allowed headers, origins, HTTP methods, from anywhere you wish, such as an XML configuration file or a data store. You would then still apply the attribute the same way as EnableCorsAttribute would be applied, that is directly on the controller/action or globally using the EnableCors extension method on the HttpConfiguration, but the settings themselves are no longer hardcoded in the source code, but rather they are retrieved using the logic you defined.

Listing 8-10. Definition of an ICorsPolicyProvider Interface

```
public interface ICorsPolicyProvider
{
    Task<System.Web.Cors.CorsPolicy> GetCorsPolicyAsync(HttpRequestMessage request,
    CancellationToken cancellationToken);
}
```

ASP.NET Web API CORS implementation internally relies on a message handler to provide CORS policy settings. That handler uses ICorsPolicyProviderFactory to gather information about the providers it should use to collect CORS configuration information.

Out of the box, the default implementation of the ICorsPolicyProviderFactory is AttributeBasedPolicyProviderFactory, which simply looks at attributes that decorate your controllers and actions, or that are globally registered using the EnableCors extension method. Therefore, when you create a custom ICorsPolicyProvider and mark it as an Attribute at the same time, it will be automatically picked up without having to modify the ICorsPolicyProviderFactory.

On the other hand, by creating a custom ICorsPolicyProviderFactory you may break out of the established approach of applying CORS rules via attributes and provide a completely different mechanism of matching individual policy rules to actions.

CORS policy settings are represented in ASP.NET Web API by the CorsPolicy class (Listing 8-11), which is also the return type from the GetCorsPolicyAsync method of the ICorsPolicyProvider interface.

Listing 8-11. Definition of CorsPolicy

```
public class CorsPolicy
{
    public CorsPolicy();

    public bool AllowAnyHeader { get; set; }
    public bool AllowAnyMethod { get; set; }
    public bool AllowAnyOrigin { get; set; }
    public IList<string> ExposedHeaders { get; }
    public IList<string> Headers { get; }
    public IList<string> Methods { get; }
    public IList<string> Origins { get; }
    public long? PreflightMaxAge { get; set; }
    public bool SupportsCredentials { get; set; }

    public override string ToString();
}
```

The Code

In this example, you'll use the same sample application as in Recipe 8-2. You don't need to read through that recipe; just have a look at the server side (Listings 8-7 and 8-9) and client side (Listing 8-8) code. You'll modify it so that instead of hardcoding the CORS settings inline in the attribute, you will now create a custom ICorsPolicyProvider, which will read the relevant settings from the configuration file—App.config or Web.config depending on where you are hosting your Web API. Listing 8-12 shows the CORS configuration structure that you'll set out to support in this recipe.

Listing 8-12. Configuration of CORS from app.config/web.config

```
<configuration>
  <configSections>
    <section name="cors" type="Apress.Recipes.WebApi.RemoteServer.CorsSection,
    Apress.Recipes.WebApi.RemoteServer" />
  </configSections>
  <cors>
    <corsPolicies>
      <add name="setup1" origins="http://localhost:43641" headers="*" methods="get" />
    </corsPolicies>
  </cors>
</configuration>
```

In order to achieve this, let's first add a reference to the System.Configuration assembly and declare all of the necessary classes required for reading a custom configuration section. CorsSection will inherit from System.Configuration.ConfigurationSection and will expose a collection of CORS policies. This is shown in Listing 8-13.

Listing 8-13. Definition of CorsSection

```
public class CorsSection : ConfigurationSection
{
    [ConfigurationProperty("corsPolicies", IsDefaultCollection = true)]
    public CorsElementCollection CorsPolicies
    {
        get { return (CorsElementCollection)this["corsPolicies"]; }
        set { this["corsPolicies"] = value; }
    }
}
```

The CorsElementCollection (Listing 8-14), representing a list of individual CORS policy definitions, will inherit from System.Configuration.ConfigurationElementCollection.

Listing 8-14. Definition of CorsElementCollection

```
[ConfigurationCollection(typeof(CorsElement))]
public class CorsElementCollection : ConfigurationElementCollection
{
    protected override ConfigurationElement CreateNewElement()
    {
        return new CorsElement();
    }

    protected override object GetElementKey(ConfigurationElement element)
    {
        return ((CorsElement)element).Name;
    }
}
```

Finally, each policy will be represented by a CorsElement, inheriting from System.Configuration.ConfigurationElement. This will allow you to configure headers, origins, and HTTP methods, as you'd do using the EnableCorsAttribute and its primary constructor. To keep things simple, each of these settings will be represented by a string, which you'll split at a semicolon to extract multiple values should you wish to provide them. Each policy will also need to provide a unique name that will act as a unique key. CorsElement is shown in Listing 8-15.

Listing 8-15. Definition of CorsElement

```
public class CorsElement : ConfigurationElement
{
    [ConfigurationProperty("name", IsKey = true, IsRequired = true)]
    public string Name
    {
        get { return (string)this["name"]; }
        set { this["name"] = value; }
    }

    [ConfigurationProperty("origins", IsRequired = true)]
    public string Origins
    {
        get { return (string)this["origins"]; }
        set { this["origins"] = value; }
    }

    [ConfigurationProperty("methods", IsRequired = true)]
    public string Methods
    {
        get { return (string)this["methods"]; }
        set { this["methods"] = value; }
    }

    [ConfigurationProperty("headers", IsRequired = false)]
    public string Headers
    {
        get { return (string)this["headers"]; }
        set { this["headers"] = value; }
    }
}
```

From your custom ICorsPolicyProvider you should inspect these configuration settings and configure the Web API CORS settings accordingly. This is done by creating an instance of the CorsPolicy class. The whole process is shown in Listing 8-16. It can take place in the constructor of the attribute, and the CorsPolicy instance can be stored in a private field.

Listing 8-16. Implementation of ICorsPolicyProvider Which Loads CORS Settings From a Configuration File

```
public class ConfigurableCorsPolicyAttribute : Attribute, ICorsPolicyProvider
{
    private readonly CorsPolicy _policy;

    public ConfigurableCorsPolicyAttribute(string name)
    {
        _policy = new CorsPolicy();
```

```
        var corsConfig = ConfigurationManager.GetSection("cors") as CorsSection;
        if (corsConfig != null)
        {
            var policy = corsConfig.CorsPolicies.Cast<CorsElement>().FirstOrDefault(x =>
            x.Name == name);
            if (policy != null)
            {
                if (policy.Headers == "*")
                    _policy.AllowAnyHeader = true;
                else
                    policy.Headers.Split(';').ToList().ForEach(x => _policy.Headers.Add(x));

                if (policy.Methods == "*")
                    _policy.AllowAnyMethod = true;
                else
                    policy.Methods.Split(';').ToList().ForEach(x => _policy.Methods.Add(x));

                if (policy.Origins == "*")
                    _policy.AllowAnyOrigin = true;
                else
                    policy.Origins.Split(';').ToList().ForEach(x => _policy.Origins.Add(x));
            }
        }
    }

    public Task<CorsPolicy> GetCorsPolicyAsync(HttpRequestMessage request, CancellationToken
    cancellationToken)
    {
        return Task.FromResult(_policy);
    }
}
```

If the configuration contains a star for any of the settings, you should respect it by setting AllowAnyHeader, AllowAnyMethod, or AllowAnyOrigin to true.

Note that in this example the returned CorsPolicy is wrapped in a completed Task, and there is nothing wrong with that, since your policy is immediately available. Should you need to read the settings from a remote server or using I/O, it will come in handy to perform that operation in an asynchronous way.

You can now apply the newly created attribute to your actions and controllers, replacing the original EnableCorsAttribute.

```
[ConfigurableCorsPolicy("setup1")]
public class BooksController : ApiController {}
```

8-4. Support Streaming and Push from ASP.NET Web API
Problem

You would like to be able to stream bytes of data from your ASP.NET Web API application, return the response as soon as possible, and then continue to progressively write to the response stream which the client can consume.

Solution

ASP.NET Web API provides an implementation of HttpContent called PushStreamContent, which allows you to synchronously or asynchronously write data to the response Stream. When using PushStreamContent, the HttpResponseMessage is sent immediately and can be consumed by the user, while the Stream representing the body of the response remains open and can be written to.

Listing 8-17 shows a sample usage of a PushStreamContent. Notice that the Web API action doesn't need to be async because it's actually the lambda passed to PushStreamContent representing the operation on the Stream that's marked as async.

Listing 8-17. Sample Usage of a PushStreamContent from a Web API Action

```
var response = new HttpResponseMessage
{
    Content = new PushStreamContent(async (respStream, content, context) =>
    {
        using (var writer = new StreamWriter(respStream))
        {
            //Read data from somewhere and write to response stream
            await writer.WriteLineAsync(<some data>);
            await writer.FlushAsync();
        }
    }, "text/plain")
};
```

How It Works

From your ASP.NET Web API action, you are able to return an HttpResponseMessage with the content set to an instance of PushStreamContent. The definition of that HttpContent class is shown in Listing 8-18.

PushStreamContent takes a Func<Stream, HttpContent, TransportContext, Task> in its constructor, which it later invokes as soon as the output response Stream becomes available. In the provided lambda, you can progressively read the source bytes from your storage (disk or database) and push them in chunks to the client by writing to the currently available Stream.

As a consequence, the client receives the initial HTTP response almost immediately (though without the body yet) and can then proceed to read the bytes of the body of the response as they are being written by the server.

PUSHSTREAMCONTENT AND WEB API 1

In version one of ASP.NET Web API, the PushStreamContent used Action<Stream, HttpContent, TransportContext> instead of a Func<Stream, HttpContent, TransportContext, Task>, which effectively meant any exceptions were impossible to be caught. This could potentially lead to even an AppDomain crash.

If you have an old version of API using PushStreamContent, it's strongly recommended to update to at least ASP. NET Web API 2. The original Action<Stream, HttpContent, TransportContext>-based constructors have not been removed in order to avoid breaking changes but they shouldn't be used anymore.

Overall, such an approach allows both of the involved sides to minimize the amount of memory used, as neither side is forced into buffering the entire representation of a resource in question. This is especially useful in transferring large blobs of data over HTTP. It is also up to you as the developer to decide whether you will write to the Stream in a synchronous or asynchronous manner, which will obviously have a consequence if the thread is being blocked or not. Finally, the Web API framework automatically applies Transfer-Encoding: chunked to your response whenever you use PushStreamContent.

Listing 8-18. Definition of PushStreamContent

```
public class PushStreamContent : HttpContent
{
    public PushStreamContent(Action<Stream, HttpContent, TransportContext> onStreamAvailable);
    public PushStreamContent(Func<Stream, HttpContent, TransportContext, Task> onStreamAvailable);
    public PushStreamContent(Action<Stream, HttpContent, TransportContext> onStreamAvailable,
                             MediaTypeHeaderValue mediaType);
    public PushStreamContent(Action<Stream, HttpContent, TransportContext> onStreamAvailable,
                             string mediaType);
    public PushStreamContent(Func<Stream, HttpContent, TransportContext, Task> onStreamAvailable,
                             MediaTypeHeaderValue mediaType);
    public PushStreamContent(Func<Stream, HttpContent, TransportContext, Task> onStreamAvailable,
                             string mediaType);

    [DebuggerStepThrough]
    protected override Task SerializeToStreamAsync(Stream stream, TransportContext context);
    protected override bool TryComputeLength(out long length);
}
```

The Code

Listing 8-19 shows an example of streaming some text from the server using PushStreamContent. After each word is written to the response Stream, the program waits for 250ms.

Listing 8-19. Example of Streaming Some Text at Regular Intervals

```
public class StreamController : ApiController
{
    private const string Lipsum =
"Lorem ipsum dolor sit amet, consectetur adipiscing elit. Morbi ut urna eget est lacinia pulvinar. ";

    [Route("stream")]
    public HttpResponseMessage Get()
    {

        var resp = new HttpResponseMessage
        {
            Content = new PushStreamContent(async (respStream, content, context) =>
            {
                try
                {
                    var wordsToSend = Lipsum.Split(' ');
```

```
                    using (var writer = new StreamWriter(respStream))
                    {
                        foreach (var word in wordsToSend)
                        {
                            await writer.WriteLineAsync(word);
                            await writer.FlushAsync();
                            await Task.Delay(millisecondsDelay: 250);
                        }
                    }
                }
                catch (Exception ex)
                {
                    return;
                }
                finally
                {
                    respStream.Close();
                }
            }, "text/plain")
        };

        return resp;
    }
}
```

In order to consume such a streamed response, the key is to not wait for the entire body to arrive, but to start the processing of the response as soon as the response headers become available. On the .NET side, HttpClient allows this through the use of HttpCompletionOption.ResponseHeadersRead (the default mode is HttpCompletionOption.ResponseContentRead).

Then, using a StreamReader, you can progressively read the contents of the body until you reach the EndOfStream. Listing 8-20 shows an example of doing just that.

Listing 8-20. Reading a Streamed Response with HttpClient

```
var client = new HttpClient();
var request = new HttpRequestMessage(HttpMethod.Get, "http://localhost:9000/stream");
var response = await client.SendAsync(request, HttpCompletionOption.ResponseHeadersRead);

var body = await response.Content.ReadAsStreamAsync();

using (var reader = new StreamReader(body))
{
    while (!reader.EndOfStream)
    {
        Console.WriteLine(reader.ReadLine());
    }
}
```

Using the same principle, you could potentially stream large files or blobs of data such as music files or video files directly to the browser, which will then progressively read them over HTTP. If the relevant format supports streaming, for example MP4, your user could enjoy the playback immediately.

8-5. Support Server-Sent Events in ASP.NET Web API

Problem

You want to add support for server-sent events (JavaScript `EventSource`) in your Web API service.

Solution

While there is no out-of-the-box, plug-and-play solution, `PushStreamContent`, discussed in Recipe 8-4, makes it really easy to create a Web API-specific `EventSource` implementation, which can be used by your client applications. According to the specification of `EventSource`, the server should send messages with the `text/event-stream` media type, which can then be handled by the client.

The process ought to be a two-step one.

1. The client registers an event source (the initial handshake process between the client and the server), which in Web API would be the equivalent of creating a new, client-specific, instance of `PushStreamContent` on the server side.

2. The client then listens to the incoming events/messages from the event source, which the server sends by writing data to the response `Stream`.

How It Works

Server-sent events were first proposed back in 2006 and initially implemented by the Opera browser. Since then, they have been defined formally in the W3C Candidate Recommendation.

> *(…) specification defines an API for opening an HTTP connection for receiving push notifications from a server in the form of DOM events. The API is designed such that it can be extended to work with other push notification schemes such as Push SMS.*

> Server-Sent Events W3C
> Candidate Recommendation
> `www.w3.org/TR/eventsource/`

The specification introduces an `EventSource` interface which is used to receive server-sent events. A client establishes an HTTP connection with the server (server responds in the `text/event-stream` format), and keeps it open, waiting for the server to send events. Server-sent events are supported in all modern browsers except Internet Explorer.

The message format is very minimalistic; it could be data-only or data with some custom event.

```
data: {info: "hello world"}

event: scoreUpdate
data: {"score": 127, "date": "2014-03-14"}
```

The nature of Web API `PushStreamContent` and its ability to keep the connection open and write to the response `stream` at any time fits perfectly into the requirements for server-sent events.

▓ **Note** The ASP.NET SignalR communication framework uses server-sent events as a fallback mechanism (in case web sockets are not available and the browser has SSE support) to provide real-time client-server messaging in a similar fashion as discussed in this recipe.

The Code

To best understand the process of implementing support for server-sent events, let's write a simple ASP.NET Web API chat application powered by them. The controller is shown in Listing 8-21.

Listing 8-21. ChatController Allowing a Client to Register EventSource

```
public class ChatController : ApiController
{
    private static object locker = new object();

    private static readonly List<StreamWriter> Subscribers = new List<StreamWriter>();

    public HttpResponseMessage Get(HttpRequestMessage request)
    {
        var response = new HttpResponseMessage
        {
            Content = new PushStreamContent(async (respStream, content, context) =>
            {
                var subscriber = new StreamWriter(respStream)
                {
                    AutoFlush = true
                };
                lock (locker)
                {
                    Subscribers.Add(subscriber);
                }
                await subscriber.WriteLineAsync("data: \n");
            }, "text/event-stream")
        };
        return response;
    }
}
```

First, you have to allow the chat clients to perform the handshake with the server, registering themselves against the Web API event source. This is done by creating and returning a new instance of a PushStreamContent for each client, with the text/event-stream media type. As part of that response, the initial event sent is an empty event.

The list of connected clients is represented by a list of StreamWriter objects, created as soon as the connection with the client is established, using each client's response Stream.

The next step is to allow the client to POST chat messages. Once a client posts a message, it should then be propagated to each of the connected clients using the Subscribers list you maintain. All of that is shown in Listing 8-22.

Listing 8-22. Posting a Message to the Chat and Pushing It to All of the Connected Clients

```
public async Task Post(Message m)
{
    m.DateTime = DateTime.Now;
    await MessageCallback(m);
}
```

```
private static async Task MessageCallback(Message m)
{
    for (var i = Subscribers.Count - 1; i >=0; i--)
    {
        try
        {
            await Subscribers[i].WriteLineAsync("data:" + JsonConvert.SerializeObject(m) + "\n");
            await Subscribers[i].WriteLineAsync("");
            await Subscribers[i].FlushAsync();
        }
        catch (Exception)
        {
            lock (locker)
            {
                Subscribers.RemoveAt(i);
            }
        }
    }
}

//message model
public class Message
{
    public string Username { get; set; }
    public string Text { get; set; }
    public DateTime DateTime { get; set; }
}
```

If you encounter an exception when trying to write to the client's response Stream, you have to remove this particular StreamWriter from the list, as it means the client has disconnected. Because of that, using a typical foreach loop is not possible, as the collection could be modified while it is being iterated through. To work around that, you can use a regular for loop and iterate backwards instead.

To see this in action, you need to add a client application; in this case you will use an HTML/JavaScript one, with some Knockout.js sprinkled in to facilitate two-way bindings. Some basic HTML containing a placeholder for displaying the messages, textboxes for a username and the message, and a button are shown in Listing 8-23. Individual incoming chat messages are represented by a Knockout.js template, which will be used to inject them into the DOM as they are pushed by the server.

Listing 8-23. HTML for the Chat Application

```
<div class="row">
    <div class="col-md-4">
        <dl id="console" data-bind="template: {name: 'chatMessageTemplate',
        foreach: chatMessages }"></dl>
    </div>
</div>
<div class="row">
    <div class="col-md-4">
        <input type="text" class="form-control" placeholder="Username" data-bind="value: chatUsername">
    </div>
</div>
```

```
<div class="row">
    <div class="col-md-4">
        <textarea class="form-control" rows="3" data-bind="value: newMessage.text"></textarea>
        <button type="button" class="btn btn-primary" data-bind="click: send, enable:
        enabled()">Send</button>
    </div>
</div>

<script type="text/html" id="chatMessageTemplate">
    <dt><span data-bind="text: DateTime"></span> <span data-bind="text: Username">
        </span></dt>
    <dd><em data-bind="text: Text"></em></dd>
</script>
```

The JavaScript view model, shown in Listing 8-24, is responsible for sending the chat messages.

Listing 8-24. Knockout View Model for Handling Basic Chat Operations

```
var ChatApp = ChatApp || {};

ChatApp.Model = function () {
    var self = this;
    self.chatMessages = ko.observableArray([]);
    self.chatUsername = ko.observable("");
    self.connected = ko.observable(false);
    self.enabled = ko.computed(function() {
        return self.connected() && self.chatUsername().length > 0;
    });

    self.newMessage = {
        username: ko.computed(function () {
            return self.chatUsername();
        }),
        text: ko.observable("")
    };

    self.send = function () {
        $.ajax({
            url: "http://localhost:1300/api/chat/",
            data: JSON.stringify({
                username: self.newMessage.username(),
                text: self.newMessage.text()
            }),
            cache: false,
            type: 'POST',
            dataType: "json",
            contentType: 'application/json; charset=utf-8'
        }).success(function () {
            self.newMessage.text("");
        });
    };
};
```

Finally, let's add the relevant EventSource code. A new EventSource will be registered on page load by making a GET request to the HTTP endpoint you previously created in your Web API, which will create a new PushStreamContent for you. You need to add the following event listeners to the EventSource object:

- "message" event indicates an incoming server sent message.

- "open" is raised when the connection is successfully established.

- "close" is raised when the server explicitly closes the connection.

In Listing 8-25, you only use the default events; however, the SSE specification allows that the server can define customs ones too. Messages pushed from your Web API controller will be available in the data property of the event arguments. You can check for the browser support for EventSource by inspecting window.EventSource property.

Listing 8-25. Registering an EventSource and Relevant Event Listeners

```
$(document).ready(function () {
    var viewModel = new ChatApp.Model();
    ko.applyBindings(viewModel);

    if (window.EventSource) {
        var source = new EventSource('http://localhost:1300/api/chat/');
        source.addEventListener('message', function (e) {
            if (e.data != "") {
                var json = JSON.parse(e.data);
                viewModel.chatMessages.push(json);
            }
        }, false);

        source.addEventListener('open', function (e) {
            console.log("open!");
            viewModel.connected(true);
        }, false);

        source.addEventListener('error', function (e) {
            if (e.readyState == EventSource.CLOSED) {
                console.log("error!");
            }
        }, false);
    }
});
```

8-6. Integrate ASP.NET SignalR into ASP.NET Web API controllers
Problem

You'd like to integrate the popular real-time communication framework ASP.NET SignalR into your Web API controllers in order to notify connected clients about operations performed against your Web API resources. For example, creation of a new resource or an update to an existing one could trigger a real-time message to be sent over to the client using the SignalR infrastructure.

Solution

ASP.NET SignalR (`Microsoft.AspNet.SignalR` on NuGet) is very easy to integrate into Web API, and a very common technique to achieve this was first suggested by Brad Wilson. In this approach, you obtain an IHubContext, representing a relevant Hub, through SignalR's GlobalHost (its service locator) from inside of your controller and use it to push the relevant info to the clients. IHubContext should be a Lazy<T> since there is no need to take the penalty of resolving it on every request. This is shown in Listing 8-26.

Listing 8-26. Simple Way to Obtain IHubContext from the ApiController

```
[HubName("books")]
public class BooksHub : Hub
{}

public class BooksController : ApiController
{
    //use the hub to push message to clients
    private readonly Lazy<IHubContext> _booksHub = new Lazy<IHubContext>(() =>
    GlobalHost.ConnectionManager.GetHubContext<BooksHub>());

    //rest of the controller omitted for brevity
}
```

A variation of this approach, and a slightly more elegant implementation as it lends itself well to unit testing, is to wrap the IHubContext in a container class and inject it through the constructor instead. You'll look at that in more detail in the code section of this recipe.

How It Works

While it is outside of the scope of this book to go into detail on the inner workings of ASP.NET SignalR, let's briefly look at some of the components used in this recipe. IHubContext (Listing 8-27) provides access to hub information from outside of that hub. This is very useful in your scenario, but as a consequence, since IHubContext is resolved globally, there is no client connection information.

Listing 8-27. Definition of IHubContext

```
public interface IHubContext
{
    IHubConnectionContext Clients { get; }
    IGroupManager Groups { get; }
}
```

In other words, since IHubContext is used from outside the hub, IHubConnectionContext will not give you access to properties such as Clients.Caller or Clients.Others, which you might have been used to when calling Context property from within the hub, because there's no individual connection ID associated with the IHubContext. If you wish to work with the connection ID in this setup, you need to pass it down from the client.

IHubConnectionContext, shown in Listing 8-28, exposes a number of proxy objects, allowing you to invoke methods on the client. Since the proxies are dynamic, you are free to call any method that you wish; it will have to match one existing on your client. Each of the objects passed to those methods will be serialized to JSON using JSON.NET.

Listing 8-28. Definition of IHubConnectionContext

```
public interface IHubConnectionContext
{
    [Dynamic]
    dynamic All { get; }

    dynamic AllExcept(params string[] excludeConnectionIds);
    dynamic Client(string connectionId);
    dynamic Clients(IList<string> connectionIds);
    dynamic Group(string groupName, params string[] excludeConnectionIds);
    dynamic Groups(IList<string> groupNames, params string[] excludeConnectionIds);
    dynamic User(string userId);
}
```

An important note is that ASP.NET SignalR is entirely OWIN-based right now; therefore, after installing it from NuGet you will need to add an OWIN Startup class to wire it in. A Project Katana example is shown in Listing 8-29.

Listing 8-29. OWIN Startup Class for SignalR

```
public class Startup
{
    public void Configuration(IAppBuilder app)
    {
        app.MapSignalR();
    }
}
```

The Code

For your sample, you'll use a small book-listing application consisting of a Web API BooksController, a Book model, and an HTML/JavaScript client. Whenever a user creates a new entry in your books list, you'll push this as an update to all of the other users that are currently also looking at the list of books.

The model and the controller supporting just that is shown in Listing 8-30. You take advantage of the Lazy<T> resolution of the IHubContext that you are interested in and use it whenever a new book is created on the server in order to notify the clients about this event, by invoking the bookAdded function on the client side.

Listing 8-30. Book Model and BooksController with a Lazy<IHubContext>

```
public class Book
{
    public int Id { get; set; }
    public string Author { get; set; }
    public string Title { get; set; }
}

public class BooksController : ApiController
{
    private readonly Lazy<IHubContext> _booksHub = new Lazy<IHubContext>(() =>
    GlobalHost.ConnectionManager.GetHubContext<BooksHub>());
```

```
    private static List<Book> _books = new List<Book>
    {
        new Book {Id = 1, Author = "John Robb", Title = "Punk Rock: An Oral History"},
        new Book {Id = 2, Author = "Daniel Mohl", Title = "Building Web, Cloud, and Mobile
                  Solutions with F#"},
        new Book {Id = 3, Author = "Steve Clarke", Title = "100 Things Blue Jays Fans Should
                  Know & Do Before They Die"}
    };

    [Route("books")]
    public IEnumerable<Book> GetAll()
    {
        return _books;
    }

    [Route("books/{id:int}", Name = "GetBookById")]
    public Book GetById(int id)
    {
        return _books.FirstOrDefault(x => x.Id == id);
    }

    [Route("books")]
    public IHttpActionResult Post(Book book)
    {
        book.Id = _books.Last() != null ? _books.Last().Id + 1 : 1;
        _books.Add(book);
        _booksHub.Value.Clients.All.bookAdded(book);

        return CreatedAtRoute("GetBookById", new { id = book.Id }, book);
    }
}
```

Sticking to this approach, you could rewrite it into a more generic approach using the abstract base class ApiControllerWithHub<T>, which will expose the relevant IHubContext automatically. In this case, the modifications to the controller are very small; you just need to change the inheritance and the way you call the hub. As a bonus, you get a reusable structure, which you can utilize across different controllers with different hubs. The code is shown in Listing 8-31.

Listing 8-31. Base Class Facilitating Obtaining IHubContext from the ApiController in a Generic Way

```
public abstract class ApiControllerWithHub<T> : ApiController
    where T : IHub
{
    readonly Lazy<IHubContext> _hub = new Lazy<IHubContext>(
        () => GlobalHost.ConnectionManager.GetHubContext<THub>()
    );

    protected IHubContext Hub
    {
        get { return _hub.Value; }
    }
}
```

```
//rewritten controller declaration
public class BooksController : ApiControllerWithHub<BooksHub>

// BooksHub is now available through the Hub property on the base class
Hub.Clients.All.bookAdded(book);
```

The only caveat to this approach is that it is not very unit testable, and mocking the code responsible for resolving the IHubContext is virtually impossible at the moment. One way to solve this is to expose a setter on the Hub property on the base class (or on the _booksHub field from the earlier example), and then remember to always set it in the unit tests. But a more elegant approach is to do it properly with constructor injection.

To achieve that, let's create a BooksBroadcaster class, which will wrap your real-time functionality in a mockable interface (IBooksBroadcaster). This way you can utilize inversion of control principles to inject this functionality into your controller. This plays well into the single responsibility principle too, as the overall business logic remains the same, but the responsibility for notifying the connected clients about a specific event has been shifted from the controller into a separate, focused class. The relevant code is shown in Listing 8-32.

Listing 8-32. Injecting IHubContext Wrapped in a Container Class to Facilitate Unit Testing and to Provide Better Logic Separation

```
public class BooksBroadcaster : IBooksBroadcaster
{
    private readonly IHubContext _booksHubContext;

    public BooksBroadcaster(IHubContext booksHubContext)
    {
        _booksHubContext = booksHubContext;
    }

    public void BookAdded(Book book)
    {
        _booksHubContext.Clients.All.bookAdded(book);
    }
}

public interface IBooksBroadcaster
{
    void BookAdded(Book book);
}

public class BooksController : ApiController
{
    //use the wrapper class (interface) to push message to clients
    //in tests just inject a mock
    private readonly Lazy<BooksBroadcaster> _booksBrodacaster;

    public BooksController(Lazy<BooksBroadcaster> booksBrodacaster)
    {
        _booksBrodacaster = booksBrodacaster;
    }

     //rest of the controller omitted for brevity
}
```

259

To facilitate the dependency injection into your Web API controllers, you are obviously free to use an IoC engine of your choice, but in this example (Listing 8-33) you'll use Autofac and its `Autofac.WebApi2` NuGet package. Autofac allows you to bind to the methods, so you can bind the `IHubContext` relevant for the `BooksBrodcaster` to `BooksHub` that is being resolved from the service locator. You'll then set the Autofac container as the dependency resolution engine for your Web API, and that will automatically take care of the rest.

Listing 8-33. Registering IBooksBroadcaster in Web API DI Using Autofac

```
var builder = new ContainerBuilder();
builder.Register(
    c => new Lazy<IBooksBroadcaster>(() => new BooksBroadcaster(GlobalHost.ConnectionManager.
    GetHubContext<BooksHub>())))
    .As<Lazy<IBooksBroadcaster>>();
builder.RegisterApiControllers(Assembly.GetExecutingAssembly());

var container = builder.Build();
httpConfiguration.DependencyResolver = new AutofacWebApiDependencyResolver(container);
```

■ **Note**   Chapter 10 is dedicated entirely to dependency injection in ASP.NET Web API, so you'll skip all of the DI details here.

With the DI wired up, you can now rewrite the controller into a very clean structure, as shown in Listing 8-34. The irrelevant parts have been omitted for brevity but the code is almost identical as before.

Listing 8-34. The Modified BooksController, Using IBooksBroadcaster

```
public class BooksController : ApiController
{
    private readonly Lazy<IBooksBroadcaster> _booksBrodacaster;

    public BooksController(Lazy<IBooksBroadcaster> booksBrodacaster)
    {
        _booksBrodacaster = booksBrodacaster;
    }

    [Route("books")]
    public IHttpActionResult Post(Book book)
    {
        book.Id = _books.Last() != null ? _books.Last().Id + 1 : 1;
        _books.Add(book);
        _booksBrodacaster.Value.BookAdded(book);

        return CreatedAtRoute("GetBookById", new { id = book.Id }, book);
    }
}
```

And this is everything regarding the server side infrastructure. You can now proceed to extend the client side with real-time functionality. Recall that in all of the above examples, you were calling a bookAdded function on the client, so obviously you'll need to add it.

To enable SignalR functionality in your HTML/JS, you need to first add the appropriate JavaScript references.

```
<script src="~/Scripts/jquery.signalR-2.0.2.min.js"></script>
<script src="~/signalr/hubs"></script>
```

All the client code is shown in Listing 8-35. It provides basic capabilities of loading all books from the server and adding a new book to the book repository. The SignalR-specific bits are highlighted in bold.

Listing 8-35. Client-side Code Required to Integrate SignalR into Your Books Example

```
<script src="~/Scripts/jquery.signalR-2.0.2.min.js"></script>
<script src="~/signalr/hubs"></script>

<script type="text/javascript">
    $(document).ready(function () {
        var vm = new Apress.Books();
        var hub = $.connection.books;

        hub.client.bookAdded = function (book) {
            vm.addBook(book);
        };

        $.connection.hub.start();

        ko.applyBindings(vm);
        vm.loadBooks();
    });

    var Apress = Apress || {};
    Apress.Books = function() {
        var self = this;

        self.books = ko.observableArray([]);

        self.newBook = {
            Title: ko.observable(""),
            Author: ko.observable("")
        };

        self.addBook = function (book) {
            var existingBook = ko.utils.arrayFirst(this.books(), function (item) {
                return item.Id == book.Id;
            });
            if (!existingBook) {
                self.books.push(book);
            }
        };
```

```
        self.loadBooks = function() {
            $.ajax("http://localhost:35366/books")
                .done(function(data) {
                    $.each(data, function(idx, item) {
                        self.books.push(item);
                    });
                })
                .fail(function(xhr, status, error) {
                    alert(status);
                });
        };

        self.sendBook = function() {
            $.ajax("http://localhost:35366/books", {
                type: "POST",
                contentType: "application/json",
                dataType: 'json',
                data: JSON.stringify({ Title: self.newBook.Title(), Author: self.newBook.Author() })
            })
                .done(function(data) {
                    self.books.push(data);
                })
                .fail(function(xhr, status, error) {
                    alert(status);
                });
        };
    };
</script>

<div class="container">
    <ul data-bind="foreach: books, visible: books().length > 0">
        <li>
            <h3 data-bind="text: Title"></h3>
            <small data-bind="text: Author"></small>
        </li>
    </ul>
    <div class="input-group">
        <input type="text" class="form-control" placeholder="Title" data-bind="value: newBook.Title" />
        <input type="text" class="form-control" placeholder="Author" data-bind="value:
        newBook.Author" />
        <button type="button" class="btn btn-default" data-bind="click: sendBook">Send</button>
    </div>
</div>
```

The connection to the hub is established from within the document.ready method. Hubs are referenced by their name, through the $.connection object. Recall that you defined the name "books" on your hub using the HubNameAttribute; that's why the JS property is also called books. The client-side function that is being called from the server, bookAdded, has also been added onto the client-side hub object. It invokes a function that exists inside of your view model, which will take care of adding the received Book to the view model's observableArray and updating the UI. The rest of the client code is just some HTML and Knockout.js sprinkled on top to provide two-way bindings.

```
┌─────────────────────────────────────────────────────────────────┐
│        ASP.NET SIGNALR + ASP.NET WEB API - OWIN AND SELF-HOST     │
└─────────────────────────────────────────────────────────────────┘
```

The example shown in this recipe uses the `Microsoft.AspNet.SignalR` package which supports ASP.NET only. If you use self-host, you cannot easily combine your Web API with SignalR anymore, since classic Web API self-host (WCF based) requires exclusivity on the port it listens to, and no other listener is allowed anymore.

On the other hand, if you use Web API OWIN host (`Microsoft.AspNet.WebApi.OwinSelfHost`), all of the principles from this recipe still apply; the only difference is the OWIN `Startup` class and the SignalR package to use: `Microsoft.AspNet.SignalR.Owin`.

```csharp
public class Startup
{
    public void Configuration(IAppBuilder app)
    {
        var config = new HttpConfiguration();
        //configure Web API as you wish

        app.UseWebApi(config);
        app.MapSignalR();
    }
}
```

8-7. Use WebSockets with ASP.NET Web API

Problem

You are building a web application directly with web sockets and would like to integrate ASP.NET Web API with them.

Solution

Socket programming, as a full-duplex communication channel, is a lower-level task than doing regular HTTP work because it requires dropping down to the TCP layer. Fortunately, using the `Microsoft.WebSockets` package from NuGet makes it very easy to get started. The package ships with a couple of higher-level socket abstractions, which make working with web sockets in ASP.NET a real pleasure.

```
Install-package Microsoft.WebSockets
```

A simple example of opening up sockets from a Web API controller is shown in Listing 8-36. Notice the status code issued by your Web API action is `HttpStatusCode.SwitchingProtocols`, HTTP 101.

Listing 8-36. A Web API Action Opening Up a Socket Connection Using a Custom WebSocketHandler

```csharp
public HttpResponseMessage Get()
{
    var httpcontext = Request.Properties["MS_HttpContext"] as HttpContextBase;
    if (httpcontext == null) return new HttpResponseMessage(HttpStatusCode.InternalServerError);
```

```
    httpcontext.AcceptWebSocketRequest(new MyWebSocketHandler());
    return Request.CreateResponse(HttpStatusCode.SwitchingProtocols);
}

public class MyWebSocketHandler : WebSocketHandler
{
    //handle sockets events such as Message, Open, Close, Error
}
```

This recipe is based on a blog post from Youssef Moussaoui (http://blogs.msdn.com/b/youssefm/ archive/2012/07/17/building-real-time-web-apps-with-asp-net-webapi-and-websockets.aspx) who, at the time of writing it, was a member of the Web API team.

■ **Caution**   Microsoft.WebSockets requires WebSocket Protocol to be installed in your IIS (Control Panel ➤ Programs ➤ Turn Windows features on or off ➤ Internet Information Services ➤ World Wide Web Services ➤ Application Development Features ➤ WebSocket Protocol).

How It Works

Even though at first glance web sockets and Web API don't really overlap, you may still have plenty of scenarios where you'd like to integrate sockets with your Web API. A common use case is to perform the initial sockets handshake between the client and the server by going through the Web API pipeline and then responding with a 101 HTTP status code indicating the switch of protocols, at that point letting sockets take over. This allows you to pick up things such as user information and authorization permissions using Web API, and only dispatch to web sockets if the expected prerequisites are met.

Additionally, you may want to enable your HTTP endpoints to call into sockets to push some information to the clients as soon as it's submitted to your Web API. The notion here is similar to the integration of ASP.NET SignalR shown in Recipe 8-6. This opens up a lot of exciting scenarios; for example, you may imagine a shop order REST API that notifies an admin interface in real-time over sockets about each incoming order.

Microsoft.WebSockets supports working with sockets in ASP.NET applications; therefore it will only work with your web-hosted Web API. If you are using a different host, you will have to support sockets differently. For example, the Katana project provides a sample of how to build OWIN sockets middleware at:

http://msdn.microsoft.com/en-us/library/system.net.websockets.websocket(v=vs.110).aspx

As an additional prerequisite for the Microsoft.WebSockets package, you will have to add the following entry into the web.config. It will, among other things, ensure that the HttpContext.Current is propagated correctly onto the new threads.

```
<appSettings>
  <add key="aspnet:UseTaskFriendlySynchronizationContext" value="true" />
</appSettings>
```

Once installed, to open up a sockets connection on the server side, you have to call the AcceptWebSocketRequest extension method of the current HttpContext, and pass in a relevant WebSocketHandler. This handler will be responsible for maintaining and facilitating the actual duplex communication between you and the client. Each client is supposed to obtain its own instance of the WebSocketHandler on the server, while the collection of all connected clients is normally shared between all of the instances so that a message from one of them can be broadcasted by the server to the others.

The Code

To see this in action, let's build a small chat application similar to the one you created in Recipe 8-5 where you explore integration of server-sent events into ASP.NET Web API.

The initial handshake will be performed over Web API. In this case, you'll create an instance of a JS WebSocket object on the client side, and use the Web API endpoint as the constructor parameter; this will be the URL to which the WebSocket server responds.

Let's start your coding by adding a WebSocketHandler (Listing 8-37) responsible for handling socket operations. Each connecting client will have to go over Web API where it will register a username. From there, an instance of a ChatWebSocketHandler will be attached to a dedicated HttpContext.

Listing 8-37. ChatHandler and a Web API Controller Responsible for the Handshake and Protocol Switch

```
public class ChatHandler : WebSocketHandler
{
    private static readonly object Locker = new object();
    public static WebSocketCollection ChatClients = new WebSocketCollection();
    private readonly string _username;

    public ChatHandler(string username)
    {
        _username = username;
    }

    public override void OnOpen()
    {
        lock (Locker)
            ChatClients.Add(this);
    }

    public override void OnMessage(string message)
    {
        var msg = JsonConvert.DeserializeObject<Message>(message);
        msg.DateTime = DateTime.Now;
        msg.Username = _username;

        ChatClients.Broadcast(JsonConvert.SerializeObject(msg));
    }

    public override void OnClose()
    {
        lock (Locker)
            ChatClients.Remove(this);
    }
}
```

```
[Route("chat")]
public class ChatController : ApiController
{
    public HttpResponseMessage Get(string username)
    {
        var httpcontext = Request.Properties["MS_HttpContext"] as HttpContextBase;
        if (httpcontext == null) return new HttpResponseMessage(HttpStatusCode.InternalServerError);

        httpcontext.AcceptWebSocketRequest(new ChatHandler(username));
        return Request.CreateResponse(HttpStatusCode.SwitchingProtocols);
    }
}
```

Your ChatHandler maintains a public list of clients representing each of the users currently connected to the chat using WebSocketCollection, which is an extension of ICollection<WebSocketHandler>. Each message from the client will be sent in a JSON string format; therefore you need to deserialize it before it's usable. You then inject a timestamp and a username into the message and broadcast it to all the other clients. Remember, when the user sends a message over sockets, it's a dedicated handler on the server side that will handle it, therefore the private field holding the username will be relevant for this given user.

The big advantage of using a public collection of all of the clients is that you can now access and interact with it from outside of the handler. For example, you could expose a regular Web API HTTP endpoint allowing for messages to be POST-ed to your Web API and have them broadcasted into the chat to all of the clients. The following is an example of such an action added to the ChatController:

```
public void Post(Message msg)
{
    ChatHandler.ChatClients.Broadcast(JsonConvert.SerializeObject(msg));
}
```

This is all of the setup required on the server side. What is needed next is the HTML/JS that will act as the UI for the chat application. The code is shown in Listings 8-38 (HTML) and 8-39 (JavaScript). The key elements are highlighted in bold and discussed afterwards.

Listing 8-38. HTML Required for the Sockets Chat Application

```
<div class="row">
    <div class="col-md-4">
        <dl id="console" data-bind="template: {name: 'chatMessageTemplate', foreach: chatMessages }">
        </dl>
    </div>
</div>
<div class="row">
    <div class="col-md-4">
        <input type="text" class="form-control" placeholder="Username" data-bind="value:
        chatUsername, enable: !connected()">
    </div>
</div>
<div class="row">
    <div class="col-md-4">
        <textarea class="form-control" rows="3" data-bind="value: newMessage.text,
        enable: connected()"></textarea>
```

```html
        <button type="button" class="btn btn-primary" data-bind="click: send, enable:
        enabled()">Send</button>
        <button type="button" class="btn btn-primary" data-bind="click: connect,
        visible: !connected(), enable: chatUsername().length">Connect</button>
    </div>
</div>

<script type="text/html" id="chatMessageTemplate">
    <dt><span data-bind="text: DateTime"></span> <span data-bind="text: Username"></span></dt>
    <dd><em data-bind="text: Text"></em></dd>
</script>
```

Listing 8-39. JavaScript for the Sockets Chat Application

```javascript
<script type="text/javascript">
        var ChatApp = ChatApp || {};

        ChatApp.Model = function() {

            var self = this;
            var socket;
            self.chatMessages = ko.observableArray([]);
            self.chatUsername = ko.observable("");

            self.connected = ko.observable(false);
            self.enabled = ko.computed(function() {
                return self.connected() && self.chatUsername().length > 0;
            });

            self.newMessage = {
                text: ko.observable("")
            };

            self.connect = function() {
                var uri = "ws://localhost:4214/chat/" + self.chatUsername();
                socket = new WebSocket(uri);

                socket.onopen = function() {
                    self.connected(true);
                };

                socket.onerror = function(event) {
                    console.log("error! ");
                    console.log(event);
                };

                socket.onmessage = function (event) {
                    var parsed = JSON.parse(event.data);
                    self.chatMessages.push(parsed);
                };
            };
```

```
        self.send = function() {
            var data = JSON.stringify({
                text: self.newMessage.text()
            });
            socket.send(data);
            self.newMessage.text("");
        };
    };

    $(document).ready(function() {
        var viewModel = new ChatApp.Model();
        ko.applyBindings(viewModel);
    });
</script>
```

The WebSocket object instance exposes all the necessary events to handle duplex communication: onopen, onerror, and onmessage. The sending of messages happens via the send function exposed by WebSocket.

The "connect" button triggers the initial socket handshake and becomes available (through a Knockout binding) as soon as the user provides a username. Since a username is now maintained on the server, you use JavaScript to disable the username textbox as soon as the user connects to your chat.

As soon as the message is received from the server (inside of the onmessage event), you can parse the incoming JSON and push the message into the chatMessages observable array, which will then rely on Knockout to update the user interface and keep the chat window visually in sync with what's arrived from the server.

CHAPTER 9

■ ■ ■

Dependency Injection

This chapter covers dealing with dependency injection in Web API services. You will learn how to do the following:

- Inject dependencies into Web API controllers, filters, message handlers, and formatters (Recipe 9-1 and 9-4)

- Add support for the common DI containers (Recipe 9-2)

- Deal with per-request dependency scope (Recipe 9-3)

- Write a custom dependency resolver for ASP.NET Web API applications (Recipe 9-5)

9-1. Inject Dependencies into ASP.NET Web API Controllers
Problem

You would like to inject, through the constructor, dependencies into your ASP.NET Web API controllers.

Solution

ASP.NET Web API provides two primary mechanisms for dealing with controller dependency injection: implementing a custom IHttpControllerActivator and implementing a custom IDependencyResolver.

Since both of them can act as a bridge between the framework and your IoC container, in order to be able to inject dependencies into your controllers, you can go ahead and register an implementation of either of them, but be aware that both have strengths and weaknesses.

How It Works

IHttpControllerActivator, shown in Listing 9-1, can be thought of as a *de facto* composition root for the Web API controllers. The framework uses it to create controllers, and each controller is created on every request. On the other hand, a controller descriptor (a "pointer" to a controller for a given set of route values) is cached.

What's extremely valuable is that IHttpControllerActivator implementations also have access to the current HttpRequestMessage, and its context can be used to define dependencies. Unfortunately, this mechanism can only be used to inject controller dependencies; all other Web API pipeline members have to be treated separately.

Listing 9-1. Definition of the IHttpControllerActivator

```
public interface IHttpControllerActivator
{
    IHttpController Create(HttpRequestMessage request, HttpControllerDescriptor
controllerDescriptor, Type controllerType);
}
```

IDependencyResolver, which can be seen in Listing 9-2, on the other hand, is practically a service locator pattern which Web API uses to initialize controllers in case no custom IHttpControllerActivator is registered. This approach is very similar to how dependency resolution is done in ASP.NET MVC. Unfortunately, IDependencyResolver is completely context-less (since Web API doesn't use static objects like HttpContext.Current to provide contextual information), and because of that it has somewhat limited capacity, for example for creating per-request dependencies. It does provide a scope (BeginScope), which is even cached and reused by the framework for the duration of the request lifecycle (see Recipe 9-3) but respecting the scope is the responsibility of the adapter between IDependencyResolver and a DI container, rather than being handled by ASP.NET Web API automatically.

Listing 9-2. Definition of the IDependencyResolver

```
public interface IDependencyResolver : IDependencyScope, IDisposable
{
    IDependencyScope BeginScope();
}
```

The IDependencyScope (Listing 9-3) interface defines two methods:

- GetService: Used to fetch an instance of a specific Type.

- GetServices: Used to fetch a collection of objects of a specific Type.

Listing 9-3. Definition of the IDependencyScope

```
public interface IDependencyScope : IDisposable
{
    object GetService(Type serviceType);
    IEnumerable<object> GetServices(Type serviceType);
}
```

The Code

Let's consider the simple system shown in Listing 9-4, which is an interface that needs to be injected into a controller.

Listing 9-4. A Test Controller and a Simple Injectable Service

```
public interface IService
{
    string SaySomething();
}

public class HelloService : IService
{
```

```
    public string SaySomething()
    {
        return "HelloService";
    }
}

public class DependencyTestController : ApiController
{
    private readonly IService _service;

    public DependencyTestController(IService service)
    {
        _service = service;
    }

    public string Get()
    {
        return _service.SaySomething();
    }
}
```

The simplest imaginable implementation of the IHttpControllerActivator is shown in Listing 9-5.

Listing 9-5. Custom IHttpControllerActivator, Acting as a Composition Root

```
public class SimpleHttpControllerActivator : IHttpControllerActivator
{
    public IHttpController Create(
        HttpRequestMessage request,
        HttpControllerDescriptor controllerDescriptor,
        Type controllerType)
    {
        if (controllerType == typeof(DependencyTestController))
            return new DependencyTestController(
                new HelloService());

        return null;
    }
}
```

Since an activator has access to the controller Type information, you can use it to instantiate the relevant controller that would serve the request, as well as inject all of its dependencies from a single place. Of course, this is hardly a sustainable solution, and far from something usable in real world, but it serves the purpose really well, illustrating how the activators can control and manage the process of controller creation.

It is registered against HttpConfiguration like almost all other internal Web API services.

```
httpConfiguration.Services.Replace(typeof(IHttpControllerActivator), new
SimpleHttpControllerActivator());
```

It is very easy to change the dummy implementation into a very usable custom one. For example, consider the TinyIoC DI container shown in Listing 9-6 (this code requires installing the TinyIoC package from NuGet).

Listing 9-6. TinyIoC Implementation of IHttpControllerActivator

```
public class TinyIoCHttpControllerActivator : IHttpControllerActivator
{
    private readonly TinyIoCContainer _container;

    public TinyIoCHttpControllerActivator(TinyIoCContainer container)
    {
        _container = container;
    }

    public IHttpController Create(
        HttpRequestMessage request,
        HttpControllerDescriptor controllerDescriptor,
        Type controllerType)
    {
        var controller = _container.Resolve(controllerType);
        return controller as IHttpController;
    }
}
```

In this case, you simply use the TinyIoCContainer to resolve all dependencies. The registration process is identical to before, with the additional step of configuring the container itself.

```
var container = new TinyIoCContainer();
container.Register<IService, HelloService>();
config.Services.Replace(typeof(IHttpControllerActivator), new TinyIoCHttpControllerActivator(container));
```

In the event that Web API doesn't find a custom IHttpControllerActivator, it uses the default implementation, DefaultHttpControllerActivator. This ties into the second dependency injection possibility, IDependencyResolver, since DefaultHttpControllerActivator will use the currently available IDependencyResolver to construct the relevant controller. IDependencyResolver is registered against HttpConfiguration and is discussed in detail in Recipes 9-2 and 9-5.

9-2. Add Support for the Most Popular DI Containers
Problem

You would like to use a popular dependency injection container, such as Ninject, StructureMap, or Autofac, in your ASP.NET Web API application.

Solution

For most of the standard DI containers, the community or the core team responsible for the container has already provided an IDependencyResolver for ASP.NET Web API. Therefore, you do not have to reinvent the wheel by trying to implement the adapter yourself; it's just a matter of installing the relevant package from NuGet or from the WebApiContrib project, and registering it as your IDependencyResolver.

How It Works

The majority of the adapters are provided in the form of an IDependencyResolver, as you can learn from Recipe 9-4, which makes it possible to use the containers from outside of the controller (as opposed to using IHttpControllerActivator).

ASP.NET Web API can only have a single dependency resolver registered at a time, which means that you cannot combine two different DI containers without resorting to some heavy customizations (writing a custom wrapper IDependencyResolver, which looks up types in different containers). It was mentioned briefly in Recipe 9-1 that the DefaultHttpControllerActivator will use the current IDependencyResolver (and its IDependencyScope) to resolve the controllers. This particular mechanism is shown in Listing 9-7.

Listing 9-7. Excerpt from DefaultHttpControllerActivator Source Code, Where IDependencyResolver Is Used to Construct the Controller

```
private static IHttpController GetInstanceOrActivator(HttpRequestMessage request, Type
controllerType, out Func<IHttpController> activator)
{
    Contract.Assert(request != null);
    Contract.Assert(controllerType != null);

    // If dependency resolver returns controller object then use it.
    IHttpController instance = (IHttpController)request.GetDependencyScope().
    GetService(controllerType);
    if (instance != null)
    {
        activator = null;
        return instance;
    }

    // Otherwise create a delegate for creating a new instance of the type
    activator = TypeActivator.Create<IHttpController>(controllerType);
    return null;
}
```

The Code

The following dependency resolver implementations are available in the WebApiContrib project (also on NuGet with the same package name):

- WebApiContrib.IoC.CastleWindsor
- WebApiContrib.IoC.Mef
- WebApiContrib.IoC.Ninject
- WebApiContrib.IoC.StructureMap
- WebApiContrib.IoC.Unity

Additionally, the Autofac team provides its own dependency resolver for ASP.NET Web API, Autofac.WebApi2.

■ **Note**   Autofac is actually used internally by Microsoft to provide dependency injection for ASP.NET Web API services used in Azure Mobile Services.

Once installed, each of them is registered against your `HttpConfiguration`, and each is automatically picked up by Web API to resolve controller dependencies, and exposed for further use in other places. This is outside of the scope of this recipe, but using the dependency resolver manually will be discussed later in Recipe 9-4.

```
httpConfiguration.DependencyResolver = new AutofacWebApiDependencyResolver();
```

9-3. Deal with Request Scope
Problem

You would still like to be able to access dependencies in per-request scope in ASP.NET Web API.

Solution

For the incoming HTTP request, ASP.NET Web API begins a dependency scope (`IDependencyScope`) from the registered `IDependencyResolver`, creating a *de facto* one-to-one relationship between the scope and the request. This scope can be reused throughout the request's lifetime, and the framework will dispose of it as soon as request ends (`IDependencyScope` is disposable).

By using the relevant `HttpRequestMessage` extension method, you are able to obtain the current scope and use it to resolve dependencies. The same scope is also used internally by Web API to create an instance of the relevant `ApiController`.

```
var scope = request.GetDependencyScope(); //returns IDependencyScope
```

How It Works

By calling the `GetDependencyScope` method on the current request you get an instance of the `IDependencyScope` that is unique to this request only. Because of that, the container used to handle dependency resolution will be a child container of the main (global) registered container. Since, as mentioned, this child container is specific for the duration of the request, the framework will dispose of it once the request gets disposed of. This is shown in the excerpt from ASP.NET Web API source code shown in Listing 9-8.

Such a mechanism makes it easier for the IoC container to provide per-request dependency scope, but ultimately it all really depends on the particular implementation of the `IDependencyResolver`. For example, for the Ninject `IDependencyResolver`, you are guaranteed that dependencies obtained through `GetDependencyScope` will be in a per-request lifetime.

Listing 9-8. Extension Method Responsible for Obtaining the Dependecy Scope

```
public static IDependencyScope GetDependencyScope(this HttpRequestMessage request)
{
    if (request == null)
    {
        throw Error.ArgumentNull("request");
    }

    IDependencyScope result;
    if (!request.Properties.TryGetValue<IDependencyScope>(HttpPropertyKeys.DependencyScope, out result))
```

```
    {
        IDependencyResolver dependencyResolver = request.GetConfiguration().DependencyResolver;
        result = dependencyResolver.BeginScope();
        if (result == null)
        {
            throw Error.InvalidOperation(SRResources.DependencyResolver_BeginScopeReturnsNull,
            dependencyResolver.GetType().Name);
        }
        request.Properties[HttpPropertyKeys.DependencyScope] = result;
        request.RegisterForDispose(result);
    }

    return result;
}
```

As you can see, the GetDependencyScope method tries to grab the IDependencyScope from the HttpRequestMessage properties. If it's already been used during the current request lifetime, it's reused; otherwise, it would be created (BeginScope) and added there. In other words, the extension method is merely a wrapper around the request's properties dictionary and the HttpPropertyKeys.DependencyScope key. So the scope could also be obtained by reaching into the dictionary directly.

```
var dependencyScope = request.Properties[HttpPropertyKeys.DependencyScope] as IDependencyScope;
```

This approach is not ideal and violates basic inversion of control principles, since the class taking on dependencies is not explicit about it (does not request its dependencies via a constructor, but rather gains off the HttpRequestMessage). It is sometimes an acceptable workaround, however, given some of the framework constraints, which are discussed in Recipe 9-4.

Finally, since you know that the scope is effectively just an entry in the request's properties dictionary, it's relatively easy to mock such hidden dependencies in the unit test.

The Code

You can access dependencies through the current IDependencyResolver in two ways: through the global scope, or through the per-request scope.

If you interact directly with the resolver available through the HttpConfiguration, the scope will be global, while if you use the GetDependencyScope method (or the HttpPropertyKeys.DependencyScope key), the scope will be request-specific.

```
var globalScope = request.GetConfiguration().DependencyResolver;
var perRequestScope = request.GetDependencyScope();
```

9-4. DI with Other ASP.NET Web API Components
Problem

Aside from controller constructor injection, you would like to resolve dependencies in other ASP.NET Web API artifacts, such as message handlers, filters, and formatters.

Solution

Due to the nature of how the handlers, filters, and formatters are constructed in the API pipeline, and their varying lifetime, it is not possible to perform typical constructor injection into them. You can, however, always obtain a dependency through the registered IDependencyResolver instance with a call to GetDependencyScope via the current HttpRequestMessage.

```
var myService = request.GetDependencyScope().GetService(typeof(IService)) as IService;
```

How It Works

For performance reasons, filters are cached and reused between requests. Additionally, some filters are shared between actions (controller-scoped filters and globally-scoped filters). This effectively eliminates any possibility of constructor injection into them, unless the injected dependency is a singleton, since then its lifetime does not matter anymore. In general, this type of behavior might be somewhat surprising to developers familiar with ASP.NET MVC, where there is no such lifetime restriction, and constructor injection into filters is possible.

In order to resolve dependencies in the filters, you have to resolve them from the currently registered dependency resolver manually. While this approach is far from ideal, it works well, and when approached correctly, allows your filters to remain testable.

Message handlers are created just once in the lifecycle of a Web API application, and then they are reused between different requests. Therefore, similarly to action filters, trying to inject any dependencies other than singletons through its constructor does not make sense.

Since message handlers allow you to process the request and response in the same handler method—as it comes in and as it goes out of your Web API system—you typically only need to obtain the dependency once and it will be available on both sides of the processing pipeline.

A final element of the Web API pipeline is the collection of MediaTypeFormatters. Because individual formatters are registered in the formatters collection as instances of Type (not delegates to create an instance), constructor injection into them is not possible. However, the base MediaTypeFormatter class provides a hook (Listing 9-9) for enriching the formatter instance with a modified state on a per-request basis.

Listing 9-9. A Useful Hook for Customizing an Instance of a Formatter - GetPerRequestFormatterInstance

```
public abstract class MediaTypeFormatter
{
    //omitted for brevity
    public virtual MediaTypeFormatter GetPerRequestFormatterInstance(Type type, HttpRequestMessage
    request, MediaTypeHeaderValue mediaType)
    {
        //overrideable
    }
}
```

The GetPerRequestFormatterInstance method is called every time the framework asks for an instance of a given type of formatter. By overriding it, you can inject whatever you wish into the formatter, and since you have access to the current HttpRequestMessage, you can also obtain the dependency scope.

The Code

Let's look at how you'd deal with dependencies in filters, handlers, and formatters. Each of the following examples will take advantage of the GetDependencyScope method on the request and use its return type, IDependencyScope, to resolve services. For insight into the internal behavior of GetDependencyScope, see Recipe 9-3.

Filters

With filters, the resolution of the dependency happens directly in the relevant method in which you would need that dependency, as shown in Listing 9-10.

Listing 9-10. A Sample Filter with a Dummy IService Dependency

```
public class MyActionFilter : ActionFilterAttribute
{
    public override void OnActionExecuting(HttpActionContext actionContext)
    {
        var myService = actionContext.Request.GetDependencyScope().GetService(typeof(IService)) as
IService;
        // do stuff with myService
    }

    public override void OnActionExecuted(HttpActionExecutedContext actionExecutedContext)
    {
        var myService = actionExecutedContext.Request.GetDependencyScope().
GetService(typeof(IService)) as IService;
        // do stuff with myService
    }
}
```

Message Handlers

Handlers, similarly to filters, should resolve dependencies inline, directly obtaining the current IDependencyScope whenever they are required. An example can be seen in Listing 9-11.

Listing 9-11. A Sample Handler with a Dummy IService Dependency

```
public class MyHandler : DelegatingHandler
{
    protected override async Task<HttpResponseMessage> SendAsync(HttpRequestMessage request,
    CancellationToken cancellationToken)
    {
        var myService = request.GetDependencyScope().GetService(typeof(IService)) as IService;
        // do stuff with myService
        // before the rest of request is processed

        var response = await base.SendAsync(request, cancellationToken);

        // do stuff with MyService
        // after the request has been processed

        return response;
    }
}
```

Formatters

For the formatters, you have to perform the call to GetDependencyScope inside the GetPerRequestFormatterInstance method, since that's the only method that has access to the current HttpRequestMessage. You can then save the instance of your resolved service in a field or a property of the formatter, so that it can be accessed from other methods too. This is shown in Listing 9-12.

Listing 9-12. A Sample Formatter with a Dummy IService Dependency

```
public class MyFormatter : JsonMediaTypeFormatter
{
    public IService Service { get; set; }

    public override MediaTypeFormatter GetPerRequestFormatterInstance(Type type, HttpRequestMessage
request, MediaTypeHeaderValue mediaType)
    {
        var formatter = base.GetPerRequestFormatterInstance(type, request, mediaType);
        Service = request.GetDependencyScope().GetService(typeof (IService)) as IService;
        return formatter;
    }
}
```

9-5. Write a Custom DI Adapter
Problem

You need to write an adapter for the dependency injection container of your choice, as you cannot find a ready-made solution in the WebApiContrib project. For example, TinyIoC is a popular IoC container that doesn't have an implementation there.

Solution

You will need to add TinyIoC from NuGet.

```
Install-package TinyIoC
```

In order to support a given DI container, you need to write a custom resolver by implementing the IDependencyResolver interface (see Recipes 9-1 and 9-2 for more background). IDependencyResolver inherits from IDependencyScope, and as such, they could be implemented in a single class, but I always recommend separating them into different classes as this approach is generally more readable.

```
public class TinyIoCScope : IDependencyScope
{
    //omitted for brevity
}

public class TinyIoCResolver : TinyIoCScope, IDependencyResolver
{
    //omitted for brevity
}
```

The registration of the new TinyIoC resolver is done the same way as all of the other dependency resolvers (Recipe 9-2).

```
var container = new TinyIoCContainer();
//register dependencies in the container
config.DependencyResolver = new TinyIoCResolver(container);
```

How It Works

In ASP.NET Web API, you are able to interact with two scopes: global, represented by the IDependencyScope (remember that IDependencyResolver is an IDependencyScope) registered against your HttpConfiguration, and inner child scope, represented by the IDependencyScope (seen in Listing 9-14) returned from IDependencyResolver's BeginScope method (which is disposed at the end of the HTTP request). This one is shown in Listing 9-13.

Listing 9-13. Definition of the IDependencyResolver

```
public interface IDependencyResolver : IDependencyScope, IDisposable
{
    IDependencyScope BeginScope();
}
```

Whenever a new controller is constructed, which happens for every incoming HTTP request, the Web API framework will ask for a relevant scope using BeginScope.

Whenever you call GetDependencyScope on the HttpRequestMessage, the framework will try to get a scope for you by calling BeginScope of the IDependencyResolver, and then cache it for the duration of the HTTP request. See Recipe 9-3 for more details.

Listing 9-14. Definition of the IDependencyScope

```
public interface IDependencyScope : IDisposable
{
    object GetService(Type serviceType);
    IEnumerable<object> GetServices(Type serviceType);
}
```

Aside from using the dependency resolver as a way to auto-inject dependencies into your controllers, you are also able to manually use it as a service locator whenever you need to. Refer to Recipes 9-3 and 9-4 for details.

The Code

Let's start off a little backwards by implementing the inner interface, IDependencyScope, as it is going to be directly responsible for resolving services from TinyIoC. This can be seen in Listing 9-15.

Listing 9-15. TinyIoC-Specific IDependencyScope

```
public class TinyIoCScope : IDependencyScope
{
    protected TinyIoCContainer Container;
```

```csharp
    public TinyIoCScope(TinyIoCContainer container)
    {
        if (container == null)
            throw new ArgumentNullException("container");

        Container = container;
    }
    public object GetService(Type serviceType)
    {
        if (Container == null)
            throw new ObjectDisposedException("this", "This scope has already been disposed.");

        try
        {
            return Container.Resolve(serviceType);
        }
        catch (TinyIoCResolutionException)
        {
            return null;
        }
    }

    public IEnumerable<object> GetServices(Type serviceType)
    {
        if (Container == null)
            throw new ObjectDisposedException("this", "This scope has already been disposed.");

        try
        {
            return Container.ResolveAll(serviceType);
        }
        catch (TinyIoCResolutionException)
        {
            return Enumerable.Empty<object>();
        }
    }

    public void Dispose()
    {
        Container = null;
        GC.SuppressFinalize(this);
    }
}
```

To begin with, an instance of `TinyIoCContainer`, which will be used to resolve inversion of control requests, is passed through the constructor. By the time this container is instantiated, all the dependencies should have already been registered in it. In order to find an implementation of a specific class that had been registered against the container, you simply ask for it using the `Resolve` method. `Resolve` will return an `object`, which you can push down the Web API pipeline. To get multiple services (`IEnumerable<object>`), you can use the `ResolveAll` method. All of this is in the TinyIoC API, which you use to bridge the Web API IoC abstraction with TinyIoC's container.

■ **Caution**   In order to not break the Web API processing pipeline when implementing a custom IDependencyScope, do not throw an Exception if a dependency cannot be resolved; return null instead for GetService and an empty Enumerable for the GetServices method.

Next, you'll add the dependency resolver, which will extend the TinyIoCScope and be responsible for initiating the scope in which dependencies are going to be processed. The code is shown in Listing 9-16.

Listing 9-16. Full Implementation of IDependencyResolver for TinyIoC

```
public class TinyIoCResolver : TinyIoCScope, IDependencyResolver
{
    public TinyIoCResolver(TinyIoCContainer container) : base(container)
    {}

    public IDependencyScope BeginScope()
    {
        return new TinyIoCScope(Container.GetChildContainer());
    }
}
```

As discussed before, Web API will want to create a scope for every HTTP request (through the BeginScope method), so you will need to return a new instance of TinyIoCScope from there. Note that TinyIoC doesn't support a way to create a bounded scope, and even though you use GetChildContainer, it will still continue to resolve the dependencies based on how they were registered globally (i.e. as a singleton or as a transient dependency).

■ **Tip**   If you are using Web API on ASP.NET, you can use TinyIoC's AsPerRequestSingleton extension method on your registered object to force it into per-request mode. This won't work on any other host, though.

Registration of the resolver against the configuration is very simple; it's done against your HttpConfiguration. Suppose you have some service, registered against a TinyIoC container, like in Listing 9-17.

Listing 9-17. A Sample Service and Registration of Your Custom TinyIoCResolver

```
public interface IService
{
    string SaySomething();
}

public class HelloService : IService
{
    public string SaySomething()
    {
        return "HelloService";
    }
}
```

```
var container = new TinyIoCContainer();
container.Register<IService, HelloService>(); //singleton
container.Register<IService, HelloService>().AsMultiInstance(); //transient
container.Register<IService, HelloService>().AsPerRequestSingleton(); //per-request (ASP.NET only)

httpConfiguration.DependencyResolver = new TinyIoCResolver(container);
```

That's it. From now on, all the constructor-injected dependencies in your Web API controllers will be resolved by TinyIoC, through the use of your shiny new TinyIoC adapter. You can also get hold of the adapter at any point where you have access to an HttpRequestMessage, through the techniques discussed in Recipes 9-3 and 9-4.

■ ■ ■

CHAPTER 10

Securing an ASP.NET Web API Service

Security in software development, and more importantly in web development, is a sensitive, vast, and complex topic, but in this chapter I'll try to make sense of some of the most common techniques for securing ASP.NET Web APIs services. I'll deal with authentication, authorization, and transport security, as well as look into the Web API way of dealing with some of the common .NET concepts, such as IPrincipal.

The chapter does not aim to be an A-Z reference on Web API security. Due to the space constraint that I have here, I'll obviously only be able scratch the surface of many of the concepts. Hopefully it will get deep enough to get you going.

You will learn how to do the following:

- Use correct Web API components for security tasks, and safely deal with IPrincipal (Recipes 10-1 and 10-7)

- Use and enforce HTTPS with your ASP.NET Web API (Recipe 10-2)

- Integrate basic authentication and Windows authentication (Recipes 10-3 and 10-4)

- Use MAC-based authentication with the example of Hawk (Recipe 10-5)

- Get started with OAuth 2.0 (Recipe 10-6)

- Remove the header footprint injected by ASP.NET Web API applications (Recipe 10-8)

Should you wish to really go in-depth with the security aspects of Web API, I strongly recommend these resources as a follow-up to the recipes from this chapter:

- *"Pro ASP.NET Web API Security: Securing ASP.NET Web API"* by Badrinarayanan Lakshmiraghavan, www.apress.com/microsoft/asp-net/9781430257820

- Dominick Baier's blog at http://leastprivilege.com/. He's an identity and access control guru.

- ASP.NET Identity section at www.asp.net/identity

10-1. Use Correct Web API Components for Security-Related Tasks
Problem

You cannot decide whether to use message handlers or filters for authorization and authentication.

Solution

In the first version of ASP.NET Web API, the distinction was the following:

- Use MessageHandlers for authentication
- Use IAuthorizationFilter for authorization

Since version 2 of the framework, Web API has been OWIN-compatible. This means that you can also take advantage of OWIN security middleware, such as Microsoft.Owin.Security, when building your ASP.NET Web API applications. Additionally, ASP.NET Web API 2 enhanced its security pipeline by introducing IAuthenticationFilter, intended explicitly for handling authentication tasks. As a result, it is recommended that you now do the following:

- Use OWIN middleware for host-specific authentication
- Use MessageHandlers for cross-cutting security concerns, such as CORS (Cross-Origin Resource Sharing)
- Use IAuthenticationFilter for ASP.NET Web API-specific authentication
- Use IAuthorizationFilter for authorization

■ **Tip** These rules are not set in stone, and, technically, there is nothing wrong with using MessageHandlers for authentication purposes; however, all of the newest security components will likely be written as IAuthenticationFilters.

How It Works

The distinction between authentication and authorization is clear and applicable to any identity-driven software, regardless of the technology or framework applied.

- *Authentication* deals with a user's identity, verifying if the user, or connecting client, really is who he is claiming to be.
- *Authorization* deals with granting the user (connecting client) access to specific resources and system operations based on the user's identity.

On the Web API framework level, it's important to perform authorization and authentication in separate components to avoid coupling of the two concepts in a single class. ASP.NET Web API ships with a single, simple implementation of IAuthorizationFilter called AuthorizeAttribute. It provides support for authorizing users based on the following:

- The sole fact they are authenticated (the HttpRequestMessage carries an associated IPrincipal)
- Role name(s)
- User name(s)

The method that's responsible for this is shown in Listing 10-1, in an excerpt from the ASP.NET Web API source code. It is virtual so you are able to override this default behavior with your own custom logic, and extend the authorization mechanisms in your Web API application this way.

Listing 10-1. IsAuthorized Method of AuthorizeAttribute

```
protected virtual bool IsAuthorized(HttpActionContext actionContext)
{
    if (actionContext == null)
    {
        throw Error.ArgumentNull("actionContext");
    }

    IPrincipal user = actionContext.ControllerContext.RequestContext.Principal;
    if (user == null || user.Identity == null || !user.Identity.IsAuthenticated)
    {
        return false;
    }

    if (_usersSplit.Length > 0 && !_usersSplit.Contains(user.Identity.Name, StringComparer.
OrdinalIgnoreCase))
    {
        return false;
    }

    if (_rolesSplit.Length > 0 && !_rolesSplit.Any(user.IsInRole))
    {
        return false;
    }

    return true;
}
```

As far as the Web API execution pipeline is concerned, prior to executing the controller action relevant for the current HTTP request, ASP.NET Web API will gather all global, controller-level, and action-level filters and group them by type:

- Authentication filters
- Authorization filters
- Action filters
- Exception filters

Then a filter pipeline is formed, with global ones given the highest, and action-level the lowest, precedence. They get executed one after another, with each filter having the option to *short-circuit* (immediately return) an HttpResponseMessage. In this filter pipeline, IAuthenticationFilter is always executed before IAuthorizationFilter.

■ **Note** The filter pipeline is discussed in more detail in Chapter 5.

Core ASP.NET Web API does not ship with any concrete implementation of `IAuthenticationFilter`. The only available implementation is `HostAuthenticationFilter`, which is part of `System.Web.Http.Owin` from the `Microsoft.AspNet.WebApi.Owin` NuGet package (you will install this whenever you need an OWIN adapter for Web API), and is intended to be integrated with the host-level authentication provided by the Katana authentication middleware.

`HostAuthenticationFilter` uses `IAuthenticationManager` from `Microsoft.Owin.Security` to perform host-level authentication, and set the `IPrincipal` (in the form of `ClaimsPrincipal`) on the `HttpAuthenticationContext`. In fact, `HostAuthenticationFilter` is not even an `Attribute`, so it cannot be used to decorate actions and controllers. Instead, `HostAuthenticationAttribute` can be used as a proxy (it forwards all the calls to `HostAuthenticationFilter`).

Message handlers (`DelegatingHandlers`) are general purpose execution pipeline components that are suitable for processing raw `HttpRequestMessages` and `HttpResponseMessages`. As such, they are generally appropriate for a wide range of security-related tasks. A great example of a message handler-based Web API authentication component is the `Thinktecture.IdentityModel.WebApi.AuthNHandler` NuGet package. As a message handler, it supports

- JSON Web Token (JWT)
- Simple Web Token (SWT)
- Security Assertion Markup Language (SAML) tokens
- Basic authentication
- Client certificates
- Access keys

The handler looks for relevant credentials on every request, and if found, will create an `IPrincipal` (`ClaimsPrincipal`) and set it against the `RequestContext` of the current `HttpRequestMessage`, or deny access if needed.

The Code

Registration of message handler-based authentication components is the same as registering any other Web API message handler, and is done against the `MessageHandlers` collection hanging off the `HttpConfiguration` instance. The following code shows registration of the `AuthenticationHandler` from `Thinktecture.IdentityModel.WebApi.AuthNHandler`:

```
var authenticationConfiguration = new AuthenticationConfiguration();

//configure authenticationConfiguration according to your application's needs
httpConfiguration.MessageHandlers.Add(new AuthenticationHandler(authenticationConfiguration));
```

When running ASP.NET Web API on top of OWIN, to register the `HostAuthenticationFilter` with a specific type of Katana authentication middleware for your entire Web API, you need to add that filter to the `Filters` collection of the `HttpConfiguration`. `HostAuthenticationFilter` requires you to pass in the authentication type (corresponding to the relevant OWIN middleware). For example, this is how it would look for Facebook authentication:

```
httpConfiguration.Filters.Add(new HostAuthenticationFilter("Facebook"));
```

Obviously, this would only work if your Katana pipeline has Facebook authentication middleware already enabled, which is done against your `IAppBuilder`, in your OWIN `Startup` class.

```
app.UseFacebookAuthentication(
    appId: "{your ID}",
    appSecret: "{your secret}");
```

Since HostAuthenticationFilter can also be used as an Attribute (proxied via HostAuthenticationAttribute), it can also be applied at controller or action level, allowing you to control which specific resources in your API require authentication. For example, in Listing 10-2, the GetAll method does not require authentication, while GetSingle is available to anyone, as long as they have authenticated with Facebook.

Listing 10-2. Application of HostAuthenticationAttribute

```
public class SampleController : ApiController
{
    [HostAuthentication("Facebook")]
    public HttpResponseMessage GetAll()
    {
        //omitted for brevity
    }

    public HttpResponseMessage GetSingle(int id)
    {
        //omitted for brevity
    }
}
```

However, such a granular approach to authentication is generally not recommended, as it blurs the lines between authorization and authentication.

Instead, once authentication is enforced globally through a globally registered IAuthenticationFilter or a MessageHandler, you can use AuthorizationAttribute to enforce the requirement of being authenticated at specific API endpoints, as well as perform specific authorization tasks, such as role-based restriction. This is shown in Listing 10-3; in both cases in this example, the attribute will first check for the presence of an IPrincipal that should be populated by the authentication filter or message handler responsible for authentication, and if it's not there, the user will be denied access.

Listing 10-3. Application of AuthorizeAttribute

```
public class SampleController : ApiController
{
    [Authorize(Roles = "VIP")]
    public HttpResponseMessage GetAll()
    {
        //omitted for brevity
    }

    [Authorize]
    public HttpResponseMessage GetSingle(int id)
    {
        //omitted for brevity
    }
}
```

10-2. Add HTTPS Support to ASP.NET Web API

Problem

You would like your ASP.NET Web API service to use TLS (Transport Layer Security) and the HTTPS scheme instead of HTTP.

Solution

When running ASP.NET Web API on top of IIS, HTTPS can be enforced at the IIS level, through IIS Manager, in the Bindings ➤ Add site binding dialog shown in Figure 10-1. You will have to associate a valid SSL certificate that's installed on your machine with the HTTPS binding that you create. Afterwards, in ASP.NET Web API itself, no additional changes are necessary.

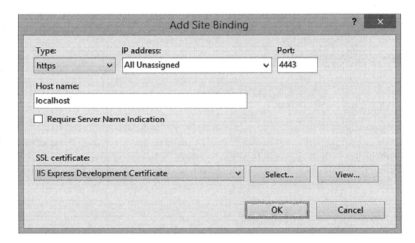

Figure 10-1. *Configuring HTTPS binding in IIS*

If you use other hosts for your Web API, you can enforce the HTTPS scheme directly from within the Web API configuration. To do that, you will first need to bind the SSL certificate (certificate creation is beyond the scope of this recipe) to a specific port on your machine using netsh, a command-line Windows utility, allowing you to modify network settings.

```
netsh http add sslcert ipport=0.0.0.0:4443 certhash={certificate hash} appid={application Guid}
```

You can then use the HTTPS scheme when creating a new hosted instance of your Web API, both in self-hosed Web API and in OWIN (for example, using Katana) outside of System.Web/IIS. This is shown in Listing 10-4.

Listing 10-4. Configuration of HTTPS in Self-hosted and OWIN-hosted Web API, Outside of IIS

```
//self host
var config = new HttpSelfHostConfiguration("https://localhost:4443/");

//owin - configuration of Web API done in the Startup class
using (WebApp.Start<Startup>("https://localhost:4443/"))
{
    //omitted for brevity
}
```

■ **Note**   Additionally, you may need to reserve the URL and port using the following `netsh` command: `netsh http add urlacl url=https://localhost:4443/ user={domain}\{username}`

How It Works

The HTTPS scheme was defined in RFC 2818 as a blueprint for providing security for HTTP-based communication, and stands for "HTTP over TLS."

> *HTTP [RFC2616] was originally used in the clear on the Internet. However, increased use of HTTP for sensitive applications has required security measures. SSL and its successor TLS [RFC2246] were designed to provide channel-oriented security.*

> Internet Engineering Task Force, RFC 2818,
> `http://tools.ietf.org/html/rfc2818`

When the communication between the client and the server happens over HTTPS, the HTTP protocol is layered on top of a secure protocol, such as SSL (predecessor to TLS) or TLS (Transport Layer Security), instead of just the raw TCP.

The current TLS version, 1.2, was introduced by RFC 2246 and defined bidirectional, private, reliable, and secure communication. TLS is flexible in terms of cryptographic algorithms, combining both asymmetric and symmetric encryption; public key cryptography is used to authenticate the server to the client, while the majority of data is encrypted using symmetric encryption.

On the Web API level, in addition to globally enabling your ASP.NET Web API to use HTTPS, you can also introduce relevant components into the ASP.NET Web API pipeline that will ensure that a given request has been sent over an HTTPS scheme. This can be done as a message handler or an authentication filter. There is no base class for authentication filters so you will have to implement the IAuthenticationFilter, shown in Listing 10-5, by hand.

Listing 10-5. Defitinion of IAuthenticationFilter

```
public interface IAuthenticationFilter
{
    void OnAuthentication(AuthenticationContext filterContext);
    void OnAuthenticationChallenge(AuthenticationChallengeContext filterContext);
}
```

The Code

If you decide to go with a handler, you can plug it into the `HttpConfiguration` to enable HTTPS enforcement against your entire API. With the filter approach, you may choose only specific endpoints as requiring HTTPS by decorating the relevant controller or action method with a filter attribute. See Listings 10-6 and 10-7 for examples of these approaches.

Listing 10-6. An Authentication Filter Enforcing HTTPS

```
public class RequireHttpsAttribute : IAuthenticationFilter
{
    public bool AllowMultiple
    {
        get { return true; }
    }

    public Task AuthenticateAsync(HttpAuthenticationContext context, CancellationToken
cancellationToken)
    {
        if (context.Request.RequestUri.Scheme != Uri.UriSchemeHttps)
        {
            context.ActionContext.Response = new HttpResponseMessage(System.Net.HttpStatusCode.
Forbidden)
            {
                ReasonPhrase = "HTTPS Required"
            };
        }

        return Task.FromResult(true);
    }

    public Task ChallengeAsync(HttpAuthenticationChallengeContext context, CancellationToken
cancellationToken)
    {
        return Task.FromResult(true);
    }
}
```

Listing 10-7. A Message Handler Enforcing HTTPS

```
public class RequireHttpsHandler : DelegatingHandler
{
    protected override Task<HttpResponseMessage> SendAsync(HttpRequestMessage request,
CancellationToken cancellationToken)
    {
        if (request.RequestUri.Scheme != Uri.UriSchemeHttps)
        {
            return Task.FromResult(new HttpResponseMessage(System.Net.HttpStatusCode.Forbidden)
```

```
        {
            ReasonPhrase = "HTTPS Required"
        });

    }
    return base.SendAsync(request, cancellationToken);
    }
}
```

If you are running a version of Web API older than version 2, IAuthenticationFilter will not be available to you. In that case, you can provide the same type of functionality by extending the AuthorizeFilterAttribute base class, such as in the example in Listing 10-8. However, authentication filters run earlier in the pipeline, and therefore, from the textbook security standpoint are more suitable.

Listing 10-8. Enforcing HTTPs with AuthorizeFilterAttribute

```
public class RequireHttpsAttribute : AuthorizationFilterAttribute
{
    public override void OnAuthorization(HttpActionContext actionContext)
    {
        if (actionContext.Request.RequestUri.Scheme != Uri.UriSchemeHttps)
        {
            actionContext.Response = new HttpResponseMessage(System.Net.HttpStatusCode.Forbidden)
            {
                ReasonPhrase = "HTTPS Required"
            };
        }
        else
        {
            base.OnAuthorization(actionContext);
        }
    }
}
```

With the message handler approach, you then need to register the handler in the HttpConfiguration.

```
var config = new HttpConfiguration();
config.MessageHandlers.Add(new RequireHttpsHandler());
```

If you opt to use filters, you can use them directly on the relevant actions or a controller, like so:

```
[RequireHttps]
public class MyController : ApiController
{
    //omitted for brevity
}
```

▓ **Tip**   If you are using an invalid certificate with `HttpClient`, requests will fail, making development and testing very frustrating. To mitigate that, you can introduce the following line of code, which instructs `System.Net` to ignore all SSL errors:

```
ServicePointManager.ServerCertificateValidationCallback += (sender, certificate, chain, sslErrors)
=> true;
```

10-3. Use Basic Authentication
Problem

You want to secure your ASP.NET Web API resources with Basic authentication.

Solution

While it's definitely possible to roll out your own Basic authentication support in the form of OWIN middleware, a Web API `MessageHandler`, or a Web API authentication filter, there is no need to reinvent the wheel.

The `Thinktecture.IdentityModel` library already provides an excellent and very flexible Basic authentication support (and other types of authentication mechanisms too, via the same package). To get started, install the Web API version of the library from NuGet.

```
Install-Package Thinktecture.IdentityModel.WebApi.AuthenticationHandler
```

You then have to configure the Basic authentication settings (such as enforcing SSL, header name, logic responsible for validating username and password, and so on) and register a Thinktecture `AuthenticationHandler` against your `HttpConfiguration`.

Alternatively, if you are using Katana (OWIN), you can choose to handle Basic authentication outside your Web API and opt to use the Thinktecture Basic Authentication OWIN middleware instead. This is done through a separate package.

```
Install-Package Thinktecture.IdentityModel.Owin.BasicAuthentication
```

This package contains the `BasicAuthenticationHandler` Katana middleware, which extends `AuthenticationHandler` middleware from `Microsoft.Owin.Security`.

How It Works

Basic authentication is the simplest, and arguably most commonly used, technique for securing HTTP APIs. With Basic authentication, the username and password are sent unencrypted (only `base64` encoded) in the `Authorization` header of every request the client makes to the server. This automatically means that in order to ensure that the credentials are not compromised, Basic authentication must be used together with TLS or SSL.

Basic authentication was first introduced by RFC 1945, back in 1996, as part of Hypertext Transfer Protocol HTTP/1.0.

The "basic" authentication scheme is based on the model that the user agent must authenticate itself with a user-ID and a password for each realm. The realm value should be considered an opaque string which can only be compared for equality with other realms on that server. The server will authorize the request only if it can validate the user-ID and password for the protection space of the Request-URI. There are no optional authentication parameters.

Hypertext Transfer Protocol — HTTP/1.0, RFC 1945,
`www.rfc-base.org/txt/rfc-1945.txt`

Requests to API endpoints protected by Basic authentication should contain an `Auhorization` header and `base64` encoded username and password, concatenated with a colon, and preceded by a `Basic` keyword.

`Authorization: Basic ZmlsaXA6YWJj`

On the server side, in case the client tries to access an endpoint without passing in the correct (or any) credentials, the server issues a 401 Not Authorized response containing a `WWW-Authenticate` header.

`WWW-Authenticate: Basic realm="Apress"`

By default, the Thinktecture implementation of basic authentication requires SSL, automatically sets the `IPrincipal` object on the incoming HTTP request, and sends back the proper `WWW-Authenticate` header in case the authentication fails. All of that and more is controlled via the `AuthenticationConfiguration` class, an overview of which is shown in Listing 10-9. As a result, you are able to easily customize the Basic authentication behavior to suit your application's needs.

Listing 10-9. Overview of AuthenticationConfiguration

```
public class AuthenticationConfiguration
{
    public void AddMapping(AuthenticationOptionMapping mapping);
    public bool TryGetAuthorizationHeaderMapping(string scheme, out SecurityTokenHandlerCollection
    handler);
    public bool TryGetHeaderMapping(string headerName, out SecurityTokenHandlerCollection handler);
    public bool TryGetQueryStringMapping(string paramName, out SecurityTokenHandlerCollection handler);
    public bool TryGetClientCertificateMapping(out SecurityTokenHandlerCollection handler);
    public List<AuthenticationOptionMapping> Mappings { get; set; }
    public bool SendWwwAuthenticateResponseHeaders { get; set; }
    public ClaimsAuthenticationManager ClaimsAuthenticationManager { get; set; }
    public bool InheritHostClientIdentity { get; set; }
    public bool EnableSessionToken { get; set; }
    public SessionTokenConfiguration SessionToken { get; set; }
    public bool RequireSsl { get; set; }
    public bool SetPrincipalOnRequestInstance { get; set; }
    public bool HasAuthorizationHeaderMapping { get; }
    public bool HasHeaderMapping { get; }
    public bool HasQueryStringMapping { get; }
    public bool HasCookieMapping { get; }
    public bool HasClientCertificateMapping { get; }
}
```

The Thinktecture library also provides helpers (`HttpClientExtensions`) for `HttpClient` so that you can easily add Basic authentication credentials if you are making HTTP requests from .NET code.

The Katana version of the library uses BasicAuthenticationOptions as a model to configure Basic authentication in your application. It inherits from an abstract AuthenticationOptions class (shown in Listing 10-10), which is part of Microsoft.Owin.Security.

Listing 10-10. Definition of AuthenticationOptions Class (Comments Come From Katana Source Code)

```
public abstract class AuthenticationOptions
{
    private string _authenticationType;

    /// <summary>
    /// Initialize properties of AuthenticationOptions base class
    /// </summary>
    /// <param name="authenticationType">Assigned to the AuthenticationType property</param>
    protected AuthenticationOptions(string authenticationType)
    {
        Description = new AuthenticationDescription();
        AuthenticationType = authenticationType;
        AuthenticationMode = AuthenticationMode.Active;
    }

    /// <summary>
    /// The AuthenticationType in the options corresponds to the IIdentity AuthenticationType
property. A different
    /// value may be assigned in order to use the same authentication middleware type more than once
in a pipeline.
    /// </summary>
    public string AuthenticationType
    {
        get { return _authenticationType; }
        set
        {
            _authenticationType = value;
            Description.AuthenticationType = value;
        }
    }

    /// <summary>
    /// If Active the authentication middleware alter the request user coming in and
    /// alter 401 Unauthorized responses going out. If Passive the authentication middleware will
only provide
    /// identity and alter responses when explicitly indicated by the AuthenticationType.
    /// </summary>
    public AuthenticationMode AuthenticationMode { get; set; }

    /// <summary>
    /// Additional information about the authentication type which is made available to the
application.
    /// </summary>
    public AuthenticationDescription Description { get; set; }
}
```

The Code

Setting up HttpConfiguration to use a Thinktecture Basic Authentication library is shown in Listing 10-11.

Listing 10-11. Configuring Basic Authentication with Thinktecture.IdentityModel for Web API

```
var config = new HttpConfiguration();
config.MapHttpAttributeRoutes();

//use defaults
var authenticationConfiguration = new AuthenticationConfiguration();
authenticationConfiguration.AddBasicAuthentication((userName, password) =>
{
    //your logic for validating username/password
    //in this example, only user "filip" is allowed
    return userName == "filip" && password == "abc";
});

config.MessageHandlers.Add(new AuthenticationHandler(authenticationConfiguration));
```

The process is three-fold:

1. An authentication configuration object is set up, in this particular case using all of the default settings.

2. A username/password validation logic is introduced in the form of a Func<string,string,bool>. This can be any logic, including ASP.NET Membership, ASP.NET Identity, or any other custom user management implementation that's used by your application.

3. Thinktecture AuthenticationHandler is registered into the MessageHandlers collection of the HttpConfiguration object.

As mentioned, all core behavior of the library is customizable. For example, the following example introduces validation against an instance of a custom (hypothetical) UserService class, with MyAuthorizationHeader (instead of the standard Authorize) and using an Apress realm:

```
authenticationConfiguration.AddBasicAuthentication((userName, password) => myUserService.
Validate(userName, password), AuthenticationOptions.ForHeader("MyAuthorization"), realm: "Apress");
```

The setup of the Katana version of the Thinktecture Basic Authentication library is done through an IAppBuilder extension method and is shown in Listing 10-12. The semantics are similar to previous examples: Basic authentication is configured to use Apress realm, and a very simple username/password validation logic is included. The only difference is that in this case, you are responsible for returning a list of System.Security.Claims.Claim objects yourself.

Listing 10-12. Configuring Basic Authentication with Thinktecture.IdentityModel for OWIN (Katana)

```
public class Startup
{
    public void Configuration(IAppBuilder appBuilder)
    {
        //this would be your username validation service
        var myUserService = new UserService();
```

```
        var authOpts = new BasicAuthenticationOptions("Apress", async (username, pwd) =>
        {
            if (myUserService.Validate(username, pwd))
            {
                return new[]
                {
                    new Claim(ClaimTypes.Name, username)
                }.AsEnumerable();
            }

            return null;
        });

        appBuilder.UseBasicAuthentication(authOpts);

        //continue with IAppBuilder set up, add Web API etc.
    }
}
```

10-4. Integrate Windows Authentication

Problem

You want to enable Integrated Windows Authentication against your ASP.NET Web API service.

Solution

At the time of writing there is no Katana middleware supporting Windows Authentication; however, both of the most popular ASP.NET Web API hosts, IIS and HttpListener, do have built-in support for it.

To enable Windows Authentication in an IIS-hosted Web API, add the following entry to the <system.webServer /> section of your web.config file:

```
<security>
    <authentication>
        <anonymousAuthentication enabled="false" />
        <windowsAuthentication enabled="true" />
    </authentication>
</security>
```

For new ASP.NET Web projects created in Visual Studio 2013, you can also select Windows Authentication as the authentication option from the One ASP.NET wizard, as shown in Figure 10-2.

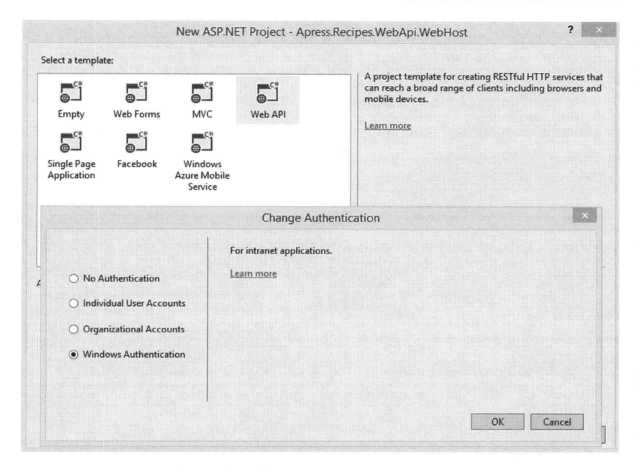

Figure 10-2. *New ASP.NET Web API with Windows Authentication*

When running on top of HttpListener, you need to set the AuthenticationSchemes property on the listener instance to AuthenticationSchemes.IntegratedWindowsAuthentication. This approach is the way to go when you use the new OWIN Self-host Web API NuGet package (Microsoft.AspNet.WebApi.OwinSelfHost).

If you still use the WCF-wrapped HttpListener, HttpSelfHostServer, from the older Web API self-host package (Microsoft.AspNet.WebApi.SelfHost), then the HttpSelfHostConfiguration exposes a ClientCredentialType property that you need to set to HttpClientCredentialType.Windows.

How It Works

Negotiation of security through the use of Windows credentials is done over the SPNEGO (Simple and Protected Negotiation) protocol. The protocol determines whether NTLM or Kerberos should be used for authentication purpose and is responsible for establishing a secure session between server and client. The HTTP Authentication for Microsoft Windows is performed via the Negotiate scheme and it builds upon the Basic authentication mechanism.

■ **Note**   A complete reference, "SPNEGO-based Kerberos and NTLM HTTP Authentication in Microsoft Windows" can be found in RFC 4559, at www.ietf.org/rfc/rfc4559.txt

---

The Negotiate scheme is supported in all of the major Windows web browsers, as well as in the .NET HttpClient, where client Windows credentials can be included by simply passing the client's requests through an HttpClientHandler with UseDefaultCredentials set to true.

```
var client = new HttpClient(new HttpClientHandler() {
    UseDefaultCredentials = true
});
```

On IIS, when Windows Authentication is enabled in your application, each request will pass through a WindowsAuthenticationModule, which will set the User on the HttpContext object to the current Windows identity.

On the OWIN self-host, interaction with the instance of the HttpListener is possible because Katana will keep the reference to it in the OWIN dictionary, under System.Net.HttpListener key. You can retrieve the listener this way, and enforce specific authentication (in this case Windows) on it through the relevant AuthenticationSchemes enumeration member (shown in Listing 10-13).

Listing 10-13. Definition of AuthenticationSchemes Enumeration

```
public enum AuthenticationSchemes
{
    None = 0,
    Digest = 1,
    Negotiate = 2,
    Ntlm = 4,
    IntegratedWindowsAuthentication = Ntlm | Negotiate,
    Basic = 8,
    Anonymous = 32768,
}
```

Of course, you could easily question this approach. Relying on the underlying server's capabilities for authentication defeats the purpose of OWIN in the first place because the application is no longer portable to a different server.

With HttpSelfHostServer, Windows Authentication is handled via WCF HttpBinding. Some of the Web API sources suggest overriding the virtual OnConfigureBinding method of the HttpSelfHostConfiguration and set ClientCredentialType and HttpBindingSecurityMode (enforce basic authentication) there.

This is definitely possible, but not necessary; simply setting ClientCredentialType on the HttpSelfHostConfiguration to anything other than HttpClientCredentialType.None results in HttpBindingSecurityMode to be internally set to TransportCredentialOnly. This is shown in Listing 10-14, which is an excerpt from the HttpSelfHostConfiguration source code.

Listing 10-14. Automatic Adjustment of HttpBindingSecurityMode in HttpSelfHostConfiguration

```
if (_clientCredentialType != HttpClientCredentialType.None)
{
    if (httpBinding.Security == null || httpBinding.Security.Mode == HttpBindingSecurityMode.None)
    {
        // Basic over HTTP case
        httpBinding.Security = new HttpBindingSecurity()
        {
            Mode = HttpBindingSecurityMode.TransportCredentialOnly,
        };
    }

    httpBinding.Security.Transport.ClientCredentialType = _clientCredentialType;
}
```

The Code

An example of enabling Windows Authentication on WCF Web API self-host by configuring HttpSelfHostConfiguration is shown in Listing 10-15, with the key line of code highlighted.

Listing 10-15. Using Windows Authentication with HttpSelfHostServer

```
var addr = "http://localhost:925";
var config = new HttpSelfHostConfiguration(addr)
{
    ClientCredentialType = HttpClientCredentialType.Windows
};

config.MapHttpAttributeRoutes();
using (var server = new HttpSelfHostServer(config))
{
    server.OpenAsync().Wait();
    Console.ReadLine();
}
```

An example of enabling Windows Authentication on Katana self-hosted Web API (HttpListener) is shown in Listing 10-16. This time, you have to extract the instance of HttpListener from the OWIN Properties dictionary.

Listing 10-16. Katana Startup Class Supporting Windows Authentication in Web API

```
class Startup
{
    public void Configuration(IAppBuilder app)
    {
        var listener = app.Properties["System.Net.HttpListener"] as HttpListener;
        if (listener != null)
        {
            listener.AuthenticationSchemes = AuthenticationSchemes.IntegratedWindowsAuthentication;
        }
```

```
        var config = new HttpConfiguration();
        config.MapHttpAttributeRoutes();
        app.UseWebApi(config);
    }
}
```

On the web host, as mentioned, it is done through an authentication configuration element. Normally, enabling Windows Authentication is done together with disabling anonymous authentication.

```
<system.webServer>
   <security>
      <authentication>
         <anonymousAuthentication enabled="false" />
         <windowsAuthentication enabled="true" />
      </authentication>
   </security>
</system.webServer>
```

■ **Tip**   For detailed information about windowsAuthentication IIS configuration element, check the official documentation at www.iis.net/configreference/system.webserver/security/authentication/windowsauthentication.

For development activities, you normally need to configure IIS Express (used by Visual Studio) to use Windows authentication as well. This is done directly from Visual Studio, in the Project Properties window, under the Development Server section, as shown in Figure 10-3. Anonymous authentication can be disabled from there too.

Figure 10-3. *Configuring Windows authentication in IIS Express*

10-5. Use the Hawk Authentication Scheme

Problem

You'd like to use the Hawk authentication scheme to provide partial HTTP request verification for your ASP.NET Web API service.

Solution

Pablo Cibraro has created an excellent open source implementation of Hawk for .NET. His project includes both an ASP.NET Web API-specific implementation (using a message handler, HawkMessageHandler) and a Katana-compatible one, built as OWIN middleware: HawkAuthenticationMiddleware. Either one of those can easily be integrated into your Web API projects, depending on which approach is more convenient for you.

To install the ASP.NET Web API version from NuGet, use the following command:

```
Install-Package HawkNet.WebApi
```

The OWIN version, for Katana, is available at

```
Install-Package HawkNet.Owin
```

The Web API package also contains a HawkClientMessageHandler, which can be used on the client side in conjunction with HttpClient.

How It Works

Hawk is a MAC-based (message authentication code) authentication scheme for HTTP. It's a great alternative for all of the scenarios where the HTTP-exposed services are unable to be offered over TLS (Transport Layer Security). It covers both the HTTP request and response, and provides built-in replay protection. Hawk requires a symmetric key to be shared between the client and the server.

With Hawk, a MAC is calculated from the key, timestamp, nonce (a unique string across the same timestamp and key) and a combination of HTTP method, request URI, and, if present, the payload of the message (including content type as part of the concatenated representation).

Replay protection is achieved by using both a timestamp window and a nonce to compute the MAC. A nonce is any string that can be generated by the client, that is unique for a given key-timestamp combination. The server is then responsible for storing the nonce for the duration of a timestamp window (by default 1 minute). Each nonce can only be used once.

When using the Hawk authentication scheme, the following fields need to be passed as part of the HTTP Authorization header, under the Hawk scheme:

- ID, as the id field

- timestamp, as the ts field

- nonce, as the nonce field

- calculated MAC, as the mac field, base64 encoded

- (optionally) hash of the request payload, as the hash field

- (optionally) extra data, which could be any application-specific data not contained in the body of the request, as the ext field

The other side of the communication process (the server) can recalculate the MAC using the provided fields and the symmetric key, and verify the validity of the incoming request.

In general, HMAC-based authentications mechanisms, such as Hawk, are often used in machine-to-machine APIs, such as the interaction between your application's backend with Amazon Web Services or between different systems that are part of your enterprise application landscape.

■ **Tip**   You can read more about Hawk at the project's official Github repository at
https://github.com/hueniverse/hawk.

The Code

Listing 10-17 shows an example of configuring an ASP.NET Web API service (in this case a self-hosted one) to use Hawk. Since HawkMessageHandler is a subclass of DelegatingHandler, it has to be added to the MessageHandlers collection on your HttpConfiguration. In this example, the server is configured to use a predefined key and SHA256 algorithm. The time skew is the second parameter passed to HawkMessageHandler and it defines the length of the window that the timestamp between the client and the server can drift apart.

Listing 10-17. Web API Self-host Using HawkNet

```
const string address = "http://localhost:925/";

var config = new HttpSelfHostConfiguration(address);
config.MapHttpAttributeRoutes();
var handler = new HawkMessageHandler(
    async id => new HawkCredential
    {
        Id = id,
        Key = "abcdefghijkl",
        Algorithm = "sha256",
        User = "filip"
    }, 30, true);

config.MessageHandlers.Add(handler);

using (var server = new HttpSelfHostServer(config))
{
    server.OpenAsync().Wait();
    Console.ReadLine();
}
```

HawkMessageHandler will create a new ClaimsPrincipal and a ClaimsIdentity, set to "Hawk", and inject it into the Web API pipeline so that you can access it all across the ASP.NET Web API service. In the example from Listing 10-17, the ClaimTypes.Name will be set to "filip" since the username is explicitly set as HawkCredential.

It is now enough for you to decorate the relevant controllers/action in your Web API with AuthorizeAttribute to prevent access of unauthorized or anonymous clients.

An example of calling the Hawk-protected endpoint using HttpClient is shown in Listing 10-18. On this side of the equation, HawkNet also provides some helpers: HawkClientMessageHandler can be used together with

HttpClient to simplify its configuration. It will deal with all the Hawk-related responsibilities, such as converting a HawkCredential instance into relevant Authorization header value, introducing a timespan value, generating a nonce, calculating MAC, and so on.

Listing 10-18. Calling a Hawk-Protected Web API Endpoint from HttpClient

```
var credential = new HawkCredential
{
    Id = "this-is-my-id",
    Key = "abcdefghijkl",
    Algorithm = "sha256",
    User = "filip"
};

var clientHandler = new HawkClientMessageHandler(new HttpClientHandler(), credential, ts: DateTime.Now);
var client = new HttpClient(clientHandler);
var request = new HttpRequestMessage(HttpMethod.Get, "http://localhost:925/test");
var response = await client.SendAsync(request);
//process response
```

Of course, calling the endpoint will work from any client, not just HttpClient, as long as the Authorization header is properly set. The raw HTTP request from your example should look like this:

```
GET http://localhost:925/test HTTP/1.1
Host: localhost:925
Hawk id="this-is-my-id", ts="1401189959", nonce="MWPwhT", mac="vAJD3BDSYUVUg/C4u+3g2d1oJ6eJs8QRxTrf
gHhCRR8=", ext=""
```

■ **Tip** The GitHub repository for HawkNet is full of many detailed, interesting samples at https://github.com/pcibraro/hawknet/.

10-6. Use OAuth 2.0 with ASP.NET Web API
Problem

You would like to use your ASP.NET Web API application as an OAuth 2.0 server, as well as enable OAuth bearer authentication for consuming OAuth bearer tokens.

Solution

Project Katana provides the middleware necessary for running an OAuth2 server as part of the Microsoft.Owin. Security.OAuth NuGet package. To get up and running, you need to use two primary extension methods as part of your Katana configuration:

- UseOAuthBearerAuthentication, to enable OAuth bearer token support (token consumption)
- UseOAuthAuthorizationServer, to enable your Web API OWIN-hosted application to act as an OAuth server, performing the credentials validation and granting a bearer token allowing access to specific resources

How It Works

The OAuth 2.0 Authorization Framework is defined in RFC 6749, and succeeds OAuth 1.0 (RFC 5849).

> *The OAuth 2.0 authorization framework enables a third-party application to obtain limited access to an HTTP service, either on behalf of a resource owner by orchestrating an approval interaction between the resource owner and the HTTP service, or by allowing the third-party application to obtain access on its own behalf.*

> Internet Engineering Task Force (IETF), RFC 6749,
> http://tools.ietf.org/html/rfc6749

OAuth 2.0 supports two primary authentication variants: *three-legged* (originally developed as part of OAuth 1.0) and *two-legged*. In a three-legged approach, a resource owner (a user), can assure a third party client (for example a mobile application) about his identity through a content provider (OAuth server) without having to share any credentials with that third-party client. A two-legged approach is a typical client-server approach, where a client can directly authenticate the user with the content provider.

Configuration of the Katana-based OAuth Authorization Server is primarily done through the IOAuthAuthorizationServerProvider and OAuthAuthorizationServerOptions classes.

An outline of OAuthAuthorizationServerOptions is shown in Listing 10-19. It extends the abstract AuthenticationOptions from Microsoft.Owin.Security and is used to set the core server options such as enforcing HTTPS, error detail level, token expiry, or endpoint paths. You can also use it to control the security of data contained in the access tokens and authorization codes. Out-of-the-box the security is host-specific; System.Web will use machine key data protection, while HttpListener will rely on the data protection application programming interface (DPAPI).

Listing 10-19. Outline of OAuthAuthorizationServerOptions

```
public class OAuthAuthorizationServerOptions : AuthenticationOptions
{
    public OAuthAuthorizationServerOptions()
        : base(OAuthDefaults.AuthenticationType)
    {
        AuthorizationCodeExpireTimeSpan = TimeSpan.FromMinutes(5);
        AccessTokenExpireTimeSpan = TimeSpan.FromMinutes(20);
        SystemClock = new SystemClock();
    }

    public PathString AuthorizeEndpointPath { get; set; }

    public PathString TokenEndpointPath { get; set; }

    public IOAuthAuthorizationServerProvider Provider { get; set; }

    public ISecureDataFormat<AuthenticationTicket> AuthorizationCodeFormat { get; set; }

    public ISecureDataFormat<AuthenticationTicket> AccessTokenFormat { get; set; }

    public ISecureDataFormat<AuthenticationTicket> RefreshTokenFormat { get; set; }

    public TimeSpan AuthorizationCodeExpireTimeSpan { get; set; }
```

```
        public TimeSpan AccessTokenExpireTimeSpan { get; set; }

        public IAuthenticationTokenProvider AuthorizationCodeProvider { get; set; }

        public IAuthenticationTokenProvider AccessTokenProvider { get; set; }

        public IAuthenticationTokenProvider RefreshTokenProvider { get; set; }

        public bool ApplicationCanDisplayErrors { get; set; }

        public ISystemClock SystemClock { get; set; }

        public bool AllowInsecureHttp { get; set; }
}
```

IOAuthAuthorizationServerProvider is responsible for processing events raised by the authorization server. Katana ships with a default implementation of IOAuthAuthorizationServerProvider called OAuthAuthorizationServerProvider, which you can see in Listing 10-20. It is a very convenient starting point for configuring the authorization server, as it allows you to either attach individual event handlers as Funcs or to inherit from the class and override the relevant method directly.

Listing 10-20. Outline of OAuthAuthorizationServerProvider

```
public class OAuthAuthorizationServerProvider : IOAuthAuthorizationServerProvider
{
    public OAuthAuthorizationServerProvider();
    public Func<OAuthMatchEndpointContext, Task> OnMatchEndpoint { get; set; }
    public Func<OAuthValidateClientRedirectUriContext, Task> OnValidateClientRedirectUri
    { get; set; }

    public Func<OAuthValidateClientAuthenticationContext, Task> OnValidateClientAuthentication
    { get; set; }
    public Func<OAuthValidateAuthorizeRequestContext, Task> OnValidateAuthorizeRequest { get; set; }
    public Func<OAuthValidateTokenRequestContext, Task> OnValidateTokenRequest { get; set; }
    public Func<OAuthGrantAuthorizationCodeContext, Task> OnGrantAuthorizationCode { get; set; }
    public Func<OAuthGrantResourceOwnerCredentialsContext, Task> OnGrantResourceOwnerCredentials
    { get; set; }
    public Func<OAuthGrantClientCredentialsContext, Task> OnGrantClientCredentials { get; set; }
    public Func<OAuthGrantRefreshTokenContext, Task> OnGrantRefreshToken { get; set; }
    public Func<OAuthGrantCustomExtensionContext, Task> OnGrantCustomExtension { get; set; }
    public Func<OAuthAuthorizeEndpointContext, Task> OnAuthorizeEndpoint { get; set; }
    public Func<OAuthTokenEndpointContext, Task> OnTokenEndpoint { get; set; }
    public virtual Task MatchEndpoint(OAuthMatchEndpointContext context);
    public virtual Task ValidateClientRedirectUri(OAuthValidateClientRedirectUriContext context);
    public virtual Task ValidateClientAuthentication(OAuthValidateClientAuthenticationContext
    context);
    public virtual Task ValidateAuthorizeRequest(OAuthValidateAuthorizeRequestContext context);
    public virtual Task ValidateTokenRequest(OAuthValidateTokenRequestContext context);
    public virtual Task GrantAuthorizationCode(OAuthGrantAuthorizationCodeContext context);
    public virtual Task GrantRefreshToken(OAuthGrantRefreshTokenContext context);
```

```
    public virtual Task GrantResourceOwnerCredentials(OAuthGrantResourceOwnerCredentialsContext
    context);
    public virtual Task GrantClientCredentials(OAuthGrantClientCredentialsContext context)
    public virtual Task GrantCustomExtension(OAuthGrantCustomExtensionContext context);
    public virtual Task AuthorizeEndpoint(OAuthAuthorizeEndpointContext context);
    public virtual Task TokenEndpoint(OAuthTokenEndpointContext context);
}
```

THE DEPTHS OF OAUTH

While OAuth 2.0 aims to simplify some of the concepts of OAuth 1.0, it is still a very broad and complex authorization framework. It is far beyond the scope and format of this book to go into details of OAuth; in this particular recipe I merely scratch the surface.

Why? There is a whole complicated security world of dealing with token providers, token types, refreshing tokens, redirect URI validations, authorization code grants, and a lot more—which you will definitely have to deal with in more complex OAuth usage scenarios.

To help you get going, the ASP.NET team provides an excellent, free-to-use (Apache 2 licensed), end-to-end sample of OAuth2 with OWIN and ASP.NET Web API at
http://code.msdn.microsoft.com/OWIN-OAuth-20-Authorization-ba2b8783.

In addition to that, Badrinarayanan Lakshmiraghavan dedicated a couple of chapters in his *Pro ASP.NET Web API Security* book (www.apress.com/microsoft/asp-net/9781430257820) exclusively to ASP.NET Web API and OAuth 2.0 integration.

The Code

When working with three-legged OAuth, the resource server (consuming tokens and exposing data based on them) and the authorization server (issues access tokens) are separate from each other, often controlled by different parties too (i.e. a sing Twitter as authorization server).

However, in simpler scenarios, resource and authorization servers can be combined into what's known as an "embedded authorization server." Listing 10-21 shows a Katana Startup class, configured to issue the tokens, use the bearer tokens for authentication and host ASP.NET Web API at the same time.

Listing 10-21. Katana Startup Configured as OAuth Server and a Web API Server

```
public class Startup
{
    public void Configuration(IAppBuilder app)
    {
        var oauthProvider = new OAuthAuthorizationServerProvider
        {
            OnGrantResourceOwnerCredentials = async context =>
            {
                //sample! validate credentials here
                if (context.UserName == "filip" && context.Password == "test")
```

```
            {
                var claimsIdentity = new ClaimsIdentity(context.Options.AuthenticationType);
                claimsIdentity.AddClaim(new Claim("user", context.UserName));
                context.Validated(claimsIdentity);
                return;
            }
            context.Rejected();
        },
        OnValidateClientAuthentication = async context =>
        {
            string clientId;
            string clientSecret;

            //sample! validate clientId and secret here
            if (context.TryGetBasicCredentials(out clientId, out clientSecret))
            {
                if (clientId == "filipClient" && clientSecret == "secretKey")
                {
                    context.Validated();
                }
            }
        }
    };

    var oauthOptions = new OAuthAuthorizationServerOptions
    {
        AllowInsecureHttp = true, //this is set to avoid having to setup TLS in the demo
        TokenEndpointPath = new PathString("/accesstoken"),
        Provider = oauthProvider
    };

    app.UseOAuthAuthorizationServer(oauthOptions);
    app.UseOAuthBearerAuthentication(new OAuthBearerAuthenticationOptions());

    var config = new HttpConfiguration();
    config.MapHttpAttributeRoutes();
    app.UseWebApi(config);
    }
}
```

In the sample, you attach two event handlers to the OAuthAuthorizationServerProvider. First is OnValidateClientAuthentication, which is used when requesting the access token. Inside that event handler, client ID and secret are extracted from the Authorization header (basic authentication) and validated. Then OnGrantResourceOwnerCredentials is used to validate the credentials of the resource owner and create a concrete ClaimsIdentity based on that. The credentials are passed in as regular application/x-www-form-urlencoded form data.

After the authorization server has been configured, you can proceed to configure the resource server, which is done by calling the UseOAuthBearerAuthentication method and passing in OAuthBearerAuthenticationOptions. Similarly to the authorization server, it can also be customized to use specific token providers or have specific event handlers attached as Funcs (i.e. to handle challenge or token validation). However, for the example in Listing 10-21, the default settings are sufficient.

```
app.UseOAuthBearerAuthentication(new OAuthBearerAuthenticationOptions());
```

This means that connecting clients should use an Authorization header with the type Bearer, and pass in the access token value as the rest of the header. Please note that you absolutely have to apply HTTPS (TLS or SSL) yourself!

Now that all the pieces are in place, you can start calling and interacting with the service over the network. Since the sample from Listing 10-21 contained a hardcoded client/secret as filipClient and secretKey, and username/password as filip:test, these are exactly the parameters you'll need to use when requesting the token and then accessing the protected resource. Listing 10-22 shows this process done from .NET using HttpClient.

Listing 10-22. Accessing Web API With Embedded OAuth 2.0 Server from HttpClient

```
var client = new HttpClient();
var authorizationHeader =
Convert.ToBase64String(Encoding.UTF8.GetBytes("filipClient:secretKey"));

//client and secret should be sent using Basic Authentication
client.DefaultRequestHeaders.Authorization = new AuthenticationHeaderValue("Basic",
authorizationHeader);

var form = new Dictionary<string, string>
{
    {"grant_type", "password"},
    {"username", "filip"},
    {"password", "test"}
};

var tokenResponse = await client.PostAsync("http://localhost:925/accesstoken",
new FormUrlEncodedContent(form));

var token = await tokenResponse.Content.ReadAsAsync<Token>(new[] {new JsonMediaTypeFormatter()});

//now reset Authorization header to a Bearer token
client.DefaultRequestHeaders.Authorization = new AuthenticationHeaderValue("Bearer", token.
AccessToken);

//this is the actual response from a secured Web API resource
var authorizedResponse = client.GetAsync("http://localhost:925/api/test");
```

The code should be quite easy to follow. First, a basic authentication header is set based on the client_id and secret; this needs to have base64 format. A prepared request is then sent to the /accesstoken endpoint, along with the form data composed of username, password, and grant_type (password). In response, an access token is returned (by default valid for 20 minutes, since you do not specify a custom TimeSpan in the OAuthAuthorizationServerOptions), which is then used for the next request in the Bearer scheme.

This is how you are allowed to access the protected Web API resource. Both the sample Web API resource and the Token helper class, which is used to deserialize the responses containing the access token, are shown in Listing 10-23. Since all OAuth configuration happens at OWIN level in Web API, it's enough to just decorate a resource with AuthorizeAttribute.

Listing 10-23. Token Helper Class and a Sample Web API Resource

```
public class Token
{
    [JsonProperty("access_token")]
    public string AccessToken { get; set; }

    [JsonProperty("token_type")]
    public string TokenType { get; set; }

    [JsonProperty("expires_in")]
    public int ExpiresIn { get; set; }

    [JsonProperty("refresh_token")]
    public string RefreshToken { get; set; }
}

[Authorize]
public class TestController : ApiController
{
    [Route("test")]
    public HttpResponseMessage Get()
    {
        return Request.CreateResponse(HttpStatusCode.OK, "hello from a secured resource!");
    }
}
```

Even though the sample here used HttpClient, the whole process of accessing your secured Web API resource through an embedded OAuth 2.0 server is obviously compatible with any HTTP-capable client.

■ **Tip** For more sophisticated scenarios, it is definitely recommended to use an existing OAuth2 client library, such as Thinktecture.IdentityModel.Client, rather than go through the cumbersome process of manually dealing with HttpClient.

10-7. Safely Access Current IPrincipal
Problem

You would like to access the current IPrincipal object from various components of your Web API pipeline, in a safe and unit test-friendly way.

Solution

The recommended way of accessing the current IPrincipal is through the RequestContext object, which is available from every instance of HttpRequestMessage. This is contrary to the traditional approach of using Thread. CurrentPrincipal in self-hosted or HttpContext.Current.User in web-hosted scenarios.

```
var requestContext = request.GetRequestContext();
//use requestContext.Principal
```

The.e are a number of benefits here. When doing asynchronous work, the thread context can easily switch and there is no guarantee that using Thread.CurrentPrincipal will synchronize correctly. Moreover, the static nature of Thread.CurrentPrincipal or HttpContext.Current.User introduces unnecessary complexity when it comes to maintaining and testing your code.

How It Works

HttpRequestContext was introduced into ASP.NET Web API 2 to provide a more organized approach to the request-specific data and metadata that was normally stored inside of the request Properties dictionary (i.e. flag whether the request is local), in static objects (i.e. IPrincipal on the Thread.CurrentPrincipal), or was disconnected from the request instance (i.e. UrlHelper) at all.

HttpRequestContext, shown in Listing 10-24, is a POCO and does not provide any behavior. All of its properties are explicitly hydrated at various stages of the Web API pipeline. The comments used in the listing come directly from the ASP.NET Web API source, and have been left here as they provide a good insight into the use of each property.

Listing 10-24. Definition of HttpRequestContext

```
public class HttpRequestContext
{
    public HttpRequestContext()
    {
        // This is constructor is available to allow placing breakpoints on //construction.
    }

    /// <summary>Gets or sets the client certificate.</summary>
    public virtual X509Certificate2 ClientCertificate { get; set; }

    /// <summary>Gets or sets the configuration.</summary>
    public virtual HttpConfiguration Configuration { get; set; }

    /// <summary>
    /// Gets or sets a value indicating whether error details, such as //exception messages and
    stack traces,
    /// should be included in the response for this request.
    /// </summary>
    public virtual bool IncludeErrorDetail { get; set; }

    /// <summary>Gets or sets a value indicating whether the request //originates from a local
    address.</summary>
    public virtual bool IsLocal { get; set; }
```

```
/// <summary>Gets or sets the principal.</summary>
public virtual IPrincipal Principal { get; set; }

/// <summary>Gets or sets the route data.</summary>
public virtual IHttpRouteData RouteData { get; set; }

/// <summary>Gets or sets the factory used to generate URLs to other APIs.</summary>
public virtual UrlHelper Url { get; set; }

/// <summary>Gets or sets the virtual path root.</summary>
public virtual string VirtualPathRoot { get; set; }
}
```

From the developer's standpoint, the most important security information about HttpRequestContext is that the IPrincipal is guaranteed to flow across the threads in case context switching happens, such as when an asynchronous operation starts on one thread and completes on another.

An instance of the HttpRequestContext is actually held inside the Properties dictionary of the HttpRequestMessage, under HttpPropertyKeys.RequestContextKey key. As a consequence, you will not be surprised to hear that the GetRequestContext method, used to obtain the HttpRequestContext from the current request, is simply an extension method that retrieves the context instance from the request's Properties. A similar SetRequestContext extension method is publicly available too, and is used by the framework to initially set the context on the request. Additionally, it's perfect to be used in unit testing scenarios where you might want to mock some of the objects carried by the HttpRequestContext, like in your specific case, an IPrincipal.

Additionally, if you are working with IAuthenticationFilter in the AuthenticateAsync method, you will have access to HttpAuthenticationContext (shown in Listing 10-25). It also exposes an IPrincipal, through a Principal property. When building a custom authentication solution using IAuthenticationFilter, you only need to set the Principal on the HttpAuthenticationContext; the framework will ensure that it gets synced to the HttpRequestContext automatically.

Listing 10-25. Overview of the HttpAuthenticationContext

```
public class HttpAuthenticationContext
{
    public HttpAuthenticationContext(HttpActionContext actionContext, IPrincipal principal);

    public HttpActionContext ActionContext { get; private set; }
    public IPrincipal Principal { get; set; }
    public IHttpActionResult ErrorResult { get; set; }
    public HttpRequestMessage Request {get; }
}
```

Finally, the base ApiController exposes a User property, which also returns the current IPrincipal, so whenever you are working in the controller, you can use that to interact with the current IPrincipal. However, under the hood the property is simply a shortcut to HttpRequestContext too, as shown in Listing 10-26.

Listing 10-26. User Property on the ApiController

```
public IPrincipal User
{
    get { return RequestContext.Principal; }
    set { RequestContext.Principal = value; }
}
```

The Code

Listing 10-27 shows accessing the HttpRequestContext from a simple Basic authentication MessageHandler. The code extracts user name and password from the Authorization header and creates a new ClaimsPrincipal based on that. Then, the principal object is set on the RequestContext, which is enough to complete the authentication process. The big advantage of working with IPrincipal this way is that the message handler can now be easily unit tested because RequestContext can be stubbed.

Listing 10-27. A Sample Message Handler, Setting IPrincipal on the HttpRequestContext

```
public class BasicAuthHandler : DelegatingHandler
{
    private const string BasicAuthResponseHeaderValue = "Basic";
    private const string Realm = "Apress";

    protected override Task<HttpResponseMessage> SendAsync(HttpRequestMessage request,
    CancellationToken cancellationToken)
    {
        bool identified = false;
        if (request.Headers.Authorization != null && string.Equals(request.Headers.Authorization.
        Scheme, BasicAuthResponseHeaderValue, StringComparison.CurrentCultureIgnoreCase))
        {
            var credentials = Encoding.UTF8.GetString(Convert.FromBase64String(request.Headers.
            Authorization.Parameter));
            var user = credentials.Split(':')[0].Trim();
            var pwd = credentials.Split(':')[1].Trim();

            //validate username and password here and set identified flag
            //omitted for brevity

            if (identified)
            {
                var identity = new ClaimsIdentity(new[] {new Claim(ClaimTypes.Name, user)},
                BasicAuthResponseHeaderValue);
                request.GetRequestContext().Principal = new ClaimsPrincipal(new[] { identity });
            }
        }

        if (!identified)
        {
            var unauthorizedResponse = request.CreateResponse(HttpStatusCode.Unauthorized);
            unauthorizedResponse.Headers.WwwAuthenticate.Add(new AuthenticationHeaderValue(BasicAuth
            ResponseHeaderValue, Realm));
            return Task.FromResult(unauthorizedResponse);
        }

        return base.SendAsync(request, cancellationToken);
    }
}
```

▩ **Note** The Basic authentication implementation used here is not complete and is shown purely to illustrate working with `HttpRequestContext` and `IPrincipal`. Please refer to Recipe 10-3 for a detailed discussion on adding Basic authentication support to your Web API.

Once the `IPrincipal` is set, you can access it through the `HttpRequestContext`. The example is shown in Listing 10-28, where three different approaches are shown, all going through `HttpRequestContext`.

Listing 10-28. Accessing IPrincipal from the Controller

```
[Authorize]
public class TestController : ApiController
{
    public HttpResponseMessage Get()
    {
        //all approaches are equally valid
        var user = Request.GetRequestContext().Principal;
        var user = RequestContext.Principal;
        var user = User;

        //rest of the action omitted for brevity
    }
}
```

10-8. Remove ASP.NET Web API Server Footprint
Problem

You want to remove all of the extra headers injected by the server on which your ASP.NET Web API application is running, such as Server, X-Powered-By, or X-AspNet-Version.

Solution

The behavior of the default headers is different when running Web API on IIS (web hosting) and on `HttpListener` (self-hosting and OWIN self-hosting), so they need to be tackled separately. When hosting on top of IIS, you have to deal with all three of the headers, while `HttpListener` only issues an extra Server header.

On IIS, you can solve this issue in a proactive or in a reactive way. In a reactive approach, you can simply add an `IHttpModule` that will pluck the unnecessary headers just prior to the response being sent to the client. In a proactive approach, you need to modify the IIS settings and your web.config to ensure none of the extra headers are issued at all.

In `HttpListener` scenarios, there is no way to plug in a component like `IHttpModule`, therefore only a proactive approach is viable. However, since there is only a single header to deal with, it's relatively easy to do via a registry configuration, since it can only be done on a per-machine basis, not per-project basis.

How It Works

While the default ASP.NET headers have no value for you as the developer of the application, they are used by Microsoft to measure the spread and outreach of ASP.NET-based solutions. This can then be used by them to quantify the severity of potential security bugs or in general provide feedback of the adoption of the platform.

On the other hand, by removing the default headers, you are making it more difficult for the potential attacker to identify the technology on which your API is running. While disguising the response headers is effectively a so-called "security by obscurity," and is definitely not enough to protect you from attackers, it is absolutely a good security practice to remove everything that you do not need (in this case all of the excessive headers that are not directly required by your application).

The headers are injected into the HTTP response by the following components:

- Server: Added by IIS (web host, value is `Microsoft-IIS/{version}`) or HTTP.SYS (any host using `HttpListener`, value is `Microsoft-HTTPAPI/2.0`)

- X-AspNet-Version: Added by `System.Web`. Since self-hosted Web API doesn't reference `System.Web`, the problem does not exist there

- X-Powered-By: Added by IIS

The Code

Let's walk through the necessary steps required to disable each of the headers.

Server

When running on IIS, it is not possible to remove the `Server` header through any configuration setting; instead, it has to be done reactively, by stripping the header before it is sent to the client. This can be done via the `Application_PreSendRequestHeaders` event in the `Global.asax`, as shown in Listing 10-29, or through a custom `IHttpModule`, which will be discussed later.

Listing 10-29. Stripping Away a Server Header from IIS-based Web Applications

```
protected void Application_PreSendRequestHeaders(object sender, EventArgs e)
{
    HttpContext.Current.Response.Headers.Remove("Server");
}
```

To disable the `Server` header issued by HTTP.SYS, you will need to modify the registry: add a DWORD entry `DisableServerHeader` with value 1 to `HKLM\SYSTEM\CurrentControlSet\Services\HTTP\Parameters`. You can do it using the standard `regedit` GUI tool, or from a PowerShell command, as shown:

```
reg add HKEY_LOCAL_MACHINE\SYSTEM\CurrentControlSet\services\HTTP\Parameters /v
DisableServerHeader /t REG_DWORD /d 00000001
```

A reboot is required for the change to take effect.

X-Powered-By

This can be removed from your responses by navigating to the HTTP Response Headers setting of your web site in the IIS Manager. This is shown in Figure 10-4.

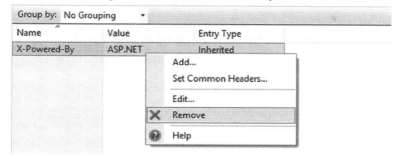

 HTTP Response Headers

Use this feature to configure HTTP headers that are added to responses from the Web server.

Figure 10-4. *Removing the X-Powered-By Header*

Alternatively, you can axe this particular header through a `web.config` file under the `<system.webServer />`section:

```
<httpProtocol>
    <customHeaders>
      <remove name="X-Powered-By" />
    </customHeaders>
</httpProtocol>
```

X-AspNet-Version

This header can be removed by adding the following configuration entry to your `web.config/machine.config` file, under `<system.Web />`section:

```
<httpRuntime enableVersionHeader="false"/>
```

All Headers Through IHttpModule

An `IHttpModule` that clears all of the unnecessary headers is shown in Listing 10-30. You can simply register it against your IIS-based application and forget about any other extra configuration. IIS and `System.Web` will still keep issuing the headers, but they will always get cleared prior to reaching the client. This approach is useful when you have no direct access to IIS Manager.

Listing 10-30. IHttpModule Responsible for Removing Default Headers

```
public class ClearHeaderModule : IHttpModule
{
    private static readonly string[] Headers = new string[3]
    {
        "Server",
        "X-AspNet-Version",
        "X-Powered-By",
    };
```

```csharp
    public void Init(HttpApplication context)
    {
        context.PreSendRequestHeaders += OnPreSendRequestHeaders;
    }

    static void OnPreSendRequestHeaders(object sender, EventArgs e)
    {
        if (HttpContext.Current == null) return;

        for (var i = 0; i < 3; i++)
        {
            HttpContext.Current.Response.Headers.Remove(Headers[i]);
        }
    }

    public void Dispose() { }
}
```

You register this module same way as any other IHttpModule in ASP.NET, in web.config, under <system.webServer />:

```xml
<modules>
  <add name="ClearHeaderModule" type="{namespace}.ClearHeaderModule, {assembly name}"/>
</modules>
```

■ **Tip**   In addition to the methods discussed in this recipe, you can also disable the default headers using a combination of Microsoft's URLScan tool (www.iis.net/downloads/microsoft/urlscan) and URLRewrite tool (www.iis.net/downloads/microsoft/url-rewrite).

CHAPTER 11

Testing Web API Services

This chapter covers testing your ASP.NET Web API service. It will take a comprehensive look at both isolated unit testing of the individual Web API components and at broadly scoped end-to-end integration tests.

You will learn how to do the following:

- Test controllers, message handlers, filters, and formatters (Recipes 11-1, 11-2, 11-3, and 11-4)

- Take advantage of the testability benefits of IHttpActionResult (Recipe 11-5)

- Test Web API routes (Recipe 11-6)

- Run Web API in memory to perform complex integration tests (Recipes 11-7 and 11-8)

All the code samples used in this chapter rely on xUnit as the testing framework and Moq as a mocking framework, but obviously you can easily apply the techniques discussed here to the test suite of your choice.

11-1. Unit Test ASP.NET Web API Controllers
Problem

You would like to unit test the controllers used in your Web API.

Solution

ASP.NET Web API allows unit testing of the controllers; however, depending on the complexity and amount of contextual information you use in the actions, you will need to perform the appropriate controller setup beforehand. Listing 11-1 shows a basic controller testing infrastructure.

Listing 11-1. A General Controller Test Setup

```
[Fact]
public async void WhenItemIsPostedResponseShouldBe201AndLocationHeaderShouldBeSet() {
    var controller = new ItemsController()
    {
        Configuration = new HttpConfiguration(),
        Request = new HttpRequestMessage
        {
            Method = HttpMethod.Post,
            RequestUri = new Uri("http://apress.com/items")
        }
    };
```

```
//depending on the context and complexity of your action
//setup controller.Configuration
//setup controller.Request
//setup controller.RequestContext

var result = await controller.Post(new Item());

//assert
}
```

How It Works

In ASP.NET Web API, controllers are the focal point of a rich processing pipeline, and their isolation for unit testing has not always been that straightforward.

The difficulty and complexity of controller unit testing in Web API has evolved considerably since the original release of the framework, where you had to understand lots of internal details of the controller execution pipeline as well as be familiar with lower-level objects such as HttpControllerContext in order to set up your controllers for testing. From version 2 of the framework, testing has been much easier, and while the base controller class in Web API, ApiController, still relies heavily on lots of dependencies such as the HttpRequestMessage, HttpRequestContext, and HttpConfiguration, those can normally be relatively easily configured in order to allow the unit testability of your actions. All of them are exposed as public properties on the ApiController and can be set in the "arrange" part of your test.

■ **Tip** It is advisable to keep controllers as lean as possible, and only let them act as a bridge between your HTTP endpoint and the business layer. As a result, when unit testing controllers, you should only have to focus on verifying most basic operations, rather than any sophisticated logic.

The Code

Let's have a look at testing a sample controller from Listing 11-2, one that allows you to get a resource by ID and to add one to the underlying repository.

Listing 11-2. Sample Controller to be Tested

```
public class ItemsController : ApiController
{
    private readonly IItemService _itemService;

    public ItemsController(IItemService itemService)
    {
        _itemService = itemService;
    }

    [Route("items/{id:int}", Name = "ItemById")]
    public async Task<Item> Get(int id)
    {
        var result = await _itemService.GetById(id);
        return result;
    }
```

```
    [Route("items")]
    public async Task<HttpResponseMessage> Post(Item item)
    {
        if (!ModelState.IsValid) return Request.CreateErrorResponse(HttpStatusCode.BadRequest,
        ModelState);

        await _itemService.SaveAsync(item);
        var response = new HttpResponseMessage(HttpStatusCode.Created);
        response.Headers.Location = new Uri(Url.Link("ItemById", new { id = item.Id }));
    }
}
```

The core logic invoked through these API endpoints is delegated to a separate IItemsService, which is a good practice. Instead, the controller only focuses on the most fundamental task, providing an HTTP gateway and doing basic sanity checks.

To test the Post method, you need to set up the HttpRequestContext and its RouteData, as the action uses the UrlHelper to generate a link, which in turn relies on RouteData. This is shown in Listing 11-3.

Listing 11-3. Unit Testing a Fairly Complex Post Action

```
[Fact]
public async void WhenItemIsPostedResponseShouldBe201AndLocationHeaderShouldBeSet()
{
    var item = new Item
    {
        Id = 1,
        Name = "Filip"
    };
    var service = new Mock<IItemService>().Object;
    var controller = new ItemsController(service)
    {
        Configuration = new HttpConfiguration(),
        Request = new HttpRequestMessage
        {
            Method = HttpMethod.Post,
            RequestUri = new Uri("http://localhost/items")
        }
    };
    controller.Configuration.MapHttpAttributeRoutes();
    controller.Configuration.EnsureInitialized();
    controller.RequestContext.RouteData = new HttpRouteData(
        new HttpRoute(), new HttpRouteValueDictionary { { "controller", "Items" } });

    var result = await controller.Post(item);

    Assert.Equal(HttpStatusCode.Created, result.StatusCode);
    Assert.Equal("http://localhost/items/1", result.Headers.Location.AbsoluteUri);
}
```

■ **Tip**   In Web API 2 it is also possible to mock `IUriHelper` directly, instead of relying on `RouteData`. See Recipe 11-5 for more details.

In order to enable the routes on the tested controller, you either have to add them manually using the `MapHttpRoute` method (the same way as you would deal with centralized routes), or if, as in this case, your controller uses attribute routing, you have to call two methods on the `HttpConfiguration` in this particular order:

```
controller.Configuration.MapHttpAttributeRoutes();
controller.Configuration.EnsureInitialized();
```

This code makes sure the routes from the attributes have been initialized correctly. If you don't add the relevant routes, the test code will throw an exception, complaining that "the route `ItemById` cannot be found."

You also have a failure path in the controller; if the `ModelState` is invalid, you should throw an `HttpResponseException` and respond to the user with HTTP status code 400. The easiest way to test if this behavior is correct is to configure `ModelState` by hand: add an error into it manually. Normally, `ModelState` only gets populated by the Web API when performing model binding, which is not happening in unit tests, as you call the controller directly. Testing `ModelState` is shown in Listing 11-4.

Listing 11-4. *Unit Testing the ModelState-driven Exception Path*

```
[Fact]
public void WhenItemIsPostedAndIsInvalidThrowsBadRequest()
{
    var item = new Item
    {
        Id = 1
    };
    var service = new Mock<IItemService>().Object;
    var controller = new ItemsController(service)
    {
        Configuration = new HttpConfiguration(),
        Request = new HttpRequestMessage
        {
            Method = HttpMethod.Post,
            RequestUri = new Uri("http://localhost/items")
        }
    };
    controller.ModelState.AddModelError("Name", "Name is required");

    var ex = AssertEx.TaskThrows<HttpResponseException>(async () => await controller.Post(item));
    Assert.Equal(HttpStatusCode.BadRequest, ex.Response.StatusCode);
}
```

In Listing 11-4, the `ModelState` will trigger the failure path and throw an `Exception`. You can take advantage of the terrific AssertEx library from NuGet, which, contrary to default xUnit assertions, allows you to assert using an async lambda (since your action is async). As everything is awaited, there is no need to unwrap the `HttpResponseException` from an `AggregateException` anymore.

Unit testing of the GetById action (Listing 11-5) is very simple and boils down to verifying if the underlying service has been called, and in case it returns null, that the Exception representing a 404 HTTP response has been thrown. Interestingly, since the code inside that action does not rely on any Web API context (such as current request or route information), you can skip that part in your arrange altogether and test the action as if it was a regular method on a typical .NET class.

Listing 11-5. Unit Testing GetById Action

```
[Fact]
public async void WhenGetByIdIsCalledUnderlyingServiceIsCalled()
{
    var item = new Item {Id = 1, Name = "Filip"};
    var service = new Mock<IItemService>();
    service.Setup(x => x.GetById(1)).Returns(Task.FromResult(item));
    var controller = new ItemsController(service.Object);
    var result = await controller.Get(1);

    Assert.Equal(item, result);
}

[Fact]
public void WhenIdCalledByGetByIdIsNotFound404IsThrown()
{
    var service = new Mock<IItemService>();
    service.Setup(x => x.GetById(1)).Returns(Task.FromResult<Item>(null));
    var controller = new ItemsController(service.Object);

    var ex = AssertEx.TaskThrows<HttpResponseException>(async () => await controller.Get(1));
    Assert.Equal(HttpStatusCode.NotFound, ex.Response.StatusCode);
}
```

11-2. Unit Test Message Handlers
Problem

You would like to unit test the message handlers used in your ASP.NET Web API application.

Solution

ASP.NET Web API message handlers cannot be called directly in the unit tests as their only member, SendAsync, is not public. However, the System.Net.Http library contains an HttpMessageInvoker class, which can be used to invoke the handler. It allows you to pass in a handler through the constructor and itself exposes a SendAsync method, which calls SendAsync on the wrapped handler.

```
var handler = new MyMessageHandler();
var invoker = new HttpMessageInvoker(handler);
var result = await invoker.SendAsync(new HttpRequestMessage(), CancellationToken.None);
```

■ **Tip**   The popular HttpClient is actually a subclass extending the HttpMessageInvoker. As a result, you can also use HttpMessageInvoker to perform integration testing, as discussed in detail in Recipe 11-7.

How It Works

The signature of HttpMessageHandler is shown in Listing 11-6.

Listing 11-6. Definition of HttpMessageHandler

```
public abstract class HttpMessageHandler
{
        protected internal abstract Task<HttpResponseMessage> SendAsync(HttpRequestMessage request,
        CancellationToken cancellationToken);
}
```

While in Web API you would normally extend the DelegatingHandler (a subclass of HttpMessageHandler, providing default pipelining behavior), rather than implement HttpMessageHandler, either way the SendAsync will not be public.

The reason why HttpMessageInvoker is able to call into that method is that its access modifier is protected internal, and all three classes (HttpMessageInvoker, DelegatingHandler, and HttpMessageHandler) are defined in the same System.Net.Http assembly. As a result, the invoker, being a friend class, is free to call the SendAsync method whenever it is required.

Web API itself heavily relies on HttpMessageInvoker to facilitate the pipeline functionality and message handler chaining. What is also worth mentioning is that in unit testing Web API-specific HttpMessageHandlers, such as HttpServer or HttpRoutingDispatcher, HttpMessageInvoker is used by the ASP.NET Web API team in the same manner as described in this recipe.

The Code

Let's take a simple example of the logging message handler from Listing 11-7.

Listing 11-7. Message Handler to be Unit Tested

```
public class LoggingHandler : DelegatingHandler
{
    public ILoggingService LoggingService { get; set; }

    protected override Task<HttpResponseMessage> SendAsync(HttpRequestMessage request,
    CancellationToken cancellationToken)
    {
        var loggingService = LoggingService ?? request.GetDependencyScope().GetService
        (typeof (ILoggingService)) as ILoggingService;
        if (loggingService != null)
        {
            loggingService.Log(request.RequestUri.ToString());
        }

        return base.SendAsync(request, cancellationToken);
    }
}
```

In this handler, you probably want to verify that the logger is invoked with the relevant request URI. The message handler will try to resolve an ILoggingService from the request's DependencyScope (see Recipe 10-4 for more details); as a consequence, it's a good idea to keep the service public with a setter, so that you can easily mock it in the unit test.

Since it's already been mentioned that HttpMessageInvoker is the go-to-guy for unit testing message handlers, let's write the test. See Listing 11-8.

Listing 11-8. Unit Test for a Message Handler

```
[Fact]
public async void WhenCalledShouldLogTheRequestUrl()
{
    var mockLogger = new Mock<ILoggingService>();
    var handler = new LoggingHandler
    {
        LoggingService = mockLogger.Object
    };

    var invoker = new HttpMessageInvoker(handler);
    await invoker.SendAsync(new HttpRequestMessage(HttpMethod.Get,
    new Uri("http://apress.com/resource")), new CancellationToken());

    mockLogger.Verify(x => x.Log("http://apress.com/resource"), Times.Once);
}
```

In this particular example, the response message is not interesting for us, but in case the message handler did some more sophisticated processing, the awaited output of the SendAsync method could be read into a variable and asserted accordingly.

In case your message handler does not expose its dependencies in the form of a public, settable property, you can provide a mock of an IDependencyResolver and pass it into the handler through the HttpRequestMessage and the Properties dictionary, under HttpPropertyKeys.DependencyScope key.

```
var mockResolver = new Mock<IDependencyResolver>();
//setup resolver
request.Properties[HttpPropertyKeys.DependencyScope] = mockResolver.Object;
```

■ **Note** An alternative, less elegant way of unit testing message handlers is to subclass your handler so that the fake child class can have access to the SendAsync method.

11-3. Unit Test Action Filters
Problem

You would like to unit test the action filters used in your Web API.

Solution

Testing action filters in Asp.NET Web API is relatively easy, as they can be invoked directly (no need to use a bridge class like HttpActionInvoker, discussed in Recipe 11-2).

However, action filters operate on HttpActionContext and HttpActionExecutedContext, and, depending on what your filter is doing and which context information it needs access to, those objects have to be properly set up in order for tests to execute successfully.

Similarly, in case you want to assert the modifications that the filter performed on the HttpResponseMessage object, it's the instance that is set on the HttpActionContext/HttpActionExecutedContext that needs to be inspected. All filter operations are void/Task returning and do not yield any result.

How It Works

Your action filter can perform a wide array of different tasks. Depending on what you are trying to test, some of the properties of the HttpActionContext need to be hydrated. The most common places to go are the Request and RequestContext properties.

HttpActionExecutedContext is a post-processing wrapper around HttpActionContext (Listing 11-9), so as in former case, it's the HttpActionContext that needs to be set up.

Listing 11-9. Definition of HttpActionContext and HttpActionExecutedContext

```
public class HttpActionContext
{
    public HttpActionContext();
    public HttpActionContext(HttpControllerContext controllerContext,
    HttpActionDescriptor actionDescriptor);
    public Dictionary<string, object> ActionArguments { get; }
    public HttpActionDescriptor ActionDescriptor { get; set; }
    public HttpControllerContext ControllerContext { get; set; }
    public ModelStateDictionary ModelState { get; }
    public HttpRequestMessage Request { get; }
    public HttpRequestContext RequestContext { get; }
    public HttpResponseMessage Response { get; set; }
}

public class HttpActionExecutedContext
{
    public HttpActionExecutedContext(HttpActionContext actionContext, Exception exception);
    public HttpActionContext ActionContext { get; set; }
    public Exception Exception { get; set; }
    public HttpResponseMessage Response { get; set; }.
}
```

When processing a request, Web API will group all filters it finds on your actions into four groups:

- Authorization filters
- Authentication filters
- Action filters
- Exception filters

While you can test your filters by calling their relevant public methods directly, Web API internally uses a specialized private ActionInvoker to invoke the action on the controller together with the filter pipeline.

All groups are linked together through a chain of IHttpActionResults. For example, action filters are wrapped in an ActionFilterResult, which in turn wraps around regular action invocation, and is itself wrapped by an AuthorizationFilterResult or AuthenticationFilterResult.

The Code

Let's imagine that you have an action filter in your application that sets the Cache-Control header on the responses that you'd like to be cached on the client side. The implementation used here (Listing 11-10) is trivial and doesn't do much in terms of conforming well to HTTP caching standards, but it's a useful study case nonetheless.

Listing 11-10. Sample Action Filter to be Unit Tested

```
public class CacheAttribute : ActionFilterAttribute
{
    public int ClientTimeSpan { get; set; }

    public override void OnActionExecuted(HttpActionExecutedContext actionExecutedContext)
    {
        if (actionExecutedContext.Response.StatusCode >=HttpStatusCode.InternalServerError)
        {
            return;
        }

        var cachecontrol = new CacheControlHeaderValue
        {
            MaxAge = TimeSpan.FromSeconds(ClientTimeSpan),
            MustRevalidate = true,
            Public = true
        };

        actionExecutedContext.Response.Headers.CacheControl = cachecontrol;
    }
}
```

The filter is applying an instance of CacheControlHeaderValue to the response object's headers, but only if the response status code is not a 5xx error. The rationale here is that success responses (2xx), redirects (3xx), and client side errors (4xx) could be cached, but server side errors shouldn't.

▓ **Note**   According to RFC2616, there is nothing wrong with caching error responses (4xx, 5xx). It is up to you, the developer, to decide whether you want to treat status codes higher or equal than 500 as exceptional circumstances that the client should not be expecting and should always try to revalidate.

To unit test this functionality, you need to appropriately construct the HttpActionExecutedContext. Since it takes HttpActionContext through the constructor, you will have to pass that one in too.

In the first test, shown in Listing 11-11, you can verify if the cache control is indeed not set in case of an error (5xx) from the action, while the second test checks if the cache control is equivalent to the expected values.

Listing 11-11. Unit Tests for the Action Filter

```
[Fact]
public void WhenActionErrorsOutShouldNotCache()
{
    var attribute = new CacheAttribute();
    var executedContext = new HttpActionExecutedContext(new HttpActionContext
    {
        Response = new HttpResponseMessage(HttpStatusCode.InternalServerError)
    }, null);

    attribute.OnActionExecuted(executedContext);

    Assert.Null(executedContext.Response.Headers.CacheControl);
}

[Fact]
public void WhenActionIsSuccessfulRelevantCacheControlIsSet()
{
    var attribute = new CacheAttribute {ClientTimeSpan = 100};
    var executedContext = new HttpActionExecutedContext(new HttpActionContext
    {
        Response = new HttpResponseMessage(HttpStatusCode.OK)
    }, null);

    attribute.OnActionExecuted(executedContext);

    Assert.Equal(TimeSpan.FromSeconds(100), executedContext.Response.Headers.CacheControl.MaxAge);
    Assert.Equal(true, executedContext.Response.Headers.CacheControl.Public);
    Assert.Equal(true, executedContext.Response.Headers.CacheControl.MustRevalidate);
}
```

11-4. Unit Test Formatters
Problem

You have written a custom MediaTypeFormatter and would like to write some unit tests for it.

Solution

The quick way to unit test a formatter is to use ObjectContent<T> (from ASP.NET Web API's System.Net.Http.Formatting library) as a helper class; its constructor allows you to pass in an object instance and a relevant formatter. This gives you an opportunity to verify if the given object can be serialized with your formatter and whether the content headers are set correctly. Moreover, using the HttpContent ReadAsAsync<T> extension method (HttpContentExtensions, from the same System.Net.Http.Formatting library), you can verify if the deserialization process can happen too.

Alternatively, you can also test in a more traditional, and arguably more elegant, way by invoking the relevant methods and checking properties on the formatter itself. However, to invoke the critical WriteToStreamAsync and ReadFromStreamAsync methods, you will need to mock the TransportContext and IFormatterLogger, which are required by the respective method signatures.

How It Works

ObjectContent's constructor will test for you whether the Type passed in can be serialized with the formatter (internally calling CanWriteType on that formatter). It will also invoke the formatter's SetDefaultContentHeaders method to set appropriate headers. The constructor (Listing 11-12) will not perform any actual serialization; this is done through the SerializeToStreamAsync on the HttpContent later in the pipeline.

Listing 11-12. The Constructor of ObjectContent and the Bits Useful in Testing Formatters

```
public ObjectContent(Type type, object value, MediaTypeFormatter formatter,
MediaTypeHeaderValue mediaType)
{
    if (type == null)
    {
        throw Error.ArgumentNull("type");
    }
    if (formatter == null)
    {
        throw Error.ArgumentNull("formatter");
    }

    if (!formatter.CanWriteType(type))
    {
        throw Error.InvalidOperation(Properties.Resources.ObjectContent_FormatterCannotWriteType,
        formatter.GetType().FullName, type.Name);
    }

    _formatter = formatter;
    ObjectType = type;

    VerifyAndSetObject(value);
    _formatter.SetDefaultContentHeaders(type, Headers, mediaType);
}
```

Conversely, the ReadAsAsync<T> method of the HttpContentExtensions will internally check which of the formatters that you passed can read a given Type (by calling the formatter's CanReadType).

```
public static Task<T> ReadAsAsync<T>(this HttpContent content,
IEnumerable<MediaTypeFormatter> formatters)
```

The Code

Let's write some unit tests for the Protocol Buffers formatter that's part of the WebApiContrib project (it works great, but itself does not have any unit tests!). Two major paths for unit testing a formatter were already mentioned, but there's nothing to stop you from using both of the approaches here, instead of sticking to only one of them.

In order for Types to be serializable with Protobuf-net (which is the core library powering the ProtoBufFormatter), the Type needs to be either registered with the RuntimeTypeModel or decorated with relevant attributes, [ProtoContract] or [DataContract], along with an ordering property for each member. For the sake of this example, let's use two items, one that can be serialized and the other that cannot. This is shown in Listing 11-13.

Listing 11-13. Sample Types Used to Test the Formatter

```
[ProtoContract]
public class Item
{
    [ProtoMember(1)]
    public int Id { get; set; }
    [ProtoMember(2)]
    public string Name { get; set; }
}

public class EvilItem
{
    public int Id { get; set; }
    public string Name { get; set; }
}
```

Testing Using ObjectContent<T>

The sample from Listing 11-14 utilizes ObjectContent and the ReadAsAsync extension. By relying on ObjectContent, you can easily verify if the content has been set or if the exception has been thrown (unsupported Type).

Listing 11-14. Verifying if Serialization Is Possible Using ObjectContent

```
[Fact]
public void WhenInvokedObjectContentShouldNotThrow()
{
    var item = new Item {Id = 1, Name = "Filip"};
    Assert.DoesNotThrow(() => new ObjectContent<Item>(item, new ProtoBufFormatter()));
}

[Fact]
public void WhenInvokedWithUnsupportedTypeObjectContentShouldThrow()
{
    var item = new EvilItem { Id = 1, Name = "Filip" };
    Assert.Throws<InvalidOperationException>(() => new ObjectContent<EvilItem>(item,
    new ProtoBufFormatter()));
}
```

You can also use ObjectContent to check if the headers on the HttpContent have been set correctly and if the HttpContent serialized with the formatter can be also deserialized with the formatter; this is done using the ReadAsAsync extension method. It normally takes in an IEnumerable<MediaTypeFormatter>, so in this case you can simply pass in a single item array with the formatter under test. This is shown in Listing 11-15.

Listing 11-15. Verifying Content Headers and Deserializing Type Using ObjectContnent and ReadAsAsync

```
[Fact]
public void WhenInvokedContentHeadersShouldBeSetCorrectly()
{
    var item = new Item { Id = 1, Name = "Filip" };
    var content = new ObjectContent<Item>(item, new ProtoBufFormatter());

    Assert.Equal("application/x-protobuf", content.Headers.ContentType.MediaType);
}
```

```
[Fact]
public async void WhenUsedToDeserializeShouldCreateCorrectObject()
{
    var formatter = new ProtoBufFormatter();
    var item = new Item { Id = 1, Name = "Filip" };
    var content = new ObjectContent<Item>(item, formatter);

    var deserializedItem = await content.ReadAsAsync<Item>(new[] {formatter});
    Assert.Same(item, deserializedItem);
}
```

Traditional Unit Testing

In a more traditional approach to testing the formatter, you can call each of its methods individually. Verifying whether a Type can be written/read is done by calling the CanReadType and CanWriteType methods, without any extra formatter setup. This is shown in Listing 11-16.

Listing 11-16. Testing CanReadType and CanWriteType

```
[Fact]
public void WhenCallingCanReadShouldNotBeAbleToReadTypesItDoesNotUnderstand()
{
    var formatter = new ProtoBufFormatter();
    var canRead = formatter.CanReadType(typeof (EvilItem));
    Assert.False(canRead);
}

[Fact]
public void WhenCallingCanWriteShouldNotBeAbleToWriteTypesItDoesNotUnderstand()
{
    var formatter = new ProtoBufFormatter();
    var canWrite = formatter.CanWriteType(typeof(EvilItem));
    Assert.False(canWrite);
}

[Fact]
public void WhenCallingCanReadShouldBeAbleToReadTypesItUnderstands()
{
    var formatter = new ProtoBufFormatter();
    var canRead = formatter.CanReadType(typeof(Item));
    Assert.True(canRead);
}

[Fact]
public void WhenCallingCanWriteShouldBeAbleToWriteTypesItUnderstands()
{
    var formatter = new ProtoBufFormatter();
    var canWrite = formatter.CanWriteType(typeof(Item));
    Assert.True(canWrite);
}
```

In order to test the actual serialization process, you need to create an empty MemoryStream to which the formatter will write its output, and pass that stream to WriteToStreamAsync, along with an object instance that you want to be processed by the formatter. This is equivalent to ASP.NET Web API writing to a response stream. You can then try to deserialize the object from the MemoryStream using the Protobuf-net serializer directly (no need to go through the formatter anymore), and compare to the original instance; they should be identical. Additionally, WriteToStreamAsync needs a TransportContext that can be mocked.

On the opposite end of the spectrum, when testing ReadFromStreamAsync, you simply reverse the operations order (Listing 11-17): serialize a test object instance to a MemoryStream using Protobuf-net directly, and pass in the hydrated MemoryStream to the ReadFromStreamAsync, which has a return type of object and should be casted and compared to the original instance. As before, there is an extra parameter that needs mocking, IFormatterLogger.

Listing 11-17. Testing ReadFromStreamAsync and WriteToStreamAsync

```
[Fact]
public async void WhenWritingToStreamShouldSuccessfullyComplete()
{
    var formatter = new ProtoBufFormatter();
    var item = new Item { Id = 1, Name = "Filip" };

    var ms = new MemoryStream();
    await formatter.WriteToStreamAsync(typeof (Item), item, ms, new ByteArrayContent(new byte[0]),
        new Mock<TransportContext>().Object);

    var deserialized = ProtoBufFormatter.Model.Deserialize(ms, null, typeof (Item));

    Assert.Same(deserialized, item);
}

[Fact]
public async void WhenReadingFromStreamShouldSuccessfullyComplete()
{
    var formatter = new ProtoBufFormatter();
    var item = new Item { Id = 1, Name = "Filip" };

    var ms = new MemoryStream();
    ProtoBufFormatter.Model.Serialize(ms, item);
    var deserialized = await formatter.ReadFromStreamAsync(typeof(Item),
    ms, new ByteArrayContent(new byte[0]),
        new Mock<IFormatterLogger>().Object);

    Assert.Same(deserialized as Item, item);
}
```

■ **Note**   It was mentioned that the Protocol Buffers formatter in WebApiContrib does not have any tests. Now it does, because the tests used in this recipe have been contributed back to the project. Open source is great!

11-5. Simplify Tests with IHttpActionResult

Problem

You have to perform a lot of complex setup in the tests for actions returning `HttpResponseMessage` and you would like to avoid that.

Solution

By replacing `HttpResponseMessage` with `IHttpActionResult` you can shift the responsibility for producing the response from the action itself to an external class (in this case, an implementation of `IHttpActionResult`).

This has great benefits for the testability of your actions, as lots of logic gets moved outside of them, helping you conform to the golden rule of "lean controllers."

LEAN CONTROLLERS

Lean, logic-free controllers are one of the cornerstones of architecting a maintainable web application. In the ASP.NET world, one of the strongest advocates of keeping the controllers as simple as possible has been Jimmy Bogard, who defined the following reasons for keeping the controllers lean:

- Controllers are not a proper place for your business logic.

- Actions should be declarative in nature.

- Simplicity and consistency are paramount.

- Unit testing controllers is difficult (painful).

You can learn more about lean controllers from his series of blog posts at `http://lostechies.com/jimmybogard/2013/10/10/put-your-controllers-on-a-diet-redux/`. While Jimmy focuses on ASP.NET MVC, the same design principles apply to ASP.NET Web API.

How It Works

By switching from raw `HttpResponseMessage` usage to `IHttpActionResult`, you benefit immediately in a number of ways:

- The `HttpResponseMessage` creation logic, which can get very complex, is now out of scope for the action.

- That logic can be easily reused across different actions.

- Such `IHttpActionResult` implementation only needs to be tested once, helping you avoid repetitive asserts across various tests.

- Core Web API already ships with plenty of `IHttpActionResults`, which you can freely use for some most common tasks. Since they are part of the framework, they are unit tested by the framework and as a result you do not have to do that anymore.

The Code

Consider the simple controller in Listing 11-18, which performs a redirect to another controller.

Listing 11-18. A Sample Controller with an Action Making Use of HttpResponseMessage Directly

```
public class ItemsController : ApiController
{
    [Route("items/{id:int}", Name = "Items")]
    public HttpResponseMessage Get(int id)
    {
        var response = new HttpResponseMessage(HttpStatusCode.Redirect);
        var link = Url.Link("Other", new { id = id });
        response.Headers.Location = new Uri(link);

        return response;
    }
}
public class OtherController : ApiController
{
    [Route("id:int", Name = "Other")]
    public Item Get(int id)
    {
        return new Item {Id = id, Name = "Filip"};
    }
}
```

The Get action on the ItemsController is instantiating an instance of HttpResponseMessage and setting a 302 HTTP status code on it. It then proceeds to set the appropriate Location header on the response, using UrlHelper to resolve a link to OtherController.

The whole example here is very trivial, but in the older versions of Web API, it still required a tremendous amount of setup to be able to unit test such a controller, as UrlHelper could not be mocked. Since Web API 2, things have become much easier, as you can now set the UrlHelper instance on the controller using a public setter and override its virtual members. Nevertheless, the test code for this action (Listing 11-19) is still not as simple as it could be.

Listing 11-19. Testing an Action Returning HttpResponseMessage

```
[Fact]
public void WhenGetIsCalledShouldRespondWithRedirectToOtherController()
{
    var url = "http://www.apress.com";
    var urlHelper = new Mock<UrlHelper>();
    urlHelper.Setup(x => x.Link(It.IsAny<string>(), It.IsAny<object>())).Returns(url);

    var controller = new ItemsController {Url = urlHelper.Object};

    var result = controller.Get(5);

    Assert.Equal(HttpStatusCode.Redirect, result.StatusCode);
    Assert.Equal(new Uri(url), result.Headers.Location);
}
```

The test in Listing 11-19 mocks the helper, and verifies the 302 status code and the Location header. Note that the test can easily become very complicated if you perform some advanced tasks in your actions, such as manual content negotiation.

On the other hand, the action can be quickly modified to use IHttpActionResult instead of HttpResponseMessage; the built-in RedirectToRouteResult is doing exactly the same thing as the original action did (Listing 11-20).

Listing 11-20. Same Action Rewritten to Use HttpResponseMessage

```
[Route("newItems/{id:int}", Name = "NewItems")]
public IHttpActionResult GetNewItems(int id)
{
    return RedirectToRoute("Other", new { id = id });
}
```

▌ **Tip**   In this example, you do not need to new up an instance of RedirectToRouteResult since base ApiController already provides helper methods for the built-in IHttpActionResult, and it's normally more convenient to call those.

To test such an action, you only need to verify if the return Type is RedirectToRouteResult, as the redirection functionality itself is already guaranteed by the framework (all built-in IHttpActionResults are unit tested by the framework already). An example is shown in Listing 11-21.

Listing 11-21. Testing Whether the Returned IHttpActionResult Is of the Correct Type

```
[Fact]
public void WhenGetNewItemsIsCalledReturnTypeIsRedirectToRouteResult()
{
    var controller = new ItemsController();
    var result = controller.GetNewItems(5);

    Assert.IsType<RedirectToRouteResult>(result);
}
```

While IHttpActionResult is not a silver bullet applicable in every scenario, if you shift to using it in some of your heavier actions, you can generally benefit from having to test less.

11-6. Test Routes

Problem

You would like to test routing in your ASP.NET Web API application: whether a given URL really resolves to a specific method, and whether it's actually being invoked with a correct parameter.

Solution

With Web API, it is possible to manually run the entire default mechanism responsible for controller selection and action selection based on specific data. While the whole process is a bit rough, and not as elegant as, for example, the manual content negotiation (see Recipe 4-7), it can still be packaged into a reusable tester class which you can apply to many of your projects.

Once the selection process runs, you can compare its outcome to the class/method you are expecting to be hit: HttpControllerDescriptor, to confirm the controller, and HttpActionDescriptor, to compare an action.

How It Works

For testing routes, ASP.NET Web API requires the following things to be set up:

- Some registered routes, so that a string (a URI) can be matched to some predefined routing template. Obviously, we are talking about testing a route setup here—without that, there would be nothing to test in the first place.

- An instance of HttpControllerSelector; in this recipe you assume that the default DefaultHttpControllerSelector is being used. Otherwise you'd have to cater for the logic used internally in that custom selector.

- HttpControllerSelector will allow you to get an HttpControllerDescriptor representing the selected controller Type. To do that, you need an instance of HttpRequestMessage, with some RouteData on it.

- An instance of ApiControllerActionSelector, which is used by DefaultHttpControllerSelector to select a relevant action on the controller (using ControllerDescriptor). This is done based on the route data and on the HTTP method.

With these bits in place, the whole action selection pipeline can be run in process, by hand, and used to verify your routing mechanisms.

The Code

You'll need to set up a basic routing context to perform routing tests. This is all based on the current URL and a configuration object that will have some Routes hanging off it. The RouteContext helper test class is shown in Listing 11-22.

Listing 11-22. RoutingContext Which Runs Action Selection Against Your Web API Request and Exposes the Relevant Results

```
public class RouteContext
{
    private readonly IEnumerable<HttpActionDescriptor> _actionMappings;

    public RouteContext(HttpConfiguration config, HttpRequestMessage request)
    {
        var routeData = config.Routes.GetRouteData(request);
        request.SetRouteData(routeData);

        var controllerSelector = new DefaultHttpControllerSelector(config);
        var descriptor = controllerSelector.SelectController(request);
        ControllerType = descriptor.ControllerType;

        var actionSelector = new ApiControllerActionSelector();
        _actionMappings = actionSelector.GetActionMapping(descriptor)[request.Method.
        ToString()];
    }
    public Type ControllerType { get; private set; }
```

```
        public bool VerifyMatchedAction(MethodInfo method)
        {
            return _actionMappings.Any(item => ((ReflectedHttpActionDescriptor)item).MethodInfo.
            ToString() == method.ToString());
        }
    }
```

Effectively, the class does go through the exact process mentioned in the "How It Works" section. RouteData is extracted from the configuration, where route would be matched and set on the request itself. Then the controller selector is used to find out an HttpControllerDescriptor based on that request. Finally, controller Type is exposed publicly (so that it can be used in the tests), and all action mappings for a given HTTP verb are saved in a private field, as they will be used to compare if the selected action really does have the same signature as the one you are expecting.

With this small setup, you can proceed to writing test code for your routes. Let's take a simple example of a controller, like the one in Listing 11-23 (its implementation details are completely irrelevant).

Listing 11-23. A Sample Controller That Will Be Used to Test Routes

```
[RoutePrefix("coolitems")]
public class HappyItemsController : ApiController
{
    [Route("")]
    public IEnumerable<Item> Get()
    {
        return new List<Item> {
            new Item { Id = 1, Name = "Filip" },
            new Item { Id = 1, Name = "NotFilip" }
        };
    }

    [Route("{id:int}")]
    public Item GetById(int id)
    {
        return new Item { Id = id, Name = "Filip" };
    }

    [Route("")]
    public void Post(Item item)
    {}

    [Route("{id:int}")]
    public void Delete(int id)
    {}
}
```

In case of this controller, what you would like to verify might be

- GET http://www.apress.com/coolitems ends up in the Get action of the controller

- GET http://www.apress.com/coolitems/1 ends up in the GetById action of the controller and passes in 1 as the id parameter

- POST http://www.apress.com/coolitems ends up in the Post action of the controller

- DELETE http://www.apress.com/coolitems/1 ends up in the Delete action of the controller and passes in 1 as the id parameter

Let's write the tests. Remember, in order for the attribute routing to kick in, you have to manually invoke the MapHttpAttributeRoutes method and EnsureInitialize on the HttpConfiguration. The tests are shown in Listing 11-24.

Listing 11-24. Unit Testing Routes

```
public class AttributeRouteTests
{
    readonly HttpConfiguration _config;

    public AttributeRouteTests()
    {
        _config = new HttpConfiguration();
        _config.MapHttpAttributeRoutes();
        _config.EnsureInitialized();
    }

    [Fact]
    public void ItemsControllerGetIsCorrect()
    {
        var request = new HttpRequestMessage(HttpMethod.Get, "http://www.apress.com/coolitems/");
        var routeTester = new RouteContext(_config, request);

        Assert.Equal(typeof(HappyItemsController), routeTester.ControllerType);
        Assert.True(routeTester.VerifyMatchedAction(ReflectionHelpers.GetMethodInfo
        ((HappyItemsController p) => p.Get())));
    }

    [Fact]
    public void ItemsControllerGetByIdIsCorrect()
    {
        var request = new HttpRequestMessage(HttpMethod.Get, "http://www.apress.com/coolitems/7");
        var routeTester = new RouteContext(_config, request);

        Assert.Equal(typeof(HappyItemsController), routeTester.ControllerType);
        Assert.True(routeTester.VerifyMatchedAction(ReflectionHelpers.GetMethodInfo
        ((HappyItemsController p) => p.Get(7))));
    }

    [Fact]
    public void ItemsControllerPostIsCorrect()
    {
        var request = new HttpRequestMessage(HttpMethod.Post, "http://www.apress.com/coolitems/");
        var routeTester = new RouteContext(_config, request);

        Assert.Equal(typeof(HappyItemsController), routeTester.ControllerType);
        Assert.True(routeTester.VerifyMatchedAction(ReflectionHelpers.GetMethodInfo
        ((HappyItemsController p) => p.Post(new Item()))));
    }
```

```
    [Fact]
    public void ItemsControllerDeleteIsCorrect()
    {
        var request = new HttpRequestMessage(HttpMethod.Delete, "http://www.apress.com/coolitems/7");
        var routeTester = new RouteContext(_config, request);

        Assert.Equal(typeof(HappyItemsController), routeTester.ControllerType);
        Assert.True(routeTester.VerifyMatchedAction(ReflectionHelpers.GetMethodInfo
        ((HappyItemsController p) => p.Delete(7))));
    }
}
```

▓ **Note**　The host part of your HTTP request is not important in these tests; only the relative part of the Uri is affecting the routing.

Each test is identical in terms of the setup and execution: an HttpRequestMessage is instantiated with the relevant HTTP method and a URI pointing to some resource. Then the helper RouteContext is created based on those two. Afterwards, you can compare the ControllerType on the RouteContext to the one you are expecting the request to be routed to. Additionally, each test compares an expected method to the one determined by the RouteContext object.

This particular comparison takes advantage of some reflection helpers (Listing 11-25); they are here merely so that you can grab a MethodInfo in an elegant way, off an ExpressionTree. With that, all the comparisons that are happening can be strongly typed, and the tests can be easily refactored in case some signatures change (since they won't compile anymore).

Listing 11-25. ReflectionHelpers Useful for Obtaining MethodInfo in a Strongly Typed Manner

```
public class ReflectionHelpers
{
    public static MethodInfo GetMethodInfo<T, U>(Expression<Func<T, U>>expression)
    {
        return GetMethodInfoInternal(expression);
    }

    public static MethodInfo GetMethodInfo<T>(Expression<Action<T>>expression)
    {
        return GetMethodInfoInternal(expression);
    }

    private static MethodInfo GetMethodInfoInternal(dynamic expression)
    {
        var method = expression.Body as MethodCallExpression;
        if (method != null)
            return method.Method;

        throw new ArgumentException("Expression is incorrect!");
    }
}
```

The controller and tests from Listing 11-24 use attribute routing, but if your code utilizes traditional centralized routing instead, you can test that too. The only change is to modify the test class constructor where the routes are initialized. You can either call MapHttpRoute inline, or pass the configuration to the method where you normally register all the routes (i.e. WebApiConfig.Register).

```
public RouteTests()
{
    _config = new HttpConfiguration();
    _config.Routes.MapHttpRoute(name: "Default", routeTemplate: "{controller}/{id}",
    defaults: new { id = RouteParameter.Optional });
}
```

11-7. Integration Testing

Problem

You would like to perform end-to-end integration testing of your ASP.NET Web API service.

Solution

ASP.NET Web API can be hosted entirely in memory (in process). This feature is extremely useful for integration testing, as you can easily run the whole pipeline in memory, in a very fast and efficient manner. All you need to do is just pass in a Web API HttpServer instance to the HttpClient constructor.

```
var config = new HttpConfiguration();
config.MapHttpAttributeRoutes();

var server = new HttpServer(config);
var client = new HttpClient(server);
// client can now call Web API in memory
```

■ **Tip** For even more lightweight experience, you can use HttpActionInvoker, which HttpClient extends.

How It Works

One of the key aspects of the architecture of Web API (or rather the new HTTP object model it uses) is its client-server symmetry. The entry point to Web API is an HttpServer, which itself is just a subclass of MessageHandler. As a developer, you can then chain other handlers in this pipeline.

The .NET HttpClient, on the other hand, can use MessageHandlers on the client side too, as two of its constructors actually accepts a handler as a parameter.

```
public HttpClient(HttpMessageHandler handler)
public HttpClient(HttpMessageHandler handler, bool disposeHandler)
```

The principle is similar to the server side, and handlers can be chained. You can imagine a LoggingHandler that could log requests and responses and be totally agnostic about its environment. Such a handler would be equally usable on the client and server side.

As a consequence of this design, `HttpClient` does not have to send requests over the network to communicate with Web API, since you can just pass the `HttpServer` directly through its constructor. With this type of setup, the entire Web API pipeline would run in memory, bypassing any network interfaces. This has tremendous value for testing scenarios, as well as for some highly specialized use cases beyond tests, such as local batching of requests or developing applications using techniques like CefSharp, an embedded Chromium for .NET.

INTEGRATION TESTING WITH SELF-HOSTED WEB API

While self-hosting Web API might seem like an appealing approach to integration testing, it is not a recommended practice.

Self-host (based on WCF and `HttpListener`) typically requires elevated privileges, which automatically means that every component running tests in your CI pipeline must run in admin mode (individual developer machines, test runners, CI server, and so on).

Additionally, what you really end up testing, in addition to your Web API service itself, is the underlying operating system's networking stack, and that might differ across different staging environments (for example, a given port might not be available). As a result, you might get dragged into unnecessary debugging efforts across different machines to even get the tests up and running.

Finally, due to some difference between web and self-host, testing using self-host doesn't guarantee that the service will behave and run correctly when hosted on ASP.NET and vice versa.

The Code

Let's have a look at testing a simple Web API service. Since this is an integration test, there are a number of things you might be interested in verifying.

- Does my controller respond correctly?
- Is my message handler invoked in the pipeline?
- Are my filters being executed?
- Is my API responding with XML/JSON media types correctly?

Of course, in end-to-end testing scenarios, many more of such questions should be asked—and answered.

Consider the following simple system under test: a small controller (Listing 11-28), a logging message handler (Listing 11-26), and a caching filter (Listing 11-27). For the sake of consistency with the rest of this chapter, the handler will be identical to Recipe 11-2, and the filter the same as in Recipe 11-3. It is very typical in ASP.NET Web API solutions to unit test the pieces individually and then verify them working together through an integration test.

Listing 11-26. A Sample Logging Interface and the Message Handler Using It

```
public interface ILoggingService
{
    void Log(string message);
}
```

```
public class LoggingHandler : DelegatingHandler
{
    public ILoggingService LoggingService { get; set; }

    protected override Task<HttpResponseMessage> SendAsync(HttpRequestMessage request,
    CancellationToken cancellationToken)
    {
        var loggingService = LoggingService ?? request.GetDependencyScope().GetService(typeof
        (ILoggingService)) as ILoggingService;
        if (loggingService != null)
        {
            loggingService.Log(request.RequestUri.ToString());
        }

        return base.SendAsync(request, cancellationToken);
    }
}
```

Listing 11-27. A Sample Filter Responding for Adding MaxAge to the Response

```
public class CacheAttribute : ActionFilterAttribute
{
    public int ClientTimeSpan { get; set; }

    public override void OnActionExecuted(HttpActionExecutedContext actionExecutedContext)
    {
        var cachecontrol = new CacheControlHeaderValue
        {
            MaxAge = TimeSpan.FromSeconds(ClientTimeSpan),
            MustRevalidate = true
        };

        actionExecutedContext.ActionContext.Response.Headers.CacheControl = cachecontrol;
    }
}
```

Listing 11-28. A DTO and a Simple Test Controller

```
public class MessageDto
{
    public string Text { get; set; }
}

public class HelloController : ApiController
{
    [Route("hello")]
    [Cache(ClientTimeSpan = 100)]
    public string Get()
    {
        return "Hello World";
    }
```

```
    [Route("hello")]
    public HttpResponseMessage Post(MessageDto message)
    {
        //pretend we process message here

        return Request.CreateResponse(HttpStatusCode.Created, message);
    }
}
```

Each integration test will need an in-memory server to be up and running, and have it configured with the appropriate routes and configuration. If you use an external method to configure your Web API (such as the static Register method that web host templates for Visual Studio add), you can pass the configuration object to it, but this example will do everything inline. Obviously, in case your Web API application requires some customizations of the configuration (such as replacing the default services, or changing media type support), those should be performed here too. The basic wireframe for an integration test is shown in Listing 11-29.

Listing 11-29. The Minimum Setup Required to Run Integration Tests—an Instance of HttpServer, HttpConfiguration, and Route Mapping

```
public class IntegrationTests
{
    private readonly HttpServer _server;
    private const string Url = "http://www.apress.com/";
    private readonly Mock<ILoggingService> _loggingService;

    public IntegrationTest()
    {
        _loggingService = new Mock<ILoggingService>();

        var config = new HttpConfiguration();
        config.MapHttpAttributeRoutes();

        config.MessageHandlers.Add(new LoggingHandler {LoggingService = _loggingService.Object});
        _server = new HttpServer(config);
    }

    //tests will go here

    public void Dispose()
    {
        if (_server != null)
        {
            _server.Dispose();
        }
    }
}
```

At this point, the whole Web API pipeline is set up in memory for each test run. The calls that will be made to this pipeline will happen entirely in memory. However, you still need to use an absolute URI to be able to make the calls; it does not matter which, as the HttpServer will only look at the relative part anyway.

Listing 11-30 verifies that the Get method responds correctly, that the cache attribute kicks in and sets the Cache-Control like it was expected, and that the call goes through a LoggingHandler.

Listing 11-30. Tests Veryifing Successful Execution and Response from the Get Method, Action Filter, and Message Handler

```
[Fact]
public async void GetHelloReturnsCorrectResponse()
{
    var client = new HttpClient(_server);
    var response = await client.GetAsync(Url + "hello");
    var result = await response.Content.ReadAsStringAsync();

    Assert.Equal("Hello World", result);
}

[Fact]
public async void GetHelloSetsMaxAgeTo100()
{
    var client = new HttpClient(_server);
    var response = await client.GetAsync(Url + "hello");

    Assert.Equal(TimeSpan.FromSeconds(100), response.Headers.CacheControl.MaxAge);
}

[Fact]
public async void GetHelloGoesThroughLoggingHandler()
{
    var client = new HttpClient(_server);
    var response = await client.GetAsync(Url + "hello");

    _loggingService.Verify(i => i.Log("http://www.apress.com/hello"), Times.Once);
}
```

Calling the API endpoints in memory is identical to using HttpClient against external resources; the only difference is that the client was initially instantiated by passing in the HttpServer in the constructor. Reading the response, response body, or headers is just regular usage of HttpClient API.

You can also perform more advanced tests of the content negotiation. Suppose you'd like to verify for sure that your API can respond successfully in XML and JSON formats (or support any other media type that you intend to be used with your API). In that case, you may want to write tests like the ones in Listing 11-31.

Listing 11-31. Tests Checking Media Type Support

```
[Fact]
public async void PostCanRespondInXml()
{
    var message = new MessageDto
    {
        Text = "This is XML"
    };
    var client = new HttpClient(_server);
    var response = await client.PostAsXmlAsync(Url + "hello", message);
```

```
        var result = await response.Content.ReadAsAsync<MessageDto>(new [] {new XmlMediaTypeFormatter() });

        Assert.Equal(message.Text, result.Text);
}

[Fact]
public async void PostCanRespondInJson()
{
    var message = new MessageDto
    {
        Text = "This is JSON"
    };
    var client = new HttpClient(_server);
    var response = await client.PostAsJsonAsync(Url + "hello", message);

    var result = await response.Content.ReadAsAsync<MessageDto>(new[] { new JsonMediaTypeFormatter() });

    Assert.Equal(message.Text, result.Text);
}
```

Both tests are submitting a relevant representation of a resource to the API, and then verifying whether the response comes back in the same media type format. Of course, you could easily get much more sophisticated here, but the gist of the matter is that it's extremely easy to quickly and efficiently run your entire Web API service in memory, without touching the networking stack.

11-8. Integration Testing with OWIN
Problem

You would like to perform end-to-end integration testing of your ASP.NET Web API service. However, using the HttpServer in a way discussed in Recipe 11-7 is not an option since you host Web API on the OWIN stack using Project Katana and would like the OWIN pipeline to be included in the tests too.

Solution

A Microsoft.Owin.Testing package on NuGet, which is part of the Katana project, allows you to run the OWIN pipeline in memory. The usage is almost the same as HttpServer, except you either have to configure the Katana IAppBuilder during the test setup or point the test server to your Startup class.

```
var server = TestServer.Create<Startup>();
var response = await _server.HttpClient.GetAsync("/hello");
```

How It Works

Hosting Web API with Project Katana is explained in detail in Recipe 2-2. The way it runs is memory is identical to how HttpServer operates (see Recipe 11-7).

The Katana TestServer object contains a public property Handler, which holds an HttpMessageHandler, which can be passed to the HttpClient's constructor. That handler is actually an OwinClientHandler, which is the OWIN pipeline entry and exit point. It is responsible for taking in an HttpRequestMessage (from HttpClient), dispatching it through the OWIN pipeline, and grabbing the response and producing a relevant HttpResponseMessage.

The Code

Let's use an identical configuration of the system under test as defined in Recipe 11-7 in Listings 11-26 through 11-28. However, since the idea is to have a look at running OWIN pipeline in memory, let's refactor the LoggingHandler into an OwinMiddleware, such as the one shown in Listing 11-32. The rest of the Web API components (test controller, filter) are intact.

Listing 11-32. Dummy Middleware Responsible for Logging

```
public class LoggingMiddleware : OwinMiddleware
{
    public static Lazy<ILoggingService> LoggingService = new Lazy<ILoggingService>(() => new
    SampleLoggingService());

    public LoggingMiddleware(OwinMiddleware next)
        : base(next)
    {
    }

    public override async Task Invoke(IOwinContext context)
    {
        //this is just a test implementation
        LoggingService.Value.Log(context.Request.Uri.ToString());
        await Next.Invoke(context);
    }
}
```

■ **Note** To run Web API using OWIN, you need to install the Microsoft.AspNet.WebApi.Owin package.

LoggingService is exposed publicly so that it can be easily mocked. The OWIN Startup class (Listing 11-33) adds the logging middleware into the pipeline and initializes Web API.

Listing 11-33. OWIN Startup Class Chaining the Logging Middleware and Web API

```
public class Startup
{
    public void Configuration(IAppBuilder appBuilder)
    {
        var config = new HttpConfiguration();
        config.MapHttpAttributeRoutes();

        appBuilder.Use(typeof (LoggingMiddleware));
        appBuilder.UseWebApi(config);
    }
}
```

You can now proceed to writing unit tests, and they will be remarkably similar to the ones written against Web API's HttpServer. You will have to create an instance of a TestServer using the relevant factory method (TestServer has no public constructors), and you will later use the HttpClient hanging off that TestServer to communicate with your API in memory. The latter helps you avoid having to new up an HttpClient every time, although it's not mandatory, as you can use an independent instance of HttpClient too.

The two available factory methods to create a `TestServer` are as follows:

```
public static TestServer Create<TStartup>();
public static TestServer Create(Action<Owin.IAppBuilder> startup);
```

They allow you to use the `Startup` class to initialize the OWIN pipeline, or to build it by hand in the tests.

In your particular integration test setup, in the constructor, you will also have to remember to add a `LoggingService` onto your custom `LoggingMiddleware` middleware to be able to verify when and how it's getting invoked. This is shown in Listing 11-34.

Listing 11-34. Basic Setup for OWIN Integration Tests

```
public class IntegrationTests
{
    private readonly TestServer _server;
    private readonly Mock<ILoggingService> _loggingService;

    public IntegrationTests()
    {
        _loggingService = new Mock<ILoggingService>();
        _server = TestServer.Create<Startup>();
        LoggingMiddleware.LoggingService = new Lazy<ILoggingService>(() => _loggingService.Object);
    }

    //tests go here

    public void Dispose()
    {
        if (_server != null)
        {
            _server.Dispose();
        }
    }
}
```

Since everything is in place, you can now add the tests (Listing 11-35), which are using the `TestServer` and the `HttpClient` exposed by it to make the in-memory calls to the OWIN pipeline. The usage and semantics are identical to normal usage of `HttpClient` APIs.

Listing 11-35. In-Memory Integration Tests for the OWIN Pipeline

```
[Fact]
public async void GetHelloReturnsCorrectResponse()
{
    var response = await _server.HttpClient.GetAsync("/hello");
    var result = await response.Content.ReadAsStringAsync();

    Assert.Equal("Hello World", result);
}
```

```csharp
[Fact]
public async void GetHelloSetsMaxAgeTo100()
{
    var response = await _server.HttpClient.GetAsync("/hello");
    Assert.Equal(TimeSpan.FromSeconds(100), response.Headers.CacheControl.MaxAge);
}

[Fact]
public async void GetHelloGoesThroughLoggingHandler()
{
    var response = await _server.HttpClient.GetAsync("/hello");
    _loggingService.Verify(i => i.Log("http://www.apress.com/hello"), Times.Once);
}

[Fact]
public async void PostCanRespondInXml()
{
    var message = new MessageDto
    {
        Text = "This is XML"
    };
    var response = await _server.HttpClient.PostAsXmlAsync("/hello", message);
    var result = await response.Content.ReadAsAsync<MessageDto>(new[] { new XmlMediaTypeFormatter() });

    Assert.Equal(message.Text, result.Text);
}

[Fact]
public async void PostCanRespondInJson()
{
    var message = new MessageDto
    {
        Text = "This is JSON"
    };
    var response = await _server.HttpClient.PostAsJsonAsync("/hello", message);
    var result = await response.Content.ReadAsAsync<MessageDto>(new[] { new JsonMediaTypeFormatter() });

    Assert.Equal(message.Text, result.Text);
}
```

The in-memory integration tests used here will ensure that HTTP requests can flow through your OWIN pipeline seamlessly and hit the relevant middleware components. In addition to that, they validate for you that the expected API responses are returned safely to the client.

CHAPTER 12

OData

In this chapter, I will briefly introduce ASP.NET Web API support for OData, the Open Data Protocol. You will learn how to do the following:

- Create a simple OData service in ASP.NET Web API (Recipe 12-1)

- Create centralized and attribute-based OData routes (Recipe 12-2)

- Work with OData Query Options (Recipe 12-3)

- Support OData functions and actions in ASP.NET Web API (Recipe 12-4)

12-1. Creating OData Services in Web API
Problem

You would like to create an OData service using ASP.NET Web API.

Solution

The easiest way to get started with OData in Web API is to use the ASP.NET scaffolder to generate OData controllers for you. To do that, right click on your project and choose Add ➤ New Scaffold Item.

This will pull up a dialog window such as the one shown in Figure 12-1, where you can choose either "Web API 2 OData Controller with actions, using Entity Framework" or "Web API 2 OData Controller with read/write actions." Visual Studio will then generate the relevant OData controller and download all the necessary NuGet packages to allow you to get started with OData.

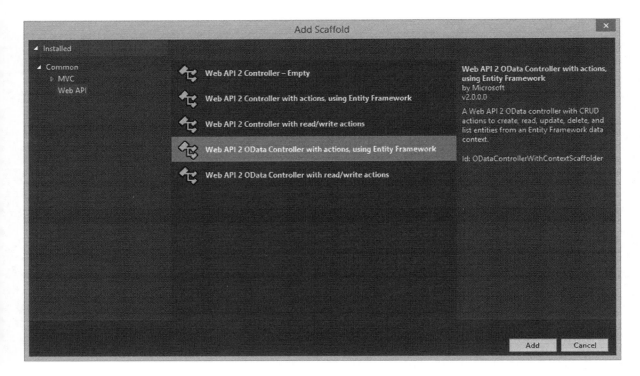

Figure 12-1. Adding OData controllers using ASP.NET scaffolder

However, the scaffolder option will only be available in web host (ASP.NET Web API hosted within an ASP.NET web application). For other types of Web API hosts, you can start developing your OData endpoints by installing the `Microsoft.AspNet.OData` package (OData 4.0 specific) from NuGet.

How It Works

OData is a standardized protocol for exposing rich APIs over HTTP. OData 4.0 is approved by the OASIS international open standards consortium and is often considered to be to the Web what ODBC (Open Database Connectivity) is to the database world.

> *The Open Data Protocol (OData) enables the creation of REST-based data services, which allow resources, identified using Uniform Resource Locators (URLs) and defined in a data model, to be published and edited by Web clients using simple HTTP messages.*
>
> OData Version 4.0
>
> `http://docs.oasis-open.org/odata/odata/v4.0/odata-v4.0-part1-protocol.html`

■ **Tip**   The OData home page at `www.odata.org` is full of interesting resources that will help you get started with the OData protocol.

ASP.NET Web API 2.2 supports OData version 4.0 (`Microsoft.AspNet.OData` NuGet package), while the earlier releases supported OData 3.0. You can still use or target OData 3.0 though, if you specifically reference the `Microsoft.AspNet.WebApi.OData` NuGet package.

OData controllers should inherit from an `ODataController` base class instead of the regular `ApiController`. ASP.NET Web API allows you to mix OData controllers with traditional controllers within the same project, so you can expose OData endpoints alongside your regular API resources.

Controllers derived from `ODataController` are configured differently by the framework. They get an OData-specific `IHttpActionSelector` called `ODataActionSelector`, which is based on OData routing conventions, as well as a specific set of media type formatters which replace the default ones. All of OData formatters are variations of `ODataMediaTypeFormatter`, which can handle OData specific request/response formats in both XML (AtomPub) and JSON (AtomPubJSON light).

The Code

Listing 12-1 shows a fully-functional, yet fairly typical, CRUD (create, read, update, delete) `ODataController`. In this case it's a class generated by the ASP.NET scaffolder from a `Player` entity and an Entity Framework data context.

Listing 12-1. A Typical ODataController

```
public class PlayerController : ODataController
{
    private PlayerContext db = new PlayerContext();

    [EnableQuery]
    public IQueryable<Player> GetPlayer()
    {
        return db.Players;
    }

    [EnableQuery]
    public SingleResult<Player> GetPlayer([FromODataUri] int key)
    {
        return SingleResult.Create(db.Players.Where(player => player.Id == key));
    }

    public async Task<IHttpActionResult> Put([FromODataUri] int key, Player player)
    {
        if (!ModelState.IsValid)
        {
            return BadRequest(ModelState);
        }

        if (key != player.Id)
        {
            return BadRequest();
        }

        db.Entry(player).State = EntityState.Modified;
```

```
        try
        {
            await db.SaveChangesAsync();
        }
        catch (DbUpdateConcurrencyException)
        {
            if (!PlayerExists(key))
            {
                return NotFound();
            }

            throw;
        }

        return Updated(player);
    }

    public async Task<IHttpActionResult> Post(Player player)
    {
        if (!ModelState.IsValid)
        {
            return BadRequest(ModelState);
        }

        db.Players.Add(player);
        await db.SaveChangesAsync();

        return Created(player);
    }

    [AcceptVerbs("PATCH")]
    public async Task<IHttpActionResult> Patch([FromODataUri] int key, Delta<Player> patch)
    {
        if (!ModelState.IsValid)
        {
            return BadRequest(ModelState);
        }

        Player player = await db.Players.FindAsync(key);
        if (player == null)
        {
            return NotFound();
        }

        patch.Patch(player);

        try
        {
            await db.SaveChangesAsync();
        }
```

```
        catch (DbUpdateConcurrencyException)
        {
            if (!PlayerExists(key))
            {
                return NotFound();
            }

            throw;
        }

        return Updated(player);
    }

    public async Task<IHttpActionResult> Delete([FromODataUri] int key)
    {
        Player player = await db.Players.FindAsync(key);
        if (player == null)
        {
            return NotFound();
        }

        db.Players.Remove(player);
        await db.SaveChangesAsync();

        return StatusCode(HttpStatusCode.NoContent);
    }

    protected override void Dispose(bool disposing)
    {
        if (disposing)
        {
            db.Dispose();
        }
        base.Dispose(disposing);
    }

    private bool PlayerExists(int key)
    {
        return db.Players.Any(e => e.Id == key);
    }
}
```

The controller is very similar to typical Web API controllers, with just a few things worth highlighting:

- OData query syntax is supported through EnableQueryAttribute. This is discussed in detail in Recipe 12-3.

- OData query syntax can be used against a single entity too (not just collections), as long as the entity is wrapped in the SingleResult<T>. This is also discussed in detail in Recipe 12-3.

- FromODataUriAttribute should be used instead of traditional Web API FromUriAttribute for binding values from a URI.

- OData controllers often allow partial update of entities. In this example, it's achieved through the HTTP PATCH verb and a Delta<T>, a special type that only works with ODataMediaTypeFormatters, and can be used to apply differentials between two instances of the entity.

Obviously the controller is not everything; the bare minimum to get started with OData is to create an Entity Data Model (EDM) for your OData service and set up at least one OData route. Both of those operations are done against an instance of the Web API HttpConfiguration, which is shown in Listing 12-2 (OData routing is explored in detail in Recipe 12-2). EDM is used to define URIs for your service as well as to provide a semantic description (metadata) for it.

Listing 12-2. Setting Up an EDM and an OData Route

```
var config = new HttpConfiguration();
//configure your Web API

var builder = new ODataConventionModelBuilder();
builder.EntitySet<Player>("Players");

//first parameter is the name of the route, second is the route prefix for OData
//players resource is now accessible at /odata/players
config.Routes.MapODataServiceRoute("odata", "odata", builder.GetEdmModel());
```

The ODataConventionModelBuilder class helps you create an EDM without having to explicitly worry about naming conventions, navigation properties, or keys. If you want to customize those default relationship conventions, you can directly use its base class, ODataModelBuilder, instead.

The EntitySet method adds an entity set to the EDM and defines a specific ODataController, in this case PlayersController, to handle HTTP requests for that resource.

12-2. Manage OData Routes

Problem

You want to have full control over your OData routes.

Solution

To register a central OData route, use a MapODataServiceRoute extension method from the HttpConfigurationExtensions class. A single route is enough, as the rest is handled by your Entity Data Model.

```
config.MapODataServiceRoute(routeName: "Default OData", routePrefix: "odata", model: myEdmModel);
```

To register a direct route, which is supported for OData since ASP.NET Web API 2.2, decorate an action method with an ODataRouteAttribute. Similarly to regular attribute routing, you can also set up route prefixing at the controller level, through ODataRoutePrefixAttribute.

```
[ODataRoute("Players")]
public IQueryable<Player> GetAllPlayers()
{
    //omitted for brevity
}
```

How It Works

Routes in the Web API implementation of OData are handled through the ODataRoute class, which is a subclass of HttpRoute. The specialized route class is needed to support ODataPathRouteConstraint, an OData-specific implementation of IHttpRouteConstraint, which ensures that all OData properties, such as EDM Model, OData path, or the OData routing conventions are set on the HttpRequestMessage after an OData route is matched.

The ODataPath class is used to wrap the parsed OData resource path and expose its segments in a strongly typed manner. By convention, ASP.NET Web API uses the resource path (part of the URI), such as /Players(1), to map to a relevant controller, based on the setup in the Entity Data Model. Then, the verb-based action selection kicks in to find a relevant action on the controller. Furthermore, OData in Web API also uses a number of custom routing conventions, all of which can impact the action selection.

■ **Tip** For more information on OData routing conventions, see the official ASP.NET documentation at www.asp.net/web-api/overview/odata-support-in-aspnet-web-api/odata-routing-conventions.

You can override the OData routing behavior and implement custom OData controller and action selection by introducing your own IODataRoutingConvention, shown in Listing 12-3.

Listing 12-3. Definition of IODataRoutingConvention

```
public interface IODataRoutingConvention
{
    string SelectController(ODataPath odataPath, HttpRequestMessage request);
    string SelectAction(ODataPath odataPath, HttpControllerContext controllerContext,
    ILookup<string, HttpActionDescriptor> actionMap);
}
```

Such a custom routing convention can then be passed to the MapODataServiceRoute extension method when you define the OData routes; one of the overloads accepts a collection of IODataRoutingConvention. If none of them are passed (such as in the usage example of MapODataServiceRoute showed before), then Web API will internally call a static ODataRoutingConventions.CreateDefaultWithAttributeRouting to use default built-in routing conventions only.

Attribute routing in OData is simply another version of IODataRoutingConvention–AttributeRoutingConvention. It will find all ODataRouteAttribute usages and build up the appropriate mappings in the form of a Dictionary<ODataPathTemplate, HttpActionDescriptor>. If the incoming request matches the ODataPath from the current HTTP request, then the controller related to this HttpActionDescriptor will be selected to handle the request.

Attribute routing is a great choice for non-standard routes, such as when using unbounded OData functions or actions. Trying to route to them with centralized routing requires a custom routing convention (so effectively, an extra class), whereas with attribute routing it can be achieved straight away by simply annotating the relevant method with the ODataRouteAttribute.

It is important to mention that, contrary to regular attribute routing, OData attribute routing is enabled by default; that is, unless you override the default IODataRoutingConventions. If you don't, then Web API calls ODataRoutingConventions.CreateDefaultWithAttributeRouting internally whenever you use the MapODataServiceRoute method, which ensures that AttributeRoutingConvention is included in the conventions collection used by Web API OData. This is shown in Listing 12-4, in the excerpt from the Web API source code.

Listing 12-4. ODataRoutingConventions Class, Ensuring That AttributeRoutingConvention Is Included

```
public static class ODataRoutingConventions
{
        public static IList<IODataRoutingConvention> CreateDefaultWithAttributeRouting(
            HttpConfiguration configuration,
            IEdmModel model)
        {
            if (configuration == null)
            {
                throw Error.ArgumentNull("configuration");
            }
            if (model == null)
            {
                throw Error.ArgumentNull("model");
            }

            IList<IODataRoutingConvention> routingConventions = CreateDefault();
            AttributeRoutingConvention routingConvention = new AttributeRoutingConvention(model,
configuration);
            routingConventions.Insert(0, routingConvention);
                return routingConventions;
        }

        public static IList<IODataRoutingConvention> CreateDefault()
        {
            return new List<IODataRoutingConvention>()
            {
                new MetadataRoutingConvention(),
                new EntitySetRoutingConvention(),
                new SingletonRoutingConvention(),
                new EntityRoutingConvention(),
                new NavigationRoutingConvention(),
                new PropertyRoutingConvention(),
                new RefRoutingConvention(),
                new ActionRoutingConvention(),
                new FunctionRoutingConvention(),
                new UnmappedRequestRoutingConvention()
            };
        }
    }
```

As a result, there is no need to invoke any extra method at your application startup to instruct the framework to scan for route attributes. In fact, the only way to get attribute routing to work in the first place is to call the central MapODataServiceRoute.

The Code

To introduce centralized routing into your OData Web API, you simply need to call `MapODataServiceRoute` against your `HttpConfiguration` and pass in the route prefix and your `IEdmModel`. A full example of a Katana `Startup` class with a single OData entity and a single central route is shown in Listing 12-5, using a `Player` entity.

Listing 12-5. Katana Startup Class Declaring a Basic OData Route

```
public class Startup
{
    public void Configuration(IAppBuilder builder)
    {
        var odataBuilder = new ODataConventionModelBuilder();
        odataBuilder.EntitySet<Player>("Players");

        var edm = odataBuilder.GetEdmModel();

        var config = new HttpConfiguration();
        config.MapODataServiceRoute("Default OData", "odata", edm);
        builder.UseWebApi(config);
    }
}

public class Player
{
    public int Id { get; set; }
    public string Name { get; set; }
    public string Team { get; set; }
}
```

This allows you to use all of the default built-in routing conventions, such as the following:

- myapi.com/odata/Players

- myapi.com/odata/Players(key)

- myapi.com/odata/Players(key)/{navigation property | property}

- myapi.com/odata/Players(key)/{function | action}

■ **Caution**   The default Web API OData routing convention uses a notion of a key, not an ID, so your controller actions should also accept a key parameter.

Listing 12-6 shows an `ODataController` with two actions methods. Both of them have OData routes enabled via attribute routing.

Listing 12-6. Sample Usage of Attribute Routing with ODataController

```
[ODataRoutePrefix("Players")]
public class PlayersController : ODataController
{
    private readonly PlayersContext _players = new PlayersContext();

    [EnableQuery]
    [ODataRoute]
    public IQueryable<Player> GetAllPlayers()
    {
        return _players.AsQueryable();
    }

    [EnableQuery]
    [ODataRoute("({key})")]
    public SingleResult<Player> GetSinglePlayers(int key)
    {
        return SingleResult.Create(_players.Where(x => x.Id == key).AsQueryable());
    }
}
```

12-3. Enable OData Queries
Problem
You want your Web API endpoints to support the common OData System Query Options, such as $select or $filter.

Solution
To enable query options on a Web API endpoint, you decorate the action with an EnableQueryAttribute.

If your action does not return a collection, but a single instance of an object, a client could still apply two of the query options, $expand and $select. However, to do that, you have to wrap the return object in a SingleResult<T>. Both examples are shown in Listing 12-7.

Listing 12-7. Enabling Querying on Two OData Routes

```
public class PlayersController : ODataController
{
    private readonly PlayersContext playersDbContext = new PlayersContext();

    [EnableQuery]
    public IQueryable<Player> GetAllPlayers()
    {
        Return playersDbContext;
    }

    [EnableQuery]
    public SingleResult<Player> GetSinglePlayers(int key)
    {
        return SingleResult.Create(playersDbContext.Where(x => x.Id == key).AsQueryable());
    }
}
```

How It Works

The query options for OData are defined in the OData specification as "query string parameters that control the amount and order of the data returned for the resource identified by the URL." ASP.NET Web API supports almost all of the query options defined in the standard:

- $expand: Allows the client to include a related resource(s) in the response, alongside the requested resource.

- $select: Allows the client to limit the properties on the returned resource.

- $filter: Allows the client to filter resources available via an OData endpoint.

- $count: Allows the client to obtain the total count of entities in a collection without actually retrieving them.

- $orderby: Allows the client to specify an ordering key for the queried collection.

- $skip: Allows the client to omit a certain amount of items from the queried collection.

- $top: Allows the client to restrict the count of entities returned from the queried collection.

- $format: Allows the client to request a response in a specific format.

The only one not supported is the free-text $search query parameter.

■ **Tip**   You can find the entire OData v4.0 specification at www.odata.org/documentation/odata-version-4-0/.

The querying options are represented in ASP.NET Web API by the ODataQueryOptions class. The way EnableQueryAttribute works is actually very straightforward. Since it's an action filter, it captures the response of your action in the OnActionExecuted method, and tries to cast its HttpContent to an ObjectContent<T>. Then, it will construct an instance of ODataQueryOptions from the HTTP request, based on the arguments supplied by the client, and try to apply it to your response. If that response is a collection, it will apply all of the query options provided by the client, and if the response is not a collection, it will expect the object wrapped within the ObjectContent to be a SingleResult<T>. If that's the case, $expand and $select will still be supported.

Instead of using EnableQueryAttribute, ODataQueryOptions can also be accepted as an argument in your action method. The way Web API supports this is through a custom HttpParameterBinding called ODataQueryParameterBinding. You can then use the information from that ODataQueryOptions instance to manually perform the relevant querying.

What is interesting is that you do not have to fully embrace OData in your Web API to be able to take advantage of the Query Options. The basic ones, such as $top, $skip, or $select can be applied to any Web API controller as long as an action is decorated with EnableQueryAttribute, not just those that are built as ODataControllers.

The Code

With your controller actions decorated with the EnableQueryAttrbute, as shown in Listing 12-7, you are able to issue any requests that rely on OData query options. For example,

- myapi.com/Players(1)?$select=Name,Team: Requesting player entity with key 1, but only its Name and Team properties. The response is shown in Listing 12-8.

Listing 12-8. Sample Query Response from OData Web API Endpoint

```
Content-Length: 115
Content-Type: application/json; odata.metadata=minimal
Date: Thu, 12 Jun 2014 21:02:17 GMT
OData-Version: 4.0
Server: Microsoft-HTTPAPI/2.0
{
    "@odata.context": "http://localhost:925/$metadata#Players(Name,Team)/$entity",
    "Name": "Filip",
    "Team": "Whales"
}
```

- myapi.com/Players?$skip=1&$top=2: Omit the first player entity, and take next two. The response is shown in Listing 12-9.

Listing 12-9. Sample Query Response from OData Web API Endpoint

```
Content-Length: 194
Content-Type: application/json; odata.metadata=minimal
Date: Thu, 12 Jun 2014 21:03:12 GMT
OData-Version: 4.0
Server: Microsoft-HTTPAPI/2.0
{
    "@odata.context": "http://localhost:925/$metadata#Players",
    "value": [
        {
            "Id": 2,
            "Name": "Felix",
            "Team": "Whales"
        },
        {
            "Id": 3,
            "Name": "Luiz",
            "Team": "Dolphins"
        }
    ]
}
```

- myapi.com/Players?$format=application/json;odata.metadata=full&$filter=Team%20 eq%20%27Whales%27: Requesting only player entities for which the Team property equals "Whales" and in the JSON format, but also including all of the OData metadata such as type information and navigation links. The response is shown in Listing 12-10.

Listing 12-10. Sample Query Response from OData Web API Endpoint

```
Content-Length: 769
Content-Type: application/json; odata.metadata=full
Date: Thu, 12 Jun 2014 20:59:59 GMT
OData-Version: 4.0
Server: Microsoft-HTTPAPI/2.0
```

```json
{
    "@odata.context": "http://localhost:925/$metadata#Players",
    "value": [
        {
            "@odata.type": "#Apress.Recipes.WebApi.Player",
            "@odata.id": "http://localhost:925/Players(1)",
            "@odata.editLink": "http://localhost:925/Players(1)",
            "Id": 1,
            "Name": "Filip",
            "Team": "Whales",
            "Stats@odata.associationLink": "http://localhost:925/Players(1)/Stats/$ref",
            "Stats@odata.navigationLink": "http://localhost:925/Players(1)/Stats"
        },
        {
            "@odata.type": "#Apress.Recipes.WebApi.Player",
            "@odata.id": "http://localhost:925/Players(2)",
            "@odata.editLink": "http://localhost:925/Players(2)",
            "Id": 2,
            "Name": "Felix",
            "Team": "Whales",
            "Stats@odata.associationLink": "http://localhost:925/Players(2)/Stats/$ref",
            "Stats@odata.navigationLink": "http://localhost:925/Players(2)/Stats"
        }
    ]
}
```

As mentioned, you can also manually apply the query by adding ODataQueryOptions as a parameter of your action. ODataQueryParameterBinding will take care of hydrating that object and passing it into your action, where you can extract the values of relevant OData query options. The example using $top and $skip is shown in Listing 12-11.

Listing 12-11. Working with ODataQueryOptions in the Action

```csharp
public IQueryable<Player> GetAllPlayers(ODataQueryOptions queryOptions)
{
    //the client sends top and skip
    var filtered = _db.Players.Skip(queryOptions.Skip.Value);

    if (queryOptions.Top.Value > 0)
    {
        filtered = filtered.Take(queryOptions.Top.Value);
    }

    return filtered.AsQueryable();
}
```

12-4. Support OData Functions and Actions

Problem

You would like to use OData functions and actions in your Web API application.

Solution

When building an OData web service with ASP.NET Web API, you can define functions and actions through the fluent builders exposed by `ODataModelBuilder`, `EntityCollectionConfiguration`, and `EntityTypeConfiguration` classes, in the form of a `Function` and `Action` methods.

When setting up your `ODataModelBuilder`, you can specify the function or action name and define its input parameters, as well as the expected return. See Listing 12-12 for an example.

Listing 12-12. Sample Function Exposed Off a Player Entity

```
var odataBuilder = new ODataConventionModelBuilder();
odataBuilder.EntitySet<Player>("Players");
var player = odataBuilder.EntityType<Player>();

//entity function - read some data
player.Function("PercentageOfAllGoals").Returns<double>();

//entity action - invoke an operation
player.Action("TradePlayer").Parameter<string>("NewTeam");
```

The mapping between a controller action and an OData function/action name happens by convention, through the name, so you will need to add an action with a corresponding name to your OData controller.

How It Works

OData function support was introduced into ASP.NET Web API in version 2.2, even though they were already defined as part of the OData 3.0 specification. On the other hand, actions were already available in earlier Web API versions.

You are able to define OData functions/actions and expose them directly as regular Web API action methods, which can then be called by the client.

The primary advantage of using actions or functions is that they allow you to shift the responsibility of the query composition back to the server side, which, especially in the case of complex queries, can relieve the clients from a lot of unnecessary pain.

Semantically, there is little difference between OData actions and functions; they are both defined in the specifications as "extending the set of operations that can be performed on or with a service or resource." The primary difference is that functions can have no side effects and must return data, while actions can produce side effects on the server side, and do not need to return anything. Additionally, functions can be invoked from within a `$filter` predicate.

In the ASP.NET Web API implementation of OData, actions and functions are defined together with all OData conventions through an instance of your main `ODataConventionModelBuilder` object. Web API OData builder supports three types (levels) of those operations:

- service actions/functions: Defined directly against your `ODataModelBuilder`.

- collection actions/functions: Defined against an `EntityCollectionConfiguration`.

- entity actions/functions: Defined against an `EntityTypeConfiguration`.

The Code

Listing 12-13 shows a sample data set, embedded for demo purposes directly into a controller in the form of an in-memory repository, as well as the definition of the Player DTO class.

You'll use them to create all three of the OData function types: service, collection, and entity-bound ones. The examples will focus on functions, but defining and working with actions would be almost identical. The only difference would be that in all places where the Function method is used for declaration, the Action method should be used instead.

Listing 12-13. Sample In-Memory Data and Entity Model

```
public class Player
{
    public int Id { get; set; }
    public string Name { get; set; }
    public string Team { get; set; }
    public SkaterStat Stats { get; set; }
}

public class SkaterStat
{
    public int Goals { get; set; }
    public int Assists { get; set; }
    public int GamesPlayed { get; set; }
}

public class PlayersController : ODataController
{
    private static List<Player> _players = new List<Player>
    {
        new Player
        {
            Id = 1,
            Name = "Filip",
            Team = "Whales",
            Stats = new SkaterStat
            {
                GamesPlayed = 82, Goals = 37, Assists = 43
            }
        },
        new Player
        {
            Id = 2,
            Name = "Felix",
            Team = "Whales",
            Stats = new SkaterStat
            {
                GamesPlayed = 80, Goals = 30, Assists = 31
            }
        },
```

```
        new Player
        {
            Id = 3,
            Name = "Luiz",
            Team = "Dolphins",
            Stats = new SkaterStat
            {
                GamesPlayed = 78, Goals = 20, Assists = 30
            }
        },
        new Player
        {
            Id = 4,
            Name = "Terry",
            Team = "Dolphins",
            Stats = new SkaterStat
            {
                GamesPlayed = 58, Goals = 19, Assists = 30
            }
        }
    };

    // rest of controller to be added
}
```

The aforementioned Function method, hanging off ODataModelBuilder, EntityCollectionConfiguration, and EntityTypeConfiguration, returns a FunctionConfiguration instance, which can be used to configure the specifics of your function, such as whether the function should be supported in $filter, what parameters it should accept, and what should be its return. An example of a Katana Startup class defining three OData functions against the ODataModelBuilder and one of its entity types is shown in Listing 12-14.

Listing 12-14. Katana Startup Defining OData Service Function, Collection Function, and Entity Function

```
public class Startup
{
    public void Configuration(IAppBuilder builder)
    {
        var odataBuilder = new ODataConventionModelBuilder();
        odataBuilder.EntitySet<Player>("Players");
        var player = odataBuilder.EntityType<Player>();

        //collection function
        player.Collection.Function("TopPpg").ReturnsCollection<Player>();

        //entity function
        player.Function("PercentageOfAllGoals").Returns<double>();

        //service function
        var serviceFunc = odataBuilder.Function("TotalTeamPoints");
        serviceFunc.Returns<int>().Parameter<string>("team");
        serviceFunc.IncludeInServiceDocument = true;

        var edm = odataBuilder.GetEdmModel();
```

```
        var config = new HttpConfiguration();
        config.MapODataServiceRoute("Default OData", "odata", edm);
        builder.UseWebApi(config);
    }
}
```

TopPpg is a collection function, and it will return a collection of players with top points (goals + assists) per game ratio. PercentageOfAllGoals is an entity function and will return a ratio of the goals scored by a given player to all of the goals scored by all of the players. This function will require a key (player ID) to be passed by the client, but notice that being an entity key, it does not need to be explicitly specified in the function builder. Finally, TotalTeamPoints will be an unbounded service function, not related to a specific player. Instead, it will take a team name as a parameter and return all points (goals + assists) scored by all of the players of that team. Additionally, the TotalTeamPoints will be included in the service document, the /odata/$metadata, as a FunctionImport entry.

The functions are implemented as simple LINQ calculations happening inside an action method on your sample OData controller (refer to Listing 12-13) and shown in Listing 12-15. The unbounded service functions are decorated with an additional OData attribute route because the default EDM-driven routing convention would not pick it up otherwise.

Listing 12-15. Controller Actions Used to Expose the OData Functions

```
[HttpGet]
public IEnumerable<Player> TopPpg()
{
    var result = _players.OrderByDescending(x => (double)(x.Stats.Goals + x.Stats.Assists)/(double)
x.Stats.GamesPlayed).Take(3);
    return result;
}

[HttpGet]
public IHttpActionResult PercentageOfAllGoals(int key)
{
    var player = _players.FirstOrDefault(x => x.Id == key);
    if (player == null) return NotFound();

    var result = (double)player.Stats.Goals/(double)_players.Sum(x => x.Stats.Goals) * 100;
    return Ok(result);
}

[HttpGet]
[ODataRoute("TotalTeamPoints(team={team})")]
public int TotalTeamPoints([FromODataUri]string team)
{
    var result = _players.Where(x => string.Equals(x.Team, team, StringComparison.
InvariantCultureIgnoreCase))
        .Sum(x => x.Stats.Goals + x.Stats.Assists);

    return result;
}
```

With these in place, you can now call your OData functions using the function names in the URI. As per the specification, you need to include the brackets to indicate that you are calling an OData function:

- /odata/Players/Default.TopPpg()
- /odata/Players(1)/Default.PercentageOfAllGoals() - 1 is a player's key
- /odata/TotalTeamPoints(team='Whales')

Index

■ I, J, K

■ L

■ M, N

■ T, U, V

■ W

■ X, Y, Z

Get the eBook for only $10!

Now you can take the weightless companion with you anywhere, anytime. Your purchase of this book entitles you to 3 electronic versions for only $10.

This Apress title will prove so indispensible that you'll want to carry it with you everywhere, which is why we are offering the eBook in 3 formats for only $10 if you have already purchased the print book.

Convenient and fully searchable, the PDF version enables you to easily find and copy code—or perform examples by quickly toggling between instructions and applications. The MOBI format is ideal for your Kindle, while the ePUB can be utilized on a variety of mobile devices.

Go to www.apress.com/promo/tendollars to purchase your companion eBook.